Management of Biomedical Waste

Management of Biomedical Waste

Lakshmi Prasanna Jakka

RANDOM

RANDOM PUBLICATIONS
NEW DELHI (INDIA)

Management of Biomedical Waste

ISBN 978-93-5111-801-5

Published in 2016 in India by

RANDOM PUBLICATIONS

4376-A/4B, Gali Murari Lal, Ansari Road
New Delhi-110 002
Phone : +9111-43580356, 011-23289044, 011-43142548
e-mail: sales@randompublications.com, info@randompublications.com, randomexports@gmail.com

Reprinted 2026

Type Setting by : Friends Media, Delhi-110089

Preface

Biomedical waste is waste that is either putrescible or potentially infectious. Biomedical waste may also include waste associated with the generation of biomedical waste that visually appears to be of medical or laboratory origin as well research laboratory waste containing biomolecules or organisms that are restricted from environmental release. As detailed below, discarded sharps are considered biomedical waste whether they are contaminated or not, due to the possibility of being contaminated with blood and their propensity to cause injury when not properly contained and disposed of. Biomedical waste is a type of biowaste. Biomedical waste may be solid or liquid. Examples of infectious waste include discarded blood, sharps, unwanted microbiological cultures and stocks, identifiable body parts, other human or animal tissue, used bandages and dressings, discarded gloves, other medical supplies that may have been in contact with blood and body fluids, and laboratory waste that exhibits the characteristics described above.

Waste sharps include potentially contaminated used needles, scalpels, lancets and other devices capable of penetrating skin. Biomedical waste is generated from biological and medical sources and activities, such as the diagnosis, prevention, or treatment of diseases. Common generators of biomedical waste include hospitals, health clinics, nursing homes, medical research laboratories, offices of physicians, dentists, and veterinarians, home health care, and funeral homes. In healthcare facilities, waste with these characteristics may alternatively be called medical or clinical waste. Biomedical waste is distinct from normal trash or general waste, and differs from other types of hazardous waste, such as chemical, radioactive, universal or industrial waste. Medical facilities generate waste hazardous chemicals and radioactive materials. While such wastes are normally not infectious, they require proper disposal. Some wastes are considered multihazardous, such as tissue samples preserved in formalin.

– Author

Contents

1

Biomedical Waste Treatment and Disposal Principles

BIOMEDICAL WASTE

Biomedical Healthcare Waste incinerators generally have a primary combustion chamber operating at 800–1000°C and a secondary chamber operating at 850–1100°C with gas retention times of two seconds. The incinerator plant includes gas-cleaning equipment to reduce emissions to air and comply with the EU Waste Incineration Directive.

Pyrolysis

Pyrolysis Involves the high temperature (545–1000°C) combustion of waste in the absence of oxygen. This treats the waste, destroys pathogens and reduces the volume of clinical waste.

Plasma Technology

IN A plasma system, an electric current is passed through an inert gas (eg., argon) to ionise it and this causes an electric arc to create temperatures as high as 6000°C. The clinical waste within the system is brought to temperatures of 1300–1700°C, destroying pathogenic microbes and converting the waste into a glassy rock or slag, ferrous metal and inert gases.

Non-Burn/Low-Temperature Treatments

Thermal Disinfection Systems

- *The Autoclave*: Saturated steam is introduced into a vessel above atmospheric pressure. Some autoclaves shred the waste during treatment whilst others require the waste to be macerated before treatment.
- *The Steam Auger:* Waste is shredded prior to introduction into a steam auger at atmospheric pressure.
- *Dry Heat*: Pathogens are destroyed by electrically generated hot oil.

- *Microwaves*: Electromagnetic waves with a frequency between radio waves and infrared waves, thermally destroy pathogens. It is important for the waste to be wet, either as a result of moisture naturally occurring in the waste stream or by the addition of moisture in the form of steam. The combination of the two-microwaves and moisture-creates the thermal process.
  "Dry" microwave systems are also available, which use direct microwave energy in a nitrogen atmosphere to treat the waste and produce higher treatment temperatures.
- *Macrowaves*: Low-frequency radio waves inactivate microbes by heating the waste from the inside of the materials to the outer surface.

Gasification

The Waste materials are thermally decomposed in an oxygen-starved atmosphere during gasification. No additional fuel is required except for that required to initiate combustion. The decomposition results in the generation of volatile gases and, depending on the waste content, various vapourised tar-oil substances. The waste gas is passed through a series of scrubbers, filters and cyclonic separators to provide a clean "producer gas".

BIOMEDICAL WASTE TREATMENT PLANT

In past, Management of waste generated during diagnosis, treatment or immunization of human bodies or animals or research activities has never been an integral part of the health care programme.

These wastes, if not managed properly pose a serious threat to human health. Bio Medical Waste (Management and Handling) Rules, 1998 notified under Environment (Protection) Act, makes it compulsory for medical professionals and organizations that the waste generated by their activities is properly segregated, collected, treated and disposed as per provisions of the Rules.

Our Work

Surat Municipal Corporation, recognizing the need of hour and took up the task of proper disposal of the medical waste generated from medical institution. A BOOT contract was awarded to M/s Envision Enviro Engineers Pvt. Ltd. to set up a centralized Bio Medical Waste Treatment Facility in a plot measuring approximately 2400 sq mt. with state of art technology at Bhatar Solid Waste Disposal Site. Transportation of biomedical waste from 27 designated health centres upto facility is carried out by Envision Enviro Engineers Pvt. Ltd. Treatment option adopted are incineration of biomedical waste of categories 1, 2, 3 and 5 and sterilization by means of autoclaving and shredding for biomedical waste of categories 3, 4, 6 and 7. Incineration ash and

shredding waste sent to landfill site of Surat Municipal Corporation for ultimate disposal.

WASTEWATER TREATMENT PLANT

The wastewater treatment is a broad term that applies to any process, operation or combinations of processes and operations that can reduce the objectionable properties of water carried waste and render it less dangerous and repulsive to man.

Thus, the wastewater should be effectively treated before its ultimate disposal in order to:

- Reduce the spread of communicable diseases caused by the pathogenic organisms.
- Prevent the pollution of surface and ground water.

Wastewater treatment is a combination of physical, chemical and biological processes. We are one of the leading firms in South Gujarat for the consultancy and complete turnkey solution for the wastewater treatment and disposal problem. We excel in the ETP designing, construction and commissioning with the experience of above 70 units fully in working condition.

The effluent from each of the industry is unique with reference to the effluent generated by it, which by and large depends on the type of the production. We cover the entire spectrum of industrial units as far as the ETP designing and commissioning is concerned. Thus we offer highly case specific solution for the treatment of the waste water of each industries, covering dyeing and printing units, pharmaceuticals, sugar, dairy, glass, agrochemicals, chemicals etc. The effluent design is made according to the local norm of effluent discharge. We also offer complete zero discharge solution for waste water treatment in certain industries. This zero discharge solution reaffirms our mission of creating better environment and controlling pollution.

SOLID AND LIQUID INCINERATION SYSTEMS

Incineration is a waste treatment technology that involves the combustion of waste at high temperature. Incineration figures as an alternative to the land filling, and biological treatment technology like composting and anaerobic digestion.It is a furnace for burning refuse. Modern incinerators include pollution mitigation equipments like flue gas cleaning. We are one of the very few firms in south Gujarat proficient in the designing and maintaining of the incineration systems.

We design incinerator to handle all kinds of waste like hazardous waste, solid, liquid, municipal, biomedical waste etc. Considering the scale of cost and type of incoming effluent our designing team takes into considerations all the pros and cons for the unit and thereby provides the client with best suitable solution. Over and above all the units designed for each of the particular type

of waste our incinerator system encompasses all the pollution control equipments like venturi scrubber, demisters, deduster, cyclone separtor, heat exchanger, gas coolers, and waste gas separation through ID fan and Stack.

SECURED LANDFILL SITES FOR HAZARDOUS WASTES

A landfill, also known as a dump (US) or a tip (UK), is a site for the disposal of waste materials by burial and is the oldest form of waste treatment. Historically, landfills are the most common methods of organized waste disposal and remain so in many places around the world. Landfills may include internal waste disposal sites (where a producer of waste carries out their own waste disposal at the place of production) as well as sites used by many producers. Many landfills are also used for other waste management purposes, such as the temporary storage, consolidation and transfer, or processing of waste material (sorting, treatment, or recycling). Most modern landfills are classified according to the type(s) of waste material disposed of into them.

Hazardous Waste Landfill

Waste disposal units constructed to specific design criteria and which receive wastes meeting the local definition of hazardous waste. These landfills are generally constructed to be secure repositories for material that presents a serious hazard to human health, such as high-level radioactive waste. They are restricted, by permit or law, to the types of waste that they may handle (chemical vs. radioactive, liquid vs. dry). We have had firsthand experience in developing the secured landfill site right from the site selection phase upto the closure point.

The site selection, hauling of waste etc are all given a complete circle of thoughts to provide the clients with the most feasible solution for their waste disposal as well as no disturbance to the local authorities. Our site development is based on the type and quantity of waste to be handled. We provide the solutions for waste handling which are of international standard taking in view all the possible alternatives for the problems. We cater to the needs of client, giving them the value added for their resources employed.

PYROLYSIS

DESCRIPTION

Pyrolysis is a form of incineration that chemically decomposes organic materials by heat in the absence of oxygen. Pyrolysis typically occurs under pressure and at operating temperatures above 430°C (800°F). In practice, it is not possible to achieve a completely oxygen-free atmosphere. Because some oxygen is present in any pyrolysis system, a small amount of oxidation occurs. If volatile or semi-volatile materials are present in the waste, thermal desorption

will also occur. Organic materials are transformed into gases, small quantities of liquid, and a solid residue containing carbon and ash. The off-gases may also be treated in a secondary thermal oxidation unit. Particulate removal equipment is also required. Several types of pyrolysis units are available, including the rotary kiln, rotary hearth furnace, and fluidized bed furnace. These units are similar to incinerators except that they operate at lower temperatures and with less air supply. A molten salt process may also be used for waste pyrolysis. In molten-salt oxidation (MSO), combustible waste is oxidized in a bath of molten salts (at 500–950°C). There is no direct flame, and this prevents many of the problems associated with incineration. Shredded solid waste is injected with air under the surface of a molten salt bath. Hot gases rise through the molten salt bath. The salt, being alkaline, scrubs acids from the gases. The heat of the molten salt degrades and melts the waste material. Because the salt bath is liquid, it also removes some particles in the gas. Byproducts are retained in the melt. Gases exiting the salt bath are treated before discharge to the atmosphere. Spent molten salt is tapped from the reactor, cooled, and placed in a landfill.

LIMITATIONS AND CONCERNS

The technology requires drying of soil prior to treatment. Limited performance data are available for systems treating hazardous wastes containing polychlorinated biphenyls (PCBs), dioxins, and other organics. There is concern that systems that destroy chlorinated organic molecules by heat have the potential to create products of incomplete combustion, including dioxins and furans. These compounds are extremely toxic in the parts per trillion range. The MSO process reportedly does not produce dioxins and furans.The molten salt is usually recycled in the reactor chamber.

However, depending on the waste treated (especially inorganics) and the amount of ash, spent molten salt may be hazardous and require special care in disposal. Pyrolysis is not effective in either destroying or physically separating inorganics from the contaminated medium. Volatile metals may be removed as a result of the higher temperatures associated with the process, but they are not destroyed. Byproducts containing heavy metals may require stabilization before final disposal. When the off-gases are cooled, liquids condense, producing an oil/tar residue and contaminated water. These oils and tars may be hazardous wastes, requiring proper treatment, storage, and disposal. There are a wide variety of thermal treatment systems incorporating 'advanced' or 'emerging' technologies for the treatment of municipal wastes. The most prevalent being Pyrolysis and Gasification processes. Pyrolysis, often incorporating gasification, is a thermal process where organic materials in the waste are broken down under pressure and in the absence of oxygen. The process works best when the input waste is carbon-rich, preferably sorted or pre-sorted. Best results

are obtained from single stream wastes such as sewage sludge, plastics, wood, tyres, or agricultural wastes. Where MSW is to be used it should be pre-sorted to remove the majority of the non-organics and processed to homogenise the feedstock. The Pyrolysis process produces a liquid residue and gaseous output which may be combusted to generate electricity. A solid slag is also produced which may require disposal or additional processing.

SCHEMATIC OF INPUTS AND OUTPUTS OF A TYPICAL PYROLYSIS PROCESS

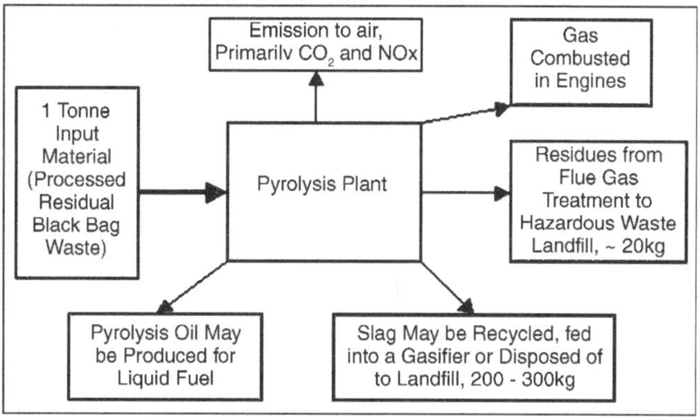

Gasification usually operates at a higher temperature range to pyrolysis, with the addition of an oxidant (either air or oxygen) and the output from a pyrolysis plant may be fed into this process.

Gasification of organic derived wastes will produce a gas which can be combusted to generate electricity and a char which usually requires disposal if no markets are available.

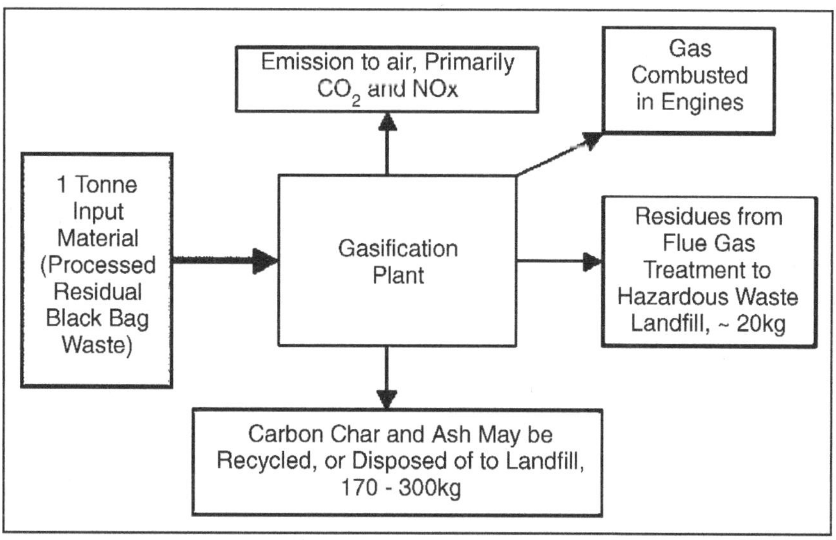

Fig. Schematic of Inputs and Outputs of a Typical Gasification Process

Theses processes are still at the development stage, with no full scale plants operating commercially in the UK. European experience is limited and mixed.

- *Typical capacity*: Typically 20,000 tpa—100,000 tpa (tend to be modular, so larger capacities may be achieved through multiples of facilities on one or more sites).
- *Land Requirements*: Typically 0.5–1.75Ha for a 50,000–60,000 tpa sized plant. 6Ha for 225,000t facility in Germany
- *Capital Costs*: £ for 100,000tpa plant (process dependent).
- *Operating Costs*: Limited data available. Example from one system shows gate fee of/tonne for RDF and processed MSW for a 60Ktpa plant, if supplemented by higher gate fee materials such as clinical waste.
- *Staffing Requirements*: Staffing levels, including technical competence, management and administrative resources will required and will vary depending on the size of the facility. Typically 30–40 employees for plants of 60,000–200,000 tpa

Table. Strengths and Weaknesses of Pyrolysis and Gasification Processes

Strengths	Weaknesses
Not Incineration! perception as incineration, some evidence	May suffer from the same negative of this overseas, yet to be tested in the UK
Qualifies for the Renewabsles Obligation for a substantial proportion of the feedstock processed	Requires extensive pre-treatment to be able to handle MSW
Efficient electricity generation through combustion of gas through engines	Many processes will still have residues to be disposed of, some of which (from flue gas treatment) will be hazardous in nature
Potential to recycle a large proportion of residues depending on the process	Unproven on a commercial scale on MSW in the UK, patchy experience overseas
High temperatures may make the system more flexible for other waste streams such as clinical	More sensitive system than moving grate incineration technology
Smaller units more acceptable and part of an integrated system	More expensive (in terms of gate fee) than Energy from Waste
Capable of being integrated with other processes such as the output from MBT /Refuse Derived Fuel (RDF) production	

Other Issues

Key issues with regards to these 'advanced' thermal treatment technologies are:

- Their relatively unproven performance on MSW;
- Whether they will be perceived as 'incineration by another name';

and issues of cost and commercial application of the systems in the UK waste management market.

There is considerable potential for these systems, if proven reliable, to act as components in integrated municipal waste management. They may be complementary in processing specific 'problematic' waste streams or to link in with other pre-processing MSW facilities such as MBT, RDF manufacture or steam reformation processes. Their smaller scale implementation as envisaged to date, makes them compliant with the proximity principle and should help in public perception and in gaining planning permission over larger facilities. The efficient energy production aspects of the processes and the eligibility for Renewables Obligations Certificates are also positive characteristics of these facilities.

LANDFILL

Landfills have been the standard answer for disposing of waste for many years-not because they are a good solution but because the alternatives were not viewed as being economically viable. For many years no one understood the "true" cost of operating a landfill. Initially we just dumped waste in open pits and covered them up. After a number of years we learned that contaminants in the waste were leaching into the ground water and contaminating aquifers.

Landfill gas was escaping into surrounding neighbourhoods and into basements of homes. We then began to line the landfills and over time have developed fairly sophisticated liner systems. However, even the best liner system will eventually leak and cause environmental damage. During this time a variety of programmes have been developed to reduce the amount of waste going into landfills. We have developed recycling programmes, composting, anaerobic digestion and a variety of other techniques to reduce the waste. However, we are still dumping most of our waste into landfills because of a lack of viable economic alternatives.

There is no other technology that can compete with the cost of a landfill, when considering only the cost to construct and operate the landfill. However, when we consider the cost of transporting waste to a distant landfill, or the cost to society for the environmental damage caused by the landfill, or the value of the land that could be used for other purposes, or the future liability of a landfill, then the "real" cost of a landfill starts to grow. Many municipalities do not look at the "life cycle" cost of operating a landfill and are only concerned about this year's budget shortfall. Other municipalities have not found viable alternatives that can adequately solve the entire problem. In many cases municipalities would like another alternative but are locked into existing contracts with private landfill owners.

Landfills are now being banned or phased out by many communities. Cities like New York City and Toronto have stopped using landfills and are exporting their waste to other communities. These other communities are starting to realise the long-term cost of taking the waste. The world society is now awakening to the detrimental effects of landfills and are earnestly seeking viable alternatives.

The public rarely hears of landfill gas emissions. Since landfills occupy large areas of land, emissions control for these areas are more difficult to manage than a point source at a Recovered Energy System™ plant. The biodegradable waste in the landfill produces among other things methane gas. As a greenhouse gas methane is twenty-three times more potent than carbon dioxide. Landfill gas to energy receives renewable energy credits for providing the valuable service of converting methane into carbon dioxide.

With the Recovered Energy System™ system there is an immediate and thorough conversion of the biodegradable waste in a controlled manner. Unless properly capped the emissions from landfills go largely uncontrolled. Landfills also produce a leachate that needs to be monitored and treated.

The Recovered Energy System™ system eliminates landfills and the associated environmental issues. The Recovered Energy System™ system can also be used in conjunction with an existing landfill to process the landfill gas and leachate.

SAFE DISPOSAL OF MEDICAL WASTE

MEDICAL WASTE DISPOSAL

Biohazardous Waste (Regulated Medical Waste)

Some wastes associated with biological materials must be disposed of in special ways because they may have been contaminated with infectious organisms or agents. These potentially infectious or biohazardous materials are defined by NJ regulations as Regulated Medical Waste.

These wastes include the following:

- All sharps, *e.g.* glass implements, needles, syringes, blades, etc. coming from facilities using infectious materials
- Biologically-cultured stocks and plates, human blood or tissues

For disposal of these wastes, the lab personnel:

- Sterilize or disinfect waste materials associated with viral, bacterial or other agents infectious to humans (by autoclave or chemical treatment equivalent to 1:10 bleach solution).
- Place all biohazardous wastes, except for sharps, directly into the red bag-lined medical waste boxes provided by Building Services.
- Place sharps into labeled sharps containers which when filled are placed into the medical waste box.
- When the Medical Waste box is filled, seal the bag liner and box and notify janitor for pick-up.

IMPORTANT LABELLING REQUIREMENT

Lab personnel must apply an adhesive-backed label completed with generator information to each bag or container (such as autoclaved bags or filled sharps containers) placed into the medical waste box. Building Services provides such a label that has space to record Date and Building. Apply this label to all containers placed inside the medical waste box AND to the exterior of the sealed medical waste box before it is made available for pick-up by Building Services. Alternatively, the inner bags and containers can be marked clearly with a permanent marker to indicate "Princeton University, Princeton, New Jersey."

- Where pick-ups are infrequent or limited, contact Building Services to arrange for pick-up.

Other wastes generated in these facilities that are not contaminated with biological agents or materials are nottreated as biohazardous and may be discarded in the regular trash container, with recyclables, or into other specially designated waste containers. These include such items as recyclable and non-recyclable waste glass, gloves, unused plates or tubes, fly media or embryo plates, etc. In order to clarify how these various wastes are to be handled in laboratories using biological materials, the waste stream chart has been developed and put into use for all departments generating research waste. It is intended for laboratories using biological and/or chemical materials. Choose the waste model that most clearly fits the waste being generated and follow the indicated management procedures. Call the Biosafety Officer or Chemical Programme Manager at 8-5294 for clarification.

Animal Bedding Waste

Animal bedding waste that has been exposed to biosafety level 2 agents is autoclaved prior to disposal or, if an autoclave is not available in the animal facility, is packaged as infectious waste in cardboard fibre drums or boxes by Laboratory Animal Resources (LAR) staff. Any container of bedding that is labeled as infectious waste is closed by LAR staff to prevent spills or leakage. Containers of infectious waste are picked up by Building Services and transported to a weather-protected shelter for holding until they are picked up by the University's infectious waste vendor, for incineration. Spills from containers of animal bedding labeled as infectious waste are to be cleaned up by LAR staff.

Animal bedding that has not been labeled as infectious is bagged and collected for disposal by LAR staff. After bagging the waste, it is placed into gray carts for movement by LAR staff to the pick-up location. This waste is picked up by Princeton University Building Services personnel and is not to be mixed with other waste. Bags are filled only to a depth and weight that will allow for effective tying of the bag by animal facility staff and for ease of handling by one person. For example, several partially-filled bags should be tied and placed in the gray carts rather than one or two full bags (bag weight should not exceed 40 pounds). This will help to prevent repetitive motion injury to staff and prevent bags from being ripped open while being handled. The carts are maintained clean and in sanitary condition by the animal facility staff. Any spills of (non-infectious) bedding when loading the truck are cleaned up by the Building Services trash crew.

Animal Carcasses

Freezers are provided in each animal facility for storage of carcasses that have been bagged and sealed. All animal carcasses that have been exposed to biosafety level 2 agents are placed into an infectious waste bag. All carcasses are packed and incinerated as infectious waste through a licensed, contracted firm. Freezers are cleaned and defrosted as necessary by animal laboratory personnel to keep them in a sanitary condition.

Animal Waste from BSL2 Animal Room LTL 41

Rodents housed in this animal space are considered to be potentially infectious because as part of the research protocol they are infected with Biosafety Level 2 (BSL2) animal and/or human viruses. Animal bedding, carcasses, and tissue are placed in biohazard bags by the research staff. All animal bedding is autoclaved before being placed in medical waste boxes by animal care staff and disposed of in the medical waste stream. Bagged animal carcasses and tissue are placed in the provided storage freezer in room 41 and removed by animal care staff to medical waste boxes for pick-up by Building Services as part of the medical waste stream.

Patient Care Waste Disposal

All disposable wastes generated at McCosh Health Center from patient rooms and as part of direct patient care are considered potentially infectious and are disposed of in the medical waste stream. Syringes, needles, and other sharps are placed in the provided sharps container which, when filled and sealed are placed in the provided medical waste box. When boxes are filled and sealed, they are removed by the custodial staff outside to the locked storage shed for later pick-up by Building Services.

Patient care waste generated at other sites on campus by medical response personnel (*i.e.* Public Safety) are placed in biohazard bags and brought to McCosh Health Center for medical waste disposal or handled by responding EMS personnel. A programme is in place to ensure that needles and syringes generated as part of personal diabetes care will not be an exposure hazard to others. Collection containers are available from McCosh Health Center which, when filled, are returned to Health Center for proper disposal in the medical waste stream.

PROPER MEDICAL WASTE DISPOSAL IS GREEN

Green is the colour of the century. Every person and business across the country is trying to find new and easy ways to go green. If you're a hospital or just a building that has medical waste, you can turn that garbage into something positive. Don't just toss the medical waste in the trash bin. It's neither safe nor efficient. Choosing to use medical waste services, such as Med Assure, is an easy way to help out the environment.

First, you should separate any regular garbage from the medical waste. Also separate anything that can be recycled like cardboard or glass. When it comes to choosing medical waste services, only choose a company that is environmentally friendly like Med Assure. Their services are emission free, use no chemicals, and it is safe for landfill disposal. Never choose companies that use incinerators. They release harmful carcinogens into the air. A little research into a company can go a long way.

MANAGEMENT OF BIOMEDICAL WASTE IN INDIA AND OTHER COUNTRIES

'Bio-medical waste' means any waste generated during diagnosis, treatment or immunization of human beings or animals. Management of healthcare waste is an integral part of infection control and hygiene programs in healthcare settings. These settings are a major contributor to community-acquired infection, as they produce large amounts of biomedical waste. Biomedical waste can be categorized based on the risk of causing injury and/or infection during handling and disposal.

Wastes targeted for precautions during handling and disposal include sharps , pathological wastes (anatomical body parts, microbiology cultures and blood samples) and infectious wastes (items contaminated with body fluids and discharges such as dressing, catheters and I.V. lines). Other wastes generated in healthcare settings include radioactive wastes, mercury containing instruments and polyvinyl chloride (PVC) plastics.

These are among the most environmentally sensitive by-products of healthcare. WHO stated that 85% of hospital wastes are actually non-hazardous, around 10% are infectious and around 5% are non-infectious but hazardous wastes. In the USA, about 15% of hospital waste is regulated as infectious waste. In India this could range from 15% to 35% depending on the total amount of waste generated. The management of bio-medical waste is still in its infancy all over the world. There is a lot of confusion with the problems among the generators, operators, decision-makers and the general community about the safe management of bio-medical waste. The reason may be a lack of awareness. Hence resource material on the environment for hospital administrators, surgeons, doctors, nurses, paramedical staff and waste retrievers, is the need of the hour.

SOURCES OF BIO-MEDICAL WASTE

While urban solid waste has attracted the attention of town planners, environmental activists and civic administrators, there is yet lack of concern for some special sources of waste and its management. One such waste is bio-medical waste generated primarily from health care establishments, including hospitals, nursing homes, veterinary hospitals, clinics and general practitioners, dispensaries, blood banks, animal houses and research institutes. The other sources of biomedical waste are the following: Households, Industries, education institutes and research centres, Blood banks and clinical laboratories, Health care establishments. The sector generates all the types of waste listed under the bio-medical waste are shown in Figure.

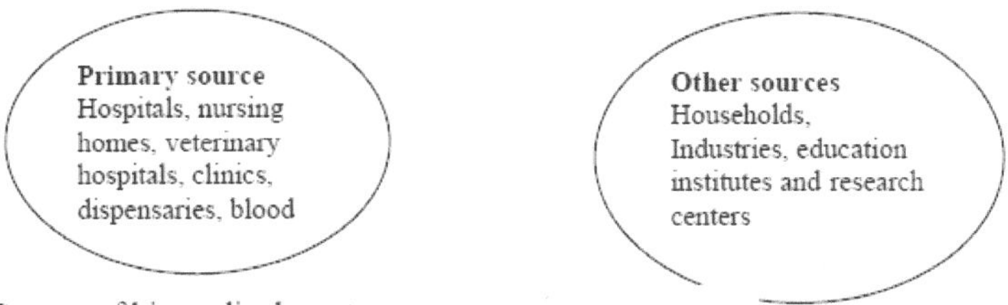

Figure Source of biomedical wastes

EFFECTS OF BIOMEDICAL WASTE

The improper management in bio-medical waste causes stern environmental problems that causes to air, water and land pollution. The pollutants that cause damage can be classified into biological, chemical and radioactive. There are several legislations and guidelines in India concerning environmental problems, which can be addressed. The classification of radioactive waste generated as part of bio-medical waste is covered. Some of the effects of pollution on air, radio activities, land, health and hazards are discussed.

AIR POLLUTION

Air pollution can be caused in both indoors and outdoors atmosphere. Biomedical waste that generated by air pollution are been classified in three types namely-Biological, Chemical and radioactive.

IN-DOOR AIR POLLUTION

Pathogens present in the waste can enter and remain in the air for a long period in the form of spores or as pathogens Segregation of waste, pre-treatment at source etc., can also reduce this problem to a great extent. Sterilizing the rooms will also help in checking the indoor air pollution due to biological. The indoor air pollution caused due to the above chemicals from poor ventilation can cause diseases like Sick Building Syndrome (SBS). Proper building design and well-maintained air conditioners can reduce the SBS. Chemicals should be utilized as per prescribed norms. Over use of chemicals should be avoided .

OUT-DOOR AIR POLLUTION

Outdoor air pollution can be caused by pathogens. The biomedical waste without pre-treatment if transported outside the institution, or if it is dumped in open areas, pathogens can enter into the atmosphere. Chemical pollutants that cause outdoor air pollution have two major sources-open burning and incinerators. Open burning of bio-medical waste is the most harmful practice. When inhaled can cause respiratory diseases. Certain organic gases such as dioxins and furans are carcinogenic. The design parameters and maintenance of such treatment and disposal technology should be as per the prescribed standards .

RADIOACTIVE EMISSIONS

Research and radio-immunoassay activities may generate small quantities of radioactive gas. Gaseous radioactive material should be evacuated directly to the outside. The use of such device requires maintenance of the trap and monitoring of the off-gas .

WATER POLLUTION

The liquid waste generated when let into sewers can also lead to water pollution if not treated properly . Water pollution can alter parameters such as pH, BOD, DO, COD, *etc*. There are instances where dioxins are reported from water bodies near incinerator plants. Dioxins enter the water body from the air.

RADIOACTIVE EFFLUENT

Radioactive waste in liquid form can come from chemical or biological research, from body organ imaging, from decontamination of radioactive spills, from patient's urine and from scintillation liquids used in radioimmunoassay. Under normal circumstances, urine and faeces can be handled as no radioactive waste so long as the patient's room is routinely monitored for radioactive contamination.

LAND POLLUTION

Soil pollution from bio-medical waste is caused due to infectious waste, discarded medicines, chemicals used in treatment and ash and other waste generated during treatment processes. Heavy metals such as cadmium, lead, mercury etc., which are present in the waste will get absorbed by plants and can then enter the food chain. Nitrates and phosphates present in leachates from landfills are also pollutants. Excessive amounts of trace nutrient elements and other elements including heavy metals in soil are harmful to crops and are also harmful to animals and human beings. Minimizing the waste and proper treatment before disposal on land are the only ways of reducing this kind of pollution.

HEALTH HAZARDS

According to the WHO, the global life expectancy is increasing year after year. However, deaths due to infectious disease are increasing. A study conducted by the WHO in 1996, reveals that more than 50,000 people die everyday from infectious diseases. One of major causes for the increase in infectious diseases is improper waste management. List of infections and diseases documented to have spread through bio-medical waste. Tuberculosis, pneumonia, diarrhoeal diseases, tetanus, whooping cough etc., are other common diseases spread due to improper waste management.

OCCUPATIONAL HEALTH HAZARDS

Occupational health concerns exist for janitorial and laundry workers, nurses, emergency medical personnel, and refuse workers. Injuries from sharps and exposure to harmful chemical waste and radioactive waste also cause health hazards to employees in institutions generating bio-medical waste. Proper management of waste can solve the problem of occupational hazards to a large extent .

HAZARDS TO THE GENERAL PUBLIC

The general public's health can also be adversely affected by bio-medical waste. Improper practices such as dumping of bio-medical waste in municipal dustbins, open spaces, water bodies etc., leads to the spread of diseases. Emissions from incinerators and open burning also lead to exposure to harmful gases which can cause cancer and respiratory diseases. Plastic waste can choke animals, which scavenge on openly dumped waste. Injuries from sharps are common feature-affecting animals. Harmful chemicals such as dioxins and furans can cause serious health hazards to animals and birds. Certain heavy metals can affect the reproductive health of the animals .

ENVIRONMENTAL MANAGEMENT SYSTEM

The EMS is a broad framework aimed at providing effective direction for an institution in response to the changing external and internal factors. Waste system of the hospital was studied by. Figure shows the waste management flow chart and process flow chart of the existing indicated the sequence from generation of waste to its final disposal.

Figure shows the interference of the points and data. Colour coding and type of container for disposal of biomedical wastes. Biomedical waste solutions specialize are in three categories namely:

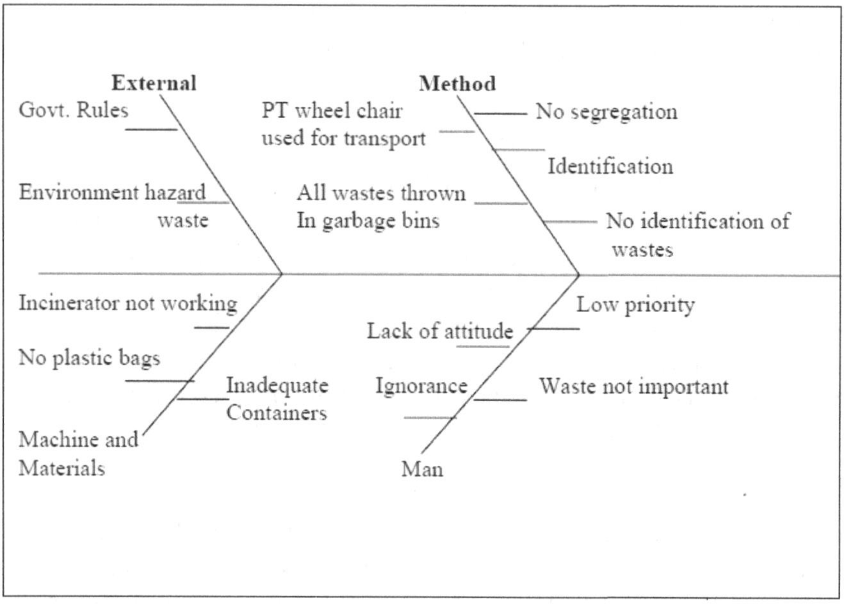

Figure Waste management flow chart*

DISPOSAL METHODS

Different methods are used for the disposal of bio medical waste and are discussed below: *Incineration:* It is a controlled combustion process where waste is completely oxidized and harmful microorganisms present in it are destroyed/ denatured under high temperature. An article regarding plasma pyrolysis of medical waste was reported by Neema and Gareshprasad. The authors stated that the operating cost of the system would be Indian Rupees 13 per kilogramme (kg), and the energy recovered would cost Indian Rupees 8 per kg; thus the net cost would be Rs 7 per kg. Incineration is popular in countries such as Japan where land is a scarce resource, as they do not consume as much area as a landfill. Sweden has been a leader in using the energy generated from incineration over the past 20 years. Denmark also extensively uses waste-to-energy incineration in localised combined heat and power facilities supporting district heating schemes .

- *Autoclaving:* Autoclaving is a low-heat thermal process where steam is brought into direct contact with waste in a controlled manner and for sufficient duration to disinfect the wastes. For ease and safety in operation, the system should be horizontal type and exclusively designed for the treatment of bio-medical waste. For optimum results, pre-vacuum based system be preferred against the gravity type system. It shall have tamper-proof control panel with efficient display and recording devices for critical parameters such as time, temperature, pressure, date and batch number etc.

- *Microwaving*, microbial inactivation occurs as a result of the thermal effect of electromagnetic radiation spectrum lying between the frequencies 300 and 300,000 MHz. Microwave heating is an inter-molecular heating process. The heating occurs inside the waste material in the presence of steam .
- *Hydroclaving* is similar to that of autoclaving except that the waste is subjected to indirect heating by applying steam in the outer jacket. The waste is continuously tumbled in the chamber during the process.
- Shredder: Shredding is a process by which waste are deshaped or cut into smaller pieces so as to make the wastes unrecognizable. It helps in prevention of reuse of bio-medical waste and also acts as identifier that the wastes have been disinfected and are safe to dispose off. A shredder is to be used for shredding in bio-medical waste with minimum requirements.

2

Handling, Ttorage, and Transportation of Health-care Waste

INTRODUCTION

Health care (or healthcare) is the diagnosis, treatment, and prevention of disease, illness, injury, and other physical and mental impairments in humans. Health care is delivered by practitioners in allied health, dentistry, midwifery-obstetrics, medicine, nursing, optometry, pharmacy and other care providers. It refers to the work done in providing primary care, secondary care, and tertiary care, as well as in public health.

Access to health care varies across countries, groups and individuals, largely influenced by social and economic conditions as well as the health policies in place. Countries and jurisdictions have different policies and plans in relation to the personal and population-based health care goals within their societies.Health care systems are organizations established to meet the health needs of target populations. Their exact configuration varies from country to country. In some countries and jurisdictions, health care planning is distributed among market participants, whereas in others planning is made more centrally among governments or other coordinating bodies. In all cases, according to the World Health Organization (WHO), a well-functioning health care system requires a robust financing mechanism; a well-trained and adequately-paid workforce; reliable information on which to base decisions and policies; and well maintained facilities and logistics to deliver quality medicines and technologies.

Health care can contribute to a significant part of a country's economy. In 2011, the health care industry consumed an average of 9.3 percent of the GDP orUS$ 3,322 (PPP-adjusted) per capita across the 34 members of OECD countries. The USA (17.7%, or US$ PPP 8,508), the Netherlands (11.9%, 5,099), France (11.6%, 4,118), Germany (11.3%, 4,495), Canada (11.2%, 5669), and Switzerland (11%, 5,634) were the top spenders, however life expectancy in total population at birth was highest in Switzerland (82.8 years), Japan and Italy

(82.7), Spain and Iceland (82.4), France (82.2) and Australia (82.0), while OECD's average exceeds 80 years for the first time ever in 2011: 80.1 years, a gain of 10 years since 1970. The USA (78.7 years) ranges only on place 26 among the 34 OECD member countries, but has the highest costs by far. All OECD countries have achieved universal (or almost universal) health coverage, except Mexico and the USA.

Health care is conventionally regarded as an important determinant in promoting the general health and well-being of people around the world. An example of this is the worldwide eradication of smallpox in 1980—declared by the WHO as the first disease in human history to be completely eliminated by deliberate health care interventions.

DELIVERY OF MODERN HEALTH CARE

The delivery of modern health care depends on groups of trained professionals and paraprofessionalscoming together as interdisciplinary teams. This includes professionals in medicine, nursing, dentistry,midwifery-obstetrics and allied health, plus many others such as public health practitioners, community health workers and assistive personnel, who systematically provide personal and population-based preventive, curative and rehabilitative care services. While the definitions of the various types of health care vary depending on the different cultural, political, organizational and disciplinary perspectives, there appears to be some consensus that primary care constitutes the first element of a continuing health care process, that may also include the provision of secondary and tertiary levels of care. Healthcare can be defined as either public or private.

PRIMARY CARE

Primary care refers to the work of health care professionals who act as a first point of consultation for all patientswithin thc hcalth carc system. Such a professional would usually be a primary care physician, such as ageneral practitioner or family physician, or a non-physician primary care provider, such as a physician assistant ornurse practitioner. Depending on the locality, health system organization, and sometimes at the patient's discretion, they may see another health care professional first, such as a pharmacist, a nurse (such as in the United Kingdom), a clinical officer (such as in parts of Africa), or an Ayurvedic or other traditional medicine professional (such as in parts of Asia). Depending on the nature of the health condition, patients may then bereferred for secondary or tertiary care.

Primary care is often used as the term for the health care services which play a role in the local community. It can be provided in different settings, such as Urgent care centres which provide services to patients same day with appointment or walk-in bases.

Primary care involves the widest scope of health care, including all ages of patients, patients of all socioeconomic and geographic origins, patients seeking to maintain optimal health, and patients with all manner of acute and chronic physical, mental and social health issues, including multiple chronic diseases. Consequently, a primary care practitioner must possess a wide breadth of knowledge in many areas.

Continuity is a key characteristic of primary care, as patients usually prefer to consult the same practitioner for routine check-ups and preventive care, health education, and every time they require an initial consultation about a new health problem. The International Classification of Primary Care (ICPC) is a standardized tool for understanding and analyzing information on interventions in primary care by the reason for the patient visit.

Common chronic illnesses usually treated in primary care may include, for example: hypertension, diabetes, asthma, COPD, depression and anxiety, back pain, arthritis or thyroid dysfunction. Primary care also includes many basic maternal and child health care services, such as family planning services andvaccinations. In the United States, the 2013 National Health Interview Survey found that skin disorders (42.7%), osteoarthritis and joint disorders (33.6%), back problems (23.9%), disorders of lipid metabolism (22.4%), and upper respiratory tract disease (22.1%, excluding asthma) were the most common reasons for accessing a physician. In context of global population aging, with increasing numbers of older adults at greater risk of chronic non-communicable diseases, rapidly increasing demand for primary care services is expected around the world, in both developed and developing countries. The World Health Organizationattributes the provision of essential primary care as an integral component of an inclusive primary health care strategy.

PHC AND POPULATION AGING

Given global demographic trends, with the numbers of people age 60 and over expected to double by 2025, PHC approaches have taken into account the need for countries to address the consequences of population ageing. In particular, in the future the majority of older people will be living in developing countries that are often the least prepared to confront the challenges of rapidly ageing societies, including high risk of having at least one chronic non-communicable disease, such as diabetes and osteoporosis. According to WHO, dealing with this increasing burden requires health promotion and disease prevention intervention at community level as well as disease management strategies within health care systems.

PHC AND MENTAL HEALTH

Some jurisdictions apply PHC principles in planning and managing their health care services for the detection, diagnosis and treatment of common mental health conditions at local clinics, and organizing the referral of more complicated mental health problems to more appropriate levels of mental health care.

SECONDARY CARE

Secondary care is the health care services provided by medical specialists and other health professionals who generally do not have first contact withpatients, for example, cardiologists, urologists and dermatologists. It includes acute care: necessary treatment for a short period of time for a brief but serious illness, injury or other health condition, such as in a hospitalemergency department.

It also includes skilled attendance during childbirth, intensive care, and medical imaging services. The "secondary care" is sometimes used synonymously with "hospital care". However many secondary care providers do not necessarily work in hospitals, such as psychiatrists, clinical psychologists, occupational therapists or physiotherapists, and some primary care services are delivered within hospitals. Depending on the organization and policies of the national health system, patients may be required to see a primary care provider for a referral before they can access secondary care.

For example in the United States, which operates under a mixed market health care system, some physicians might voluntarily limit their practice to secondary care by requiring patients to see a primary care provider first, or this restriction may be imposed under the terms of the payment agreements in private/group health insurance plans. In other cases medical specialists may see patients without a referral, and patients may decide whether self-referral is preferred. In the United Kingdom and Canada, paticnt sclf-rcfcrral to a mcdical specialist for secondary care is rare as prior referral from another physician (either a primary care physician or another specialist) is considered necessary, regardless of whether the funding is from private insurance schemes or national health insurance. Allied health professionals, such as physical therapists, respiratory therapists, occupational therapists, speech therapists, and dietitians, also generally work in secondary care, accessed through either patient self-referral or through physician referral.

TERTIARY CARE

Tertiary care is specialized consultative health care, usually for inpatients and on referral from a primary or secondary health professional, in a facility that has personnel and facilities for advanced medical investigation and treatment, such as a tertiary referral hospital. Examples of tertiary care services are cancer management, neurosurgery, cardiac surgery, plastic surgery, treatment for severe burns, advanced neonatology services, palliative, and other complex medical and surgical interventions.

QUATERNARY CARE

The term quaternary care is sometimes used as an extension of tertiary care in reference to advanced levels of medicine which are highly specialized and not widely accessed. Experimental medicine and some types of uncommon diagnostic or surgical procedures are considered quaternary care. These services are usually only offered in a limited number of regional or national health care centres. This term is more prevalent in the United Kingdom, but just as applicable in the United States. A quaternary care hospital may have virtually any procedure available, whereas a tertiary care facility may not offer a sub-specialist with that training.

HOME AND COMMUNITY CARE

Many types of health care interventions are delivered outside of health facilities. They include many interventions of public health interest, such as food safety surveillance, distribution of condoms and needle-exchange programmes for the prevention of transmissible diseases. They also include the services of professionals in residential and community settings in support of self care, home care, long-term care, assisted living, treatment for substance use disorders and other types of health and social care services. Community rehabilitation services can assist with mobility and independence after loss of limbs or loss of function. This can include prosthesis, orthotics orwheelchairs.

Many countries, especially in the west are dealing with aging populations, and one of the priorities of the health care system is to help seniors live full, independent lives in the comfort of their own homes. There is an entire section of health care geared to providing seniors with help in day-to-day activities at home, transporting them to doctor's appointments, and many other activities that are so essential for their health and well-being. Although they provide home care for older adults in cooperation, family members and care workers may harbor diverging attitudes and values towards their joint efforts. This state of affairs presents a challenge for the design of ICT for home care.

With obesity in children rapidly becoming a major concern, health services often set up programs in schools aimed at educating children in good eating habits; making physical education compulsory in school; and teaching young adolescents to have positive self-image.

HEALTH CARE INDUSTRY

The health care industry incorporates several sectors that are dedicated to providing health care services and products. As a basic framework for defining the sector, the United Nations' International Standard Industrial Classification categorizes health care as generally consisting of hospital activities, medical and dental practice activities, and "other human health activities". The last class involves activities of, or under the supervision of, nurses, midwives, physiotherapists, scientific or diagnostic laboratories, pathology clinics, residential health facilities, or other allied health professions, e.g. in the field of optometry, hydrotherapy, medical massage, yoga therapy, music therapy, occupational therapy, speech therapy, chiropody, homeopathy, chiropractics, acupuncture, etc.

In addition, according to industry and market classifications, such as the Global Industry Classification Standard and the Industry Classification Benchmark, health care includes many categories of medical equipment, instruments and services as well as biotechnology, diagnostic laboratories and substances, and drug manufacturing and delivery. For example, pharmaceuticals and other medical devices are the leading high technology exports of Europe and the United States. The United States dominates the biopharmaceutical field, accounting for three-quarters of the world's biotechnology revenues.

HEALTH CARE FINANCING

There are generally five primary methods of funding health care systems:

1. general taxation to the state, county or municipality
2. social health insurance
3. voluntary or private health insurance
4. out-of-pocket payments
5. donations to health charities

In most countries, the financing of health care services features a mix of all five models, but the exact distribution varies across countries and over time within countries. In all countries and jurisdictions, there are many topics in the politics and evidence that can influence the decision of a government, private sector business or other group to adopt a specific health policy regarding the financing structure.

For example, social health insurance is where a nation's entire population is eligible for health care coverage, and this coverage and the services provided are regulated. In almost every jurisdiction with a government-funded health care system, a parallel private, and usually for-profit, system is allowed to operate. This is sometimes referred to as two-tier health care or universal health care.

PRACTICE CONDITIONS AND REGULATIONS

SHORTAGES OF HEALTH PROFESSIONALS

Many jurisdictions report shortfalls in the number of trained health human resources to meet population health needs and/or service delivery targets, especially in medically underserved areas. For example, in the United States, the 2010 federal budget invested $330 million to increase the number of doctors, nurses, and dentists practicing in areas of the country experiencing shortages of health professionals.

The Budget expands loan repayment programs for physicians, nurses, and dentists who agree to practice in medically underserved areas. This funding will enhance the capacity of nursing schools to increase the number of nurses. It will also allow states to increase access to oral health care through dental workforce development grants. The Budget's new resources will sustain the expansion of the health care workforce funded in the Recovery Act.

In Canada, the 2011 federal budget announced a Canada Student Loan forgiveness programme to encourage and support new family physicians, nurse practitioners and nurses to practise in underserved rural or remote communities of the country, including communities that provide health services to First Nations and Inuit populations.

In Uganda, the Ministry of Health reports that as many as 50% of staffing positions for health workers in rural and underserved areas remain vacant. As of early 2011, the Ministry was conducting research and costing analyses to determine the most appropriate attraction and retention packages for medical officers, nursing officers, pharmacists, and laboratory technicians in the country's rural areas.

At the international level, the World Health Organization estimates a shortage of almost 4.3 million doctors, midwives, nurses, and support workers worldwide to meet target coverage levels of essential primary health care interventions. The shortage is reported most severe in 57 of the poorest countries, especially in sub-Saharan Africa.

HEALTH AND STRESS AMONG HEALTH CARE PRACTITIONERS

Some studies suggest that workplace stress is pervasive in the health care industry because of inadequate staffing levels, long work hours, exposure toinfectious diseases and hazardous substances leading to illness or death, and in some countries threat of malpractice litigation.

According to a report from the United States' National Institute for Occupational Safety and Health, "health care workers have higher rates of substance abuse and suicide than other professions and elevated rates of depression and anxiety linked to job stress."

Elevated levels of stress were also linked to high rates of burnout,absenteeism and diagnostic errors, and to reduced rates of patient satisfaction. In Canada, a national report Canada's Health Care Providers also indicated higher rates of absenteeism due to illness or disability among health care workers compared to the rest of the working population, although those working in health care reported similar levels of good health and fewer reports of being injured at work. Female health care workers may face specific types of workplace-related health conditions and stress. According to the World

Health Organization, women predominate in the formal health workforce in many countries, and are prone to musculoskeletal injury (caused by physically demanding job tasks such as lifting and moving patients) and burnout. Female health workers are exposed to hazardous drugs and chemicals in the workplace which may cause adverse reproductive outcomes such as spontaneous abortion and congenital malformations. In some contexts, female health workers are also subject to gender-based violence including from coworkers and patients.

Violence in the workplace subjects almost every healthcare worker to higher risk of on-the-job injury. Drunk, confused, and hostile patients and visitors are a continual threat to providers attempting to treat patients. Frequently, assault and violence in a healthcare setting goes unreported and is wrongly assumed to be part of the job.

PRACTICING WITHOUT A LICENSE

Practicing without a license that is valid and current is typically illegal. In most jurisdictions, the provision of health care services is regulated by government, and individuals found to be providing medical, nursing or other professional services without the appropriate certification or licence may face sanctions including even criminal charges leading to prison. The number of professions subject to regulation, requisites for individuals to receive professional licensure, and nature of sanctions that can be imposed for failure to comply vary across jurisdictions.

For instance, in the United States, under Michigan state laws, an individual is guilty of a felony if found to be practicing a health profession subject to regulation without a valid license or registration of their own, or exceeding what a limited license or registration allows. The state laws define the scope of practice for medicine, nursing, and a number of allied health professions. In Florida, practicing medicine without the appropriate license is a crime classified as a third degree felony, which may give imprisonment up to five years. Practicing a health care profession without a license which results in serious bodily injury classifies as a second degree felony, providing up to 15 years' imprisonment. In the United Kingdom, healthcare professionals are regulated by the state; the UK Health Professions Council (HPC) protects the 'title' of each profession it regulates. For example, it is illegal for someone to call themself an Occupational Therapist or Radiographer if they are not on the register held by the HPC.

APPLICATIONS IN HEALTHCARE

As well as seeking to improve population health through the implementation of specific population-level interventions, public health contributes to medical care by identifying and assessing population needs for health care services, including:

- Assessing current services and evaluating whether they are meeting the objectives of the health care system.
- Ascertaining requirements as expressed by health professionals, the public and other stakeholders.
- Identifying the most appropriate interventions.
- Considering the effect on resources for proposed interventions and assessing their cost-effectiveness.
- Supporting decision making in health care and planning health services including any necessary changes.
- Informing, educating, and empowering people about health issues.

IMPLEMENTING EFFECTIVE IMPROVEMENT STRATEGIES

To improve public health, one important strategy is to promote modern medicine and scientific neutrality to drive the public health policy and campaign, which is recommended by Armanda Solorzana, through a case study of the Rockefeller Foundation's hookworm campaign in Mexico in the 1920s. Soloranza argues that public health policy can't concern only politics or economics. Political concerns can lead government officials to hide the real numbers of people affected by disease in their regions, such as upcoming elections.

Therefore, scientific neutrality in making public health policy is critical; it can ensure treatment needs are met regardless of political and economic conditions.

The history of public health care clearly shows the global effort to improve health care for all. However, in modern day medicine, real, measurable change has not been clearly seen, and critics argue that this lack of improvement is due to ineffective methods that are being implemented. As argued by Paul E. Farmer, structural interventions could possibly have a large impact, and yet there are numerous problems as to why this strategy has yet to be incorporated into the health system. One of the main reasons that he suggests could be the fact that physicians are not properly trained to carry out structural interventions, meaning that the ground level health care professionals cannot implement these improvements.

While structural interventions can not be the only area for improvement, the lack of coordination between socioeconomic factors and health care for the poor could be counterproductive, and end up causing greater inequity between the health care services received by the rich and by the poor. Unless health care is no longer treated as a commodity, global public health can ultimately not be achieved. This being said, without changing the way in which health care is delivered to those who have less access to it, the universal goal of public health care cannot be achieved.

HEALTH CARE SYSTEM AND MANAGEMENT

HEALTHCARE INFORMATION SYSTEM STANDARDS

E-health basically comprises health services and information delivered or enhanced through the Internet and related technologies. The future healthcare system and its services, enabling e-health, are based on the communication between all information systems of all participants of an integrated treatment. Connecting the elements of each healthcare system (general practitioners, hospitals, health insurance companies, pharmacies, and so on)—even across national boarders—is an important issue for information systems research in healthcare.

Current developments, such as upcoming or already-deployed electronic healthcare chip cards (that are to be used across Europe), show the need for Europe-wide standards and norms. After the introduction of communication standards, we present their comparison with the aim to support the different functions in the healthcare information systems. Subsequently, we describe the documentation standards, and discuss the goals of existing standardization approaches. Implications conclude the article.

BACKGROUND

The advantages of generally accepted standards for the processes in healthcare and the medical market can be summarized as follows:

- Standards increase competition and reduce costs;
- Standardized products could easily be replaced or updated;
- Standardized products of various suppliers could easily exchange medical information;
- Healthcare institutions are able to iteratively extend their offers/ capabilities;
- Standardized products could reduce errors and make healthcare services safer.

Several national and international committees, German as well as European or American, have been founded to ensure unified standardization of national and international healthcare systems. Accordingly, there are numerous standardization attempts, which partly correspond to, but also disagree with, each other.

Two main objectives of these committees can be distinguished: the development of standards for communication, and standards for documentation in healthcare. The former focuses on enabling an efficient and effective combination of medical information systems, in order to enable the exchange of data between different medical information systems.

The latter are supposed to ensure the right interpretation of the content of electronically exchanged information.

IT-STANDARDS IN HEALTHCARE

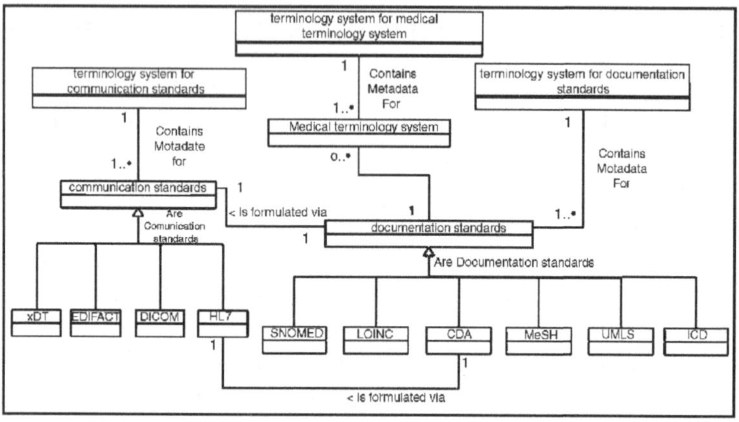

Fig. Medical Communication and Documentation Standards

The transmission of data between heterogeneous and isolated medical information systems requires interoperability of systems and data. The interoperability on its side is composed of norms, interfaces, and standards—the basis for data exchange and communication between participating applications. For an overview of common interoperability standards in the healthcare sector, and the graphical classification of its relations.

COMMUNICATION STANDARDS

Communication standards, also called syntactical standards, ensure a correct transmission of medical and administrative data between different information systems. In the clinical area, one can distinguish them worldwide, mainly between the established standards of Health Level 7/Clinical Document Architecture, (HL7/CDA), Digital Imaging and Communications in Medicine (DICOM), and Electronic Data Interchange for Administration, Commerce and Transport (EDIFACT). The reason for their acceptance is mainly the openness of these standards.

Health Level 7 is an international, vendor-independent, and main communication standard in healthcare for the exchange of information between systems and institutions. The Version 2 family of this standard is based on events that trigger the exchange of data. Beginning from Version 3 XML1, data structure is supported, alleviating the integration of data into information systems, since adequate libraries for XML handling are available.

HL7 operates at the application layer of the ISO/OSI reference model (ISO7498-1, International Organization of Standardization (ISO), 2006). The Clinical Document Architecture amplifies the HL7-standard with the description of the structure and the contents of clinical documents (e.g., discharge summaries and progress notes), based on an XML-format. HL7/CDA also offers a model for the exchange or the common use of information, and the option to individually reuse this information. Digital Imaging and Communications in Medicine is an open standard for the exchange of images in healthcare. Besides the image, it can also contain additional meta-information, such as the patient's name, date of admission, device parameters, or attending physician. The standard lists the data fields (e.g., images, diagnosis, patients, studies, series, and so on), functions of network services, as well as syntax and semantics for the commands and messages. DICOM can store the images with or without loss of information, in accordance to TIFF and JPEG formats, and enables electronic archiving of images in all medical information systems.

Electronic Data Interchange For Administration, Commerce and Transport (EDIFACT) standardizes the formats for the electronic exchange of administrative data amongst others in healthcare information systems. Orders, calculations, and payment orders in the health service are often based on it. EDIFACT is, unlike the other introduced communication standards, not specifically designed for the healthcare field- it is used globally by business partners of different kinds of business areas to exchange accounting-relevant data.

In the sector of general practitioners in Germany, there are additionally specific standards, so called xDT-standards (KBV, 2006). xDT is a set of several German standards, which are supposed to simplify the communication and the data exchange between healthcare providers (i.e., physician's offices, hospitals, and so on) and health insurance companies. As a result, xDT aims at the reduction of waste of paper by applying information technology using the following data formats:

- *ADT:* AbrechnungsDatenTransfer (invoice data for medical services)
- *AODT:* AmbulantesOperierenDatenTransfer (securing the quality of out-patient surgery)
- *BDT:* BehandlungsDatenTransfer (for the communication between general practitioners)
- *KVDT:* KassenacrztlichcVcrcinigungDatcn- Transfcr (standard for communication between physician's offices and health insurances)
- *LDT:* LaborDatenTransfer (communication with laboratories)
- *GDT:* GeraeteDatenTransfer (communication with medical devices)
- *ODT:* OnkologischerDatenTransfer (oncological data carrier for the documentation of tumor information)

Even though all of these xDT-standards serve different purposes, they are structured according to the same basic rules and principles.

There are currently efforts to harmonize the introduced communication standards on an XML-basis: HL7/CDA incorporates already the XML-format for structuring clinical documents; additionally, there are also XML-based specifications for the DICOM standard, for the xDT-standards, and for

EDIFACT. The advantages of introducing XML-based data structures can be described as follows:

- Automatic processing can be simplified when using established XML programming libraries.
- XML is an open and platform-independent standard.
- XML can be read and understood by users.

The introduced communication standards support different functions in healthcare information systems (Table 1: "x" connotes that the standard supports the function, "-" connotes the opposite case). Such a use of miscellaneous standards in several healthcare service sectors is the most current problem in electronic communication in medicine.

IT'S IMPACT ON DESIGN OF HEALTHCARE SYSTEMS

IT enables new ways of working and organising work locally, nationally and globally. IT is an important consideration in the design of public health systems in less developed countries where governments need to simultaneously pursue agenda related to healthcare, development, and trade.

Declining budgets and rising costs of healthcare encourage these innovations also in developed countries. This has significantly enhanced trade potential. Medical costs in OECD countries have risen. High cost medical procedures, increased longevity, ageing populations, and costly medicines are the main reasons patients, national public health systems and health maintenance organisations seek cross-border supplies offering more advantageous price/quality ratios.

Within domestic economies of U.S.A., Canada and Japan, TeleMedicine services halved traditional costs and increased the productivity of medical professionals. TeleExpertise has evolved as the basis for branded healthcare chains with an international scope.

Cross-border trade also flourishes within enterprises following the establishment of foreign affiliates. Corresponding to innovations in products and services introduced by IT, designs of healthcare systems could be simplified to reflect organisational forms based on syndication to reduce financial and administrative burdens. Resource combinations needed for vast undertakings such as development of new vaccines, testing new procedures for isolating genes and proteins or proving new specific treatments become organizable, bypassing difficulties associated with movement of natural persons and foreign commercial presence that restrict inter-firm and intra-firm service deliveries across national borders.

Problems of transferring patient records, communication of new medical know-how through dissemination of scientific publications and sharing in peer group fora among medical practitioners are solved. Instant portability is organised at low cost and electronic storage makes physical acquisition and storage redundant.

Public healthcare systems can be significantly rationalised with IT. Robotics and Artificial Intelligence applications enable the positioning of automatic analysers of biotic material such as blood, oral fluids and excretions at remote locations. Radiological scanners in rural areas enable distance consultations with organ specialists. Delivery of healthcare expertise can be networked through health centres in villages and beyond extending the reach of healthcare to places where it does not exist. Emergencies can also be handled more efficiently in countries deficient in transport infrastructure.

Medical professionals such as doctors, nurses, surgeons, anaesthetists, laboratory pathologists and medical technicians can pool their expertise in new forms and link in ways that save costs and time. IT enables inexpensive arrangements directly and indirectly through partnerships, branches, representation offices, subsidiaries, affiliates, franchises, licences and alliances through on-line tele-services and data transfers and there are numerous ventures in India, Pakistan, Srilanka, Kenya, and Mexico where transfers of know-how have been so arranged.

The TELEMED project in the European Union has promoted collaborations in Europe and among African, Carribean and Pacific Basin countries. New arrangements of profit-sharing are also being structured between medical practitioners, chemists, pharmaceutical firms, those providing medico-technical services and medical education institutions. Facilities in developing countries have been quick to seek affiliation with well known medical schools and hospitals to be able to offer superspecialisations and also to enhance their image as in the case of Duncan Gleneagles, Apollo Hospitals and Escorts in India.

The greatest impact is and would remain on the way healthcare development is organised where the most significant transformative role of IT is observed in how it induces:

- New ways of discovering, synthesising and testing therapeutic products where IT enables scale, speed, simulation and synergies;
- Intra-firm cross-border transfers as a source of profitability and growth with important implications for how costs are absorbed under differential pricing; and,
- Through the design of collaborations that support (a) and (b).

Trade in healthcare development is typically characterised by firm to firm arrangements. Less developed countries are weak in basic telecom and energy infrastructure and do not have many scientific laboratories endowed with adequate financial and human capital. In the past, this made them less likely nodes for linking in healthcare development networks. Three aspects have changed this now. The drug discovery process in the new biotechnologies is IT-intensive. It is necessary to process vast amounts of information at high speeds by distributing the work. Secondly, the drug development process involves clinical trials in targeted pre-selected populations based on isolating disease genes among populations with higher than normal susceptibility to disease.

Thirdly, in trying to exclude those contra-indicated by the composition of a therapeutic substance to prove a drug's safety within limits of notified exclusions calls for IT-intensity in global trials where IT-assisted screening reduces the scale of clinical trials as in the case of Genentech's Herceptin drug for breast cancer treatment. Such developments increase IT intensity in healthcare development and promote trade across borders to developed and developing countries. Intra-firm cross-border transfers are the preferred mode in the design of such healthcare development networks and contribute to the feasibility of differential pricing when final products are developed and test-marketed.

IT enables many different forms of cross-border cooperation that could bring down the high costs of innovation from about $500 million per medicinal drug developed to less than half of that cost while reducing the lead time of about twelve to fifteen years, on average, to less than five years in many cases. The logic of profitability in this situation warrants a calculus that increases consumer spending and margins while costs of development and delivery are brought down.

Firms syndicate risks in the design, development, production and distribution of healthcare products and services where profits are indicated. This is particularly the case with new drug developments and new treatment procedures for non-communicable diseases [such as cardio-vascular diseases with respiratory complications and malignant neo-plasms], which cause three times more deaths than communicable diseases8.

In communicable diseases, an important application of IT has arisen in mapping out characterised vectors using satellite remote sensing data to study the spread of vector-borne diseases such as Malaria and Plague. IT contributes profoundly in expansion of choice for design of research networks in discovery of new medicines, design of partnerships for testing new therapeutic methods, in marketing and distribution of prescription drugs, instruments, medical systems as well as investments by successful health maintenance organisations, managed care systems, and incorporated forms of general and special healthcare facilities.

Insurers can use IT to pool information and syndicate risk through consolidation if the insurance sector is open to foreign trade and investment. Cross-border mergers in the insurance industry for life and non-life businesses are prompted by new ways to assess acturial risks based on more reliable data and larger data sets through IT. The price differences for health insurance reduce. Insurers have an incentive to encourage "managed care" facilities to harmonise standards, standardise costs, and reduce the power of other service providers through consolidated contracts with or as Health Maintenance Organisations (HMOs). The policy implications of this are discussed in a later part of this chapter.

Trade in healthcare administration is, typically, a business to business activity in which "covered entities" in developed countries (and elite institutions in urban centres of less developed countries) meet obligations related to record-keeping and support services by farming out work to "business affiliates" at lower wage locations or to the informal sector in their own countries in a bid to reduce their costs.

The role of IT is significant here because time and cost advantages accrue from distributed enterprising across two or more time zones. Data processing and transfers can go on 24 hours a day, 7 days a week, 365 days in a year with increased efficiency and reduced cost. Whether this reduction in cost is passed on to the consumer or not would depend on policies governing such transactions and regulations governing prices where applicable.

Governments in services exporting countries also need policies to encourage innovation so that wage cost differentials are not the only reason for trade and the trade remains sustainable with positive spillover effects.

The dominant mechanism of cooperation in drug discovery is driven by economies of scale. Consolidation of enterprises of similar business profiles through mergers and acquisitions is replacing affiliates with more intra-firm transfers among developed countries. In drug testing, principal firms located mainly in developed countries do most of the research and development.

They are now able to organise division of work differentiating tasks of different stages and outsource some of the stages to establishments functioning as affiliates and agents. Human clinical trials are typically first conducted in developing countries due to fewer restrictions and lower costs. While positive spillover effects occur in all value chains and consolidations, investments in healthcare development were unnevenly spread. This is partially offset by research and development capacities created in developing countries like India aided by technology and scale acquired through process patent regimes and generic manufacturing for domestic market and exports. Policies can ensure that developing countries have incentives to undertake IT investments and participate in international networks of collaborators for drug discovery and development.

The demand for increased IT-intensity in healthcare development is stimulated by service providers who stand to gain from 'biopower' when databases designed by or on behalf of pharmaceutical firms, managed care enterprises and insurance agencies become available to a large transient population of commercial subscribers. New information increases the number of target molecules at which drugs are aimed. This reduces the cost of drug development if the identified target molecules could be proved or disproved quickly. The rate at which candidate molecules are disproved is presently twice the rate at which new candidate molecules are reported. At a global level, the value of IT in healthcare development (and its costs) exceeds the value of IT in healthcare delivery and healthcare administration put together.

There are significant differences in the composition of IT in healthcare development, delivery and administration between developed and developing countries. Differences in ways in which healthcare services trade is accounted and recorded make comparisons difficult. Decentralised networks and IT reinforce each other, whereas IT costs and risks require syndication.

These two contrary tendencies pull in different directions. When higher IT intensity affects the creation of value in the industry, it is pertinent to investigate whether this is associated with concentration of economic power, given the incentives for syndication of risk under conditions of higher IT intensity. Healthcare as an industry could undergo restructuring away from what are termed "cathedral" kind of corporate structures towards more "bazaar" kind of networks. There are a number of reasons for IT-intensive distributed enterprising to become the norm.

Firstly, international production and trade in healthcare services is designed around the concept of sharing in innovation through networks where the registered office is typically located in a country other than country of origin, with multiple share listings, cross-holdings based on alliances, sourcing of inputs from multiple sources and the extensive use of transfer pricing on intra-firm trade to minimise tax exposure.

Secondly, policies conducive to such arrangements require bargaining power with host governments, and well established intellectual property rights. Trends towards increased consolidation through mergers and acquisitions and divestments for arms length relationships to satisfy competition policies and anti-trust legislation are part of acquiring size and scale to be both cost-efficient and profitable.

Biotech is a high risk-high payoff business where IT intensity can make or break a company. There are over 150 biotech drugs on the market. Some biopharmaceuticals have sales of over $ 1 billion. About a third of all new drugs in Year 2001 arose from biotechnology.

However, the number of new medicines approved in the U.S. was down from 53 in 1996 to 27 in 2000 to just 9 in 2001. In Europe, biotech firms like Cybio, Genescan, Lion Bioscience and Medigene lost over 90 % of their value in Year 2001 whereas many U.S. biotech firms continued to command higher price-earnings ratios than traditional pharma companies17. However, the biotech firms havent yet grown to the size of pharma firms (Table for a comparison of the top five firms).

Table. Biotech and Pharma Firms:A Comparisson

Sales of top five biotech firms,2002-03 ($ BLN)		*Sales of top five pharma Firms,2002-03 ($ BLN)*	
Amgen	6.3	Merck	53.0
Genentech	2.8	Johnson	37.4
Serono	1.7	Pfizer	33.0
Biogen	1.2	Novartis	32.3
Chiron	1.2	Roche	29.7

IT has enabled licensing of drug development including the phases of its clinical trials. When a promising pharmaceutical compound is discovered, it is now the norm to auction rights to its development. An obesity-related gene discovered by scientists at a University was auctioned for about $20 million.

In this case, the buying firm then contracted out its clinical trials and recouped on its investment by value-adding into the asset with each progressive phase of clinical trials. In another case, Pfizer paid Searle $225 million to develop *celecoxib*, an anti-arthritis compound and farmed out the job. Inlicensing by firms for rights to development is regarded more profitable than out-licensing of know-how for a fee. The bigger firms usually have large sales and distribution networks worldwide to exploit their investments on a global scale. Out of fifty five "blockbuster drugs" (each contributing to revenues exceeding $500 million in a year) marketed in 1998, fourteen drugs were developed this way. Among these fourteen drugs, the cholesterol reducing Lipitor tops the list with sales of $2.2 billion.

Almost half of the profits of the world's ten largest pharmaceutical firms arise from such arrangements over externally sourced products and externally sourced services brokered together to gain time and cost advantages through substantial cross-border supply of services through IT. In some cases, as much as 95 % of revenues are derived from such arrangements.

It is apparent that this model is sustainable only if firms quickly spot and capture compounds. If contract R&D organisations become credible with IT, biotechnology firms would not sell out their discoveries. IT also enables large firms to target molecules through bigger networks and laboratories in situations where asset specificities and past human capital investments matter.

From the published financial statements of pharmaceutical firms, it is noticeable that the five largest pharma firms significantly increased overseas presence as measured by foreign assets to total assets ratios, taking advantage of cross-border supply of services.

According to the National Human Genome Resource Institute in U.S.A., genes contain codes for more than 50,000 proteins in the human body and drugs on the market presently target only 10 per cent of these. Moreover, the functions of 95 per cent of human genes are not yet known. This means that firms need to go beyond narrowly researching one gene at a time and investigate the interplay of genes and proteins along the entire cellular pathway of a disease. This calls for unprecedented co-operation across a range of locatiions, and a range of sciences, using gigantic data-sets at different locations.

Insurers and actuaries are able to use IT to pool records and databases for cost-effectiveness analysis. Bio-information and medical databases have been commodified and are tradable. Comparisons of relative efficacy of alternative treatments on a large scale adds to knowledge that brings down costs of diagnosis and treatment, besides enabling effective risk syndication by health insurers-domestic and international.

This is trade-promoting because there is a growing demand for private insurance in all countries where public healthcare systems are weak or non-existent (including those developing countries where incomes are rising and there is demand from urban elites).

The use of IT in structuring premia and settling claims encourages firms to set up 24-hour helplines offering year-round health insurance coverages, which may extend from national to international through partnerships and direct commercial presence involving foreign direct investments.

The consolidation of micro-insurance units for healthcare can be enabled the same way as IT enabled dairy co-operatives in rural areas of less developed countries to achieve economic scale. Schools that have IT infrastructure readily become nodal points for adult literacy and adult healthcare too. School-based health insurance schemes with IT systems have been tested successfully in Egypt in remote locations Field studies from Uganda and Philippines suggest that reinsurance possibilities can also be introduced in such ventures although the cost-neutrality in such schemes is not easily achieved 20.

IT has made it possible for moral hazards and adverse selection to be regulated so that insurance firms can take into consideration pre-existing disease conditions and public health vulnerabilities to structure risks properly and yet be supervised for not profiling only those insurance targets that have low health costs, in the interests of consumer protection.

IT'S FACILITATING ROLE IN STRENGTHENING PUBLIC-PRIVATE PARTNERSHIPS

Private sector participation in financing, production and delivery of healthcare products and services is a welcome addition to the resource-starved healthcare sector but also a challenge to the regulation of public health and in ensuring equitable access to the poor and needy.

The sharing of information about facilities, performance, resources, costs and prices among health authorities, planners, contributors, governments, service providers and patients is an important aid to promoting better management of healthcare systems with shared perspectives developed through interactive communications. This reduces the chance of missing opportunities of trade promotion in healthcare that require businesses and governments to act in concert.

The capacity of different people and organisations to work together across complex networks is an important element in novel and experimental advances. If communities of expertise can be connected and resources mobilised together with public interest, political energies and accountability, IT diffusion could play an important role in public-private partnerships in managed healthcare23. Success in any form of accountable and responsible public-private partnership is based on ongoing reviews, feedbacks and consultations where informed particpation is the key to success.

IT connectivity provides an interactive platform to exchange ideas and information at low cost which encourages participation and acts against exclusion. By this process, IT facilitates participation in collaborations by spawning communications networks with strong incentives to move away from isolated systems towards risk syndications and risk exchanges, harvesting value through designs of communications networks. Aided by IT, the success of Merck's *Ivermectin* drug donation for curing river blindness enabled a hundred million people to be treated in 31 countries with credibility of the programme based on communications networks which enabled wide participation and lots of feedback. This success later spawned one of the biggest public-private partnerships when Merck joined hands with the Gates Foundation for more such initiatives.

In contrast, Glaxo-Wellcome's anti-Malaria*M alarone* drug donation programme in Kenya suffered from inadequate communication and participation and lack of sufficient information to conduct a reasoned discourse24 Failures experienced in drug donation programmes due to communication gaps could bc easily remedied by IT 25.

IT connectivity would have enabled facts of the Malarone case to be known at the time it happened with scope for timely intervention by all concerned instead of the public remaining unaware for four years until details were published by scholarly journals like Lancet. Electronic archiving accessible through internet could simplify dissemination of new knowledge published by scientific journals.

The core role of IT in healthcare may be understood from the way designs of healthcare development and delivery enabled and supported by IT include or exclude people and encourage or discourage their participation in influencing decisions about allocation of healthcare resources. Participation is a vital aspect of healthcare because health consumption requires participation in its production at every level starting from individual persons (diet, hygiene, lifestyle, belief and trust in one or more medical systems) to communities (safety, pollution control, sanitation, public hygiene), and nations (healthcare standards, budgetary allocations, medical education, support to research and innovation in diagnosis and treatment, and availability of medicines) rendering it uniquely amenable to communicative technologies, horizontally and vertically in and between these aggregations.

Public-private partnerships are also required to cope with trading in bioinformatics and clinical databases. Significant transactions costs arise when contributions are sourced from a wide range of value creators using different platforms of data transfers and with multiple claims to proprietary rights over fragments of a whole process before a marketable product arises. This creates incentives for venture capital, pharmaceutical firms, biotech start-ups and the State (and its marketised counterparts such as health maintenance organisations) to make new forms of partnerships in predictive medicine and treatments.

Alliances of universities and research centres with drug developing and clinical trial enterprises are being established within developed and developing countries and also between organisations in developed and developing country locations. IT-intensity sustains such networks contributing to efficiency and equity through rationalisation of financial constraints as well as non-financial constraints.

IT-INDUCED VULNERABILITIES AND IT-AGGRAVATED RISKS

IT is distinguishable from other technologies because it is process oriented and transformative in its effects on production, consumption and organisation. Connection speeds are constrained by availability of bandwidth spectra and the risk of data loss from contamination by viruses and bugs can only be minimised but not altogether eliminated.

While information that IT produces is easily commodified, much of the knowledge that IT driven biotechnology incubates is tacit and not eassily reducible as information. This is the reason that biotech requires science parks and trustful networking anchored in a location.

Placing information on the web poses risks to ownership of intellectual property. Nor can all information belong to everyone being unsustainable even in its elements, without being hosted or sponsored. IT products are excludable, divisible and ownable through introduction of filters, but cyberspace does not create a domain governed from within itself insulated from other jurisdictions26.

The reliance on IT obliges adaptation to ever-changing new technical norms and to new rules introduced by regulators or censors. Policies and safeguards need to be envisaged to harmonise private and public interest so that IT is not used as a tool to propagate harmful substances and drugs. There could be four different ways in which IT as a media channel could be protected from undesirable traffic:

- International legal agreements on e-commerce prohibiting certain products and services as "global public bads" from the purview of e-commerce.

- Introduction of rules by regulators with enforceable penalties.
- The use of IT itself to neutralise the canvassing of "sins and bads" with counter-campaigns disclosing more information on health hazards.
- Censorship of cyberspace through filters.

IT has enabled screening of people for susceptibility to diseases and also the targeting of new drugs to pre-defined genetic profiles. Policies must ensure that genetic stratification does not create new social class structures with genetic upper classes and genetic lower classes. Priorities of healthcare developers and deliverers would need to be harmonised within the budgetary constraints of healthcare contributors and recipients in different countries with different quanta of healthcare resource availability.

Healthcare needs, resources and IT capacities in less developed countries differ from developed countries although IT-enabled resource linkages and exchanges could impact quality, efficiency and equity dimensions of healthcare everywhere. The globalised healthcare industry is growing faster than any other industry and offers incentives to participate in its designs. Imminent restructuring of authority and responsibility in national spaces forces all concerned to respond in self-interest.

Resource constraints in less developed countries pull investments into IT to the extent allocation of scarce resources can be improved on efficiency and quality considerations in private healthcare and on grounds of efficiency and equity in public healthcare. Safeguards are needed to ensure that global solutions for market standardisation and control (of health norms or IT standards and specifications) are not limited to a few players with greater access to healthcare or IT resources.

Since IT-intensity is one of the causes of rising healthcare expenditures, policies would need to ensure, through appropriate cost-benefit analysis, justifications and affordability of such increases on grounds of efficiency or postive externalities, particularly in the case of less developed countries27. If IT attracts resources away from actions which have large positive externalities (or the benefits to those who derive livelihoods from IT's role in healthcare are less than the increased costs of healthcare commodities and services), Specific regional studies at the level of local communities would be useful to understand and evaluate these processes because the available data is meagre.

IT has enabled certain kinds of abuses that would have previously not been possible to execute on a large scale. Pharmaceutical firms provide incentives to pharmacies to sell prescription drugs over the counter without prescriptions in less developed countries. IT has made it possible for chemists, pharmacies, and extension counters of clinics and hospitals to build databases and push products using retail store models of incentives -something that would be impossible in developed countries where firms target doctors, not individual chemists or pharmacies. This is also a source of concern to health insurers organising the contribution side of such a market through health insurance schemes. Overconsumption of medical products and services is one of the leading causes of rising healthcare costs. Health insurance schemes get dragged into bearing the burden due to improvements in medical procedures to prolong life, ageing populations and the tendency of buying insurance according to needs without necessarily contributing to it on the basis of means. There is also the danger of supply-induced demand.

For instance, schools that introduce school-wide healthcare insurance schemes are pressurised in direct marketing campaigns to dispense medicines and treatments with little regard to needs. The marketing of Ritalin, Metadate and Adderall (through commission agents armed with IT-databases) to school authorities for "attention deficit hyperactivity disorders" in school children to make children more docile for teachers has already occurred without parents' knowledge in some instances.

Such malpractices would be difficult to control in societies where establishments like schools have power over parents as in cities of developing countries where demand for places in private schools exceeds supply. IT-enabled databases have also been used to target school children covered by health insurance through commission agents acting together with school systems to push children into medical treatments they do not need by inducing them through small treats as incentives. Similarly, "managed care" alternatives could take perverse forms for adults too when IT promotes disease management models bypassing medical expertise by conducting what is termed in medical parlance as "wallet biopsy" (scrutiny of the means to pay).

The recording of health data does not merely concern medical histories, medicine inventories and doctors´ addresses maintained for the benefit of patients. Clinical and personal data of patients and doctors routinely stored in medical facilities could be traded without informed consent for market research, insurance and other commercial purposes to target profiles. IT has enabled this to be done in centralised databases on a large scale for whole communities, regions and countries.

Some governments already directly trade in their monopoly of control over such information as in UK and China. Other governments as in Estonia, Kenya, Nigeria, Tonga and Iceland license this trade through firms registered in offshore or other grey and distant jurisdictions28. The licensing of healthcare databases for commercial profit with or without the prior consent of individuals whose data is so traded enables collecting or trading DNA information on specific groups and communities without their knowledge or consent.

New vulnerabilities point to the need for policy safeguards to deal with the following problems:

- Rights to privacy and personal data protection are easily breached because healthcare databases have to be kept open for updating old records and for initiating new records and entries. So confidentiality cannot be secured by coding the data or disconnecting the data from personally identifiable features. Patients could lose trust in the confidentiality of their conversations with their doctors unless this problem is solved. Demands of payment for parting with bio-information could arise.
- Medical databases are easily linkable to databases of genealogy, castes, tribes, clans, ethnicity, and genetics. The principle that such data be stored only at its place of origin and used only for the original purpose for which it is collected is difficult to enforce. Personal data on whole nations and ethnic groups could be exploited in ways that endanger public health. Without enforceable international agreements, no individual or social institution is in any position to supervise the use of healthcare databases. In the hands of mercenaries and rogue states, healthcare databases could be misused to trigger complex humanitarian emergencies or for fostering permanent dependencies using biopower as a means of disruption.
- The scientific and commercial value of health databases is limited to those who have the means to maintain and update these databases and link them to other databases in their possession. This could accentuate the information and technology gaps between developed and less developed countries.
- IT enables decoding of personal data using genotypes and phenotypes as personal identifiers and the design of novel organisms against which vaccines or antibiotics would be useless. When private information held in public databases is commercially traded by privatising public domains, rights of natural persons get transposed with rights of artificial juridical entities. Since intellectual property rights are private rights, international regimes for e-commerce in healthcare and consumer protection are needed for what remains outside the public domain.
- The risk is greatest when exclusive ownership or control of healthcare databases is lawful. The entirety of medical records of a community are a non-renewable single good. Yet, the incentive for governments in less developed countries to sell or license such information to raise resources from the private sector is considerable. This is particularly the case when therapies are developed on the basis of databases of communities offered free drugs in exchange. There is growing awareness that firms need to repay communities for vital bio-information. DNA information of an individual is worth about $100,000

in commercial value which could be greater than the cumulative income receipts of individuals in poor countries over a lifetime30. This clearly points to the need for biobanks which could profitably and securely be designed and constituted under international control as independent global healthbanks or by extending WHO's mandate to accommodate them within its umbrella.

- Unrestrained IT in healthcare implies the end of privacy. If the restraining instrument is government executive control as in Malaysia and the U.K, the danger is arbitrariness. In contrast, IT restrained by parliamentary laws could lead to wasteful litigation. If restrained only by market incentives it would make it too easy and too profitable for businesses to act contrary to the interests of other constituents. This situation urgently requires new forms of public-private partnership.
- If it is known that normal data protection controls can be easily bypassed by powerful interests in a vital area like health in any particular country, it would also have consequences for trade and development in other sectors due to loss of confidence in that country's capacity to provide adequate data protection for business secrets and intellectual property rights.
- With IT, the inventory of possible symptoms, physiological and mental, is quickly recognised also in patients who suffer from minor ailments and who could recover anyhow, with or without treatment. When treated, such patients recover rapidly. This sort of change in diagnosis rather than in treatment may re-allocate healthcare resources and increase costs. IT could also increase the cost of healthcare in other ways when "internetpositive patients" confront doctors with medical information obtained from the web which doctors themselves may not have found time to evaluate.
- With reference to insurance consolidation in Section, trading in clinical and genetic databases enables insurers to acquire information to exclude beneficiaries of specific profiles who pose higher risks to predictable disease susceptibilities. Secondly, centralised healthcare databases of more than one million records cannot be securely designed and administered31. Due to these hazards, the role of IT in organising the contribution side of healthcare remains undeveloped for the present.
- The promotion of IT as a means to stimulate cross-border connectivity for growth and employment through trade and foreign investment cannot be easily accomplished when international networks bypass locations where doctors, IT specialists and other scientists and technologists do not already relate to each other. According to the

reports of the European Union's TELMED project, there is little evidence even in developed countries of any strategic development of telematic healthcare outside pilot programmes, except in medical imaging, community health applications, and health care administration systems involving smart cards and electronic patient record transfers.

FEATURES OF HEALTH CARE SYSTEMS

As governments and societies attempt to maximise the level of health care benefits generated from the resources available, the nature of health care systems and their funding mechanisms are never far from the discussions and deliberations that take place in academic, political and professional communities. Reforms and change have been the order of the day in many health care systems and, while any attempt to assess their relative success has been virtually impossible given the frequency and extent of such developments, one common thread has appeared to be transference of decision-making to a more local level. In the UK, the reforms introduced in the early 1990s paved the way for the present situation where local decision-makers are required to establish priorities and allocate resources. The separation of the agencies that commission, organise or purchase services from those that provide health care services has become a common feature of health care reforms across many European countries. As a result, patients may have to bypass their local hospitals and travel across both national and international boundaries in order to receive treatment, and NHS patients may be found in hospital beds alongside private patients, as well as the opposite scenario, which has a longer history.

The extent of private sector involvement in health care systems has been another feature in the ongoing debate about the funding and organisation of health care services.

For example, just as there is greater involvement with the private sector hospitals in the UK, the Private Finance Initiative (PFI) has become the main source of capital funds for major investment projects in the NHS, funding 85% of major capital projects since 1997.2 However, there are major concerns as to the effectiveness and efficiency of PFI as a vehicle for building new capacity within the NHS, with counter claims suggesting that it actually constrains service provision and limits future developments, and may not actually represent value for money as originally envisaged, and 'there appears to be no macroeconomic justification for preferring PFI to Exchequer financing, or for regarding one approach as any more affordable than the other'.

The organisational structure of health care systems is also subject to variation and what appears to be more or less constant change and reform. In 1989 the UK Department of Health White Paper 'Working for Patients' proposed a set of reforms in an attempt to improve the performance of the NHS, based on what came to be known as 'internal market'. Under the new arrangements, hospitals and community health units were designated as NHS Trusts and became the main 'providers' of front-line health services.

They were required to compete with each other for contracts from Health Authorities (HAs) and general practitioner (GP) Fundholders who were established as the purchasers or 'commissioners' of services. The new organisational structure, which sought to emphasise decentralisation and entrepreneurship, ran counter to other health policy initiatives of the time, most notably The Patient's Charter and the Health of the Nation strategies, which sought to impose central standards and targets. It was also argued that the experiment with a competitive quasi-market in health care for the NHS did not really succeed because in the main it was not tried, as the government was reluctant to reduce the extent of centralised control.

It was therefore no surprise that in 1997, the new Labour government declared that the internal market and the reliance on 'competition' as the basis for improving performance in the NHS would come to an end.8 In their place would come a return to collaboration, partnership, integration and the development of new structures to replace the existing HAs.

New organisations (with different nomenclatures evident in different parts of the devolved UK) in primary care were constituted to emphasise the increasingly important role of primary care in the planning of health care and to cooperate with secondary care providers. These independent trusts control a highly significant percentage of the NHS budget and have the capability of retaining budget surpluses and utilising these for the benefit of patients in their locality.

However, there remain serious capacity constraints within the NHS in the UK, particularly in terms of doctors and nurses - a problem that may intensify if some commentators are to be believed. A report in the media has suggested, for instance, that thousands of the country's most experienced doctors may quit the NHS within 3 years after the introduction of the new contract in 2005, which means they can retire early on full pensions.

The new contract boosts the salaries of top consultants by £20 000 to £92 000. Their pension contributions will rise in line with their pay, meaning that they will hit the Organisation and funding of health care services maximum achievable pension - just under half their salary - by their early sixties. Some could even retire as early as their mid-fifties with only a slight deduction in their retirement benefits. For most there will be little incentive to keep working punishing NHS schedules until mandatory retirement.

The stark warning presented is that by 2007 nearly 4000 senior consultants will have little or no financial incentive to continue working for the NHS and any mass exodus would exacerbate staffing problems in the service, which at present has a shortfall of 10 000 hospital doctors. The Wanless Report estimated that an extra 30 000 doctors, 24 000 nurses and 94 000 qualified scientific, technical and ancillary workers were needed over the next 20 years or so,10 but even this achievement would not change the position of the UK as below the EU average in the number of doctors and nurses per 1000 population.

In addition, the development of league tables, the continued use of performance indicators, the establishment of 'Foundation hospitals', the ongoing political debate surrounding so-called 'patient choice', and the role and extent of involvement of the private sector in the UK make it difficult to ignore the imperative of competitiveness within the health care system.

For example, in a comparison of the NHS with a health maintenance organisation in the USA, Kaiser Permanente, the latter achieved better performance at roughly the same cost as the NHS because of integration throughout the system, efficient management of hospital use, the benefits of competition and greater investment in information technology.

At the same time, the nature of the NHS and its financing continue to focus the attention of policymakers, politicians, academics and health care professionals. The rationale for government involvement in the organisation and funding of health care is fundamental to such discussions and is considered in the next section.

THE NECESSITY FOR GOVERNMENT INVOLVEMENT IN THE FINANCING OF HEALTH CARE

In order for the market mechanism to deliver Pareto-efficiency, a number of conditions need to exist:

1. Perfect competition:
   - A large number of consumers and suppliers, so that no one consumer or supplier can collude to exert excessive influence within the market;
   - Product or service homogeneity, so that no one product or service can be distinguished from (and possibly have an advantage over) another complete freedom of entry into the market and exit from it, so that there are no constraints on new suppliers joining the market or existing suppliers leaving.
2. Perfect knowledge on the part of consumers, so that consumers are fully aware of the characteristics of the product and/or service being provided, know whether they want it, know how much they want, know when they want it and where they can get it.
3. A certain world, where consumers can choose and plan when and where they will engage in transactions.
4. Absence of externalities, which arise when the activities of one consumer and/or supplier affect the outcome of the activities of another agent and are not covered by the market mechanism.

In the real world, perfect competition does not exist. Markets are characterised by monopolistic tendencies and other structures that allow individual suppliers to exercise considerable control over the price to be charged or the amount to be produced. Even if perfect competition did exist, there are certain types of goods that either would not be provided at all or would be provided inadequately or in insufficient quantity by private firms.

The demand side of the market mechanism is characterised by a desire for a commodity plus an ability to pay for it. For many products this may be perfectly realistic but for a range of others, it may not be. The characteristics of 'public goods' mean that such commodities are provided by central or local government (e.g. defence, street lighting) or not at all. In addition, governments intervene to finance and provide 'merit' goods, that is, goods and services that are higher on society's preference listing than on an aggregation of individuals' preference listings, alongside private suppliers. Examples of these are to be found in the provision of education, transport and health care.

It is inconceivable that many people would be prepared to directly pay for the provision of speed cameras or traffic-calming schemes, designed to reduce the number of accidents, and it is left to government to provide such schemes. Another problem associated with the operation of the market mechanism is the existence of what are called externalities. There are many examples of externalities in health care that require government intervention.

In recent years, the dangers of passive smoking have been recognised and led to the introduction of smoking bans in public places, with New York, Italy and Ireland being prime examples. Such measures to counter the 'adverse effects' resulting from the activities of some members of society on others would not be possible if there were no government intervention in the operation of the market mechanism.

Similarly, if there were no regulation and intervention on the 'supply side' to ensure that practitioners were qualified, the market would not prevent anyone from setting up as a practitioner, with potentially serious and even fatal consequences. While regulations and licensure do not necessarily guarantee that 'quacks' and 'one-offs' will not practice, the standards, skills and knowledge required for qualification go a long way in protecting the safety and interests of consumers, who are unlikely to be sufficiently informed to do so themselves.

Similarly, it is unrealistic to assume that consumers have, or can access, sufficient information relating to health care services (despite the wealth of information available from the Internet), to furnish themselves with the perfect knowledge required to make the decisions necessary when confronted by sickness and illness.

Consumers of health care services, as in other areas, are therefore reliant on agents who act on their behalf - health care professionals. Agency arises in situations in which potential consumers recognise that they are not sufficiently well equipped to make rational, informed consumption decisions. They decide to rely on experts acting on their behalf so that they have a better chance of maximising utility.

While politicians and policymakers have recognised the importance of involving patients in the decision-making processes and the role of the 'expert patient' has been developed, it is still the case that patients are generally ill-informed and that health care professionals are able to act as the more informed agent on behalf of patients, in relation to problem diagnoses, treatment availability and the effectiveness of interventions. Other reasons that necessitate government involvement in the funding of health care services, as opposed to reliance on a private insurance-based system, arise due to the existence of adverse selection and moral hazard.

Adverse selection occurs when people do not reveal the full extent of their health profile, and thereby their risk level, to the insurer. This may result in people at high risk paying lower premiums than their actual risk would indicate. As a consequence, insurers would inflate the premiums and some people may be left uninsured - those at low risk who do not bother to take up insurance as the premiums are too high and those at high risk who cannot afford the premiums.

Moral hazard arises when the attitudes and behaviours of people change once they are covered for the potential costs of treatment. They may choose to take less care of themselves and consume all health care services that they are entitled to, irrespective of whether they are needed or not. It is therefore apparent that there are powerful arguments in favour of government intervention in health care provision. What is also evident is that the market mechanism would not adequately deal with the supply of professionals.

In theory, a market for health care professionals could exist, but there would be no system of qualification and regulation, and patients would have to choose between practitioners based on their own assessments of quality and price, while there would be no curbs on overprovision of health care services, and, given the lack of knowledge and expertise among consumers of health care services, they would be utterly dependent on doctors and other health care professionals as their agents.

THE ROLE OF HEALTH CARE PROFESSIONALS

The motivation of individuals who work within public services in general and within health care in particular has been widely discussed in the literature. Much of this concentrates on the extent to which such individuals are self-interested or altruistic. However, most of the literature on organisational behaviour has made fairly simple assumptions concerning individual motivations and has concentrated on the extent to which individuals or groups of individuals with different motivational structures interact within organisations to affect organisational behaviour. The economic theory of the firm provides three models to assess the behaviour of organisations. The first group of models is based on what is known as the traditional theory, which represent the firm as a single agent in pursuit of profit maximisation.

The single firm is unable to exert any influence over the prices or levels of production, due to the fact that there are many other firms operating within the same market. Such models have very limited application in explaining the behaviour of organisations in general, yet alone those in health care services assume the existence of perfect competition in markets and bear no resemblance to the nature and complexity of the modern organisation.

The second group of models is based on the distinction between management and ownership and is known as 'managerial theories of the firm'. These models also consider firms as single agents, but ones that pursue other goals not linked to profit maximisation, such as the maximisation of revenue. Managers will have different goals and objectives in relation to the performance of organisations than the owners of the organisation. For example, it was suggested that the short-term nature of managerial contracts within the NHS could, in some cases, result in decisions being made to protect their employment rather than other desirable, longer-term goals, such as staff or service development.

The third group of models - multiple agent models, derived from behavioural theories of organisational behaviour - regards organisational behaviour as the product of multiple groups interacting within the organisation. Behavioural models take cognisance of the complexities underlying organisations and describe the firm as a coalition of groups with conflicting interests. The firm is a 'satisficing' organisation rather than a maximising entity, which aims to achieve a number of objectives, such as the 'maximisation' of production levels, sales, market share and profit, but with equal emphasis on stability and survival. These behavioural models have been further developed to acknowledge the significance of relationships and interactions within the organisation and how behaviour is influenced through contracts and other forms of incentive structures.

Another type of model has been advocated as a logical variation on the behavioural model, which suggests that organisational motivation is the product of multiple actors, but with a dominant single actor mimicking the behaviour of the atomistic firm structure with a single overriding goal.

Models of hospital behaviour have been drawn from the theoretical perspectives of organisational behaviour and the economic theories of the firm. Some have treated the hospital as a profit-maximising entity, in general assuming that clinicians are the primary decision-makers, while other models predict that other forms of maximisation exist which identify administrators as the decision-making unit.21 Within the UK, managers and health care professionals have been identified as the principal actors within the NHS, who coexist in a power coalition while harbouring different and potentially conflicting sets of interests.

There was no consensus on whether either the managerial or the professional body was dominant but, within professionals, consultants were considered to be the dominant actors, over and above, say, nurses.24 Much of the organisational change within the NHS during the 1980s and 1990s was an attempt to redefine the balance of power between doctors and managers, that is, to strengthen the role of management and to encourage participation by doctors in management, with the aim of shifting doctors' orientation and behaviour to be more like that of managers, thus strengthening the management's objective function of the NHS organisation.

However, such attempts were not without their casualties. A dramatic example of conflict between managers and medical staff took place in South Wales in 1995. An NHS Trust ran into serious financial difficulties, partly because medical staff were able to resist the implementation of a plan to make them redundant and to transfer others to another Trust when the service they were providing was to be transferred. In the battle that ensued - including a vote of no confidence in the Chairman of the Trust Board and the Chief Executive of the hospital passed by the medical staff - the Chairman and the Chief Executive of the Trust were replaced and the affair became the subject of an investigation by the Welsh Affairs Select Committee and Public Accounts Committee of the House of Commons.

More recent work has been undertaken to assess the extent to which the desire to strengthen the role of management and the participation of professionals in management had become apparent in reality and to determine whether in fact there is a dominant power base underlying decision-making in NHS Trusts. A survey of 1500 consultants and mangers (as the major power sourccs) across 100 Trusts was undertaken over a 3-year period to assess what motivating factors lay behind their agendas and eventually the performance of their Trusts.

The findings were that consultants considered production goals to be more important than financial break-even targets, but within those goals, considered quality to be more important than service volume. While the break-even target was generally found to be the primary goal of managers, they proved to be a heterogeneous group with quality ranking as the main priority among those managers who were closest to service delivery.

This was at odds with the apparent objective of Trusts, which both groups perceived as being the pursuit of financial targets, consistent with the formal, government-set requirements. The study concluded that the reforms of previous years had done nothing to reduce the power base of the hospital consultant and that the Trusts' primary objective was to maintain service quality.

But what of the primary care sector where the context is complicated by the existence of other factors and situations? While the literature has concentrated on hospitals and NHS Trusts, the same imperatives apply in terms of service quality and financial targets in primary care, but issues relating to equity, wider efficiency objectives and indeed ethical considerations also impinge significantly on the objectives and behaviour of primary care organisations. In addition, there are also the potential conflicts that arise from the different agendas, and objective functions that arise from the role of health care professionals as agents, especially in the context of primary care, with its dual functions of service commissioning and service provision.

HEALTH CARE PROFESSIONALS AS THE AGENTS OF PATIENTS

The role of the health care professional as the agent of the patient is of particular relevance to the organisation of health care services. The health care professional is in the unenviable position of wearing one hat as health care service provider and, at the same time, having to wear the hat of patient advisor.

As providers they seek to diagnose, treat and care for the health care needs and problems faced by patients. As patients' agents, they aim to put themselves in the place of the patients and provide advice, based on their greater knowledge and expertise, to inform the patients, who can then address their health care needs. In other words, the objectives and goals of health care professionals should mirror those of their patients.

This, of course, assumes close correspondence between the health care needs of patients as perceived by patients themselves and those as perceived by health care professionals. Much energy and effort has gone into the assessment of needs of patients. Needs are categorised into those that are perceived and those that are not, by the patient or agent. The former relate to those that exist when an 'abnormality' is identified by the patient which can be dealt with in one, or a combination, of three ways:

1. No action;
2. Use made of one of the informal agencies involved in health and social care, e.g. self-medication, informal carers;
3. Contact made with health care and social care services at the initial point of contact (i.e. 'expressed need').

Health care professionals may have a different perspective than that of patients, and it may be that the self-perceived needs of the patient are not acknowledged as being 'need' by health care professionals but rather as being 'neurosis'. Thus, because of this assessment by professionals, selfperceived needs would not necessarily be met with service provision. The other category of needs, namely needs unperceived by the (potential) patient, would encompass conditions that are unrecognised by an individual, the family, carers or friends but that are potentially discoverable by practitioners and professionals on careful investigation of the total physical, mental and emotional well-being of the individual.

The problem is that they only become discoverable when patients make contact with the service providers, who then take on the responsibility of agents acting on their behalf. Such needs may warrant intervention (when it is thought that prevention, management or specific therapy would be of benefit) but would also include those situations where intervention to meet such needs may prove to be unwanted by the patient, e.g. a severe warning to change lifestyle behaviour and habits if serious coronary events are to be avoided.

For some people, the ability to identify or articulate their needs is extremely difficult, while for most lay people their limited knowledge does present a major constraint in equating needs with appropriate interventions and services.

The problem is also compounded by the fact that in the case of health care, patients' reliance on professional advice may lead to potentially difficult and contentious situations. Suppliers of services are, potentially, in a very advantageous situation when needs have to be assessed, especially when the two functions (assessor and supplier) are contained within the same agency.

First described in 1953 in the US, whiplash rapidly achieved notoriety. .. within ten years it had become a subject heading in the Cumulated Index Medicus. . . and quickly became a worldwide epidemic and a multibillion-dollar industry. . . with a current estimate of £3.1 billion in UK.29

This sort of example raises the obvious question of whether service provision is patient-led, with health care professionals acting as agents of patients, or whether the supply of such services is driven by professional, organisational, political and economic interests.

Supply-induced demand has been defined as 'the extent to which a doctor provides or recommends the provision of medical services that differ from what the patient would choose if he or she had available the same information and knowledge as the physician'.

The question as to whether need exists may not be relevant, but it is important to realise that there may not be a coincidence between the views of patients and those of the professionals regarding needs. The perceptions of GPs, nurses and patients may all differ. For example, the relationship between patient and doctor has been portrayed in an amusing, but probably reasonably accurate, way:

> At the heart of clinical practice is the doctor-patient relationship. In principle this is a principal-agent relationship in which the patient is principal and the doctor the agent. If a doctor is acting as the perfect agent of his patient, their respective roles would be that the DOCTOR is there to give the PATIENT all the information the PATIENT needs in order that the PATIENT can make a decision, and the DOCTOR should implement that decision once the PATIENT has made it.

If that does not sound quite the way it usually is, try reversing the roles of DOCTOR and PATIENT, so that the relationship now gets described as the PATIENT being there to give the DOCTOR all the information the DOCTOR needs in order that the DOCTOR can make a decision, and the PATIENT should then implement that decision once the DOCTOR has made it. The question as to who should assess the needs of patients and how they should be responded to cannot be answered on empirical grounds alone.

The question is ultimately both subjective and political and goes to the very heart of the theories of moral justice. What can help in practice is for managers and professionals to be clear about their own particular values and ideas surrounding the notions of justice and equality but also to recognise that other views, in particular those of the patient, need to be borne in mind.

ORGANIZATIONAL STRUCTURE AND QUALITY MANAGEMENT

More than a decade ago, the WHO Health Promoting Hospitals (HPH) project was initiated in order to support hospitals towards placing greater emphasis on health promotion and disease prevention, rather than on diagnostic and curative services alone. The Health Promoting Hospitals strategy focuses on meeting the physical, mental and social needs of a growing number of chronically ill patients and the elderly; on meeting the needs of hospital staff, who are exposed to physical and psychological stress; and on meeting the needs of the public and the environment. Twenty hospitals in eleven European countries participated in the European pilot project from 1993 to 1997. Since then, the International Network of Health Promoting Hospitals has steadily expanded and now covers 25 Member States, 36 national or regional networks and more than 700 partner hospitals.

But, what has been achieved with regard to the implementation of health promotion services at both hospital and network level? What is the scope of health promotion activities in hospitals and how can the principles laid out in the Ottawa Charter for Health Promotion be put into practice? Is there an evidence base for health promotion and has this facilitated the expansion of health promotion services in hospitals? Is health promotion a service anyway? How does health promotion relate to quality management? And how can we evaluate the quality of health promotion activities in hospitals? Health promotion: definition and concept

Health promotion measures focus on both individuals and on contextual factors that shape the actions of individuals with the aim to prevent and reduce ill health and improve wellbeing. Health in this context not only refers to the traditional, objective and biomedical view of the absence of infirmity or disease but to a holistic view that adds mental resources and social well-being to physical health. Health promotion goes beyond health education and disease prevention, in as far as it is based on the concept of salutogenesis and stresses the analysis and development of the health potential of individuals. The scope of *disease prevention* has been defined in the Health Promotion Glossary as "measures not only to prevent the occurrence of disease, such as risk factor reduction, but also to arrest its progress and reduce its consequences once established". The same source defines the scope of *health education* as comprising "consciously constructed opportunities for learning involving some form of communication designed to improve health literacy, including improving knowledge and developing life skills which are conducive to individual and community health". Health promotion is defined as a broader concept in the WHO Ottawa Charter as "the process of enabling people to increase control over, and improve, their health".

In practice, these terms are frequently used compleme-ntarily and measures for the implementation may overlap; however, there are major conceptual differences with regard to the focus and impact of health promotion actions. Whereas the medical approach is directed at physiological risk factors (e.g. high blood pressure, immunization status), the behavioural approach is directed at lifestyle factors (e.g. smoking, physical inactivity) and the socio-environmental approach is directed at general conditions (such as unemployment, low education or poverty). Health promotion consequently includes, but goes far beyond medical approaches directed at curing individuals.

Based on the notion of health as a positive concept, the Ottawa Charter put forward the idea that "health is created and lived by people within the settings of their everyday life; where they learn, work, play and love". This settings approach to health promotion, founded on the experience of community and organizational development, led to a number of initiatives such as Health Promoting Cities, Health Promoting Schools, and Health Promoting Hospitals, etc. in order to improve people's health where they spend most of their time: in organizations.

The settings approach acknowledges that behavioural changes are only possible and stable if they are integrated into everyday life and correspond with concurrent habits and existing cultures. Health Promotion interventions in organizations therefore not only have to address changing individuals but also underlying norms, rules and cultures. The Ottawa Charter identifies five priority action areas for health promotion:

- Build healthy public policy: health promotion policy combines diverse but complementary approaches, including legislation, fiscal measures, taxation and organization change. Health promotion policy requires the identification of obstacles to the adoption of healthy public policies in non-health sectors and the development of ways to remove them.
- Create supportive environments for health: the protection of the natural and build environments and the conservation of natural resources must be addressed in any health promotion strategy.

- Strengthen community action for health: Community development draws on existing human and material resources to enhance self-help and social support, and to develop flexible systems for strengthening public participation in, and direction of, health matters. This requires full and continuous access to information and learning opportunities for health, as well as funding support.
- Develop personal skills: Enabling people to learn (throughout life) to prepare themselves for all stages and to cope with chronic illness and injuries is essential. This has to be facilitated in school, home, work and community settings.
- Re-orient health services: the role of the health sector must move increasingly in a health promotion direction, beyond its responsibility for providing clinical and curative services. Reorientation of health services also requires stronger attention to health research, as well as changes in professional education and training.

THE IMPACT OF HEALTH SERVICES ON HEALTH

Many health professionals presume that health promotion has always been the core business of medicine in general and hospitals in particular. This view may be challenged for a variety of reasons.

Although the history goes back further, the first identifiable hospitals were built during the 12th century and were religious-oriented, cloister-affiliated institutions providing support to the poor, elderly, psychologically deviant and others in need. In the foreground were the accommodation, nourishment and the isolation of infectious diseases, not the treatment of disease. Until the late 19th century hospitals were not a place where health was created, but rather a place to die. This changed with the development of the science of medicine, supported by utilitarian state philosophy and humanism.

Since then, the potential of hospital care to improve health has made rapid improvements with the development of aseptic and antiseptic techniques, more effective anaesthesia, greater surgical knowledge and skills, trauma techniques, blood transfusion, coronary artery bypass surgery, effective pharmaceuticals, transplantation techniques and minimal invasive surgery .

However, parallel to the advances in hospital procedures, questions have been raised with regard to the contribution of health care to the health of the population and the effectiveness of health care services. Various accounts have been made discarding the claims of health care for the reduction of infectious diseases, the significant decline in infant mortality, reductions in the major causes of death and resulting increase in life expectancy.

Although controversy is still continuing on details of his work, McKeown demonstrated compellingly how reductions in mortality in the United Kingdom, which were thought to be related to accomplishments of medical care, were in fact related to improvements in hygiene and nutrition. Another perspective was brought in by Ivan Illich and Rick Carlson who argued that medical care is more a cause of death, than of health. According to Illich, medicine has the potential to cause as much harm as good, as reflected in his concept of *iatrogenesis*.

He strongly criticized the medical professions of their "sick-making powers" and contended that health care institutions performed the opposite of their original purpose. Carlson argued along the same lines and forecasted that the limited effectiveness of medicine will further decline in the future. Recently, these perspectives gained a lot of prominence with the report of the Institute of Medicine, "To err is human", which estimates that in the USA about 100,000 deaths in hospitals annually are due to medical errors. A more operational perspective was brought in by the Avedis Donabedian and others who, being well aware of the limited population impact of health care, focused on strategies to improve the quality of health care services. Although major advances have been made with the outcomes movement and health technology assessment, the definition of quality as doing the right thing and doing it well, still raises fundamental questions and points to potential improvements in the provision of health care services.

The Health Promoting Hospitals network links the various perspectives above. It is driven by the strong perception that hospital services need to be more targeted towards the need of people, and not only to their organs or physiological parameters, in order to have a more substantial and lasting impact on health.

At the same time the HPH philosophy is now based on strong evidence and methods to incorporate health promotion as a core principle in the organization. Quality strategies already applied in clinical settings and for the management of health care organizations are applicable to health promotion as well. Before addressing this issue further below, the following paragraphs provide the rationale for and concrete examples of health promotion services in hospitals.

HEALTH PROMOTION ACTIVITIES IN HOSPITALS

Given the scope of possible health promotion interventions in hospitals, the WHO HPH movement focuses on four areas: promoting the health of patients, promoting the health of staff, changing the organization to a health promoting setting, and promoting the health of the community in the catchment area of the hospital. These four areas are reflected in the definition of a health promoting hospital:

"A *health promoting hospital* does not only provide high quality comprehensive medical and nursing services, but also develops a corporate identity that embraces the aims of health promotion, develops a health promoting organizational structure and culture, including active, participatory roles for patients and all members of staff, develops itself into a health promoting physical environment, and actively cooperates with its community". There is a large scope and public health impact for offering health promotion strategies in health care settings. Hospitals consume between 40% and 70% of the national health care expenditure and typically employ about 1% to 3% of the working population. These working places, most of which are occupied by women, are characterized by certain physical, chemical, biological and psychosocial risk factors. Paradoxically, in hospitals – organizations that aim to restore health – the acknowledgement of factors that endanger the health of their staff is poorly developed. Health promotion programmes can improve the health of staff, reduce absenteeism rates, and improve productivity and quality .

Health professionals in hospitals can also have a lasting impact on influencing the behaviour of patients and relatives, who are more responsive to health advice in situations of experienced ill-health. This is of particular importance for two reasons: firstly, the prevalence of chronic diseases (e.g. diabetes, cardiovascular diseases, cancer) is increasing in Europe and throughout the world; secondly, many hospital treatments today not only prevent premature death but improve the quality of life of patients. In order to maintain this quality, the patient's own behavior after discharge and effective support from relatives are important variables. Health Promotion Programmes can encourage healthy behavior, prevent readmission and maintain quality of life of patients.

Hospitals also typically produce high amounts of waste and hazardous substances. Introducing Health Promotion strategies in hospitals can help reduce the pollution of the environment and the cooperation with other institutions and professionals can help achieve the highest possible coordination of care. Furthermore, as research and teaching institutions hospital produce, accumulate and disseminate a lot of knowledge and they can have an impact on the local health structures and influence professional practice elsewhere.

A BRIEF HISTORY OF HEALTH PLANNING

Since the Second World War, governments in Western industrialised countries have engaged in the planning of health services (Rodwin 1984). Health planning institutions and approaches have varied, but they have shared a common range of concerns. These include:

- How should health needs be assessed and met?
- How should a health system be organised and financed?
- What is the appropriate role and scale of hospitals? and
- What are the appropriate responsibilities for public health programs?

Over the years the focus of health planning effort has changed. Health planning has evolved from the post-war expansionary phase to issues of cost containment and now to a concern with accountability and health outcomes. The early successes of creating a 'medical–industrial complex' have led, ironically, to a need to critically examine issues of effectiveness, efficiency and equity.

This chapter introduces the main theoretical issues and debates pertaining to planning in general and health planning specifically. It describes the different ways in which planning is conceived and practised. Definitions of key terms are provided. The fundamental dilemma of planning — whether to plan for health services or to plan for health improvement — is also raised.

WHAT IS PLANNING?

Planning can be thought of in numerous ways and is applicable to numerous activities. Most people try to arrange ahead many of the events of life. Budget planning is concerned with the allocation of limited and finite financial resources. Town planning is concerned with the control of influence on the future pattern of urban development and urban services. Most countries — at the national, state or local levels — engage in national security planning, economic planning, social planning, environmental planning and regional development planning. Dictionaries typically define the verb 'to plan' as meaning 'to arrange the parts of', 'to realise the achievement of' or 'to intend'. In the colloquial sense, then, 'planning' is concerned with deliberately achieving some objective by assembling actions into some orderly sequence. Green suggests that planning, as a separate identifiable activity in organisations, emerged from three strands of development. First, the rise of modern, complex industrial organisations in the late nineteenth century required decisions about the future to be taken in a considered and explicit manner.

Second, the Russian Revolution of 1917 led to the attempt to build an economy based on nationally determined plans and, hence, to the need for formal state planning (and planning bureaucracies). Third, the shortages experienced during the Second World War led to centralised controls in many Western countries.In Western industrialised democracies, planning as a generic activity and as a profession is commonly identified as emerging in the twentieth century, particularly after the Great Depression of the 1930s. Planning evolved as an attempt to mitigate the negative consequences of a laissez-faire market economy that was characterised by unrestrained pursuit of self-interest by individuals and corporations. The idea was for the state to intervene in markets through planning instruments in order to protect the collective interest. Public planning has thus had a long association with the notion of the welfare state and it has often been seen to be in conflict with private interests.Definitions of planning often reflect a tension between the technical tasks undertaken by the profession and the end objectives to be achieved by the tasks. In a generic and technical sense, planning can be conceived of as:

- 'The process of preparing a set of decisions for action in the future, directed at achieving goals by preferable means'; or
- 'Making current decisions in the light of their future effects'.

However, ways of thinking about planning have evolved with changes in society and the economy. In the 1940s, planning was concerned to set up the desired future end state in detail (that is, blueprint), but by the 1960s planning concentrated on the objectives of the plan and ways of obtaining them or systems planning. Hall suggests that, in the 1970s, planning became more heterogeneous and diffuse and it could be characterised as continuous participation in conflict. Friedmann would emphasise that planning, as the application of technical reasoning to specific problems and leading to action or policy intervention, occurs in a social and political context.

Mainstream planners typically work for the state, although increasing numbers also work within civil society. The planning profession has historically seen the discipline as 'basically a methodology, a set of procedures applicable to a variety of activities aimed at achieving selected goals by the systematic application of resources in programmed quantities and time sequences designed to alter the projected trends and redirect them toward established objectives'. Such a perspective emphasises the technical and rational aspects of planning. Taylor and Reinke expand on this perspective when they agree that 'effective planning requires stepwise application of selected multidisciplinary methods and procedures to designated programs and projects within specified time frames'. They add that 'planning is not simply a technical exercise; it is an ongoing process of learning, adapting to change and educating'.

As planners move into positions of facilitating change, the traditional model of rational planning is inserted into, if not transformed by, political practice. The values inherent in planning are made explicit by Blum. Planning, he says, 'is devoted to directing and attaining social changes of a specific and desired nature' and is the 'preferred means of achieving deliberate change'. Friedmann also sees planning practice as linking scientific and technical knowledge to processes of societal guidance, if not social transformation. In the 'societal guidance' model, planning is articulated through the state and is concerned with systematic change, while the political practice of system transformation becomes the focus on planning practice concerned with social transformation.

Parston suggests that planning is both an occupation and an idea. As an occupation, planning is work, a job. As an idea, planning is 'a process which is undertaken to meet some desired objective or to fulfil some purpose'. He argues they are inseparable. Forester also sees an activist role for the planner, in that planners are not only involved in problem solving; they are also concerned with problem finding or the mobilisation of attention to issues of concern.

As an activity that all organisations carry out with a greater or lesser degree of explicitness, planning involves making choices. When carried out by the public sector, planning is often conceived of as an intervention in the free market. In theory, the market allows equilibrium to be established between supply and demand as resources move in response to price signals. State intervention is limited and 'non-market goods' are produced in a complementary public sector. Classical economists see the market as the most efficient means of operating an economy.

However, certain key conditions have to be met. These include good knowledge by the purchaser (or consumer) of the goods or services on offer, buyers and suppliers operating independently and the market operating independently to the extent that a purchase by one consumer does not necessarily affect the decision by another to purchase.

Planning, as an instrument of state intervention, has been justified on a number of grounds since the second half of the twentieth century. Milton Friedman, an economist who champions the free market, supports state intervention in the presence of natural monopolies and externalities. The liberal perspective suggests that state intervention is justified in order to correct market failure, to redistribute income and to manipulate fiscal and monetary policies in order to affect aggregate demand. Structuralist critiques of the state suggest that the contradictory need to maintain the conditions for capital accumulation and to raise revenue to meet its own obligation creates the need to convey an image of pursuing common and general interests of society as a whole, allowing access to power and responding to justified demands.

Planning has also been more recently criticised for its utilitarianism. Modern statecraft has been described as 'devoted to rationalising and standardising ... a social hieroglyph into a legible and administratively more convenient format'. State planning schemes can be seen as a means of social engineering, greater regimentation of communities and daily lives and enhanced state capacity.

Different conceptions of thc rolc of the state will drive views on the nature and extent of state intervention required. For the health sector, views on the need for and the nature of, state intervention depend on whether the state is seen as regulator, service provider, financier or policy formulator for the health sector. In relation to health planning as a form of state intervention, the promarket position argues that health planning is likely to increase administrative controls and reduce professional autonomy and consumer choice. Health services delivery systems based on a professional model or a competitive free enterprise model would be favoured. The radical critique, in contrast, would see health as a right rather than a commodity and would prefer distribution of health resources on the basis of need. A model that requires central planning and regionalisation of health resources, such as the National Health Service in England prior to the Thatcher reforms, would be favoured. A mid-way position, represented by liberals, would accept a mixed system of public and private service provision and financing and focus state intervention on criteria such as accountability, rationality and equity.

Irrespective of their ideological positions, all governments ultimately need to make allocative decisions. Given that pure markets do not exist in the Australian context and that public sector financing and provision are dominant features, the setting of health care priorities is largely determined through health planning. The question, then, is not whether health care should be planned, but what to plan, by whom, how and when.

PLANNING TRADITIONS

Friedmann classifies the intellectual traditions of planning theory according to their political ideology as well as the intended use of knowledge.

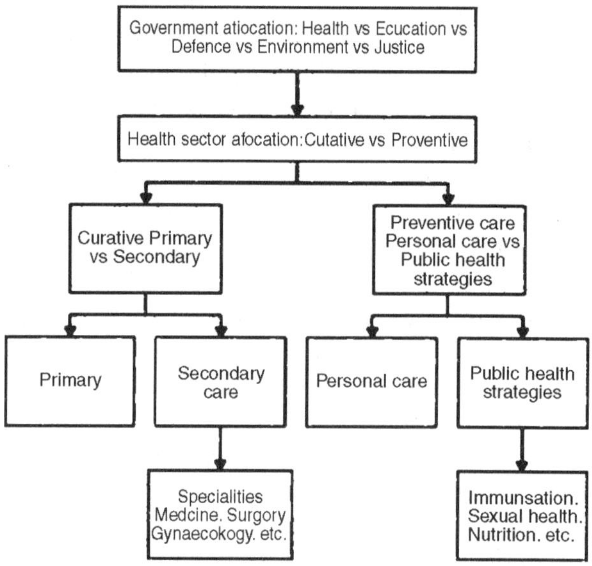

Fig. Levels of Allocative Decision Making by Government

The 'policy analysis' tradition derives from organisational theory, particularly how large organisations might improve their ability to make rational decisions. It is a rational–technical approach which builds on public administration, systems analysis and welfare and social choice theory and offers no distinctive philosophical position.

The 'social reform' tradition is concerned with institutionalising planning practice and making action by the state more effective. Planners within this tradition tend to advocate a strong role for the state, which has both mediating and authoritative functions. Building on institutional economics and political sociology, they are interested in planning instruments and technical tools that help to manage the economy in the public interest. The 'social learning' tradition is derived from organisational development approaches and focuses on the relationship between theory and practice. Rather than treating scientific knowledge as a set of building blocks for the reconstruction of society, planning is viewed as an ongoing dialectical process in which the main emphasis is on new practical undertakings.

The 'social mobilisation' tradition departs from all others by asserting the primacy of direct collective action from the grassroots (that is, the community). It is an ideology of the dispossessed, is concerned with social solidarity and aims to change the status quo. All of these traditions can be found in the brief history of health planning in Australia and they continue to co-exist. The Australian health care system has historically been characterised as a publicly planned and regulated system of supply. Even in the Australian private sector, risks are pooled through insurance arrangements and both private health care and insurance are heavily subsidised. Rational-technical planning models have been a feature of decision making about resource allocation in the health system for several decades.

At the same time, the Australian approach reflects strong cultural values about health care: that access should be determined by clinical need and not by the ability to pay; that people have a right to health care when they need it; and that health care is a key responsibility of government. Within this cultural context there have been significant shifts in policy, including a move away from institutional health care to community-based health services. Such policy debates and the ensuing processes of change often put planners within the social transformation mode. Green argues that the track record of planning internationally is often not good, as plans often fail either to be implemented or to respond to the real needs of the community. He suggests that failures arise due to:

- An emphasis on the formal process of planning, leading to it becoming a bureaucratic function or an end in itself;
- Technical failure to analyse needs appropriately or to estimate resources accurately;
- Imposition of plans from the centre in a top-down fashion, without involvement of providers and communities; and/or
- Isolation from other decision-making processes (such as budgets or human resources management).

The lessons are equally relevant to Australia and other countries — planning efforts will fail if planning is constructed as a narrow notion of apparently rational procedures being applied by a small group of technocrats who are oblivious to the broader political factors. Planning involves choices and change and, as such, will always have its opponents. Planning is neither ideology nor all powerful, but it does exist and have its effects. Understanding power structures and historical constraints, alongside the technical analysis and recognition of opportunities for action, is central to successful planning.

MODELS OF THE PLANNING PROCESS

Early planning thought is dominated by the comprehensive rational model. In this model the set of procedures essentially consists of:

- Goal setting, through identification of problems to be solved, needs to be met, opportunities to be seized and aspirations of stakeholders to be met.
- Plan formulation, through systematic analysis of alternatives, setting of criteria to choose amongst the options and examination of consequences of proposed actions.
- Plan implementation, through deploying a range of actions such as budgets, project schedules and regulatory measures.
- Monitoring and feedback, through reviewing achievements and updating the information, thus maintaining the currency of the plan.

Such understanding of the planning process implies a systems view and a systems approach. The strength of this comprehensive, rational approach is that it is analytical, information-based and allows system design to be a central concern. It also allows for the introduction of normative thinking and valuation into planning. It is a set of technocratic or analytical processes that can be applied to a range of political and social contexts. The outcomes of the planning process reflect the definition of the planning problem, the information used for planning, the governance arrangements for the planning process and the extent to which the planning process is subject to public scrutiny.

The difficulties associated with this model — recognised over time — include the fact that planners seldom start with a blank slate and often do not have access to full information. The comprehensive rational planning model essentially conceives of planning as a technical and top-down activity led by expert planners. In reality, however, planning activities tend to be iterative with various activities occurring in parallel, rather than a chronologically ordered cycle of events. Furthermore, many problems require political rather than technical solutions. Nonetheless, the essential planning skills needed to cope with complex and changing environments can still be built upon the foundation of rational planning.

An alternative approach is the mixed scanning model advocated by Etzioni. Rather than considering comprehensively the alternatives for action, mixed scanning focuses only on selected areas of interest. Once the priority areas are chosen, the analytical process hones in on the marginal changes that are possible. This model is more pragmatic than the rational comprehensive model, insofar as it is a less costly process in terms of time and information resources. The analytical process is otherwise comparable. The critique of the rational planning model rests primarily in the political nature of planning. A third and distinct model is incrementalism, or what Lindblom terms 'muddling through'. The planning process is neither cyclical nor iterative, as the model is simply one of moving from the present position to the desired objectives by acting on a series of political windows of opportunity. The essence of this model is a series of disjointed steps, in contrast with the process of pure rationalism. Its emphasis on the political dimensions more accurately reflects the real world. It is also more flexible and allows for a faster response to changing environments. However, incrementalism may serve to institutionalise existing power relations rather than encourage change, or it may lead to a lack of direction.

LEVELS OF PLANNING

Whether the model is comprehensive rationalism or mixed scanning, the analytical, problem-solving process outlined above can be applied to different levels of planning. These different levels are relevant across different fields of planning, be it health services, organisational development, urban affairs or military engagement.Dever outlines three levels of planning:

- Policy planning, which deals with what ought to be done, is the most conceptual and important in establishing system design. Planning at this level is normative and oriented towards future goals. There is also emphasis on design, on what should be rather than what is.
- Strategic planning, which deals with what can be done, is concerned with possible activities, implications for system structures and effectiveness and creation of instruments for action. The emphasis is on analysis (of need, of systems and institutions, or of stakeholders) which can lead to defining means to achieve desired goals.
- Operational planning, which deals with what will be done, is the most concrete. The focus is on specific activities to be undertaken and the resources required for implementation. The final outcome is an operational or implementation plan.

Friedmann places the levels of planning within a political and bureaucratic context. At the higher level of bureaucratic practice, planning may be focused on societal guidance and covers activities concerned with system maintenance and change. It is usually a top-down management of public affairs and incorporates policy planning and strategic planning as outlined above. The next level of bureaucratic practice is administrative planning. This involves both management of program routines and developing processes for institutional change. It is comparable to operational planning above.

STYLES OF PLANNING

Planning at the macro level can be seen as synonymous with policy making. Planning becomes a process of strategy formulation with concerns focused on power in political systems, consensus versus conflict views of how society functions and questions about issues such as the role of government, the media, interest groups, political parties and global politics.A more instrumentalist perspective tends to inform planning as strategy development at the organisational level. Mintzberg sees strategy development in organisations as occurring in one of three ways:

- Leader-driven strategy, where the strong leader determines strategy.
- Adaptive strategy, where small (often disjointed) reactive steps are taken to resolve problems/issues (incrementalism).
- Formal planning (rationalism), where analysis is used to develop explicit strategies.

Some organisations rely on the visions and strategies of a single charismatic or powerful leader who may derive their power from expertise, position, shared values or ideas, or coercion. Such a top-down approach is likely to discourage others from being innovative and creative. Further, it does not recognise the increased effectiveness associated with collaboration with communities and stakeholders.

In contrast, adaptive or power–behavioural approaches rely on negotiation, bargaining and the importance of coalitions. This approach recognises that multiple goals can co-exist in organisations and that there is a need to constantly reflect, plan and amend strategies. Incrementalism can be a useful perspective as it provides for organisational plurality, supports an analysis of organisational power and questions whose interests will be served through a particular strategy. But it may also lead to 'muddling through' without direction.

Formal planning can provide a set of concepts, directions and procedures to help people to think and act strategically, with a view to developing a comprehensive short- and long-term agenda. Formal processes can potentially provide an organised approach to developing innovative ideas and for involving people at all levels. A plan, however, is best seen as just one building block in a series of events that determine macro-level strategy (Quinn 1991). Moreover, there is a wide variety of values and approaches to formal planning which may be more or less participatory, planned or impulse-driven, top-down or bottom-up, implicit or explicit, focused on the past or on the future, or concerned with both.

Macro-level strategic planning often involves a mixture of formal planning, incrementalist (power–political) processes and management techniques, depending on the issue and context. There may even be times when openness to new ideas, information and approaches and a strong commitment to a particular issue or goal are more important than a brilliant strategic analysis. Hall et al. suggest that when an issue has high legitimacy, feasibility and support, it is likely to become an agenda item.Insofar as planning is an activity concerned with effecting change, the planner is not a neutral technocrat. Benveniste suggests two essential approaches to planning in terms of how the planner defines his/her role:

- Advocacy planning, where planning is a means of redressing the imbalances between different groups with different power and the role of the planner is to take an active role in facilitating change.
- Apolitical planning, where planning is the use of technical knowledge to achieve political or managerial compromise.

In the classification offered by Friedmann, 'apolitical planning' is comparable to 'allocative planning', which is concerned with distribution of scare resources among competing claimants or uses. 'Advocacy planning', however, is sub-divided into 'institutional planning' and 'radical planning', with the former oriented towards facilitating institutional change and the latter attempting to draw on organised citizen power to promote social transformation. The former can also be conceived of as adopting a pluralist approach involving negotiations with key stakeholders and communities to reach an equilibrium or consensus. The latter, on the other hand, may adopt a structuralist analysis and be based on collaboration between planners and communities in order to confront and address the determinants of inequity. Sandercock offers a typology of planning approaches based on the evolution of urban planning models. These include:

- The rational comprehensive model, where the planner is indisputably the expert.
- The advocacy planning model, where the planner represents the interests of the disadvantaged (though leaving intact the workings of plural democracy).
- The radical political economy model, where planning is an instrument of the capitalist state and the planner's role is as the revealer of contradictions and an agent of social innovation.
- The equity planning model, where the planning effort consciously seeks to redistribute power, resources or participation.
- The social learning and communicative action model, which acknowledges the value of local and experiential knowledge.
- The radical or emancipatory planning model, where the planner's allegiance is to the community rather than the state and his/her role is to work for social transformation through community-based organisations.

In examining the evolution of planning practice, Sandercock suggests some new pillars for post-modern planning:

- Greater and explicit reliance on practical wisdom;
- People-centred, as opposed to focusing on the planning document;
- Need to access multiple ways of knowing (for example, community experiences);
- Greater emphasis on community empowerment; and
- Recognition of the existence of multiple publics and developing multicultural literacy.

She stresses different sources of information and evidence for planning, with the keys being: knowledge through dialogue; knowledge from experience; learning from local knowledge; learning to read symbolic and non-verbal evidence; learning through contemplative or appreciative knowledge; and learning by doing, or action planning. The inherently value-laden nature of planning thus raises some critical questions about who should be involved in the planning process, how they should be involved and when they should be involved. The answers to these questions are often informed by an understanding of why a planning process is being undertaken. It can be asked:

- Is planning an aid or replacement to political decision making?
- Is planning a means of improving social justice?
- Is planning a means of getting some focus on the future?
- Is planning a gentle, persuasive route to turn ideas into action?
- Is planning a method for shared decision making?
- Is planning a means of improving the quality of effort applied to problem solving?
- Is planning a means of control?

Clarity about the answers to the above questions will result in different ways to resolve the issues which frequently occur in 'doing' planning, such as:

- What should be the process for developing a plan?
- Who should write the plan (for example, consultants, planners or managers)?
- What are the merits of a centralised versus decentralised approach?
- Who should be involved in the planning activities (for example, managers or consumers)?
- What should be the governance arrangement for the planning process?
- What are the merits of group consultation versus individual consultation?

Some of these questions may appear to be purely technical, yet most embody notions about the distribution of power, the winners and losers in any changes to the status quo and the legitimacy of the planning exercise as perceived by the stakeholders.

PARTICULAR FEATURES OF HEALTH PLANNING

The particular features that distinguish health planning from other forms of planning relate to the peculiarity of the health system. Palmer and Short suggest that the distinctiveness of health policy results from three broad defining factors:

- The unique role of the medical profession;
- The complexity of health care; and
- The nature of community expectations and values associated with health.

Some see that health care is distinguished by its hierarchical nature and by the dominance of the medical profession. Medical dominance is seen as being achieved through professionalism (freedom from scrutiny), authority over other health workers and professionals and by shaping social beliefs and understandings about health. Furthermore, the orientation towards curative care, including resource allocation to this area, is reinforced by the nature of the medical profession. Shortell and Kaluzney identify a number of operational features that distinguish health care organisations. While they recognise that many other organisations may possess one or more of these features, health care organisations will display a combination of these factors. Amongst these are:

- Definition and measurement of output is difficult.
- Work is variable and complex.
- Work is likely to be emergency work.
- There is little capacity for error.
- Activities require considerable coordination amongst a range of professional groups.
- Work is highly specialised.
- Workers are highly professionalised with strong allegiances to their profession.
- There is little control over doctors, yet they generate the costs.
- Dual lines of authority often operate.

Hospitals, of all health service organisations, may be particularly impervious to changes in the external environment. As 'closed systems', hospitals have what Taylor described as the hospital's 'cult of efficiency': long-established work patterns, routines, roles and power relations.

The hierarchy is maintained with tight scheduling, numerous rules and regulations and control mechanisms.

The rigidity, control, tight scheduling and official rules and regulations in health service institutions have long been critiqued. Health service agreements, awards, commitments and understandings also serve to mitigate against organisational change. The bureaucratic culture is determined by the accumulation of the decisions of clinicians.

In more recent times, the traditional power base of doctors may have been partly eroded in the face of health care reform, managerialism, the strengthening power base of other professions in the health field (including economists, planners, nurses, lawyers and alternative medicine), unremitting cost control and the growth of active consumer interest groups. Organisational boundaries are also being blurred with horizontal integration and collaboration between hospitals and community-based health services and between the private and public sectors. Networks of services are increasingly becoming more useful descriptions of the health system.

The complexity of promoting health in the face of increasing societal inequity and environmental degradation is challenging health professionals to work in different ways.Health planning has also been challenged by the rapid pace of change. Public sector reforms, including the introduction of purchaser–provider split models, initially raised questions about whether there is a role for state planning.

Experience with formula-based output payments, however, still suggests that the state health authority has to plan for the volume and types of services to be purchased.

More recently, purchasers have learned that their planning needs to be at a finer level, since the need for health services is a more specific concept than the need for health.The particular features of the health system described above have several implications.

One is the relationship between health management, health planning and clinical practice. Should health planning be an integral component of health management? Should health planning be the bridge between clinical practice, health management and the political process? Should health planning be the process by which clinical knowledge is channelled to drive health system reform? Another important issue is the relationship between health planning and health financing and accounting.

Should health planners be advocates for health and for patients? Should health planners be technicians involved in the distribution of finite health dollars? Should health planners be the decision makers who decide what to purchase in a purchaser–provider relationship? In practice, all of these roles are present in health planning to a greater or lesser extent. Health planning is thus practised in an environment where technical and bureaucratic traditions exist simultaneously with complexity and change on both technological and social dimensions.

MODELS OF HEALTH PLANNING

Health planning is essentially concerned with improving health and with improving health services delivery or system performance. These two aims, however, require somewhat different approaches to planning. A planning effort concerned with improving population health (also called population-based planning) usually employs the following iterative process:

- Select health issue(s) of concern.
- Identify risks.
- Evaluate population risk levels (at present and in future).
- Select programs to eliminate or reduce risks.
- Compare needed programs with existing programs.
- Adjust resources.
- Evaluate.

A planning exercise focused on improving health services delivery (also known as institution-based or resource-based planning) is also iterative and may use similar logic but has different starting points. The general model is:

- Select health service(s) of concern.
- Determine current demand.
- Forecast potential demand.
- Compare forecast with present resource capacity.
- Adjust resources.
- Evaluate.

Despite comparable logic, there are significant differences between the two models in orientation and methodological requirements. The population-based planning model establishes resource requirements based upon assessment of the risk levels and the health status of a given population. As such, it incorporates a broader understanding of the determinants of health, particularly the social and environmental factors influencing health outcomes. Its tendency is to focus on preventive programs and reorientate the health care system towards primary health care. It also gives recognition to the need for intersectoral collaboration and for community action in achieving health status improvement. Its main problems rest with gaining an accurate assessment of health status and risk levels and testing the capacity of the health sector to influence broader determinants of health.

The resource-based planning model can be applied to a service or a facility. It is largely an attempt to match supply with demand and its implementation is concerned with adjustments within the existing delivery system, most commonly with rationalisation of existing resources. This form of health planning is the dominant approach.

At a broader level, the differences in population-based and resource-based planning models also reflect different political interests. The resource-based approach is largely concerned with institutional growth and development and serves the dominant interests of the institutional sector. In the health sphere, the dominant institution is the hospital and the dominant interest it serves is the medical profession. The population-based approach, on the other hand, is concerned (by definition) with community and societal interests. It requires the planner (and the planning body) to address the needs of the population as the central issue in the planning process and, as such, to become an advocate for community interests.

The history of health planning is characterised by movement from facilitybased planning to a focus on health outcomes. This reflects a number of important trends. First, there has been a shift in health policy, from expansion of hospital facilities to the need to rationalise resources, through to a concern for the health return on the investment. Second, this shift in orientation itself has reflected the contest in policy space between dominant professional interests and community and consumer interests, supported by 'corporate rationalisers'. Third, there has been a shift from relegating planning to a technical analytical function, to becoming an integral part of management if not an approach to management. It can be expected, then, that the judicious combination of resource-based planning and population-based planning will be the direction for future development.

Health planning operates in a complex and changing environment. Planning can be highly technical or solely political. It can be done to help with 'muddling through' of daily decision making or with a radical envisioning of the future system. The essential problem faced by health planners is as follows. While there is general agreement among policy makers and the community that all people should enjoy good health and have access to health care, planners are not and have not been, able to specify what constitutes an optimal system of health and related services for keeping the population healthy.

The challenge is not solely in the technical design of a health system. Insofar as a health system reflects societal norms and expectations as well as the resources available, planning is a political process and requires a multitude of tools for implementation. The planning predicament, then, embodies the tasks associated with leveraging support for action.

CORE HEALTH PLANNING PRINCIPLES

There are a number of planning parameters which are commonly used and essentially form the 'language' of health planning. The core health planning principles include equity, accessibility, efficiency, quality and effectiveness. Each is discussed in turn.

EQUITY

Equity in health planning is often defined as equity of access, which means that an individual will receive an equal opportunity to receive health care, irrespective of personal characteristics such as income, race, gender or place of residence. Equity may be assessed through consideration of the definition of the target group, the methods for promoting access and analysis of the geographical or locational equity. An important alternative concept is equity of outcome, which refers to the fairness of the outcomes from a particular health care intervention or service. This approach to equity takes into account the range of sociological, economic and other factors that may mitigate against a fair distribution of health chances. Equity of outcome implies the need for redistribution such that new or additional resources are targeted to redress inequity.

ACCESSIBILITY

Access is the capacity or potential to obtain a service or benefit. Access incorporates notions of geographical access, physical/architectural access, cultural/ linguistic access, service acceptability and affordability. Service accessibility may refer to several things: geographical accessibility (for example, travel time to the service, or transport routes); cultural accessibility (for example, availability of interpreters for non-English-speaking background (NESB) immigrants, Aboriginal health workers, or the appropriateness of the environment for young people); physical accessibility (for example, ramps for disabled people or people with prams); service availability (for example, waiting times, opening hours, access for people working and so on); or financial access (that is, whether the cost of a service constitutes a barrier).

EFFICIENCY

Efficiency focuses on the maximisation of total benefits from the use of a given amount of resources. Technical efficiency, or productive efficiency, refers to maximising service or strategy outputs by using minimal inputs. In some social services, measures of efficiency are defined as being synonymous with costeffectiveness in that they relate outcome to input (such as the cost of obtaining one extra year of life). In this book, efficiency will be related to service outputs, not to outcomes.

The efficiency of a particular service or strategy can be assessed or planned for in a number of ways. One approach is to compare the service or strategy to other similar services/strategies on the basis of agreed outputs. It may be important that these output indicators be adjusted to reflect casemix, where such information is available.

Allocative efficiency is concerned with maximising the health and welfare of the community through ensuring an appropriate distribution of benefits. This is particularly important in considering the balance of investment between inpatient and community-based services, between preventive and curative services and between ongoing professional care and the self-help and support services provided by lay volunteers.

Dynamic efficiency is concerned with adaptability of the system over time. It is an economic concept that has yet to come to the fore in the health arena, but it can be expected to assume greater prominence as issues of sustainability attract greater attention.

QUALITY

Quality measures the degree to which a health care professional or service conforms to pre-set standards. Quality measures may include process measures (that is, the activities undertaken as a part of the service) or outcome measures (that is, the result). Ideally, both process and outcome measures would be used.

Information on the quality of processes can be obtained through analysing selected performance measurements (for example, casemix adjusted measures of complication errors, medication errors, transfers to higher levels of care, readmission rates, customer satisfaction, employee surveys, timeliness, waste and defects) or by generating information on a particular issue (for example, the proportion of people with acute myocardial infarction who receive streptokinase treatment within an hour of arriving at hospital).

EFFECTIVENESS/OUTCOMES

Effectiveness is the level of benefit when a service is rendered under ordinary circumstances by average practitioners for typical patients. This is distinct from the concept of efficacy (the level of benefit expected when health services are applied under ideal conditions). A health outcome is a change in the health of individuals or a group of people or populations that can be attributed wholly or partially to a health intervention or a series of interventions. The key issue is how to identify the best indicators or measures of benefit or health gain. Health gain indicators, or 'outcome measures', should be directly relevant both to the health needs and to the health intervention. For instance, the percentage of the infant population immunised is a relevant indicator for an immunisation campaign. When the immunisation level can be attributed to the intervention (in this case, the immunisation campaign), it can constitute a 'health outcome'. When it cannot be attributed to the intervention, the percentage immunised is a 'health status' measure and not a 'health outcome' measure.

A service should ideally collect and analyse its own data on the outcomes of its interventions. If the service is provided as part of a broader treatment/care stream (for example, physiotherapy post-orthopaedic surgery), it is difficult to undertake outcome evaluation as outcome evaluation is best undertaken across a whole service intervention. Services should identify whether the target group is an individual or a population. Consumers/communities should ideally be involved in deciding the value of the outcomes of the service/intervention. There are often difficulties in obtaining valid information about outcomes in ordinary service settings, due to differences in consumers/target groups/communities and the multiple factors that may influence outcomes.

As reflected by the core principles of health planning, most of the planner's work is concerned with the efficient and effective delivery of health care services. Does health planning actually make a difference to health status or the level of health experienced by individuals and communities? The answer to this question is complicated by differing understandings of what health is and what health planners do.

DEFINITIONS OF HEALTH

There are many definitions of health. Health can be defined by its presence or its absence and it can have individual or societal parameters. In 1946 the World Health Organisation (WHO) defined health as 'a state of complete physical, mental and social well-being and not merely the absence of disease or infirmity' (WHO 1946). In this definition, health is defined as a positive experience rather than the absence of sickness and as a social rather than a solely individual phenomenon. Critics argue that it defines health as 'perfect health', a concept which is unable to be measured or obtained and is always future-oriented.

Definitions of health and what health planners do, however, vary according to the frames of reference used. Doctors, administrators and consumers may view health differently and therefore have different views on how health needs should be met, what health services are needed and how they should be delivered. Major health frames of references include biological/biomedical, clinical health sciences, population health, ecological public health, social health and everyday life. Planners typically focus on population issues, morbidity and demography.

DETERMINANTS OF HEALTH

The causes of illness are complex and the social, cultural and environmental impacts on health are now well documented. The determinants of health interact in complex ways, with diseases sharing common risk factors and risk factors clustered in socioeconomic groups.

Broad determinants of health may include socioeconomic structures, physical, human-made and ecological environments, health service access or quality, individual biology, cultural beliefs, personal behaviour and lifestyle choices. Specific determinants may include nutrition, infectious agents, trauma, congenital or inherited problems, the physical environment (sun, radiation, altitude), tobacco and alcohol consumption, age, gender, occupation, stress and social isolation. Epidemiological evidence increasingly points to the importance of social factors in explaining health status differences across populations.

Epidemiology is at the core of contemporary understanding of the distribution and causation of health and disease at the population level. Over the past 150 years, epidemiological concepts have undergone a number of shifts, from infectious disease epidemiology (based on germ theory) to the 'classic triad' (physical, genetic and environment causes), to the current interest in chronic diseases and multiple risk factors.

Contemporary public health approaches critique both the biomedical model and an 'illness-centred' focus on the physical risk factors of individuals and groups. The more comprehensive 'web of causation' takes biological and social factors and interventions into account and may span the genetic to the societal. The central concept in the web of causation is that many variables may be related to a single effect through direct and indirect causes. The main evidence for determinants of health comes from the prevalence of disease differences between different population sub-groups. The available data about the distribution of determinants are often poor, however and this makes planning for health (with any sophistication) difficult.

If the ultimate goal of health planning activities is to impact positively on health status, then decisions have to be taken about which of the myriad of factors/determinants are priorities for action and what can be done about them. Certainly, it is not necessary (even were it possible) to understand causal mechanisms fully in order to undertake prevention. The knowledge of small components in the web of causation can significantly contribute to prevention or improved treatment/therapy.

The Ottawa Charter suggests five core strategies for health improvement: building healthy public policy; creating supportive environments; strengthening community action; developing personal skills; and reorienting health services. The challenge in health planning is to act successfully on the social determinants of health.

HEALTH SERVICES AND THEIR IMPACT ON HEALTH STATUS

The importance of public health measures in improving health has long been recognised. The dramatic decline in mortality in the last 100 years has been widely attributed to the first public health revolution resulting in environmental improvements, including sanitation, nutrition, water supply, housing and education.

These improvements led to significant overall declines in infectious diseases such as tuberculosis, typhus-typhoid, cholera, dysentery and diarrhoea, smallpox and scarlet fever. Medical and scientific advances such as the development of antibiotics, the development of the Salk and Sabin vaccines for poliomyelitis and developments in surgery contributed to reduced death rates in the 1950s; however, these only marginally improved mortality rates. The decline in population mortality in the last century has coincided with, rather than been caused by, the rise of modern medicine.

The impact of medical access on overall health status is likely to be less than the impact of improving working and living conditions. Current studies estimate that 60–80 per cent of current disease is preventable through social change. The Center for Disease Control in the United States attributed only 10 per cent of premature mortality to inadequate health care.

Despite the contention that medical interventions have a relatively marginal impact on the overall mortality levels of a community, medicine generally enjoys great community credence. Science and the scientific method is most frequently credited with having the explanations for illness and health and the 'curative' health system continues to consume the bulk of the health budget.

Nevertheless, whilst national mortality rates tend not to respond to increases in hospital and medical resources, medical care does contribute to the reduction of non-fatal diseases, disability, discomfort and distress. Health services extend life through interventions such as immunisation, accident and trauma services and cancer treatments. Quality of life may also be improved through relief of pain, improved mobility (joint replacements) and effective treatment of many non-life-threatening conditions. The challenge for health planning is to ensure equitable access to costeffective health care while harnessing complementary strategies for health improvement.

PLANNING FOR EQUITY AND HEALTH

Equity or fairness in health has been defined as a 'focus on the distributional impact of health policies on different individuals and families'. Health inequality can be defined as differences in health status, whereas health inequity links differences in health to social injustice and implies unfairness and the need for amelioration. Equity in health, whilst often appearing in the rhetoric of plans or policies, is rarely adequately examined and is differentially understood and applied, despite being generally applauded as a planning goal.

There are (at least) three main approaches to equity in health: equity as the minimum standard equity of access; and equity of outcome.

EQUITY OF ACCESS AND EQUAL HEALTH CARE

Equity is achieved when an individual receives equal health care irrespective of personal characteristics such as income, race, gender or place of residence. This does not imply equal treatment in the sense of the same treatment. Rather, the treatment or care should be tailored to meet diverse individual needs and circumstances (for example, providing an interpreter for a patient who does not speak English). This approach has been the goal of much policy and planning in the last 30 years.

EQUITY OF OUTCOME

Equity is achieved when the outcomes from a health care intervention — regardless of whether it is intersectoral, prevention, treatment or palliation — are fairly distributed across population groups and individuals. Where the current distribution of outcomes is unfair, this approach provides for redistribution. Consistent with this view, a public health approach, for example, would define equity as 'affirmative action on any resource differentially distributed in the community — for example, housing, education, income and political power. It implies access to these resources by those with the least opportunities at present'.Key questions in health planning therefore include:

- Should plans focus solely on the health care sector, or is a broad-based multisectoral approach required?
- Should equity of outcome replace equity of access? As a corollary, should a goal be to simply maintain (but not improve) the current health standing of advantaged Australians whilst new resources are targeted to improve the health status of the most disadvantaged groups?

A BRIEF HISTORY OF HEALTH PLANNING

Health planning trends have followed the prevailing and shifting policy paradigms of the last 30 years. An initial focus on equity and access had shifted by the 1980s to a concern with equity and efficiency. By the 1990s/2000s the accelerated efficiency drive led to a concern about the quality and effectiveness of health interventions.

Planning has evolved from an initial concern with developing much-needed data and information, through to developing normative planning standards which sought to define system and service inputs and then to a concern with outcomes, effectiveness and change management.

The changes in the paradigms have been complemented by ongoing tensions between community/public health services and traditional hospital and institutional approaches, between prevention and treatment, between the bureaucracy versus health providers and, inevitably and most recently, between market forces and planning. The dilemmas associated with developing a broader community-centred, consultative and ecological approach to health have also emerged.

This chapter provides an overview of health planning in Australia, concentrating on its evolution since the 1970s. Health planning practice has essentially developed in three streams. Hospital planning has focused on locational distribution and efficiency of service delivery. Community health services planning has been concerned with equity and population health need. The presence of more specialised planning practice — be it workforce or technology — has reflected policy demands. The planning skills of the health planner have increasingly moved into the corporate planning arena.

EARLY HISTORY OF HEALTH PLANNING

At the start of the twentieth century there was little other than basic population information on which to plan and there was considerable political interference in priority setting. Indeed, hospitals and health services were generally established for political gain, just prior to an election. Until the 1970s, special interest and advocacy groups (aside from medical and professional interest groups) were rare.

Hospitals were established with little detailed planning and without regard to related services. Bed numbers and roles were contrived by comparison with existing hospitals. In the major cities, hospitals were generally built in the inner city areas. In the rural areas, it was expected that each town should have its own hospital and that a town should be 'no more than a horse ride away' (fifteen minutes by motor vehicle). Irrespective of the size of their catchment population, rural towns generally had an acute hospital that also provided nursing home type services. Hospitals, at this time, were relatively inexpensive to operate and when budgets were overspent the government simply increased the budget.

There was a political view that hospital costs had to be met and there was little pressure on health administrators or politicians to contain costs.

Up to the 1970s, public health issues were largely dominated by a biomedical approach. Mass immunisations and screening had been undertaken in the post-war period to eradicate or control diseases such as tuberculosis and polio. By the 1970s, awareness had developed about the problems associated with an 'affluent society': smoking, drinking, obesity and traffic accidents.

Prior to the 1970s, governments tended to respond to concerns about health care direction or decision making by establishing commissions of inquiry or special senate task forces, comprising medical experts and politicians who would identify key recommendations for future action. Whilst significant changes occurred in health services during these first seven decades of the last century, little formal planning was involved. Planning was effectively entwined with the political process.

COMPREHENSIVE HEALTH PLANNING DEVELOPS

A Division of Planning and Research and began to assess the equity of service provision in the state. This process highlighted the lack of health services in the west of Sydney in comparison to the inner city areas. The first comprehensive service plan was a plan for the rapidly growing south-west of Sydney, incorporating Campbelltown and Liverpool. This plan was revolutionary for its day in that it demonstrated the existing health service's locational inequities and also planned for the full range of services, including hospitals, community health, a new generalist community nurse service and mental health. A similar planning exercise was undertaken for the Mt Druitt area, where a polyclinic rather than a hospital was planned. By the late 1970s the unit had developed the first metropolitan-wide health service plan. Such plans required enormous technical effort, as there was little readily available data.

With the incoming Whitlam government a reformist agenda was introduced at the national level, with the introduction of national health insurance and the Community Health Program (CHP) as key features. Sidney Sax moved from New South Wales to the Commonwealth to head up the newly established Hospitals and Health Services Commission (HHSC) in 1973. This body developed policies concerning the supply and distribution of health services and established a national health service planning model. The model envisaged a network of services comprised of primary care, private specialist care, hospitals, nursing homes, hostels and rehabilitation and domiciliary care. Of central importance were the primary care teams.

The Commission also developed the first national normative planning standards for health service provision, which were particularly pertinent for the development of the CHP. Amongst these standards were that a community of 6000 people should have two to three general practitioners and two community nurses and that communities with 40 000 people should have a community health centre, with facilities and services to support the primary care teams. The impact of the CHP on health planning was far-reaching, extending beyond the Commonwealth in that it required the introduction of populationbased planning into the state-based health system.

In response to the Whitlam government's policy of augmenting and upgrading hospitals, the Commonwealth HHSC undertook a national study of the needs and distribution of Australian hospitals. The survey highlighted the inequitable distribution of hospital beds between inner city areas and newly developed outer areas in several states. The report found an oversupply of beds in rural areas. The study suggested that the number of beds per 1000 population in Australia (6.3 beds per 1000) was too high. It recommended that Commonwealth financial assistance should be based on assessed need (that is, policy), rather than being merely a per capita distribution. This effectively constituted the first comprehensive national plan for health care in Australia. However, as often occurs in health planning, the government preempted the report and announced capital grants for the development of Westmead Hospital in Sydney, Western Suburbs Geriatric Centre and Hospital in Melbourne and the Mt Gravatt Hospital in Brisbane.

DATA DEVELOPMENT BECOMES IMPORTANT

During the planning process the Commonwealth identified a 'serious shortage of the kind of information that is essential for the planning and evaluation of health services at all levels'. In 1973, the Commonwealth responded by providing a matched grant program of $1.025 million a year. This comprised $500 000 to support the development of state-based health services planning and research, $500 000 to universities and colleges and $25 000 for seminars on data collection, record systems, planning and evaluation. Specific research training programs were included in later years.

These funds were to be used by the states to develop their planning and research capacities. Until this time, health services planning and research outside New South Wales was poorly developed. It was hoped that biomedical researchers would be enticed into health service planning and teach research skills to bureaucrats involved in planning. The role envisaged for research was to study need, access to services, productivity, efficiency and cost control. The role envisaged for planning was one of providing research findings to health service administrators, with the view that providing such advice might facilitate more rational policy. These grants provided an impetus for the development of health planning as a profession and for the establishment of state and regional planning functions.

In the 1970s there was little planning data other than population statistics. Annual reports of health authorities were only able to report the states' bed capacity, the average length of stay and the daily average, the number of newborn babies and the numbers who attended outpatient services. The hospital billing system provided additional basic data sets, as did hospital surveys. There was, however, no health status or diagnosis information and no patient information. Therefore, for health planning to be taken seriously by health administrators and politicians, significant technical and research effort was required. Consequently, the development of planning tools, including information systems, became an important priority for most planning units. For example, in its annual report in 1977/78, the Commonwealth's proud boast was that it had developed its 'computer based information bank. It now contains demographic and statistical information on hospitals, nursing homes and other institutions ... inappropriate levels of services can thus be identified' (Commonwealth Department of Health).

The first Hospital Morbidity Data Collection was developed in the Riverina area of New South Wales in the early 1960s. The departmental officer representing the NSW Health Commission successfully argued the case for statewide hospital morbidity collection, health surveys and perinatal statistics on the basis that it was 'reprehensible that the state knew more about its sheep than its people!'. By 1977 the completion of hospital morbidity data became mandatory in New South Wales and by 1978 this requirement was extended to private hospitals. The general and psychiatric collections were integrated at this time. This provided a prototype for data on the health status of populations. The data items included in the collection were demographic variables, diagnoses and operations.

There was considerable negative reaction to the requirement to complete data returns from hospitals, as it was considered that this would take medical resources away from clinical care. There was also suspicion about how the data would be used. There was, at this time, no national agreement on definitions and approaches. The process of collecting and entering data was laborious. Data would arrive on paper and had to be transferred to punch cards. Data were all centrally processed by the Australian Bureau of Statistics.

The need for more uniform approaches to hospital capital works led to the establishment of a variety of planning bodies. In New South Wales, the Hospital Planning Advisory Council was established in 1973 to develop key capital planning parameters, undertake planning research and develop tools such as the 'hospital planning units' which provided capital planning standards relating to the size, location and general functionality of hospital and health services.

In 1975 a Household Health and Welfare Survey was conducted in the Gosford–Wyong and Illawarra areas of New South Wales by the NSW Division of Planning and Research in conjunction with the Commonwealth Bureau of Statistics. The survey aimed to assess acute and chronic health problems and the health services used by the people. This became the pilot National

Health Survey, which is now an important regular source of health status information.

Linking resource allocation issues to health planning was also recognised. In 1975, New South Wales developed a rudimentary 'resource allocation formula' based on the approach undertaken in Britain. Again, this formula provided a model for future population-based resource allocation exercises.

The 1970s witnessed significant new directions for health system development that began to require the advice of 'experts'. Planners were initially innovative researchers who had to 'order spreadsheets from central office by mail. They hand-drew column graphs and scatter charts and added up large numbers of hospital separations on pocket calculators to assess admission trends'.

With these beginnings, planning emerged as a technical support to the bureaucracy. Planners developed new data and information sources and began to develop normative planning standards which could define service and system inputs. Planners became experts in analysing hospital separation, mortality and demographic data as a means of assessing a community's health needs.

PRIORITY SETTING AS A PLANNING ROLE EMERGES

During the second half of the 1970s the economic environment began to change. In 1975 the incoming Liberal Fraser government questioned the efficiency of public hospitals and developed policies to force the states to establish cost control mechanisms. Health care costs had increased from about 5 per cent of GDP in 1963/64 to 7.7 per cent in 1975/76.

Planning remained in the service of decision makers, but the goal was to discourage hospital use. Bed planning ratios of four acute beds per 1000 people were established and in 1978 the Commonwealth–State cost-sharing agreement required that equal numbers of beds should be closed if new beds or services were to be opened.

The Fraser government instigated a range of cost control measures designed to regulate the expansion of hospital beds and services, the supply of practitioners, the development of community health and the consumer contribution to health care. The significant changes in the health policy environment meant that planning was not a means of developing comprehensive new services but a tool to assist in or to justify cost cutting. Planning became more integrated into management decision making.

PLANNING FOCUSES ON INCREASING HOSPITAL EFFICIENCY

In 1980 The Commission of Inquiry into the Efficiency and Administration of Hospitals reported that health information systems were inadequate and that hospital administration appeared to be inefficient. It recommended a reduction in the number of hospital beds per 1000 population and that states develop comprehensive health service plans which would outline the development of all components of the health system on a regional and statewide basis.

Increasing pressure on the hospital budget, leading to greater support for non-hospital care, resulted from several factors: reduced hospital revenues arising from Medicare changes in 1981; the introduction by the Commonwealth of the '35 day rule' which limited acute hospital coverage to 35 days; increasing hospital staffing costs associated with the 38-hour week; requirements for improved health and safety; quality control procedures; and the safeguarding of patients' rights to informed consent.

Hospital cost control measures implemented at this time concentrated mainly on instruments such as patient payments to deter use and budgetary controls. In the 1970s, hospital administrators who spent in excess of their budget would be regularly 'bailed out' by the central-leveladministration, but by the 1980s this had changed (that is, 'come in on budget or your job may be on the line'). There was increased productivity in public hospitals during this time.

Hospital productivity improvements arose from a decrease in length of stay, an increase in same day procedures (both due in large part to the development of less invasive surgical techniques and anaesthetics and improved diagnostic technologies), early and supported discharge for some types of care (especially ophthalmology and obstetrics) and an increase in non-inpatient or ambulatorycare as an alternative to admission (for example, home dialysis, community-basedpalliative care and diabetic management).

Information systems developed significantly. Planners and managers were able to question the variability between different hospitals and within a hospital: the costs of individual patient care; average length of stay; number of admissions; waiting times; numbers of operations; admissions through emergency departments and so on. However, the hospitals invariably claimed that such variability was due to variations in the age and complexity of the patient mix.

At this time, information tools which had the capability for controlling for patient mix were being developed in the United States. By the mid-1980s the Victorian Health Department and the South Australian Health Commission initiated studies into the usage of the US Diagnosis Related Group (DRG) classification as an approach to allocating funds to hospitals. By the end of the 1980s the Commonwealth had introduced the Casemix Development Program as part of its Medicare agreement with the states to establish systems and parameters for the use of casemix classification systems within Australia.

PUBLIC/PRIVATE SECTOR BLURRING

Whilst the private hospital sector had a long history in Australia, interest in public sector technical efficiency led to an increasing interest in a range of private health sector roles. Health planners began to become involved in experimentation in providing health care in the private sector so as to develop competitive markets, improve efficiency (for example, through substitutability) and, in line with the current trends, develop ways of shifting costs from the public capped system to the private uncapped system. Such approaches included planning for primary care treatment centres attached to public hospitals, planning for day surgeries and contracting out services such as pathology and radiology.

In the 1980s, state governments legislated for greater planning and regulatory control of private hospitals. The Private Health Establishments Act was passed in New South Wales in 1982 and proclaimed in 1988. Similar legislation was passed in Victoria in 1982. These Acts provided for a planned development of private services. Licensing of hospitals would be subject to planning guidelines.

A DOSE OF EQUITY

In the 1980s, initially with support from the Whitlam Labor government and with the development of civil rights movements internationally, interest groups began to emerge as political and policy forces in Australia. Health interest groups concerned with mental health, ageing and disability and other particular health issues developed or moved from a charitable emphasis to become advocacy groups. Specific health services — such as Aboriginal medical services, women's health centres, community mental health and disability services, women's refuges, rape crisis centres and ethno-specific health workers and interpreters — were funded to address equity and access issues. Access and equity plans and policies designed to overcome access barriers began to be considered by Commonwealth and state bureaucracies.

INTEGRATED HEALTH SERVICES PLANNING DEVELOPS

cnal- or area-based organisation was that planning for super-speciality services began to be undertaken at the central or national level, planning for secondary and primary care services was undertaken at the area/regional level and operational or business planning was undertaken at the local level. During this period, specialist planners were appointed at the central and regional/area tiers of administration and occasionally at the local level.

Systemic issues which began to be evaluated and addressed included: the level of integration of hospital and community care; the historical patterns of service delivery; traditional hospital management structures as compared to more 'responsive' area and regional structures; population locational access and equity issues, particularly as they related to hospital facilities; the possible range of private health sector roles; and the need for information tools to more effectively assess health service outputs. These systemic changes in health care management were accompanied later in the 1980s by interest in health care quality and in epidemiology. By the end of the 1980s the public health movement again began to have a voice and to provide a countervailing influence to the developing corporatist efficiency paradigm.

Changes in mental health, aged care and disability legislation and policy in the 1980s particularly supported deinstitutionalisation. The relatively large institutional or nursing home bed numbers were inappropriately concentrated in metropolitan areas, there was a lack of adequate community homes and hostel beds and, in general, there was a lack of appropriate assessment and community- and home-based alternatives. In mental health and disability services, the introduction of psychotropic drugs in the 1960s and 1970s had given impetus to community care. Important changes in mental health legislation and policy occurred during the 1980s, such that mental illness was legally redefined and procedures were improved for involuntary incarceration, as were mechanisms for appeal and review. This range of legislative, human rights, treatment improvement and cost consideration changes led to a considerable shift in the numbers of people being institutionalised.

There was considerable activity in service planning, variously supported by policies and program funding designed to develop more integrated community-based service models. Questions about the level of community resources required for community-based treatment, rehabilitation, palliation and care were frequently raised.

STATES START TO ACT ON LOCATIONAL EQUITY

During the 1980s the planning processes highlighted locational inequity in many states. In some states, historical spending patterns were questioned through the use of needs-based indicators and early resource allocation formulae.

In New South Wales, for example, the Minister for Health, the Hon. Kevin Stewart, announced in 1979 the closure of 879 hospital beds in Sydney and 1200 in rural New South Wales and the redistribution of the savings to growth areas. In 1983 the NSW Minister for Health, the Hon. Laurie Brereton, further announced the closure of two medium-sized hospitals and the downgrading of the Sydney and War Memorial Hospitals in order to fund beds in Sydney's rapidly growing western suburbs. These latter changes created much greater furore than the previous closures. Such redistributions also occurred to a lesser extent in Melbourne and Adelaide and they continue today as major themes in hospital services planning.

PLANNING TOOLS DEVELOP

Health planners gradually began to be involved in developing sophisticated technical approaches to forecasting needs and trends. In the mid-1980s, role delineation of services was developed as a planning process. Role delineation of health services allowed planners and managers to assess the support services, staffing profile, minimal safety standards and other requirements for each health care service and facility. Role delineation supported the provision of specific services outside of the hospital grounds in a more efficient or effective networked arrangement. Making such clinical requirements explicit provided a more consistent way of ensuring that patients received safe care in the most appropriate facility and service.

By the late 1980s, computer modelling became firmly established. In 1985 a forecasting model was used by the Western Metropolitan Health Region of New South Wales. This set the framework for the development of teaching facilities and further redistribution of hospital beds, within the region. In the early 1990s, HOSPIM, a locational optimisation model, was used for metropolitan hospital planning in South Australia; the Victorians developed HOSPLOC, a simulation model, for reconfiguring metropolitan hospital services; and New South Wales developed the APPI Planner. In Western Australia the epidemiological contribution to planning was enhanced in the mid-1990s through record linkage of six main health databases.

DEVELOPMENT OF SPECIALISED PLANNING

The increasing use of technologies and the use of high-cost drugs in the 1970s contributed to higher health costs. Unlike other industries, where technology reduces costs, most medical technology has not been labour displacing and often results in the creation of additional jobs. Health technology planning was begun in earnest by a sub-committee of the Standing Committee of Health Ministers (SCOHM), a predecessor to the Australian Health Ministers Advisory Committee (AHMAC). Planning ratios for services such as cardiac surgery, renal dialysis and computer tomography (CT) scanners were all issues of concern.

The application of these ratios at the state level was not easy, due to political lobbying for new and expansive technology. In the 1980s, Victoria put into legislation a planning approach to regulate the diffusion of CT scanners, linear accelerators, lithotripters and Magnetic Resonance Imaging (MRIs), whereby a need had to be demonstrated before licence would be granted. Enshrining technology planning into legislation was ultimately abandoned in the 1990s when placing financial limitations — either through Commonwealth payments or through national pooled funding via AHMAC — on technology diffusion became the preferred approach. Magnetic resonance imaging and transplantations (heart, liver, lung and pancreas) were the primary targets of funding restrictions during the early 1990s.

Health manpower (sic) planning began in earnest at both state and Commonwealth levels when AHMAC was asked to report on an 'oversupply' of doctors. The supply of doctors had increased in the 1970s due to the expansion of medical schools, as recommended by the Karmel report into medical education. Furthermore, from the 1960s, 'foreign doctors' or overseas-trained doctors gradually began to be licensed to practise in various states.

Since then, workforce planning has re-emerged at times when workforce issues have been characterised by tensions between specialisation and multiskilling, or due to contests between different professional groups (especially medicine and nursing), perceived tensions between equity principles such as equal employment opportunity (EEO) and the efficiency drive and an emerging concern with professional standards and quality care.

During the 1980s the medical profession regularly went to battle with various governments and the bureaucracy on issues which included pharmaceutical benefits, staffing of community health centres, health insurance, registration of alternative health care practitioners, medical fees and the differential between general practitioner and specialist charges. Medicare had resulted in declining revenues for hospitals and for some private physicians. These factors contributed to the development of a 'festering and periodically explosive doctor' dispute' from 1984 onwards.

In the 1990s the battles between the medical profession and governments resulted in medical workforce planning as a process to negotiate the supply of specialist doctors. The Australian Medical Workforce Advisory Council (AMWAC), a sub-committee of AHMAC, is the forum where representatives of the various specialities come to agreement about shortages and oversupplies and how these might be addressed.

The recruitment and retention of nurses, allied health and a number of other health disciplines also emerged as problems from time to time throughout the 1970s and 1980s. The fluctuations in these workforce categories reflected more the position of women in the economy and workforce.

The 1980s also heralded significant changes in the nursing profession. Since the Second World War, nursing had been beset with recurring labour shortages, poor remuneration, inadequate training and poor working conditions. The patient care context for nursing had significantly shifted, such that individual nurses rather than just the hospital matron (as under the Nightingale system) now had responsibility to independently solve clinical problems. This led inevitably to tensions between greater specialisation and multiskilling in nursing. During the 1980s, nurses' wages and conditions improved and the gradual transfer of nurse education from the hospital setting to the higher education sector provided for increasing professionalism. These changes also increased the overall costs of health care, since nursing labour represented about half the total costs of health care.

With involvement in workforce planning issues, planning moved beyond its role of the early 1980s when designated health planners had mainly been involved in developing service and strategic plans for the health system. By the end of the 1980s, in keeping with the rise of managerialism at that time, corporate and business plans derived from the US private sector began to be fashionable. These plans differed from previous strategic plans in that they defined goals, objectives and strategies for the whole organisation. Planning's corporate role became intimately tied up with its service planning role. The first state corporate plan was developed in Western Australia in 1986. In 1989 the Western Australia Strategic Plan for the Health Department fully integrated the previous corporate, strategic and service plans. Corporate plans were developed in the late 1980s and early 1990s in most other states.

RATIONING, EFFECTIVENESS AND OUTCOMES

In the 1990s, planning moved from a concern with inputs to a concern with outcomes. This movement signalled a change of focus, from measuring the services that are provided to measuring the health gain achieved from those services. An outcome focus in planning related to issues surrounding quality management, the establishment of national health goals and targets and an interest in outcome evaluation.

This shift was also consistent with the move of the planning role into organisational management and improving performance monitoring and accountability. Planning became increasingly concerned with resource allocation issues, or with organisational, capital or service planning which required an 'outcomes focus' or a focus on 'health improvement'. Whilst a traditional service planning approach allowed planners to retreat to data collection, sophisticated forecasting and computer modelling, the health outcomes approach required evidence of relative need, knowledge of the best available evidence of the effectiveness of interventions and evidence of appropriate community, intersectoral and stakeholder consultation. It incorporated an economic component and required integrated planning processes.

At one level the outcomes paradigm provided a new set of principles on which to ration health care — merely another way for administrators to take control of the knife, wield it and then justify its use. At another level, in combination with improved information systems, the outcomes approach had potential to further challenge traditional practices and routines in health care and to develop more cost-effective, patient/community-centred and broad-based approaches to improving health.

The adoption of 'evidence-based medicine' began to be advocated both for clinical practice and in policy and planning. Such an approach required the planning process to take account of the findings of research and data and to develop skills in analysing effectiveness, safety and acceptability, the quality of evidence and the generalisability and local applicability of research and data. The outcomes movement contributed to increasing involvement of frontline health workers in clinical research, business planning and information gathering.

At the same time, designated planning units were often abandoned in favour of private consultants or market forces. Where planning was totally abandoned in favour of market forces, a commitment to distributional equity was also substantially abandoned.

Policy and planning documents became replete with both the language of economic rationalism and the public health and health outcomes lexicon. Tensions between public health and biomedicine, between outputs and outcomes and between planning and market forces characterised the health planning environment. Whereas in the previous decade the planning process could often be topdown, the public health approach and market assessment required a more rigorous and intersectoral approach to needs assessment and applied epidemiology. Health planning required a more eclectic approach that integrated processes which had previously been discrete and sequential, including service planning, economic appraisal and capital and asset planning. Planning was essentially concerned with change management and economics. Planning also became a skill expected of most health care managers and administrators.

THE FUTURE OF HEALTH PLANNING

The future is likely to see further cost restraint, new approaches to resource allocation, the predicted ageing of the population, the predicted ethical and financial difficulties for the health care system of delivering equitable services to the 'old old', an increase in technology and new treatments, a further blurring of the public and private components of health care and greater community and consumer involvement in health care.

Key questions for the system are whether to focus resources on improving the health of 'the many' (equity of access), or to focus resources, activities and interventions on those with the poorest health, thereby attempting to equalise their health outcomes with those of the rest of the population (equity of outcome). Questions must also arise as to whether health services and facilities remain at the forefront of health planning activity, or whether broader social and intersectoral approaches become pivotal.

Certainly, the current political, economic and scientific environment is replete with individualistic approaches to prevention and treatment issues. The march of bio-medical approaches to health care and health improvement remains strong and constant. A reductionist approach to improving health is ever more likely as scientists and the general community become increasingly fascinated with genetics, genetic manipulation and molecular approaches to improving health. Public health has been identified as being at the crossroads, with the inevitable clash of reductionist and broad visions of health. As health planning develops the change mechanisms that are consistent with prevailing outcomes policy paradigms, it is also at a crossroads, with individualistic, top-down approaches down one road and intersectoral, inclusive, health improvement and equity planning down the other.

HEALTH AND SUSTAINABILITY

At one of the project management team meetings to discuss the development of this book, a profound question was put to the group: why sustainability? In other words, for what reason were we working so hard? The answer is not as simple as you might imagine. The people at the meeting did not say things such as, 'because our planet is warming', 'our resources are running out', or 'our environments are becoming toxic waste dumps'.

Those answers were too simplistic and, as time has shown, there are no simple solutions. After a great deal of discussion, one of the group simply said, 'When in 20 years' time one of my grandchildren asks me why our generation let things go on for so long when everything was telling them time was running out, I want to be able to tell them I did all I could.'

As Capra (1983) suggested in The Turning Point, we are at a point in history where the essential nature of our relationship to the environment is changing. Like Capra, we believe the next generation will not understand the motivations for our purely growth-driven actions today, just as we found it hard to understand the mid-20th century motivation for tolerating the spread of fascism. We would like readers to begin this book by contemplating answers for the children of 2020.

Baum's The New Public Health (2002) puts the argument for a new approach to public health based on the increase in globalisation and decrease in equity in and between populations. This book takes this new direction one step further and argues that if public health is to consider its full responsibility to the health of the public, it has no choice but to give major consideration to global sustainability.

Survey results are indicating most people believe the environment is an important consideration and that the community has good knowledge of environmental issues. If this is so, why is there no corresponding increase in action for the environment, even in simple issues such as waste recycling? This conundrum is also true of the response of public health practice in general: while there is an obvious connection between health and a state of global ecological integrity, there seem to be only isolated reactions on behalf of public health practitioners toward global ecological integrity.

Such a reorientation of public health is nothing new. Public health has always been regarded as a response to changes in the biophysical landscape. Hippocrates of Kos and his school supported the idea that nature—which included the human body—could cure itself, and that the quality of the environment had an important bearing on this process. The beginning of public health as a formal practice was a courageous response by Snow to prevent water being pumped from a cholerainfected supply and was carried out in the face of extensive disapproval from the local community.

His removing the pump handle, acting on indicative but not final evidence (that is, applying the precautionary principle) halted the epidemic ... but raised the fury of the water-deprived population. These characteristics—acting for the public good when there is a risk too great not to act on, even if the evidence is not all in and before the public is aware of the risks—are still part of public health practice today.

We are now in the third of three phases in public health practice arising from health risks of the industrial revolution, economic development and the current concern about sustainable development. Each era has called on different responses from public health practitioners and their colleagues. In the first phase reducing the risks of infectious disease epidemics lay in the hands of the civic authorities, who made decisions about urban renewal, sewerage and hygiene.

Legal action saw the emergence of restraints on public freedom of some to safeguard the health of all, including quarantine, condemned housing and controls on contamination of water sources and waterways. After major epidemics of infectious diseases had been controlled (at least in developed countries) by changes in public infrastructure, the second phase of public health emerged with the industrial byproducts and wastes of economic development.

Technical testing capacities for monitoring air, water and soils became major professional skills of public health practitioners. By the last quarter of the 20th century, public health practice was faced with an even greater change in its application. As well as increases in its existing responsibilities there came the added responsibility of protecting local environmental life-support systems.

Moreover, this responsibility is also for the future; not only for the local population but also for that population as a unit of the planetary environment. Long-term protection has always been the concern of public health, but single localities can no longer be protected in isolation from their neighbours.

The long shadows of the major cities, the rapid transport of goods and services mean that collaborative regional and national action is required. Local issues still offer the unit of action when dealing with global concerns, leading practitioners to seek to widen their links with a range of professions, expert advisors and community interests at other scales of action. Contamination of city air by transport exhausts, blue-green algae affecting many waterways and the leaching of nitrates into groundwater from crop runoff are examples of unsolved health risks arising from environmental disruption.

Maintaining sustainable ecosystems as essential prerequisites for human health is now beginning to be accepted as part of the responsibility of public health. This is designed to stimulate a new generation of public health workers to recognise the connections between the health of the ecosystem and the health of populations.

It is the first phase of a continuing dialogue about how public health practitioners can participate in action for sustainability as an essential consideration in promoting the health of populations. It should not be viewed as a new dogma, but rather as the first step in a critical review of the role public health practitioners play currently in sustainability along with actions they can take to improve the situation in the future.

Global ecological integrity

The term global ecological integrity refers to the maintenance of the complex relationship between life on the planet and the ecosystem that supports this life. The concept suggests that for the existing life-support system to remain fully functional, it must be able to regenerate itself in its entirety after addressing any ecological crisis threatening this integrity.

The public health practitioner needs to consider a suite of emerging ecological issues around these threats. These should be viewed as a list of symptoms that result from humanity's poorly considered hunger for rapid growth and unsustainable development, as a result of which ecological symptoms are affecting human wellbeing and resulting in global disintegrity.

Human changes to the environment have altered the continuity of global cycles, and the rate of change is expected to increase. Ozone depletion, global warming, urban pollution, non-degradable industrial waste, fresh water contamination and biodiversity depletion are bringing serious and increasing risks to sustainability of the planet's life-support systems and so to human health and wellbeing. Pimentel et al. (1998) claim that 40 per cent of the human disease burden now arises from environmental sources. In a report to the 2002 World Summit, the World Health Organisation (WHO) calculates the figure as closer to 25 per cent—still an amount to be reckoned with (World Summit on Sustainable Development 2002). McMichael (2001) considers structural change is needed in public health practice and in the larger community's cultural and technological processes to recreate a functioning ecosphere that can continue to support biological and social needs.

In 1986 the World Commission on Environment and Development explored ways in which human impact on the environment has endangered the sustainability of global systems (World Commission on Environment and Development 1987). Environmental sustainability was acknowledged as crucial to preserving human health in its own right, not merely as a support system.

Despite this recognition the rate of disruption of global air, water, soil and living systems—that is, of the traditional concerns of public health —has increased. International conventions have failed to arrest the escalating rates of environmental degradation. The Kyoto Protocol for reducing the production of greenhouse gas emissions causing global warming was not unanimously supported; global temperatures are rising, the ozone hole reappears every year and irrigation and the resulting soil salinisation is increasing. Food production per head is falling, and species are disappearing at the same time that population is rising (although the rate of increase is slowing). Fossil fuel use is increasing, though the proportion of renewable energy use is rising.

The question we need to ask in any teaching/learning programme on sustainability and health is: Since all the responsible agencies confirmed those trends in 1995, why is it that those trends continue in 2002? The answer has to lie in re-thinking the solutions we are currently applying. In the context of this book we consider public health practice needs to take these trends into account and act accordingly.

Reports on the state of the global environment suggest that increasing risks from degraded environmental resources of air, water and soil (particularly water) are approaching thresholds beyond which the damage may be irreversible.

Thus, risks to the sustainability of environmental systems have become risks to human health in themselves, through:

- Directly damaging human systems, for example, through contaminated drinking water;
- Degrading small-scale environmental systems on which human systems depend, for example, through forest clearing that reduces local rainfall and so local water supplies;
- Disrupting global environmental systems on which all species depend, for example, through contributing to global warming; and
- Diminishing biodiversity and indigenous plant knowledge systems, reducing the stock of potential medicines for future generations.

Defining sustainable development

'Sustainable development' has been the generally preferred response to human-generated environmental changes as they affect our wellbeing. The usual working definition is taken from the World Commission on Environment and Development as 'development which meets the needs of the present without compromising the capacity of future generations to meet their own needs'.

It is doubtful whether this definition can hold up today, with global systems already significantly changed. The WCED also included global ecological integrity and human collaborative social systems in its recommendations, so perhaps it is time for a new look at this definition. Principles of sustainable development have been adopted by the United Nations and their relevant family of organisations as the basis for policy development, programme design, programme delivery and monitoring of the outcomes of global and local environmental changes.

These principles have also been incorporated in the health, environmental and public health policies of the United Kingdom, Canada and Australia.

Sustainable development principles have been translated into action in many different ways. They are referred to in the 27 action groups in Agenda 21. In the Bellagio principles they are set out as modes of action, and in the Australian Ecologically Sustainable Development Strategy and the Australian National Public Health Strategy and Implementation Plan they are set out as five strategic goals.

There is much discussion in the literature on whether sustainable development is an oxymoron (a pair of irreconcilable opposites), a paradox (a contradiction in terms), or a newly derived concept in the process of being developed. There are also debates on whether it is a tangible goal, a mode of action or an ideal. We are assuming here that it is a necessary goal, one toward which all professions and practitioners must work, not public health alone. The most generally accepted working definition of sustainable development is that it is a set of principles, issues and processes.

While Australia is the only country that has added 'ecologically' to sustainable development, in all other respects the terms are applied internationally in exactly the same way. Publications as various as those of the United States Research Council and the World Bank have moved to use 'sustainability' as a more appropriate concept than sustainable development.

This move reflects the progression from working to resolve two conflicting agendas (ecological sustainability and economic development) to that of reconciling both these and social agendas such as health in a co-ordinated long-term solution. Understanding and describing sustainability has been one of the issues of continuing consideration and dialogue for the group engaged in this project.

However, at this stage we have settled with a description for sustainability and health proposed by our expert advisors who have agreed that sustainability in public health is about transformational change in environmental governance; it is neither about revolution nor is it about 'business as usual':

Sustainability in public health requires both local knowledge and strategic knowledge of environmental change as well as the specialised knowledge of the academic disciplines; and Sustainability and Health teaching programmes will need to be different from traditional courses in that they deal with the future as well as the present, and about what to change as well as how to address what to preserve.

The implementation of sustainable development principles has been extremely varied, both in individual countries and worldwide. In Britain, MacDonald (1998) evaluated 45 Agenda 21 projects that had been launched at UNCED 1992 and found only eight still proceeding, all of which were based on local action. In 1999 the United States Institute of Medicine, Research, Engineering and Science reviewed the global situation and, like many similar reviews, found there were structural barriers to the implementation of sustainable development principles in professional education and research. Their combined report, Our Common Journey, accepted that a transformation of current research and education frameworks was required if there was to be progress towards sustainable development, and recommended the following changes in direction:

- Establish research and education frameworks that integrate global and local perspectives to shape a 'place-based' understanding of the interactions between environment and society;
- Ensure that the three key decision-making groups of community, experts and government are fully involved in the research into and the delivery of sustainability programmes;
- Initiate dedicated research programmes on the under-studied questions that are central to a deeper understanding of interactions between society, environment, and the health of all life forms; and
- Promote better use of existing tools and processes to link knowledge and action in pursuit of a transition to sustainability.

These recommendations provide one of the few sets that link education, research and evaluation in the context of global change, and bring together the specialised fields of health, environment and science. They offer useful guidelines for a public health curriculum addressing sustainability and health. One thing is certain: public health initiatives, coming late into the field of sustainability practice, cannot go it alone; the diversity of interests and information means teamwork and multiple alliances will be necessary.

Nor can public health practitioners assume that health will be the lead agency in social change, as has often been the case. A place for health will need to be negotiated among the interests of environmental resource management, economic efficiencies, continuity needs of diverse social groups, and organisational territories—no mean task.

One of the early warnings of need for these changes came in the early 1970s. The Club of Rome project headed by Donella and Dennis Meadows developed a thesis titled The Limits to Growth using computer modelling to demonstrate the cumulative and interactive effects of growth in population, energy use and polluting byproducts of industry on the self-renewing capacity of the environment. Predictions of ozone depletion, global warming and water depletion date from this time.

The warning was partly heeded, with industry and governments of industrialised countries recognising that some controls and re-tooling were necessary. The lessons on social structural change and the need to reinterpret both problems and solutions were lost. The increasing rate of environmental decline has led, by 2003, to recognition that some form of global intervention and reinterpretation of growth and development is required. AtKisson (1999) recalls the impact of the Club of Rome and brings the idea of sustainable development up to date in the light of all we have learnt since then, giving us three necessary conditions for the physical survival of our species:

1. Not using up renewable natural resources (air, water, life forms) faster than they can replenish themselves;
2. Investing ahead to develop replacements for depleted non-renewable resources (fossil fuels, fertile soils) while we still have the wealth from using up the resources; and
3. Not producing wastes faster than natural processes can absorb them.

AtKisson goes on to point out that physical survival is not enough; humanely governed sustainable development is required for the survival to be worthwhile. AtKisson's messages, carrying many lessons that echo those of public health practice (making healthy choices the easy choices; turning change into routine behaviour, and moving from treatment of outcomes to prevention of risk), are explored on behalf of public health practice.

The model known as the Mandala of Health depicts the human ecosystem as a complex web of interrelationships, each component of which has potential to affect human health. In the Mandala, the social unit (individual or family) is placed as the centre of concentric circles ever-expanding out to the biosphere. Within the circles are four key factors that determine health. The form the Mandala takes serves first to illustrate that the impacts of changes in one part of the web of relationships are not restricted to that part and instead are likely to make an impact across the entire web.

The model especially makes clear that there is a very tight relationship between culture and environment, thus emphasising the risks of this tightening relationship as humans have learned to manipulate the planet. As well as acting to describe the nature of the interrelationships, the Mandala has the potential to serve as a framework for action and in its modified form has been adapted as a guide for practice.

One of the key concepts Hancock advocates as central to the process of the WHO Healthy Cities project is community action (2000):

... a concern with ecology necessarily becomes part of a social movement because the problem of reversing the present self-destructive treatment of the environment cannot be separated from the right to challenge the authoritarian decision making process invested in corporate and governmental institutions.

Hancock states that 'a shared vision can be a powerful force that brings together a community and inspires its members to take action together'. Healthy Cities begin their projects by allowing citizens to participate in a process of visualising a common future. The project works with citizens to help them establish indicators of success and participate in a process of evaluation and re-evaluation.

In parallel with Healthy Cities, Hancock with others developed the Ottawa Charter for Health Promotion, now known as the blueprint for a new public health. There are clear parallels between the New Public Health, Local Agenda 21 and the principles of sustainable development.

In Doing Less Harm, Hancock takes the medical system's ethical commitment to primum non nocere—first, do no harm—to inform the medical profession of its responsibility to make health facilities environmentally healthy. This booklet provides simple, commonsense actions for change with case studies of successful stories.

Hancock argues that hospitals are significant users of energy and that the health implications of energy use such as carbon dioxide emissions and resource depletion are greater than the health implications of all other aspects of unsustainable hospital buildings put together.

New Ideas for New Public Health

Baum addresses the strengthening links between environmental issues and the overall health of the public. In The New Public Health, she reviews current public health, especially addressing the translation of the rhetoric into public health practice. She traces the way public health has moved from its basis primarily on bio-medical models to a wider, more holistic and multidisciplinary activity.

This more encompassing perspective has been termed the 'New Public Health'. Baum provides clear evidence of the strong practice links between environmental health practitioners and public health practitioners. An assumption underpinning all her work is that of the primacy of community involvement in decisions and actions that affect members of that community.

In relating the history of public health practice, Baum shows how the values underpinning this recent perspective are developing and are still fragile. She describes how the rather paternalistic collective public health measures of the 19th and early 20th centuries, with their focus on policies and laws across society, gave way late last century to concentration on individual and personal health behaviours, with approaches echoing clinical practice in medicine.

Context, situation and locality were not seen to be of importance. Little value was given to proactive or preventive measures, with most effort and funding being directed to reactive responses addressing problems already defined. Although Baum and colleagues have moved to support the principles of the new public health, which they identify as the contemporary view, many in the public health field find any movement away from standard medical practice to be retrogressive and see the work of community-focused public health as of lesser value.

The changes in the global environment and its impact on health described by McMichael confirm the need for a further perspective on public health practice, education and research, that we believe could be termed the 'new, new public health'. Soskolne and Bertollini propose that global ecological integrity, previously taken for granted, is emerging as the cornerstone of public health. They put forward the idea that shifts in current practice and new frameworks are needed to make wise decisions governing the change. Breaches in global environmental integrity are emerging as the biggest challenge in protecting public health, greater even than the move to cities and the great plagues of past centuries, since they threaten the future of the species itself.

Soskolne and Bertollini's thesis, which includes contributions by researchers from many disciplines published in the same discussion document, provides an excellent overview of the social, economic and ecological implications of these conclusions.

Soskolne and Bertollini suggest that potential solutions lie in models that focus more on social, information and service-based development than on growth. They argue that knowledge that transcends the barriers of scientific disciplines is necessary for achieving interdisciplinary scientific understanding and consensus, and for reaching agreements among many societal interests to promote appropriate changes in policy and practice.

Participants in the Soskolne-Bertollini symposium addressed the 'principle of ecological integrity'. Rees (2000) described humans as a dominant species in the global ecological system, large, adaptable social mammals that live in groups. They have correspondingly large energy and material demands and all resources entering the human economy come from natural systems.

Very few unmodified local habitats are productive enough to support even modest groups of people living in permanent settlements for very long. In this respect we are a true 'patch disturbance' species in that we have an impact on the environments we inhabit, a distinction shared with other mammals ranging from beavers to elephants, yet it is evident that the nature of our patch disturbance has a longer lasting if not permanent impact.

Capra more recently has revisited this idea by suggesting, 'Accordingly, the appropriate way of approaching nature to learn about her complexity and beauty is not through domination and control, but through respect, cooperation and dialogue'. Prigogine (1980) describes our society as a 'dissipative structure' drawing resources from external sources to maintain the integrity of society's structures, while all the time increasing the disorder in locations where the resources are drawn.

If we accept Prigogine's hypothesis, the nature of our current society can only be maintained through destructively decreasing global ecological integrity. Not for the first time, public health practice for sustainability and health requires changes in the way we live. The context of public health education, and particularly the incorporation of sustainability and health into it, reveals a system in the process of change.

In responding to this change, continual review and re-evaluation of the application of sustainable development principles in public health is necessary.

This will allow these to meet the challenge Soskolne and Bertollini have described and become a cornerstone of public health and public health practice across the world.

Adhering personally to the principles of sustainability can be seen not only as a means of enlarging the focus of public health practice but also as an essential 'role-model' allowing not only more effective distribution of the sustainability 'message' but also encouraging more effective practice in its own right. Personal practice contributes in its own way to closing the gap between sustainability and health in theory and practice.

Hess, in the same symposium, reviews the significance of impaired ecological integrity for public health. He suggests that unintentionally and unwittingly, public health has contributed to the breaching of the planet's natural systems. The profession of public health has promoted economic development as a means of achieving health. Public health strategies have tended to disregard the ecological consequences of their various interventions.

Traditional public health interventions have focused predominantly on humanity as an independent entity and not in the context of the living environment. In both its measures and its interventions, the goal of public health has been to make people impervious to nature by making them immune to disease and by increasing longevity. In such a framework the elements of nature are implicitly reclassified into resources for and threats to human health.

New measures are required to assess health as a balanced system of individuals, communities and the environment. This changing way we view the world around us needs explicit recognition of humankind's niche in the greater environment and of our natural limitations as a species. This new, new public health perspective also requires accepting the public health practitioner as one of a multi-skilled team, a team learning together to support the changing human/ environment relationship.

An Open Learning Framework

Nothing is more certain in our lives than change. Change is all around us; every time we open our front doors to go outside it seems something else is different. Our work here does not involve stopping change, since that would be both impossible and absurd. We do advocate, however, that we become deeply involved in and help to guide a new approach to change. Each of us has ideas—good ideas for improving things—but some of us never get the chance to put those ideas into practice.

We suggest throughout this book that change is based on economic, technological, environmental and social considerations, and that somehow all these need to be considered at the same time in the change process. Below we describe a process we believe will lead to sustainable change and development that includes a humane future. The development of this process is necessarily iterative in that it is part of an ongoing dialogue. Sustainability and health practice is based on the need to respond to and manage change rather than simply follow what has gone before; therefore we need an adaptive, responsive critical learning framework, one that provides the basis for long-term learning. The framework proposed for the design of teaching programmes, course materials and field experience in this book is based on a combination of experiential inquiry-based learning principles and place-based cooperation for local sustainability.

Kolb et al. argue that all learning is about change, and adult learning is best characterised as a form of personal inquiry into real world problems. This educational approach is well suited to responding to issues of sustainability and health, requiring acceptance of the need for transformational change. Kolb outlines four steps in the experiential learning cycle, linked here with the matching step carrying individual learning into the public sphere: observation and reflection (describing), abstract conceptualisation (designing), active experimentation (doing) and testing the new ideas in fresh situations (developing).

In his applied research Kolb demonstrated that different professions concentrated on one or more of the steps of the cycle—engineers on concrete observation, scientists on active experimentation, and management on reflection and observation. He argued that an individual or a project team often did not complete the learning/problem-solving cycle; that the learning and/or the inquiry was therefore incomplete and so was unsustainable over the longer term.

The learning cycle is in practice a spiral with continual learning throughout an individual's or an organisation's lifespan. Kolb's work has influenced the field of action research, acting as a framework for lifelong learning in a number of professions and giving rise to the idea of the learning organisation, a key concept in organisational management circles.

It is becoming increasingly apparent that the future sustainability of the human species depends on adaptive, system-wide solutions to linked social, economic and ecological issues. It is becoming equally apparent that aids to understanding complex, inter-related ecological systems to improve decision-making will be needed to augment the prevailing analytical, singlefactor thinking.

Among such aids is the D4P4 decision-making framework designed to be used as a guide to local decision-making under conditions of system change toward sustainability. The framework was first developed in partnership with local government authorities as a monitoring and evaluation model for local integrated state-of-the-environment reporting.

Through the pursuit of grounded theory, which also follows the Kolb experiential learning cycle through ideas to practice to new ideas, the D4P4 framework became established as a useful tool in partnership with local government and their communities. Since then the D4P4 framework, which links knowledge to action, has been used in a range of change management processes from land care communication and redesign of a curriculum in public health to regional state-of-the environment reporting. By incorporating sustainable development principles into public health decision-making and so into public health education and practice, the change process goes through four stages of knowledge development and their related action. Kolb's experiential stages of develop, describe, design, and do enable the establishment of a knowledge base of principles, people and place, potential and practice, and subsequent review, thereby constructing a spiral learning process.

Applying New Ideas

The principles by which we live, as private citizens or as expert practitioners, are based on some set of ethical values, whether the values are explicitly acknowledged or, more usually, taken for granted. The principles (what should be) drive our actions; for example, 'Since I value the sustainability of the human species, I should follow the precautionary principle. Because the risks from climate change are too great, this will mean reducing my energy use.' In the case of emergent concerns such as sustainability and health, longstanding values are not likely to change, but a fresh understanding of the situation may alter the principles that decide the type of action; for example, the shift in response to drought in Australia.

Until a decade ago, it has been 'drought is a national disaster', with support to 'drought-stricken' families. The altered response is to 'drought as a normal event in the Australian climate', with support for 'responsibilities' of families to adopt different farming practices and/or leave the land, though some of the former response continues in parallel with the new approach.

The ethical value of humane care for humans remains, but the accompanying principle for land care has dramatically changed, and so have the appropriate actions. The values underlying the key words 'health' and 'environment' are widely debated and indeed interpreted differently in different cultures and communities. The debate on the values underlying 'health' has been only partly resolved by the widely applied WHO definition: that health is the attainment of optimum bio-psycho-social wellbeing.

This statement originally omitted 'spiritual wellbeing', leaving a gap criticised by many nation-states, formal religions and health professionals, to the extent that a recent World Health Assembly has recommended its inclusion. The definition is also seen as lacking in that it does not consider environmental wellbeing as a necessary precondition for health.

Describing People and Place

Since public health practice now needs to respond to global environmental change, it is important that information on the status of sustainable development principles is included in most if not all public health teaching programmes. Principles (what should be) will influence which aspects of health and environment (what is) are selected as content for training in evidence based practice. Learning about sustainability and health is not primarily about information transfer, though it will require the best available information on people and place.

The educational task lies in preparing for key roles as agents of change in the sustainable governance of our increasingly hazardous ecosystem. Environmental management then takes on a new significance as part of public health practice. Progress toward sustainability and health requires an accurate record of the status of inter-related changes in social, economic and environmental resources, and the cumulative effects of the interactions between them.

The chapters that follow begin with an examination of the wide range of perspectives (environment-centred, people-centred, resource-centred) on the status of sustainability and health across the globe, and how these perspectives are being incorporated into the context of public health action. The situation varies from public health programmes that fail to deal with sustainable development, to those where it is a central focus. Tools to help the public health practitioner understand the mass of background information and multiple options for action are needed in order to explore ways of moving forward.

Conceptualisation

In the emergent field of sustainability and health, practitioners are working with unpredictable outcomes and as yet largely unspecified practices. At this stage of the early 21st century, the public health community is only just beginning to accept that sustainability is an important public health goal.

Under these circumstances of uncertainty and change, the creative design of new ideas and strategic thinking, and new possibilities for practice, can well be of greater effectiveness than continuing to follow the precedents of established practice. This is not to suggest 'throwing the baby out with the bath water', but that there is a need to incorporate the new with the old, undoubted strengths of well-tried practice.

In this phase of the decision-making process, the ideas that will help realise the potential of human inventiveness and environmental resilience are also emerging. This knowledge is not already stored in libraries or professional practice records, but is being developed through the creative stimulus of changing environmental conditions, the interactions of globalisation, the technical capacity of the Internet and the warnings of impending crisis.

The foundation for 'what could be' has been laid by deciding on shared principles and describing 'what is'. For this stage it will be most productive to begin a process that will lead decision-making groups to redefine sustainability and health. Open discussion will allow many viewpoints about the way forward to be considered. Public health practitioners will gain from working with the widest possible range of colleagues.

During this phase, open dialogue in a creative, safe, non-confrontational environment as described by Bohm (1996) encourages entry of new ideas, and the synergy sparked by the interaction of different ideas provides the basis for learning. This returns the practitioner to the primary proposition underpinning Kolb's learning stages: learning is essentially individual and personal, and social learning proceeds from experiential individual learning.

Concrete Experience

Putting ideas into practice is the testing site of the whole decision-making process. Lack of such application is one of the most frequent complaints about the current management of the sustainability process, from the Kyoto principles on controlling greenhouse gases to the conclusions on lack of progress toward sustainability at the 2002 World Summit on Sustainable Development. Sustainability and health practitioners from public health cannot go it alone when it comes to practice; they need fellow practitioners from all the disciplines involved in this book.

Not only practice but also review of practice is essential for the effective practitioner. The scoping of what is intended to result from the practice and the context in which it is conducted need to be determined before the practice begins, otherwise the practitioner has no basis for making judgments on what works under what conditions; this is why the chapter on scoping is presented before the chapters on sustainability and health action.

Traditional public health scoping practices include epidemiological profiles; for sustainability practice these need to be coupled with annual state-of-the-environment reports allowing for the observation of patterns that emerge. While all adult education in a changing society is education for change, the question remains of how change is expressed in the education and practice of public health professionals in an era of unsustainable change.

The answer—or rather answers—to that question provides the foundation for the content, approaches and skills of a public health curriculum incorporating the principles of sustainable development. Such answers are emerging from a rapidly growing body of practical experience and theoretical debate on the pathways to achieving sustainability and health.

Sustainability as Public Health Practice

The move to incorporating sustainable development in socio-political structures worldwide has been slow, but is now accelerating under a new process of sustainability. Public health is one of the professions that needs urgently to reconsider its role in maintaining the health of human populations, in the light of current state of the world environment reports. Contemporary international events provide the teaching process with a clearly described and shared body of knowledge.

A recent report on public health education in the USA offers some rhetoric which could translate into producing practitioners who could comprehend the demands of these major changes. The report suggests that public health professionals 'must understand the theoretical underpinnings of the ecological model [of health] ... to more effectively address the challenges of the 21st century'. The report built on earlier work emphasising the importance of the universal competencies together with the five core disciplinary areas.

Sustainable development adds another perspective and body of content, much of it drawn from the field of environment governance, to the wide range of paradigms already existing in public health. Related fields include health risk assessment, social impact assessment, health promotion, health education, social justice, community development, epidemiology and the New Public Health and its vehicle of Healthy Cities, to name but a few.

The content and skills of environmental management are equally well established, but not usually yet considered an integral part of public health. Environmental risk and impact assessments, environmental education and law, adaptive land management and Local Agenda 21 plans are all grappling with the health implications of global and local environmental degradation. The overlapping sets of environmental and health activities described above lead inevitably to the conclusions that, of the two sets of information, each requires the other for effective decision-making; and that of the two sets of professional skills, each calls for close collaboration with the other.

Each group of professional practitioners takes pride in its expertise and may well question the intrusion of others into its field; in neither group have sustainable development principles become fully established in professional education and practice. Yet between them, the arenas of environment and health already carry the expertise to implement all five of the principles of sustainability.

In public health practice, equity within and between generations, precautionary action and monitoring play an integral part; while in environmental sciences, acting for the future, environmental integrity and monitoring form the basis of environmental management practice.

Questions arise as to how best to address this new dimension of the established two-way relationship between environment and health. If public health practice now requires skills in environmental management and environmental management is increasingly addressing public health issues, does this mean:

- Public health practice incorporates environmental management
- Environmental management incorporates public health practice

- Environmental health expands and takes responsibility for both; or
- A fresh form of all-encompassing professional practice is required?

The trend of the answers from sources in either environment or health is that all four options are waiting to be taken up. As in the Hitchhiker's Guide to the Galaxy we know the answer, but what is the question?

The degree of transformation needed to instigate well-documented strategies to move from global degradation to global sustainability requires changes not only in many professions but also in community practices and community services; so as far as the public health curriculum is concerned, sustainable development principles need to be included as:

- A recognised section of all specialised public health fields;
- A basis for collaboration with environmental professions;
- A part of core business for environmental health practitioners; and
- A form of professional expertise requiring research and development.

As well as forging a new combination from the parallel expertise of public health practice and environmental management, and supporting a strengthened environmental health profession, a sustainability and health curriculum faces a third and even more difficult task.

Public health and environmental health, both as professions and as research fields in general, remain narrowly scientifically based, while the solutions to problems in either field lie in understanding the social and environmental systems in which they operate. In both fields there is emerging exploration of transdisciplinary, systemic and futureoriented approaches to research and practice; that this remains tentative and far from the mainstream is evident in the criteria for research funding, duty statements for job applications, and most formal texts and resource files.

Many of the initiatives responding to health and environment issues and calling for ncw approaches are being described as 'sustainability science'. Lowe proposes developing inside science as an integrative method that is broadly multidisciplinary and systemic rather than the traditional unidisciplinary approach—a method that could be called sustainability science Mark 1.

Others such as the US Academy of Science and a sustainability science research group at Harvard University go further and suggest that there is a need to go outside the research sciences and link to other sources of knowledge such as the community or strategic planners in positions of leadership. This new more inclusive direction could be labelled sustainability science Mark 2.

The future for public health practice involves working with other professions, communities and governments to incorporate sustainability science Marks 1 and 2 into everyday practice:

What will be required are significant advances in basic knowledge, in the social and technological capacities to utilise it, and in the political will to turn this knowledge and know-how into action.

Public health was born out of the need for a transformation in civic responses to the movement of populations into cities in the 19th century. The effect of a global population three times the size of that of the 19th century affecting the whole planet requires an equally major extension of current capacities to respond in all the professions, not only public health.

Developing Principles and Describing People and Place

The education principles can be expressed as inquiry-based learning in sustainability and health, applying the D4P4 decision-making for change framework. Principles for guiding change are predetermined; applying sustainable development principles to public health is the aim of the enterprise. Place is also a given; sustainability and health issues arise from global environmental change.

The condition of the planet and each locality is in a state of continual change, so that while the basic reference text is McMichael (2001), particular issues will need to be re-examined for each application of the curriculum or each locality where it will be applied.

Sets of principles that are discussed in this book include the principles of sustainable development and other anthropocentric frameworks, and the emerging more integrated meaning of sustainability and its relationship with the Earth Charter as an ecocentric framework.

Designing Potential Strategies and Doing them in Practice

The many potential directions for public health professional practice have been explored in a range of strategies, including the so-called New Public Health (now 15 years old), Local Agenda 21, Sustainable Communities, Common Ground and many others. Hancock provides reviews of current public health services addressing sustainability issues; Rees offers strategies for re-examining environmental resource use that include ecological and social needs for sustainable futures.

Responding to the worldwide call for a wider scientific perspective on environment and health issues, Lowe (2001) offers an introduction to sustainability science, broadened by Brown et al. (2001) to include communities' local knowledge and government strategic directions.

At the turn of the century, many international events are addressing the adoption of sustainable development principles through the lens of structural change. It is now all but universally recognised that it is not only global economic resources and ecological balance that are at risk, but also the health of our species as a whole.

International organisations such as the United Nations, the World Bank and globalised industrial corporations such as BHP and Shell have moved to initiate structural changes addressing the principles of sustainable development in their core operations. The move to sustainability worldwide has been slow, but is now accelerating.

WASTE SEGREGATION AND PACKAGING

The key to minimization and effective management of health-care waste is segregation and identification of the waste. Appropriate handling, treatment, and disposal of waste by type reduces costs and does much to protect public health. Segregation should always be the responsibility of the waste producer, should take place as close as possible to where the waste is generated, and should be maintained in storage areas and during transport. The same system of segregation should be in force throughout the country. The most appropriate way of identifying the categories of health-care waste is by sorting the waste into colour-coded plastic bags or containers. In addition to the colour coding of waste containers, the following practices are recommended:

- General health-care waste should join the stream of domestic refuse for disposal.
- Sharps should all be collected together, regardless of whether or not they are contaminated. Containers should be puncture-proof (usually made of metal or high-density plastic) and Fitted with covers. They should be rigid and impermeable so that they safely retain not only the sharps but also any residual liquids from syringes. To discourage abuse, containers should be tamper-proof (difficult to open or break) and needles and syringes should be rendered unusable. Where plastic or metal containers are unavailable or too costly, containers made of dense cardboard are recommended ; these fold for ease of transport and may be supplied with a plastic lining.

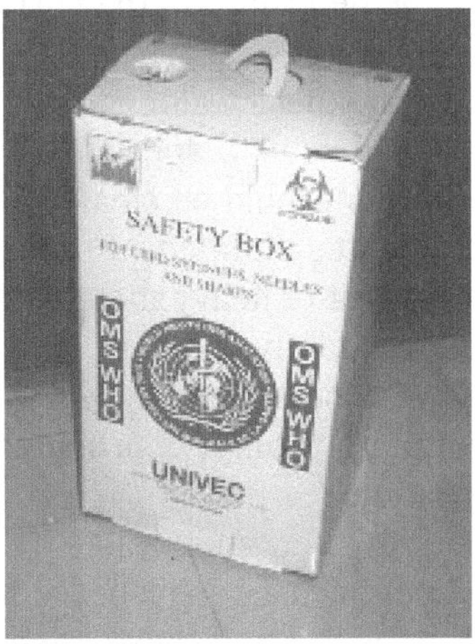

Fig. *Collapsible cardboard sharps container*

Bags and containers for infectious waste should be marked with the international infectious substance symbol.

- Highly infectious waste should, whenever possible, be sterilized immediately by autoclaving. It therefore needs to be packaged in bags that are compatible with the proposed treatment process: red bags, suitable for autoclaving, are recommended.
- Cytotoxic waste, most of which is produced in major hospital or research facilities, should be collected in strong, leak-proof containers clearly labelled "Cytotoxic wastes".
- Small amounts of chemical or pharmaceutical waste may be collected together with infectious waste.
- Large quantities of obsolete or expired pharmaceuticals stored in hospital wards or departments should be returned to the pharmacy for disposal. Other pharmaceutical waste generated at this level, such as spilled or contaminated drugs or packaging containing drug residues should *not* be returned because of the risk of contaminating the pharmacy; it should be deposited in the correct container at the point of production.
- Large quantities of chemical waste should be packed in chemical resistant containers and sent to specialized treatment facilities. The identity of the chemicals should be clearly marked on the containers: hazardous chemical wastes of different types should never be mixed.
- Waste with a high content of heavy metals (e.g. cadmium or mercury) should be collected separately.
- Aerosol containers may be collected with general health-care waste once they are completely empty, provided that the waste is not destined for incineration.
- Low-level radioactive infectious waste (e.g. swabs, syringes for diagnostic or therapeutic use) may be collected in yellow bags or containers for infectious waste if these are destined for incineration.

Since costs for safe treatment and disposal of hazardous health-care waste are typically more than 10 times higher than those for general waste, all general, i.e. non-hazardous, waste should be handled in the same manner as domestic refuse and collected in black bags. No healthcare waste other than sharps should be deposited in sharps containers, as these containers are more expensive than the bags used for other infectious waste. Measures of this sort help to minimize the costs of healthcare waste collection and treatment. When a disposable syringe is used, for example, the packaging should be placed in the general waste bin and the used syringe in the yellow sharps container.

In most circumstances, the needle should *not* be removed from the syringe because of the risk of injury; if removal of the needle is required, special care must be taken. Appropriate containers or bag holders should be placed in all locations where particular categories of waste may be generated. Instructions on waste separation and identification should be posted at each waste collection point to remind staff of the procedures. Containers should be removed when they are three-quarters full. Examples of suitable containers and bags are shown in figure.

Fig. *Waste containers recommended for small hospitals in Thailand*

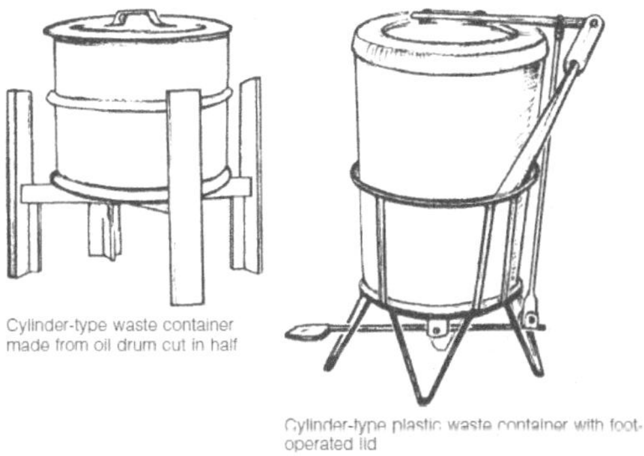

Ideally, they should be made of combustible, non-halogenated plastics. Staff should never attempt to correct errors of segregation by removing items from a bag or container after disposal or by placing one bag inside another bag of a different colour. If general and hazardous wastes are accidentally mixed, the mixture should be treated as hazardous healthcare waste. Cultural and religious constraints in certain countries make it unacceptable for anatomical waste to be collected in the usual yellow bags; such waste should be disposed of in accordance with local custom, which commonly specifies burial.

ON-SITE COLLECTION, TRANSPORT, AND STORAGE OF WASTE

COLLECTION

Nursing and other clinical staff should ensure that waste bags are tightly closed or sealed when they are about three-quarters full. Light-gauge bags can be closed by tying the neck, but heavier-gauge bags probably require a plastic sealing tag of the self-locking type. Bags should *not* be closed by stapling. Sealed sharps containers should be placed in a labelled, yellow infectious health-care waste bag before removal from the hospital ward or department. Wastes should not be allowed to accumulate at the point of production. A routine programme for their collection should be established as part of the health-care waste management plan. Certain recommendations should be followed by the ancillary workers in charge of waste collection:

- Waste should be collected daily (or as frequently as required) and transported to the designated central storage site.
- No bags should be removed unless they are labelled with their point of production (hospital and ward or department) and contents.
- The bags or containers should be replaced immediately with new ones of the same type.

A supply of fresh collection bags or containers should be readily available at all locations where waste is produced.

STORAGE

A storage location for health-care waste should be designated inside the health-care establishment or research facility. The waste, in bags or containers, should be stored in a separate area, room, or building of a size appropriate to the quantities of waste produced and the frequency of collection. Unless a refrigerated storage room is available, storage times for healthcare waste (i.e. the delay between production and treatment) should not exceed the following:

Cytotoxic waste should be stored separately from other health-care waste in a designated secure location. *Radioactive waste* should be stored in containers that prevent dispersion, behind lead shielding. Waste that is to be stored during radioactive decay should be labelled with the type of radionuclide, the date, and details of required storage conditions.

Recommendations for storage facilities for health-care waste:

- The storage area should have an impermeable, hard-standing floor with good drainage; it should be easy to clean and disinfect.
- There should be a water supply for cleaning purposes.
- The storage area should afford easy access for staff in charge of handling the waste.
- It should be possible to lock the store to prevent access by unauthorized persons.
- Easy access for waste-collection vehicles is essential.
- There should be protection from the sun.
- The storage area should be inaccessible for animals, insects, and birds.
- There should be good lighting and at least passive ventilation.
- The storage area should not be situated in the proximity of fresh food stores or food preparation areas.

- A supply of cleaning equipment, protective clothing, and waste bags or containers should be located conveniently close to the storage area.

ON-SITE TRANSPORT

Health-care waste should be transported within the hospital or other facility by means of wheeled trolleys, containers, or carts that are not used for any other purpose and meet the following specifications:

- Easy to load and unload;
- No sharp edges that could damage waste bags or containers during loading and unloading;
- Easy to clean.

The vehicles should be cleaned and disinfected daily with an appropriate disinfectant. All waste-bag seals should be in place and intact at the end of transportation. Different types of vehicle for the onsite transportation of health-care waste are shown in Plate 7.4 and Figure.

Fig. *Wheeled vehicles used for transportation of health-care waste in small hospitals in Thailand*

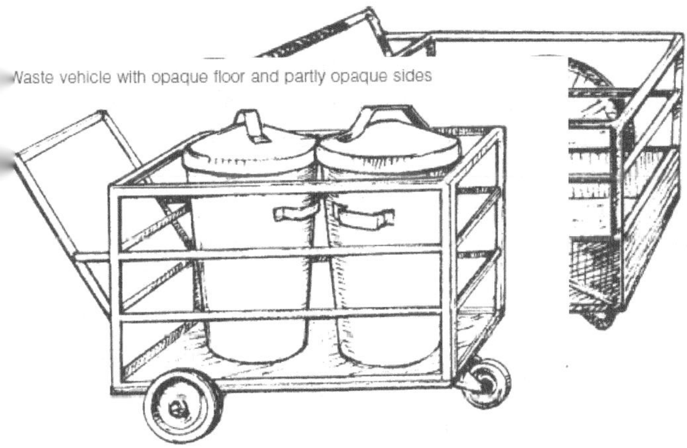

Waste vehicle that can be loaded with either containers or plastic bags

OFF-SITE TRANSPORTATION OF WASTE

REGULATION AND CONTROL SYSTEM

The health-care waste producer is responsible for safe packaging and adequate labelling of waste to be transported off-site and for authorization of its destination. Packaging and labelling should comply with national regulations governing the transport of hazardous wastes, and with international agreements if wastes are shipped abroad for treatment. In case there are no such national regulations, responsible authorities may refer to *Recommendations on the transport of dangerous goods*, published by the United Nations. The control strategy for health-care waste should have the following components:

- A consignment note should accompany the waste from its place of production to the site of FInal disposal. On completion of the journey, the transporter should complete the part of the consignment note especially reserved for him and return it to the waste producer. A typical consignment note for carriage and disposal of hazardous waste, used in the United Kingdom, and the routing of the consignment note are shown in Figure, respectively.
- The transporting organization should be registered with, or known to, the waste regulation authority.
- Handling and disposal facilities should hold a permit, issued by a waste regulation authority, allowing the facilities to handle and dispose of health-care waste.

The consignment note should be designed to take into account the waste control system in operation within the country. The ÒMultimodal Dangerous Goods FormÓ recommended by the United Nations may be taken as an example. If a waste regulation authority is sufficiently well established, it may be possible to pre-notify the agency about the planned system of transport and disposal of the health-care waste and obtain the agency's approval. Anyone involved in the production, handling, or disposal of health-care waste has a general Duty of care, i.e. an obligation to ensure that waste handling and associated documentation comply with the national regulations.

Fig. Route of the consignment note used in the United Kingdom

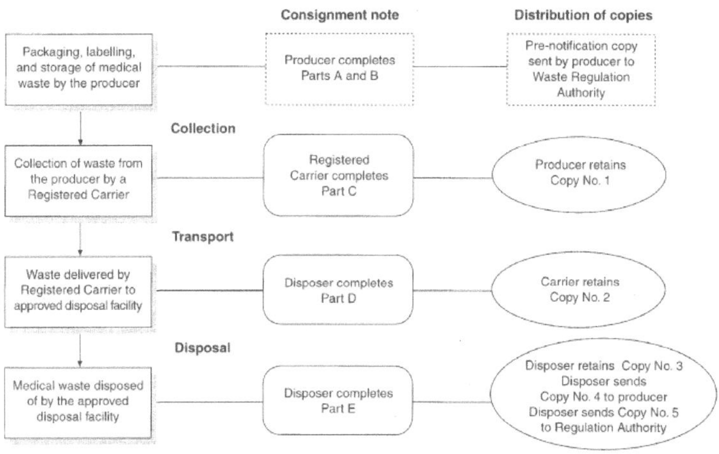

SPECIAL PACKAGING REQUIREMENTS FOR OFF-SITE TRANSPORT

In general, in sealed bags or containers, to prevent spilling during handling and transportation. The bags or containers should be appropriately robust for their content (puncture-proof for sharps, for example, or resistant to aggressive chemicals) and for normal conditions of handling and transportation, such as vibration or changes in temperature, humidity, or atmospheric pressure. In addition, radioactive material should be packed in containers whose surfaces can be easily decontaminated. The United Nations recommend further packing requirements for infectious substances. For infectious health-care wastes, it is recommended that packaging should be design type-tested and certiFIed as approved for use. The packaging recommended for most health-care wastes, with a relatively low probability that infectious substances are present and which are not likely to cause human disease. However, since these packaging requirements are relatively complex, it is suggested that the United Nations recommendations are consulted directly for further details.

LABELLING

All waste bags or containers should be labelled with basic information on their content and on the waste producer. This information may be written directly on the bag or container or on preprinted labels, securely attached. According to the United Nations recommendations for Class 6.2 substances, the following indications should appear on the label:

- The United Nations substance class, e.g. Class 6.2 for infectious waste;
- The United Nations packaging symbol, e.g. the international symbol for infectious substances;
- The proper shipping name and the UN number;
- The total quantity of waste covered by the description;
- The country authorizing the allocation of the label.

Fig. Blank label

[SYMBOL]
(UN Class/year of waste packaging)
(UN Number, proper shipping name)
(Country/name of producer)
(Waste class/date of production)
(Special remarks)
(Waste quantity—waste destination)

Fig. Example of correct labelling

[BIOHAZARD SYMBOL]
CLASS 6.2/98
(UN Class, year of waste packaging)
3291 CLINICAL WASTE, UNSPECIFIED, N.O.S.
(UN Number, proper shipping name)
GB/Queen's University Hospital London
(Country/name of producer)
Sharps/collected 04.05.1998
(Waste class/date of production)
DANGER—CONTAMINATED SHARPS
(Special remarks)
350 kg—Special incinerator ARD, London
(Waste quantity—waste destination)

Cytotoxic waste should be marked with the label ÒCYTOTOXIC WASTEÓ.

It is also recommended that the last two digits of the year of manufacture of the packaging specified by the competent authority are marked on the package, as well as a special code designating the type of packaging. For health-care waste, the following additional information should be marked on the label:

- Waste category
- Date of collection
- Place in hospital where produced
- Waste destination.

In case of problems involving questions of liability, full and correct labelling allows the origin of the waste to be traced. Labelling also warns operative staff and the general public of the hazardous nature of the waste. The hazards posed by container contents can be quickly identiFIed in case of accident, enabling emergency services to take appropriate action. Typical blank and completed labels are shown in Figures respectively.

LABELLING FOR RADIOACTIVE WASTE

Three labels have been designed by the UN/IAEA for radioactive material, providing information on the levels of activity of a given package. Unless the package is large (and it is assumed here that all packages containing radioactive waste do not exceed 1m2 in cross-sectional area). The package shall be assigned to the higher category. This categorization is as recommended in *Regulations for the safe transport of radioactive material.* For large packages or higher activity levels than those dealt with here, these regulations should be consulted directly.

PREPARATION FOR TRANSPORTATION

Before transportation of the waste, dispatch documents should be completed, all arrangements should be made between consignor, carrier, and consignee, and, in case of exportation, the consignee should have con- Firmed with the relevant competent authorities that the waste can be legally imported and that no delays will be incurred in the delivery of the consignment to its destination.

TRANSPORTATION VEHICLES OR CONTAINERS

Waste bags may be placed directly into the transportation vehicle, but it is safer to place them in further containers (e.g. cardboard boxes or wheeled, rigid, lidded plastic or galvanized bins). This has the advantage of reducing the handling of FIlled waste bags but results in higher disposal costs. These secondary containers should be placed close to the waste source. Any vehicle used to transport health-care waste should fulfill the following design criteria:

- The body of the vehicle should be of a suitable size commensurate with the design of the vehicle, with an internal body height of 2.2 metres.

- There should be a bulkhead between the driver's cabin and the vehicle body, which is designed to retain the load if the vehicle is involved in a collision.
- There should be a suitable system for securing the load during transport.
- Empty plastic bags, suitable protective clothing, cleaning equipment, tools, and disinfectant, together with special kits for dealing with liquid spills, should be carried in a separate compartment in the vehicle.
- The internal Finish of the vehicle should allow it to be steam-cleaned, and the internal angles should be rounded.
- The vehicle should be marked with the name and address of the waste carrier.
- The international hazard sign should be displayed on the vehicle or container, as well as an emergency telephone number. A vehicle used for the transportation of health-care waste in the United Kingdom is shown in Figure.

Fig. *Example of vehicle used for transportation of health-care waste in the United Kingdom*

Vehicles or containers used for the transportation of health-care waste should not be used for the transportation of any other material. They should be kept locked at all times, except when loading and unloading. Articulated or demountable trailers (temperature-controlled if required) are particularly suitable, as they can easily be left at the site of waste production. Other systems may be used, such as specially designed large containers or skips; however, open-topped skips or containers should never be used for transporting health-care waste.

Where the use of a dedicated vehicle cannot be justiFIed, a bulk container that can be lifted on to a vehicle chassis may be considered. The container may be used for storage at the health-care establishment and replaced with an empty one when collected. The Finish of these bulk containers should be smooth and impervious and permit easy cleansing or disinfection.

The same safety measures should apply to the collection of hazardous health-care waste from scattered small sources. Health-care establishments that practise minimal programmes of health-care waste management should either avoid off-site transportation of hazardous waste or at least use closed vehicles to avoid spillage. The internal surfaces of any vehicle used for this purpose should be easy to clean.

ROUTING

Health-care waste should be transported by the quickest possible route, which should be planned before the journey begins. After departure from the waste production point, every effort should be made to avoid further handling. If handling cannot be avoided, it should be pre-arranged and take place in adequately designed and authorized premises. Handling requirements can be specified in the contract established between the waste producer and the carrier.

3

Solid and Liquid Biomedical Waste Disposal Procedures

SOLID WATSE

The sight of a dustbin overflowing and the stench rising from it, the all too familiar sights and smells of a crowded city. You look away from it and hold your nose as you cross it.

Have you ever thought that you also have a role to play in the creation of this stench? That you can also play a role in the lessening of this smell and making this waste bin look a little more attractive if you follow proper methods of disposal of the waste generated in the house?

Since the beginning, humankind has been generating waste, be it the bones and other parts of animals they slaughter for their food or the wood they cut to make their carts. With the progress of civilization, the waste generated became of a more complex nature.

At the end of the 19th century the industrial revolution saw the rise of the world of consumers. Not only did the air get more and more polluted but the earth itself became more polluted with the generation of nonbiodegradable solid waste. The increase in population and urbanization was also largely responsible for the increase in solid waste.

Each household generates garbage or waste day in and day out. Items that we no longer need or do not have any further use for fall in the category of waste, and we tend to throw them away. There are different types of solid waste depending on their source. In today's polluted world, learning the correct methods of handling the waste generated has become essential. Segregation is an important method of handling municipal solid waste. Segregation at source can be understood clearly by schematic representation. One of the important methods of managing and treating wastes is composting.

As the cities are growing in size and in problems such as the generation of plastic waste, various municipal waste treatment and disposal methods are now being used to try and resolve these problems. One common sight in all cities is the rag picker who plays an important role in the segregation of this waste. Garbage generated in households can be recycled and reused to prevent creation of waste at source and reducing amount of waste thrown into the community dustbins.

FOUR RS (REFUSE, REUSE, RECYCLE, REDUCE) TO BE FOLLOWED FOR WASTE MANAGEMENT

- Refuse: Instead of buying new containers from the market, use the ones that are in the house. Refuse to buy new items though you may tzhink they are prettier than the ones you already have.
- Reuse: Do not throw away the soft drink cans or the bottles; cover them with homemade paper or paint on them and use them as pencil stands or small vases.
- Recycle: Use shopping bags made of cloth or jute, which can be used over and over again [will this come under recycle or reduce?].Segregate your waste to make sure that it is collected and taken for recycling.
- Reduce: Reduce the generation of unnecessary waste, *e.g.* carry your own shopping bag when you go to the market and put all your purchases directly into it.

Solid waste can be classified into different types depending on their source:

- Household waste is generally classified as municipal waste,
- Industrial waste as hazardous waste, and
- Biomedical waste or hospital waste as infectious waste.

MUNICIPAL SOLID WASTE

Municipal solid waste consists of household waste, construction and demolition debris, sanitation residue, and waste from streets. This garbage is generated mainly from residential and commercial complexes. With rising urbanization and change in lifestyle and food habits, the amount of municipal solid waste has been increasing rapidly and its composition changing. In 1947 cities and towns in India generated an estimated 6 million tonnes of solid waste, in 1997 it was about 48 million tonnes. More than 25% of the municipal solid waste is not collected at all; 70% of the Indian cities lack adequate capacity to transport it and there are no sanitary landfills to dispose of the waste. The existing landfills are neither well equipped or well managed and are not lined properly to protect against contamination of soil and groundwater.

Garbage: The four broad categories

1. *Organic waste*: Kitchen waste, vegetables, flowers, leaves, fruits.
2. *Toxic waste*: Old medicines, paints, chemicals, bulbs, spray cans, fertilizer and pesticide containers, batteries, shoe polish.
3. *Recyclable*: Paper, glass, metals, plastics.
4. *Soiled*: Hospital waste such as cloth soiled with blood and other body fluids.

Over the last few years, the consumer market has grown rapidly leading to products being packed in cans, aluminium foils, plastics, and other such nonbiodegradable items that cause incalculable harm to the environment. In India, some municipal areas have banned the use of plastics and they seem to have achieved success. For example, today one will not see a single piece of plastic in the entire district of Ladakh where the local authorities imposed a ban on plastics in 1998. Other states should follow the example of this region and ban the use of items that cause harm to the environment. One positive note is that in many large cities, shops have begun packing items in reusable or biodegradable bags. Certain biodegradable items can also be composted and reused. In fact proper handling of the biodegradable waste will considerably lessen the burden of solid waste that each city has to tackle. There are different categories of waste generated, each take their own time to degenerate.

Table. The Type of Litter we Generate and the Approximate Time it Takes to Degenerate

Type of Litter	Approximate Time it Takes to Degenerate the Litter
Organic waste such as vegetable and fruit peels, leftover foodstuff, etc.	A week or two.
Paper	10–30 days
Cotton cloth	2–5 months
Wood	10–15 years
Woolen items	1 year
Tin, aluminium, and other metal items such as cans	100–500 years
Plastic bags	One million years?
Glass bottles	undetermined

HAZARDOUS WASTE

Industrial and hospital waste is considered hazardous as they may contain toxic substances. Certain types of household waste are also hazardous. Hazardous wastes could be highly toxic to humans, animals, and plants; are corrosive, highly inflammable, or explosive; and react when exposed to certain things *e.g.* gases. India generates around 7 million tonnes of hazardous wastes every year, most of which is concentrated in four states: Andhra Pradesh, Bihar, Uttar Pradesh, and Tamil Nadu. Household waste that can be categorized as hazardous waste include old batteries, shoe polish, paint tins, old medicines, and medicine bottles. Hospital waste contaminated by chemicals used in hospitals is considered hazardous. These chemicals include formaldehyde and phenols, which are used as disinfectants, and mercury, which is used in thermometers or equipment that measure blood pressure. Most hospitals in India do not have proper disposal facilities for these hazardous wastes. In the industrial sector, the major generators of hazardous waste are the metal, chemical, paper, pesticide, dye, refining, and rubber goods industries. Direct exposure to chemicals in hazardous waste such as mercury and cyanide can be fatal.

Plastic with its exclusive qualities of being light yet strong and economical, has invaded every aspect of our day-to-day life. It has many advantages: it is durable, light, easy to mould, and can be adapted to different user requirements. Once hailed as a 'wonder material', plastic is now a serious worldwide environmental and health concern, essentially due to its nonbiodegradable nature. In India, the plastic industry is growing phenomenally. Plastics have use in all sectors of the economy—infrastructure, construction, agriculture, consumer goods, telecommunications, and packaging. But the good news is that along with a growth in the use, a country-wide network for collection of plastic waste through rag pickers, waste collectors and waste dealers and recycling enterprises has sprung all over the country over the last decade or so. More than 50% of the plastic waste generated in the country is recycled and used in the manufacture of various plastic products.

Conventional plastics have been associated with reproductive problems in both wildlife and humans. Studies have shown a decline in human sperm count and quality, genital abnormalities and a rise in the incidence of breast cancer. Dioxin a highly carcinogenic and toxic by-product of the manufacturing process of plastics, is one of the chemicals believed to be passed on through breast milk to the nursing infant. Burning of plastics, especially PVC releases this dioxin and also furan into the atmosphere. Thus, conventional plastics, right from their manufacture to their disposal are a major problem to the environment.

Table. Source of Generation of Waste Plastics

Source	Waste plastics
Household	Carrybags Bottles Containers Trash bags
Health and Medicare	Disposable syringes Glucose bottles Blood and uro bags Intravenous tubes Catheters Surgical gloves
Hotel and Catering	Packaging items Mineral water bottles Plastic plates, glasses, spoons
Air/Rail Travel	Mineral water bottles Plastic plates, glasses, spoons Plastic bags

Plastics are so versatile in use that their impacts on the environment are extremely wide ranging. Careless disposal of plastic bags chokes drains, blocks the porosity of the soil and causes problems for groundwater recharge. Plastic disturbs the soil microbe activity, and once ingested, can kill animals. Plastic bags can also contaminate foodstuffs due to leaching of toxic dyes and transfer of pathogens. In fact, a major portion of the plastic bags *i.e.,* approximately 60–80% of the plastic waste generated in India is collected and segregated to be recycled. The rest remains strewn on the ground, littered around in open drains, or in unmanaged garbage dumps. Though only a small percentage lies strewn it is this portion that is of concern as it causes extensive damage to the environment.

The plastic industry in the developed world has realised the need of environmentally acceptable modes for recycling plastics wastes and has set out targets and missions. Prominent among such missions are the Plastic Waste Management Institute in Japan, the European Centre for Plastics in Environment, the Plastic Waste Management Task Force in Malaysia.

Manufacturers, civic authorities, environmentalists and the public have begun to acknowledge the need for plastics to conform to certain guidelines/standards and code of conduct for its use. Designing eco-friendly, biodegradable plastics is the need of the hour. Though partially biodegradable plastics have been developed and used, completely biodegradable plastics based on renewable starch rather than petrochemicals have only recently been developed and are in the early stages of commercialization.

SEGREGATION

Certain things that are not needed around the house are kept aside to be sold to the *kabadiwala* or the man who buys old items. These items are newspapers, used bottles, magazines, carry bags, old exercise books, oilcans, etc. This is one form of segregation, which is done as a routine in all households in India. Separating our waste is essential as the amount of waste being generated today causes immense problem. Segregation of municipal solid waste can be clearly understood by schematic representation. Certain items are not biodegradable but can be reused or recycled.

In fact, it is believed that a larger portion can be recycled, a part of it can be converted to compost, and only a smaller portion of it is real waste that has no use and has to be discarded. Household waste should be separated daily into different bags for the different categories of waste such as wet and dry waste, which should be disposed of separately. One should also keep a bin for toxic wastes such as medicines, batteries, dried paint, old bulbs, and dried shoe polish.

Wet waste, which consists of leftover foodstuff, vegetable peels, etc., should be put in a compost pit and the compost could be used as manure in the garden. Dry waste consisting of cans, aluminium foils, plastics, metal, glass, and paper could be recycled. If we do not dispose of the waste in a more systematic manner, more than 1400 sq. km of land, which is the size of the city of Delhi, would be required in the country by the year 2047 to dispose of it.

Segregation of Waste

Waste can be segregated as:

- Biodegradable and
- Nonbiodegradable.

Biodegradable waste include organic waste, *e.g.,* kitchen waste, vegetables, fruits,

flowers, leaves from the garden, and paper.

Nonbiodegradable waste can be further segregated into:

- *Recyclable waste*: Plastics, paper, glass, metal, etc.
- *Toxic waste:* Old medicines, paints, chemicals, bulbs, spray cans, fertilizer and pesticide containers, batteries, shoe polish.

- *Soiled:* Hospital waste such as cloth soiled with blood and other body fluids.

Toxic and soiled waste must be disposed of with utmost care.

Door-to-door collection of waste is another method of segregation, but it is not a common practice as yet in India except in the metros where some private organizations are doing such work. The rag picker plays a very important part in the segregation of waste. It is now becoming more and more essential to look for methods by which the garbage load on the land can be reduced. It has been seen that at present segregation of waste at source level seems to be the best. A large number of NGOs (non-governmental organizations) are working in the field of solid waste management such as Clean Ahmedabad Abhiyan in Ahmedabad, Waste-Wise in Bangalore, Mumbai Environmental Action Group in Mumbai, and Vatavaran and Srishti in Delhi. They are all successfully creating awareness among the citizens about their rights and responsibilities towards solid waste and the cleanliness of their city. These organizations promote environmental education and awareness in schools and involve communities in the management of solid waste.

Role of the Rag Picker

Rag pickers are the people who are actually going through the garbage bins to pick out the 'rags'. These rag pickers, women, children, and men from the lowest rung in the society, are a common sight in most cities and towns around the country. Rag picking is considered the most menial of all activities and it is people who have no other alternative that are generally driven to it. Rag pickers contribute a great deal to waste management as they scavenge the recyclable matter thereby saving the municipality of the cost and time of collecting and transporting this to the dumps.

The rag picker has a special role to play in the segregation of waste in India. He is one of the focal points for the recycling of waste. He is the person who, in spite of all the dangers that he faces, goes on relentlessly picking through the garbage bin, looking for waste that could be useful to him. He sells all the material he picks to the whole sellers and retailers who in turn sell it to the industry that uses this waste matter as raw material. The main items of collection are plastics, paper, bottles, and cans. Rag pickers are well coordinated in their method of working. Among themselves, they have a good understanding for operating by area. Each group takes specific items from the bins.

It has been observed that more and more women and children are getting involved in the business of rag picking. This is a matter of concern as these children who should be spending their time in schools either studying or playing are instead putting themselves at risk by handling waste. While picking through waste, the rag picker puts himself at a great risk and is always prone to disease as the waste that he rummages through can be infected. We can indirectly help the rag picker by carefully segregating the waste that is generated at our homes, thereby facilitating his search for materials that are useful to him. He will not have to scavenge in the bins for long hours.

RECYCLING AND REUSE

Recycling involves the collection of used and discarded materials processing these materials and making them into new products. It reduces the amount of waste that is thrown into the community dustbins thereby making the environment cleaner and the air more fresh to breathe.

Surveys carried out by Government and non-government agencies in the country have all recognized the importance of recycling wastes. However, the methodology for safe recycling of waste has not been standardized. Studies have revealed that 7%-15% of the waste is recycled.

If recycling is done in a proper manner, it will solve the problems of waste or garbage. At the community level, a large number of NGOs (Non Governmental Organizations) and private sector enterprises have taken an initiative in segregation and recycling of waste (EXNORA International in Chennai recycles a large part of the waste that is collected). It is being used for composting, making pellets to be used in gasifiers, etc. Plastics are sold to the factories that reuse them.

The steps involved in the process prior to recycling include:

- Collection of waste from doorsteps, commercial places, etc.
- Collection of waste from community dumps.
- Collection/picking up of waste from final disposal sites.

Table. Some Items that can be Recycled or Reused

Paper	Old copies Old books Paper bags Newspapers Old greeting cards Cardboard box
Plastic	Containers Bottles Bags Sheets
Glass and ceramics	Bottles Plates Cup Bowls
Miscellaneous	Old cans Utensils Clothes Furniture

Most of the garbage generated in the household can be recycled and reused. Organic kitchen waste such as leftover foodstuff, vegetable peels, and spoilt or dried fruits and vegetables can be recycled by putting them in the compost pits that have been dug in the garden.

Old newspapers, magazines and bottles can be sold to the *kabadiwala* the man who buys these items from homes.

In your own homes you can contribute to waste reduction and the recycling and reuse of certain items.

To cover you books you can use old calendars; old greeting cards can also be reused. Paper can also be made at home through a very simple process and you can paint on them.

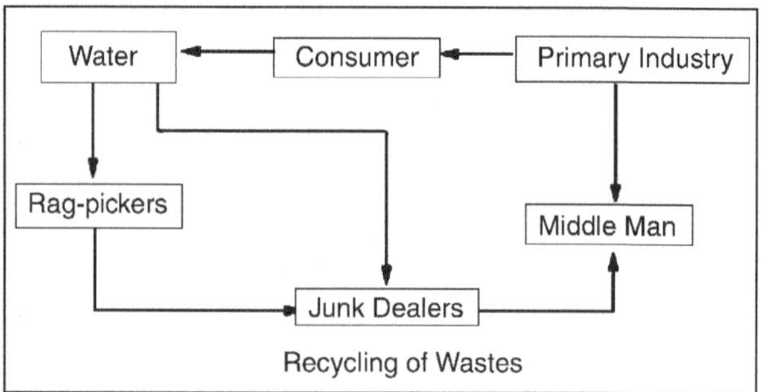

Fig. The Schematic Diagram Depicts Recycling of Wastes

Waste recycling has some significant advantages. It,

- Leads to less utilization of raw materials.
- Reduces environmental impacts arising from waste treatment and disposal.
- Makes the surroundings cleaner and healthier.
- Saves on landfill space.
- Saves money.
- Reduces the amount of energy required to manufacture new products.

In fact recycling can prevent the creation of waste at the source.

TREATMENT AND DISPOSAL

As cities are growing in size with a rise in the population, the amount of waste generated is increasing becoming unmanageable. The local corporations have adapted different methods for the disposal of waste—open dumps, landfills, sanitary landfills, and incineration plants. One of the important methods of waste treatment is composting.

Open Dumps

Open dumps refer to uncovered areas that are used to dump solid waste of all kinds. The waste is untreated, uncovered, and not segregated. It is the breeding ground for flies, rats, and other insects that spread disease. The rainwater run-off from these dumps contaminates nearby land and water thereby spreading disease. In some countries, open dumps are being phased out.

Landfills

Landfills are generally located in urban areas where a large amount of waste is generated and has to be dumped in a common place. Unlike an open dump, it is a pit that is dug in the ground. The garbage is dumped and the pit is covered thus preventing the breeding of flies and rats. At the end of each day, a layer of soil is scattered on top of it and some mechanism, usually an earth-moving equipment is used to compress the garbage, which now forms a cell.

Thus, every day, garbage is dumped and becomes a cell. After the landfill is full, the area is covered with a thick layer of mud and the site can thereafter be developed as a parking lot or a park. Landfills have many problems. All types of waste is dumped in landfills and when water seeps through them it gets contaminated and in turn pollutes the surrounding area. This contamination of groundwater and soil through landfills is known as leaching.

Sanitary Landfills

An alternative to landfills which will solve the problem of leaching to some extent, is a sanitary landfill which is more hygienic and built in a methodical manner. These are lined with materials that are impermeable such as plastics and clay, and are also built over impermeable soil. Constructing sanitary landfills is very costly and they are have their own problems. Some authorities claim that often the plastic liner develops cracks as it reacts with various chemical solvents present in the waste. The rate of decomposition in sanitary landfills is also extremely variable. This can be due to the fact that less oxygen is available as the garbage is compressed very tightly. It has also been observed that some biodegradable materials do not decompose in a landfill. Another major problem is the development of methane gas, which occurs when little oxygen is present, *i.e.* during anaerobic decomposition. In some countries, the methane being produced from sanitary landfills is tapped and sold as fuel.

Incineration Plants

This process of burning waste in large furnaces is known as incineration. In these plants the recyclable material is segregated and the rest of the material is burnt. At the end of the process all that is left behind is ash. During the process some of the ash floats out with the hot air. This is called fly ash. Both the fly ash and the ash that is left in the furnace after burning have high concentrations of dangerous toxins such as dioxins and heavy metals. Disposing of this ash is a problem. The ash that is buried at the landfills leaches the area and cause severe contamination. Burning garbage is not a clean process as it produces tonnes of toxic ash and pollutes the air and water. A large amount of the waste that is burnt here can be recovered and recycled. In fact, at present, incineration is kept as the last resort and is used mainly for treating the infectious waste.

COMPOSTING

Organic matter constitutes 35%–40% of the municipal solid waste generated in India. This waste can be recycled by the method of composting, one of the oldest forms of disposal. It is the natural process of decomposition of organic waste that yields manure or compost, which is very rich in nutrients. Composting is a biological process in which micro-organisms, mainly fungi and bacteria, convert degradable organic waste into humus like substance.

This finished product, which looks like soil, is high in carbon and nitrogen and is an excellent medium for growing plants. The process of composting ensures the waste that is produced in the kitchens is not carelessly thrown and left to rot. It recycles the nutrients and returns them to the soil as nutrients. Apart from being clean, cheap, and safe, composting can significantly reduce the amount of disposable garbage. The organic fertilizer can be used instead of chemical fertilizers and is better specially when used for vegetables. It increases the soil's ability to hold water and makes the soil easier to cultivate. It helped the soil retain more of the plant nutrients.

Compost allows the soil to retain more plant nutrients over a longer period:

- It supplies part of the 16 essential elements needed by the plants
- It helps reduce the adverse effects of excessive alkalinity, acidity, or the excessive use of chemical fertilizer.
- It makes soil easier to cultivate.
- It helps keep the soil cool in summer and warm in winter.
- It aids in preventing soil erosion by keeping the soil covered.
- It helps in controlling the growth of weeds in the garden.

Vermi-composting has become very popular in the last few years. In this method, worms are added to the compost. These help to break the waste and the added excreta of the worms makes the compost very rich in nutrients. To make a compost pit, you have to select a cool, shaded corner of the garden or the school compound and dig a pit, which ideally should be 3 feet deep. This depth is convenient for aerobic composting as the compost has to be turned at regular intervals in this process. Preferably the pit should be lined with granite or brick to prevent nitrite pollution of the subsoil water, which is known to be highly toxic. Each time organic matter is added to the pit it should be covered with a layer of dried leaves or a thin layer of soil which allows air to enter the pit thereby preventing bad odour. At the end of 45 days, the rich pure organic matter is ready to be used.

WHAT YOU CAN DO TO REDUCE SOLID WASTE

- Carry your own cloth or jute bag when you go shopping.
- Say no to all plastic bags as far as possible.
- Reduce the use of paper bags also.
- Reuse the soft drinks polybottles for storing water.
- Segregate the waste in the house–keep two garbage bins and see to it that the biodegradable and the nonbiodegradable is put into separate bins and dispose off separately.
- Dig a compost pit in your garden and put all the biodegradables into it.
- See to it that all garbage is thrown into the municipal bin as the collection is generally done from there.
- When you go out do not throw paper and other wrappings or even leftover food here and there, make sure that it is put in the correct place, that is into a dustbin.
- As far as possible try to sell all the recyclable items that are not required to the Kabariwala.

HEALTH IMPACTS OF SOLID WASTE

Modernization and progress has had its share of disadvantages and one of the main aspects of concern is the pollution it is causing to the earth—be it land, air, and water. With increase in the global population and the rising demand for food and other essentials, there has been a rise in the amount of waste being generated daily by each household. This waste is ultimately thrown into municipal waste collection centres from where it is collected by the area municipalities to be further thrown into the landfills and dumps. However, either due to resource crunch or inefficient infrastructure, not all of this waste gets collected and transported to the final dumpsites. If at this stage the management and disposal is improperly done, it can cause serious impacts on health and problems to the surrounding environment.

Waste that is not properly managed, especially excreta and other liquid and solid waste from households and the community, are a serious health hazard and lead to the spread of infectious diseases. Unattended waste lying around attracts flies, rats, and other creatures that in turn spread disease. Normally it is the wet waste that decomposes and releases a bad odour. This leads to unhygienic conditions and thereby to a rise in the health problems. The plague outbreak in Surat is a good example of a city suffering due to the callous attitude of the local body in maintaining cleanliness in the city. Plastic waste is another cause for ill health. Thus excessive solid waste that is generated should be controlled by taking certain preventive measures.

IMPACTS OF SOLID WASTE ON HEALTH

The group at risk from the unscientific disposal of solid waste include—the population in areas where there is no proper waste disposal method, especially the pre-school children; waste workers; and workers in facilities producing toxic and infectious material. Other high-risk group include population living close to a waste dump and those, whose water supply has become contaminated either due to waste dumping or leakage from landfill sites. Uncollected solid waste also increases risk of injury, and infection.

In particular, *organic domestic waste* poses a serious threat, since they ferment, creating conditions favourable to the survival and growth of microbial pathogens. Direct handling of solid waste can result in various types of infectious and chronic diseases with the waste workers and the rag pickers being the most vulnerable.

Exposure to hazardous waste can affect human health, children being more vulnerable to these pollutants. In fact, direct exposure can lead to diseases through chemical exposure as the release of chemical waste into the environment leads to chemical poisoning. Many studies have been carried out in various parts of the world to establish a connection between health and hazardous waste. *Waste from agriculture and industries* can also cause serious health risks. Other than this, co-disposal of industrial hazardous waste with municipal waste can expose people to chemical and radioactive hazards.

Uncollected solid waste can also obstruct storm water run-off, resulting in the forming of stagnant water bodies that become the breeding ground of disease. Waste dumped near a water source also causes contamination of the water body or the ground water source. Direct dumping of untreated waste in rivers, seas, and lakes results in the accumulation of toxic substances in the food chain through the plants and animals that feed on it. *Disposal of hospital and other medical waste* requires special attention since this can create major health hazards.

This waste generated from the hospitals, health care centres, medical laboratories, and research centres such as discarded syringe needles, bandages, swabs, plasters, and other types of infectious waste are often disposed with the regular non-infectious waste.

Waste treatment and disposal sites can also create health hazards for the neighbourhood. Improperly operated incineration plants cause air pollution and improperly managed and designed landfills attract all types of insects and rodents that spread disease. Ideally these sites should be located at a safe distance from all human settlement. Landfill sites should be well lined and walled to ensure that there is no leakage into the nearby ground water sources.

Recycling too carries health risks if proper precautions are not taken. Workers working with waste containing chemical and metals may experience toxic exposure. Disposal of health-care wastes require special attention since it can create major health hazards, such as Hepatitis B and C, through wounds caused by discarded syringes. Rag pickers and others who are involved in scavenging in the waste dumps for items that can be recycled, may sustain injuries and come into direct contact with these infectious items.

Occupational hazards associated with waste handling:

- Infections
  - Skin and blood infections resulting from direct contact with waste, and from infected wounds.
  - Eye and respiratory infections resulting from exposure to infected dust, especially during landfill operations.
  - Different diseases that results from the bites of animals feeding on the waste.
  - Intestinal infections that are transmitted by flies feeding on the waste.
- Chronic diseases
  - Incineration operators are at risk of chronic respiratory diseases, including cancers resulting from exposure to dust and hazardous compounds.
- Accidents
  - Bone and muscle disorders resulting from the handling of heavy containers.
  - Infecting wounds resulting from contact with sharp objects.
  - Poisoning and chemical burns resulting from contact with small amounts of hazardous chemical waste mixed with general waste.
  - Burns and other injuries resulting from occupational accidents at waste disposal sites or from methane gas explosion at landfill sites.

DISEASES

Certain chemicals if released untreated, *e.g.* cyanides, mercury, and polychlorinated biphenyls are highly toxic and exposure can lead to disease or death. Some studies have detected excesses of cancer in residents exposed to hazardous waste. Many studies have been carried out in various parts of the world to establish a connection between health and hazardous waste. The unhygienic use and disposal of plastics and its effects on human health has become a matter of concern. Coloured plastics are harmful as their pigment contains heavy metals that are highly toxic.

Some of the harmful metals found in plastics are copper, lead, chromium, cobalt, selenium, and cadmium. In most industrialized countries, colour plastics have been legally banned. In India, the Government of Himachal Pradesh has banned the use of plastics and so has Ladakh district. Other states should emulate their example.

Proper methods of waste disposal have to be undertaken to ensure that it does not affect the environment around the area or cause health hazards to the people living there. At the household-level proper segregation of waste has to be done and it should be ensured that all organic matter is kept aside for composting, which is undoubtedly the best method for the correct disposal of this segment of the waste. In fact, the organic part of the waste that is generated decomposes more easily, attracts insects and causes disease. Organic waste can be composted and then used as a fertilizer.

WASTE DISPOSAL METHODS

Most solid waste is either sent to landfills (dumped) or to incinerators (burned). Ocean dumping has also been a popular way for coastal communities to dispose of their solid wastes. In this method, large barges carry waste out to sea and dump it into the ocean. That practice is now banned in the United States due to pollution problems it created. Most municipal and non-municipal waste (about 60%) is sent to landfills. Landfills are popular because they are relatively easy to operate and can handle of lot of waste material.

There are two types of landfills:

1. Sanitary landfills and
2. Secure landfills.

In a sanitary landfill solid wastes are spread out and compacted in a hole, canyon area or a giant mound. Modern sanitary landfills are lined with layers of clay, sand and plastic. Each day after garbage is dumped in the landfill, it is covered with clay or plastic to prevent redistribution by animals or the wind. Rainwater that percolates through a sanitary landfill is collected in the bottom liner. This liquid leachate may contain toxic chemicals such as dioxin, mercury, and pesticides. Therefore, it is removed to prevent contamination of local aquifers. The groundwater near the landfill is closely monitored for signs of contamination from the leachate.

As the buried wastes are decomposed by bacteria, gases such as methane and carbon dioxide are produced. Because methane gas is very flammable, it is usually collected with other gases by a system of pipes, separated and then either burned off or used as a source of energy (*e.g.,* home heating and cooking, generating electricity). Other gases such as ammonia and hydrogen sulfide may also be released by the landfill, contributing to air pollution. These gases are also monitored and, if necessary, collected for disposal. Finally, when the landfill reaches its capacity, it is sealed with more layers of clay and sand. Gas and water monitoring activities, though, must continue past the useful life of the landfill.

Secure landfills are designed to handle hazardous wastes. They are basically the same design as sanitary landfills, but they have thicker plastic and clay liners. Also, wastes are segregated and stored according to type, typically in barrels, which prevents the mixing of incompatible wastes. Some hazardous waste in the United States is sent to foreign countries for disposal. Developing countries are willing to accept this waste to raise needed monies. Recent treaties by the U.N. Environment Programme have addressed the international transport of such hazardous wastes.

Federal regulation mandates that landfills cannot be located near faults, floodplains, wetlands or other bodies of water. In many areas, finding landfill space is not a problem, but in some heavily populated areas it is difficult to find suitable sites. There are, of course, other problems associated with landfills. The liners may eventually leak and contaminate groundwater with toxic leachate. Landfills also produce polluting gases, and landfill vehicle traffic can be a source of noise and particulate pollutants for any nearby community.

About 15 per cent of the municipal solid waste in the United States is incinerated. Incineration is the burning of solid wastes at high temperatures (>1000°C). Though particulate matter, such as ash, remains after the incineration, the sheer volume of the waste is reduced by about 85 per cent. Ash is much more compact than unburned solid waste. In addition to the volume reduction of the waste, the heat from the trash that is incinerated in large-scale facilities can be used to produce electric power. This process is called waste-to-energy. There are two kinds of waste-to-energy systems: mass burn incinerators and refuse-derived incinerators.

In mass burn incinerators all of the solid waste is incinerated. The heat from the incineration process is used to produce steam. This steam is used to drive electric power generators. Acid gases from the burning are removed by chemical scrubbers. Any particulates in the combustion gases are removed by electrostatic precipitators. The cleaned gases are then released into the atmosphere through a tall stack. The ashes from the combustion are sent to a landfill for disposal.

It is best if only combustible items (paper, wood products, and plastics) are burned. In a refuse-derived incinerator, non-combustible materials are separated from the waste. Items such as glass and metals may be recycled. The combustible wastes are then formed into fuel pellets which can be burned in standard steam boilers. This system has the advantage of removing potentially harmful materials from waste before it is burned. It also provides for some recycling of materials. As with any combustion process, the main environmental concern is air quality. Incineration releases various air pollutants (particulates, sulfur dioxide, nitrogen oxides, and methane) into the atmosphere. Heavy metals (*e.g.*, lead, mercury) and other chemical toxins (*e.g.*, dioxins) can also be released. Many communities do not want incinerators within their city limits. Incinerators are also costly to build and to maintain when compared to landfills.

SOLID WASTE CLASSIFICATION

Solid waste can be classified into 3 categories:

1. Organic and inorganic
2. Burnable and non burnable
3. Recyclable and non-recyclable

ORGANIC MATERIAL

It consists of matter that was once alive. It is made up of chemical compounds based especially on carbon, excluding Carbon Dioxide

Ex: Food waste, garden waste, wood and so on.

Inorganic material:

Consists of chemical compounds that are not based on carbon.

Ex: Minerals

BURNABLE MATERIAL

- It is similar to organic materials. It is used in the process of burning or combustion heat to degrade these materials.

RECYCLABLE MATERIAL

- These are materials that still have useful physical or chemical properties after serving their original purpose, and therefore, can be re-used or converted into raw material for the manufacture of new products.

Examples: Paper, plastic, glass, wood, etc

WASTE MINIMIZATION

Purdue University is committed to preserving a balance between protecting the health of people and the environment, while accommodating increasingly sophisticated and productive research operations. As specified in Executive Memorandum C36, University faculty, staff and students must comply with environmental, health, and safety laws and regulations issued by federal, state, and local agencies. Faculty, staff and students are required to comply with related University policies, procedures, and instructions. The Chemical Management Committee (CMC) requires each principal investigator/generator to certify their waste minimization efforts annually.

Waste minimization is any action that reduces the amount and/or toxicity of chemical wastes that must be shipped off-site for disposal as hazardous waste. This is a national policy specifically mandated by the U.S. Congress in the national hazardous waste law, the Resource Conservation and Recovery Act (RCRA). There is clear intent in RCRA, the Clean Air Act, and the Pollution Prevention Act to focus attention on source reduction and recycling as preferred environmental management approaches over the treatment, disposal, or release of harmful chemicals to the environment. The U.S. Environmental Protection Agency (EPA) has established its hierarchy of waste minimization approaches: reduce, recycle, and treatment.

METHODS OF WASTE MINIMIZATION

- *Source Reduction (Pollution Prevention)*: The most desirable method of waste minimization is source reduction, which reduces the impact of chemical wastes on the environment to the greatest extent. This is an activity that reduces or eliminates the generation of chemical waste at the source.
- *Recycling*: The next most desirable approach is waste minimization through recycling. When a waste material is used for another purpose, treated and reused in the same process, or reclaimed for another process, this is called recycling.
- *Treatment*: The last minimization method is treatment. The most common treatment that can be performed in laboratories is elementary neutralization. Other kinds of treatment may involve chemical, physical or biological methods.

Substitution of hazardous chemicals with non-hazardous ones is a simple way to minimize waste. For example: use Alconox for cleaning glassware instead of chromic acid based cleaners, and avoid mercury containing equipment whenever possible. Modification of procedures, processes or equipment can also lead to waste minimization. In laboratories where high volumes of spent solvents are generated, distillation would provide a cost effective means of re-using these solvents. Good laboratory practices such as computer modeling and small scale experiments can minimize waste, as well as purchasing only the amount and type of chemical needed for the experiment. Keeping hazardous waste separate from non-hazardous will reduce waste as will good inventory control, housekeeping, and training of personnel.

POLLUTION PREVENTION AND WASTE MINIMIZATION PROGRAMMES

Battery Recycling

Batteries are found in countless devices used across campus. Cordless power tools, laptop computers, cellular and cordless telephones, digital cameras, laboratory equipment, and many other hand held devices are used throughout campus facilities and departments. Purdue recycles the following types of batteries: Nickel cadmium (Ni-Cad), nickel metal hydride (Ni-MH), lithium ion, sealed lead acid, and mercury. When broken, these batteries can release heavy metals that damage the environment. Used batteries may be classified as hazardous waste due to their heavy metal content and are thus regulated under the Resource Conservation and Recovery Act (RCRA). These regulations provide for management of hazardous wastes. The Universal Waste Rule is designed to reduce regulatory management requirements. The University manages used batteries as universal waste. The Universal Waste Rule promotes pollution prevention and waste minimization by encouraging the recycling of used batteries instead of less desirable methods of disposal such as land filling or incineration.

Management

Used batteries can be picked by completing a Hazardous Waste Pickup Request Form.

- Training is mandatory of all personnel handling batteries for recycling.
- All batteries must be intact.
- Leaking or damaged batteries shall be placed in a suitable, closed container and labeled accordingly.
- All batteries will be placed in the appropriately labeled container inside the trailer.
- Alkaline batteries shall be placed in the trash.

CHEMICAL REDISTRIBUTION PROGRAMME

Occasionally REM receives chemicals of good enough quality that they can be redistributed to you. These chemicals will be materials in the original container with original labeling. The container may have been opened or never opened, half full or more, and uncontaminated.

The most common chemicals available for redistribution are listed:

- Mineral acids
- Acetic acid and trifluoracetic acid
- Hydrogen Peroxide 30%
- Solid oxidizers (permanganates, chlorates, chromates, nitrates)
- Reactives (alkali metals, metal hydrides, hydrazones, sulfides)
- Phenol crystallized
- Non-halogenated solvents
- Bromine

COMPUTER AND ELECTRONIC EQUIPMENT RECYCLING

Many people today are still unaware of the federal and state requirements for computer and electronic equipment disposal. Computer monitors contain materials that should be recycled. The Cathode Ray Tube or CRT is the viewing portion of computer monitors and televisions.

The CRT contains hazardous material that needs to be recycled. In your discarded computer monitors, televisions, and other electronic equipment there are traces of lead, phosphorus, cadmium, barium, and mercury. As a product, these hazardous materials are safely sealed.

When the CRT is left on a loading dock or in an outdoor storage area the potential for breakage is increased, and the hazardous materials may be released creating a potential hazard to faculty, staff, students and visitors. Placing these units outdoors is an unacceptable management practice.

In addition, data in electronic storage media may be sensitive or restricted. If this equipment is not repurposed within the university, then equipment with usable life is resold to the general public. Otherwise, the equipment is recycled.

To ensure the university manages this equipment in a secure and environmentally sound manner, please follow these steps:

- For data security, follow ITaP Media Disposal Guidelines.
- Purdue Universities Internal Audit approves the University Warehouse and Surplus as an official site for performing DOD wipes of computer hard drives.
- Complete and submit a Property Accounting Equipment Change in Status form.
- *Send equipment to University Warehouse and Surplus for processing:*
  - Contact the University Warehouse and Surplus supervisor at 742-4414 or 742-7386 to request a pick up for the equipment. The supervisor will make arrangements with the General Labour crew if necessary.
  - Departments may also deliver the equipment to the University Warehouse and Surplus at 3601 Sagamore Parkway North, Suite K, Lafayette, IN 47904; access from North 9th Street.

For questions, concerns, or equipment pick up, please contact University Warehouse and Surplus at 742–4414 or 742–7386 or Radiological and Environmental Management at 49–63712.

FLUORESCENT BULB AND BALLAST RECYCLING

Fluorescent lamps illuminate countless classrooms, laboratories, and buildings on campus. HID lamps (mercury-vapour, metal-halide and high-pressure sodium) are used for streetlights, floodlights and shop lights. When broken, these lamps release mercury and other metals that damage the environment.

Note: Broken Fluorescent lamps must be managed as hazardous waste. submit a completed Hazardous Waste Pickup Request for proper disposal. The University manages used fluorescent lamps as universal waste. The Universal

Waste Rule is designed to reduce regulatory management requirements. The Universal Waste Rule promotes pollution prevention and waste minimization by encouraging the recycling of used lamps instead of less desirable methods of disposal such as land filling or incineration.

Academic Areas/Buildings, and Physical Facilities Shops

- Purdue personnel can send an e-mail requesting pickup of bulbs/ ballasts. Please indicate in this e-mail the quantity (number of boxes, buckets or bins), type of material (bulbs or ballasts), and location (building loading dock) of the pickup.
- A Crew Chief or Lighting Technician will pickup requested bulbs/ ballasts from the loading dock indicated on the pickup request as time allows during the workweek.

Residence Halls, Memorial Union, Graduate Houses, and Athletic Department

- A Crew Chief or Lighting Technician can pickup bulbs/ballasts from the designated area as time allows during the workweek. Usually every two weeks on Wednesday. An e-mail request is required for this pickup.

Important Reminders

- University personnel can bring bulbs/ballasts from their buildings/ shops to the trailer located near HMMT on Ahlers Road.
- Training is mandatory for all personnel that handles used fluorescent bulbs.
- All lamp containers must be closed and labeled with the words "Universal Waste Bulbs".
- All buckets/boxes containing ballasts must be labeled with the words "Non-PCB" ballasts or "PCB" ballasts depending on the type of ballasts in the container(s).

USED OIL

Used oil can be a valuable resource when it is properly managed to avoid release to the environment and recycled for utilization of its lubricant or fuel value. The State of Indiana has adopted Used Oil Management Standard; codified in Indiana Administrative Code 329 IAC 13, to encourage the recycling of used oil and promote its environmentally sound collection, storage, and management. The University also recognizes the need for waste minimization and proper management of used oil. University shops, farms, and other generators from campus generate on average 5,000 gallons of recyclable used oil annually. An outside vendor recycles this material at minimal cost to the University. All faculty and staff should participate in pollution prevention and waste minimization by recycling their used oil. Used oil is defined as any oil that has been refined from crude oil, or synthetic, and has been used and as a result of such use is contaminated by physical or chemical impurities.

Use Oil for Recycling

- Lubricants
- Hydraulic Fluids
- Motor Oil
- Metalworking Oil
- Wire Drawing Solutions

Note: All containers used shall be closed at all times except to empty or fill the container. The words "Used Oil" shall appear on the outside of the container in plain view. A pickup request shall be submitted to REM prior to container removal

Used oil that must be collected separately and cannot be recycled include:

- Refrigeration oil
- Heat Transfer oil
- *Any oil contaminated with any quantity of the following items:*
  - Fuels (gasoline, diesel, kerosene, fuel oil, jet fuels
  - Creosote
  - Solvents (lacquer thinner, mineral spirits, turpentine, paint thinner, degreaser solvents, Stoddard solvent, varsol, white spirits, oleum, naphtha, petroleum naphtha)
- Duplicating Fluid
- Aromatic Hydrocarbons
- Petroleum Distillates

PARTS WASHERS

A parts washer is used to remove residues such as, grease, wax and oil from metal parts, assemblies, and other fabricated products. Sink-type parts washers are a common site in shops across campus. Cleaning solutions used in parts washers include solvents and aqueous cleaners. Solvents clean by dissolving away dirt. Solvents include petroleum-based solvent mixtures such as mineral spirits, Stoddard solvent, petroleum naphtha, and pure organic solvents such as trichloroethane, trichloroethylene, benzene, and xylenes.

Aqueous cleaners are pH-neutral or alkaline water-based solutions that break down and remove dirt from part surfaces. Semi-aqueous solutions that contain small amounts of solvents are also available. The University has found that solvent substitutes with lower volatility and higher flash points combined with simple changes in shops cleaning operations reduce waste generation, improve compliance, and increase safety, while saving money at the same time.

The University is using three different sink-type parts washers. The first is a solvent exchange service. Waste (dirty) solvent is removed and reused as a roofing material component. The second sink–type parts washer uses a low volatile, high flash point solvent and a filter that cleans the solvent. The clean solvent is then re-circulated through the machine for reuse.

The third sink-type parts washer unit uses a built-in distillation process to clean the solvent before being re-circulated for reuse. Affective use of these three (3) types of parts washers will reduce the volume and toxicity of hazardous waste generation (an excellent waste minimization/pollution prevention technique), reduce operating costs, protect employees, and improve efficiency. Never use solvents containing the following constituents, methylene chloride, perchloroethylene, trichloroethylene, 1,1,1-trichlorethane, carbon tetrachloride, or chloroform. EPA has determined that emissions from cleaning equipment using these solvents present a threat to human health and the environment. When using a solvent exchange service, use the longest service interval possible that is consistent with the shop's needs. For heavily soiled parts, consider using separate parts washers in stages. Use one for dirty parts and a second for final cleaning.

Overall, this technique extends solvent life. Do not allow any other solvents to be used in or over the parts washer. A common source of contamination is the use of spray solvents such as brake cleaner or carburetor cleaner containing tetrachloroethylene and other regulated solvents. This will cause all the solvent in the parts washer to become hazardous waste and prevent it from being recycled. Extend the parts washer solvent and filter service life (if installed) by pre-wiping parts to remove excess grease or oil. For Filtration Units, change filters and pads, frequently enough to prevent fouling.

ORGANIZATIONAL SUPPORT

Waste minimization is a process of continual improvement. All University faculty, staff and students shall be encouraged to identify opportunities for waste minimization in their daily activities. The Radiological and Environmental Management Department's (REM) Environmental Protection Specialist will support the University's waste minimization efforts by providing training in procedures, techniques, and best management practices. Additionally, REM will organize special, University-wide waste minimization efforts and facilitate information sharing by University. Waste prevention and minimization has positive environmental, human health and safety, and economic impacts.

Therefore it is an important goal at Purdue University. Implementing a "less is better" concept provides better protection of human health and safety by reducing exposures, generating less demand for disposal on the environment. Less Waste also lowers disposal cost. You can do your part helping Purdue reach this waste prevention and minimization goal by educating yourself and others about waste prevention and minimization. All faculty, staff, and students should take responsibility for educating ourselves about environmental protection as well as human health and safety.

METHODS

WASTE MANAGEMENT TECHNIQUES

Managing domestic, industrial and commercial waste has traditionally consisted of collection, followed by disposal. Depending upon the type of waste and the area, a level of processing may follow collection. This processing may be to reduce the hazard of the waste, recover material for recycling, produce energy from the waste, or reduce it in volume for more efficient disposal. Collection methods vary widely between different countries and regions. For example, in Australia most urban domestic households have a 240-litre bin that is emptied weekly by the local Council.

Many areas, especially those in less developed areas, do not have a formal waste-collection system in place. Disposal methods also vary widely. In Australia, the most common method of disposal of solid waste is to landfills, because it is a large country with a low-density population. By contrast, in Japan it is more common for waste to be incinerated, because the country is smaller and land is scarce.

Landfill

Disposing of waste in a landfill is the most traditional method of waste disposal, and it remains a common practice in most countries. Historically, landfills were often established in disused quarries, mining voids or borrow pits. A well-run landfill can be a hygienic and relatively inexpensive method of disposing of waste materials. Older or poorly managed landfills can create number of adverse environmental impacts, including wind-blown litter, attraction of vermin and soluble contaminants (leachate) leaching into and polluting groundwater.

Another product of landfills containing putrescible wastes is landfill gas (mostly composed of methane and carbon dioxide), which is produced as the waste breaks down.

Characteristics of a modern, well-run landfill should include methods to contain leachate, such as clay or plastic liners. Disposed waste should be compacted and covered to prevent vermin and wind-blown litter. Many landfills also have a landfill gas extraction system installed after they are closed to extract the gas generated by the decomposing waste materials. This gas is often burnt to generate power. Generally, even flaring the gas off is a better environmental outcome than allowing it to escape to the atmosphere, as this consumes the methane (a far more potent greenhouse gas than carbon dioxide).

Many local authorities (especially in urban areas) have found it difficult to establish new landfills, due to opposition from adjacent landowners. Few people want a landfill in their local neighbourhood. As a result, solid waste disposal in these areas has become more expensive as material must be transported further away for disposal. Some oppose the use of landfills in *any* way, anywhere, arguing that the logical end result of landfill operations is that it will eventually leave a drastically polluted planet with no canyons, and no wild space. Some futurists have stated that landfills will be the "mines of the future": As some resources become more scarce, they will become valuable enough that it would be necessary to 'mine' them from landfills where these materials were previously discarded as valueless.

This fact, as well as growing concern about the impacts of excessive materials consumption, has given rise to efforts to minimise the amount of waste sent to landfill in many areas. These efforts include taxing or levying waste sent to landfill, recycling the materials, converting material to energy, designing products that require less material, etc. A related subject is that of industrial ecology, where the material flows between industries is studied. The by-products of one industry may be a useful commodity to another, leading to reduced waste materials.

Incineration

Incineration is the process of destroying waste material by burning it. Incineration is carried out both on a small scale by individuals, and on a large scale by industry. It is recognised as a practical method of disposing of hazardous waste materials (such as biological medical waste). Though still widely used in many areas (especially developing countries), incineration as a waste management tool is becoming controversial for several reasons.

First, it may be a poor use of many waste materials because it destroys not only the raw material, but also all of the energy, water, and other natural resources used to produce it. Some energy can be reclaimed as electricity by using the combustion to create steam to drive an electrical generator, but even the best incinerator can only recover a fraction of the caloric value of fuel materials.

Second, incineration creates toxic gas and ash, which can harm local populations and pollute groundwater. Modern, well-run incinerators take elaborate measures to reduce the amount of toxic products released in exhaust gas. But concern has increased in recent years about the levels of dioxins that are released when burning mixed waste. Until recently, safe disposal of incinerator waste was a major problem. In the mid–1990s, experiments in France and Germany used electric plasma torches to melt incinerator waste into inert glassy pebbles, valuable in concrete production. Incinerator ash has also been chemically separated into lye and other useful chemicals.

VOLUME REDUCTION

This means various techniques for making the waste fit into less space and easier to handle in bulk. Usually achieved by compaction or fragmentation.

Compaction

The waste is compacted or compressed.

It also breaks up large or fragile items of waste:

- This process is conspicuous in the feed at the back end of many garbage collection vehicles.
- See car crusher
- In landfill sites, the waste is often compacted by driving over it a heavy excavator-type vehicle with spiked wheels.

Shearing

The waste is sliced with heavy metal shears.

Grinding

The waste is ground up hammer mill.

RESOURCE RECOVERY TECHNIQUES

A relatively recent idea in waste management has been to treat the waste material as a resource to be exploited, instead of simply a challenge to be managed and disposed of. There are a number of different methods by which resources may be extracted from waste: the materials may be extracted and recycled, or the calorific content of the waste may be converted to electricity. The process of extracting resources or value from waste is variously referred to as secondary resource recovery, recycling, and other terms.

The practice of treating waste materials as a resource is becoming more common, especially in metropolitan areas where space for new landfills is becoming scarcer. There is also a growing acknowledgement that simply disposing of waste materials is unsustainable in the long term, as there is a finite supply of most raw materials. There are a number of methods of recovering resources from waste materials, with new technologies and methods being developed continuously.

Recycling

Recycling means to reuse a material that would otherwise be considered waste. The popular meaning of 'recycling' in most developed countries has come to refer to the widespread collection and reuse of single-use beverage containers. These containers are collected and sorted into common groups, so that the raw materials of the items can be used again (recycled). In developed countries, the most common consumer items recycled include aluminium beverage cans,steel food and aerosol cans, HDPE and PET plastic bottles, glass bottles and jars, paperboard cartons,newspapers, magazines, and cardboard. Other types of plastic are also recyclable, although not as commonly collected. These items are usually composed of a single type of material, making them relatively easy to recycle into new products. The recycling of obsolete computers and electronic equipment is important although more costly due to the separation and extraction problems.

The recycling of junked automobiles also depends on the scrap metal market. Recycled or used materials have to compete in the marketplace with new (virgin) materials.

The cost of collecting and sorting the materials usually means that they are equally or more expensive than virgin materials. This is most often the case in developed countries where industries producing the raw materials are well-established. Practices such as trash picking can reduce this value further, as choice items are removed (such as aluminium cans).

In some countries, recycling programmes are subsidised by deposits paid on beverage containers. Not accounted for by most economic systems are the benefits to the environment of recycling these materials, compared with extracting virgin materials. It usually requires significantly less energy, water and other resources to recycle materials than to produce new materials. For example, recycling 1000 kg of aluminium cans saves approximately 5000 kg of bauxite ore being mined and 95% of the energy required to refine it.

In many areas, material for recycling is collected separately from general waste, with dedicated bins and collection vehicles. Other waste management processes recover these materials from general waste streams. This usually results in greater levels of recovery than separate collections of consumer–separated beverage containers, but are more complex and expensive.

Composting and Digestion

Waste materials that are organic in nature, such as food scraps and paper products, are increasingly being recycled. These materials are put through a composting or artificial digestion process to decompose the organic matter and kill pathogens. The organic material is then recycled as mulch orcompost for agricultural or landscaping purposes. There are a large variety of composting methods and technologies, varying in complexity from simple window composting of shredded plant material, to automated enclosed-vessel digestion of mixed domestic waste. Composting methods can be broadly categorised into aerobic or anaerobic methods, although hybrids of the two methods also exist.

Composting and Digestion Programmes

The Green Bin Programme, a form of organic recycling used in Markham, Ontario, Canada, makes use of anaerobic digestion to reduce the amount of garbage shipped to Michigan, in the United States. This is the newest facet of the 3-stream waste management system has been implemented in the town and is another step towards the goal of diverting 70% of current waste away from the landfills. Green Bins allow any organic waste that in the past would have formed landfill waste to be composted and turned into nutrient rich soil. Examples of waste products for the Green Bin are food products and scraps, soiled papers and sanitary napkins. Currently, Markham—like the other municipalities in the Greater Toronto Area—ships all of its garbage to Michigan at a cost of ₹22 CAN per metric tonne.

The Green Bin Programme is currently being studied by other Municipalities in the province of Ontario as a way of diverting waste away from the landfills. Notably, Toronto and Ottawa are in the preliminary stages of adopting a similar programme. The City of Edmonton, Alberta, Canada has adopted large-scale composting to deal with its urban waste. Its composting facility is the largest of its type in the world, representing 35 per cent of Canada's centralized composting capacity.

The ₹100-million co-composter allows Edmonton to recycle 65 per cent of its residential waste. The co-composter iself is 38,690 square metres in size, equivalent to 8 football fields. It's designed to process 200,000 tonnes of residential solid waste per year and 22,500 dry tonnes of biosolids, turning them into 80,000 tonnes of compost annually.

INCINERATION, PYROLYSIS AND GASIFICATION

Use of incinerators for waste management is controversial, and most Americans passionately oppose it. This controversy roots from the understandable conflict between short-term concerns and long-term ones, in this case between burning the wastes now, or postponing this problem by passing the waste burden to future generations. Whether any form of incineration or thermal treatment should be defined as "resource recovery" is a matter of dispute in policy-making circles.

Pyrolysis and Gasification are two related forms of thermal treatment where materials are incinerated with limited oxygen. The process typically occurs in a sealed vessel, under high temperature and pressure. Converting material to energy this way is more efficient than direct incineration, with more energy able to be recovered and used. Pyrolysis of solid waste converts the material into solid, liquid and gas products. The liquid oil and gas can be burnt to produce energy or refined into other products. The solid residue (char) can be further refined into products such as activated carbon. Gasification is used to convert organic materials directly into a synthetic gas composed of carbon monoxide and hydrogen. The gas is then burnt to produce electricity and steam. Gasification is used in biomass power stations to produce renewable energy and heat.

HOSPITAL SOLID WASTE

Hospital waste is generated during the diagnosis, treatment, or immunization of human beings or animals or in research activities in these fields or in the production or testing of biologicals. It may include wastes like sharps, soiled waste, disposables, anatomical waste, cultures, discarded medicines, chemical wastes, etc. These are in the form of disposable syringes, swabs, bandages, body fluids, human excreta, etc. This waste is highly infectious and can be a serious threat to human health if not managed in a scientific and discriminate manner.

It has been roughly estimated that of the 4 kg of waste generated in a hospital at least 1 kg would be infected. Surveys carried out by various agencies show that the health care establishments in India are not giving due attention to their waste management. After the notification of the Bio-medical Waste (Handling and Management) Rules, these establishments are slowly streamlining the process of waste segregation, collection, treatment, and disposal. Many of the larger hospitals have either installed the treatment facilities or are in the process of doing so.

Many terms are used to identify and characterize biomedical waste, such as: biohazardous, pathological, and infectious. These terms are often used interchangeably without clearly defining their subtle differences and similarities. To assist the reader these terms are defined below. For the purpose of this document biomedical waste will be used as the general term. Where the waste may be defined more specifically and require special treatment, this procedure will specify the requirements.

BIOMEDICAL WASTE

Discarded biological material from teaching, clinical and research laboratories and operations. Examples of biomedical waste include but are not limited to;

- *Animal Waste* - Animals carcasses, tissues and body parts, blood and bodily fluids and infectious bedding.
- *Biological Laboratory Waste* - Cultures, stocks or specimens of microorganisms, live or attenuated vaccines, human or animal cell cultures and laboratory material that has come into contact with these (solid and liquid).
- *Human Anatomical Waste* - any part of the human body, including tissues and organs but excluding extracted teeth, hair, and nail clippings.
- *Human Blood and Body Fluid Waste* – Human fluid blood and blood products, items saturated or dripping blood, body fluids contaminated with blood and body fluids removed for diagnosis during surgery, treatment or autopsy. This does not include urine or feces. Material

with minimal amounts of non-infectious blood (i.e. does not release blood if compressed) are not considered biomedical waste.

- *Sharps* - Needles, syringes with needles, lancets, scalpels, razor blades, and precision knives. Contaminated broken glass, pipettes, test tubes, microscope slides, blood vials or any other material capable of causing punctures or cuts.

BIOHAZARDOUS WASTE

Waste that is known or suspected to contain infectious material or which because of its physical or biological nature may be harmful to humans, animals, plants or the environment

Infectious waste

Waste which contains microorganisms in sufficient quantity which could result in the multiplication and growth of those microorganisms in a host.

Pathological waste

Any waste which contains microorganisms capable of causing disease.

ROLES AND RESPONSIBILITES

Principal Investigators

- Ensure all lab staff/students have received proper training to deal with biomedical waste. Communicate these guidelines to key personnel.
- Ensure labs are equipped with the proper containers and or bags and that they are ideally located.

Users (students, lab or clinic personnel):

- Practice due diligence at all times when handling biomedical waste (i.e. wear protective equipment)
- Ensure familiarity with the handling, treatment and disposal procedures of the waste you generate.

Service or Faculty/Department Biomedical Waste Representative:

- Arrange for pick-up/drop off of waste with users.
- Transport or assist in transport of waste to designated storage areas.
- Log waste information in the appropriate log.
- Contact ORM to arrange for pick up of full containers and for re-supply (where applicable)

OFFICE OF RISK MANAGEMENT (ORM):

- Pick up all biomedical waste from designated storage areas and arrange for off site disposal.

- Maintain records regarding the amount of waste generated.
- Ensure Principal Investigators, users, and representatives are complying with guidelines.
- Provide guidance regarding the handling treatment or disposal of biomedical waste.

GENERAL GUIDELINES

Segregation:

- Biomedical waste must be stored in a secure environment at all times.
- Whenever possible, biomedical waste must not be mixed with chemical, radioactive or other laboratory trash. This may be unavoidable (i.e. radioactive carcasses) and in such instances special handling may be required. For further information contact ORM.
- The various types of biomedical waste should be segregated from each other.
- Fluid waste should be contained separately from solid waste.

CONTAINMENT & LABELING

Containers for biomedical waste must be appropriate for its contents. There are several different kinds of containers and bags available for the containment and disposal of biomedical waste. Containers and bags are available through your faculty/service stores, your hazardous waste representative or the ORM. The various types of packaging and associated labelling used for different types of biomedical waste are outlined below. **All** containers for biomedical waste must display the biohazard symbol and the words 'Biohazard' in a colour contrasting the container.

SHARPS

- must be rigid, leak proof, puncture resistant and sealable
- University currently uses 4.5L yellow containers
- 22.5L containers are available upon request
- Label: University of Ottawa Hazardous Waste label

ANATOMICAL/ANIMAL WASTE

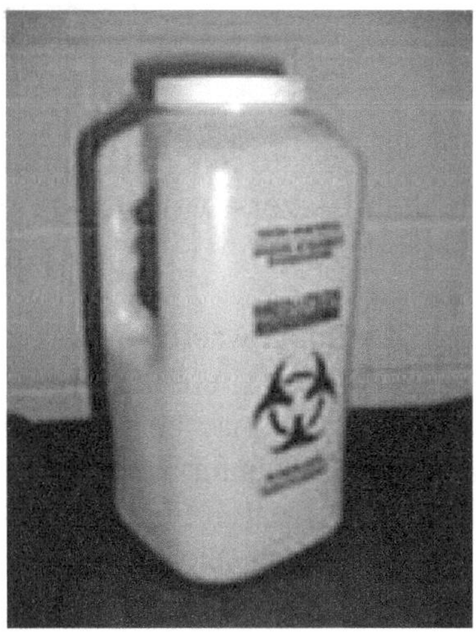

- Place waste in a red biohazard bag or a black garbage bag if the waste will immediately be stored in a barrel lined with red biohazard bags.
- Barrels are approved heavy duty rigid cardboard.
- Label: Each bag must be tagged with a completed yellow incineration (necropsy) tag.

BIOLOGICAL LABORATORY WASTE

Review of current practices indicates biological laboratory waste is treated in-house (autoclaved or chemically treated). If in-house treatment is not suitable, contact ORM to discuss other means of disposal.

Solid:

- Collect waste in a red or orange autoclavable biohazard bag
- Label: University of Ottawa Hazardous Waste label

LIQUID WASTE

There are liquid wastes in several sectors of the economy. Agriculture is an important source, where manure particularly poses an environmental burden, but where methane may be captured and used for energy production before the manure is used as fertilizer.

Wastewater treated in wastewater treatment plants can be an additional source of methane release into the atmosphere, where capture and destruction or utilisation is an obvious possibility for reducing greenhouse gas emissions. Otherwise, it may be aerated to avoid anaerobic conditions and the uncontrolled release of methane. Additionally, the food industry produces significant amounts of waste oil that is easily transformed into useful fuel.

The following are recorded as sources of liquid waste:

- Manure
- Waste Oil
- Wastewater

LIQUID WASTE MANAGEMENT

The coverage of sewerage facilities, even in the City Corporations, is extremely low of the order of 30% in Thiruvananthapuram and 5% in Kochi Corporation areas, probably one of the lowest in the country. Even in this system, the provision for treating the black liquor is almost absent. Rest of the Municipal and rural areas do not have even such a facility. Due to land constraints the septic tanks have volume constraints and due to high water table scenario, the leach pits overflows, especially during rainy season which extend up to about 150 days in a year.

Therefore, there is a requirement of clearance and removal of septage, the facilities for which are not available anywhere in the state. The practice now is to collect the septage using vacuum suction into tankers which are then emptied into open spaces and even water bodies, one of the most dangerous practices. Therefore, there is an immediate necessity of installing Sewage Treatment Plants, at least for treating the septage collected from septic tanks and leach pits, the technical aspects of which are being worked out.

COMPOSITION OF LIQUID WASTE

The destruction of sarin (GB) in the EDS using aqueous MEA (45 per cent) as the treatment chemical produces an organic-rich neutralent stream, as described. The posttreatment of this neutralent stream is the focus of this report, but there are also other liquid waste streams that must be dealt with. The other streams result from the rinsing of the EDS chamber with water after each use to remove residual MEA and solid residues and the cleaning to remove other solid and liquid residues.

These waste streams must also be prepared for ultimate disposal unless their compositions meet the feed requirements for an on-site treatment works. The diverse nature of these waste streams is illustrated.

The data indicate that there are two main types of liquid waste streams from the EDS treatment of CB as produced in the bomblet campaign at Rocky Mountain Arsenal:

1. Organic-rich neutralent derived from the MEA treatment and from the MEA rinse step used with the first two bomblets and
2. Aqueous streams resulting from water rinses of the EDS chamber and from aqueous acetic acid cleaning of the chamber.

Most of the MEA reagent and most of the GB and energetic degradation products appear in the organic-rich neutralent stream. The concentration of isopropyl methylphosphonic acid (IMPA), the major product of GB decomposition, approximates that expected from 70 to 90 per cent hydrolysis of the 1.3 pounds of GB contained in each bomblet. It is clear that the neutralents are far too organic-rich for direct treatment in a water treatment works. Some further treatment such as oxidation is needed to mineralize the organic components for disposal through a treatment works or by deposition in a hazardous waste landfill.

A further complication is the high concentrations of some metal ions such as aluminum, copper, and zinc. These metals presumably were present as materials of construction for the bomblets and were washed or extracted from the bomblet fragments by the MEA solutions. The water rinsates contain small quantities of MEA and GB degradation products that clung to the bomblet fragments and to the interior surfaces of the EDS apparatus. The metal ion concentrations are generally much lower than in the neutralents. The rinsates may be suitable for disposal through FOTW or POTW, depending on the regulations and permit requirements applying to the particular treatment facility. The spent cleaning solutions are primarily water-based and acidic. The acidity appears to have played a major role in extracting metal ions, of which mercury may be the most problematic. The protocol for cleaning liquid flow lines on the EDS appears to have been a work in progress during the RMA campaign. The concentrations of chloroform and dichloromethane in this waste stream appear to arise from a commercial lubricant used as a sealant on the EDS. The appropriate disposal of the spent cleaning solutions requires careful analysis. It may be possible to combine them with the aqueous rinsates, but care must be taken to be sure that the mixture can be handled in accordance with regulatory standards for the treatment works. There are no established treatment standards for the agent or degradation/hydrolysis products that may be of concern. Whether to establish numerical treatment standards for agents and degradation products has been the subject of intense discussions between the Army and the states. The numerical pretreatment standards listed in EPA's Clean Water Act (CWA) are a minimum requirement.

The sewerage agency must make a case-by-case determination to ensure that:

- The POTWs permit limits are not exceeded by the influent,
- The water quality standards are not exceeded as a result of the discharge,
- The toxic pollutants entering the POTW are adequately treated, and
- The influent does not cause the POTW's sludge to exceed any applicable

CLASSIFICATION OF LIQUID WASTE

CLASSIFICATION PROCEDURE OF LABORATORY WASTE

Stabilization and Protection for Liquid Waste

- Organic waste with unknown components can be classified as halogen containing organic liquid waste.
- The pH of cyanide derived liquid waste must be adjusted to 11, otherwise HCN will be released.

- Liquid waste containing fluoride or phosphorus should be stabilized with the addition of calcium salts (*e.g.* CaO, $Ca(OH)_2$, $CaSO_4$, $CaCl_2$)and pH adjustment to be greater than 7.0

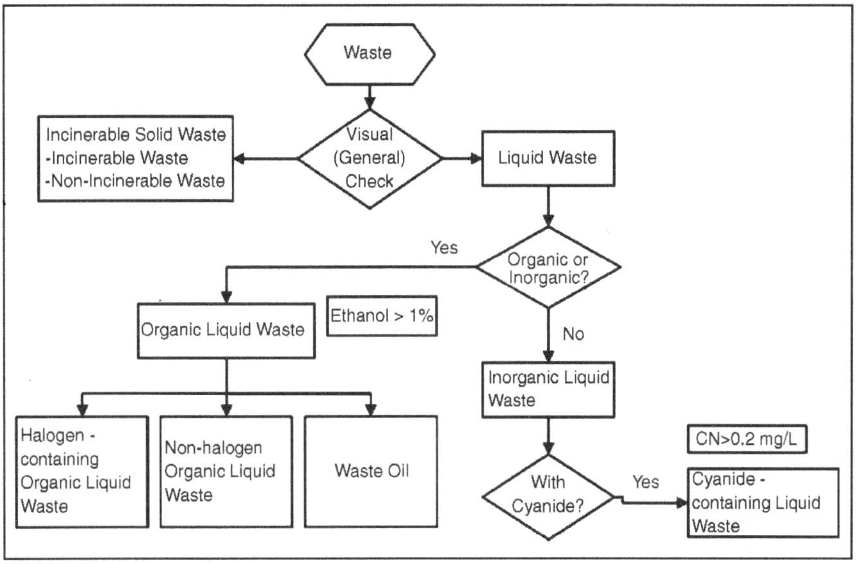

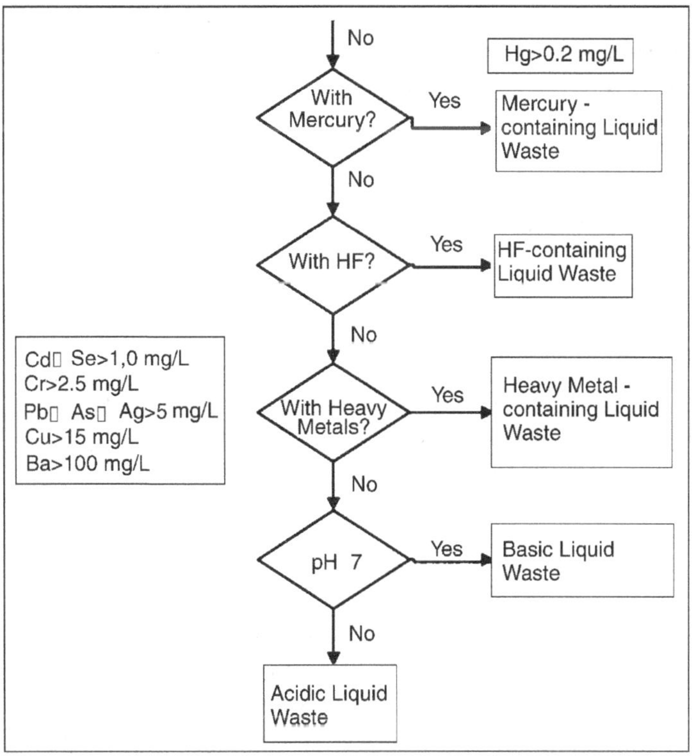

DISASTER MANAGEMENT

WHAT IS DISASTER MANAGEMENT

'Disaster management can be defined as the organization and management of resources and responsibilities for dealing with all humanitarian aspects of emergencies, in particular preparedness, response and recovery in order to lessen the impact of disasters.'

Types of Disasters

There is no country that is immune from disaster, though vulnerability to disaster varies. There are four main types of disaster.

Natural Disasters

These disasters include floods, hurricanes, earthquakes and volcano eruptions that can have immediate impacts on human health, as well as secondary impacts causing further death and suffering from floods causing landslides, earthquakes resulting in fires, tsunamis causing widespread flooding and typhoons sinking ferries

Environmental Emergencies

These emergencies include technological or industrial accidents, usually involving hazardous material, and occur where these materials are produced, used or transported. Large forest fires are generally included in this definition because they tend to be caused by humans.

Complex Emergencies

These emergencies involve a break-down of authority, looting and attacks on strategic installations. Complex emergencies include conflict situations and war.

Pandemic Emergencies

These emergencies involve a sudden onset of a contagious disease that affects health but also disrupts services and businesses, bringing economic and social costs. Any disaster can interrupt essential services, such as the provision of health care, electricity, water, sewage/garbage removal, transportation and communications.

The interruption can seriously affect the health, social and economic networks of local communities and countries. Disasters have a major and long-lasting impact on people long after the immediate effect has been mitigated. Poorly planned relief activities can have a significant negative impact not only on the disaster victims but also on donors and relief agencies. So it is important that physical therapists join established programmes rather than attempting individual efforts. Local, regional, national and international organisations are all involved in mounting a humanitarian response to disasters. Each will have a prepared disaster management plan. These plans cover prevention, preparedness, relief and recovery.

Disaster Prevention

These are activities designed to provide permanent protection from disasters. Not all disasters, particularly natural disasters, can be prevented, but the risk of loss of life and injury can be mitigated with good evacuation plans, environmental planning and design standards. In January 2005, 168 Governments adopted a 10-year global plan for natural disaster risk reduction called the Hyogo Framework. It offers guiding principles, priorities for action, and practical means for achieving disaster resilience for vulnerable communities.

Disaster Preparedness

These activities are designed to minimise loss of life and damage—for example by removing people and property from a threatened location and by facilitating timely and effective rescue, relief and rehabilitation. Preparedness is the main way of reducing the impact of disasters. Community-based preparedness and management should be a high priority in physical therapy practice management.

Disaster Relief

This is a coordinated multi-agency response to reduce the impact of a disaster and its long-term results. Relief activities include rescue, relocation, providing food and water, preventing disease and disability, repairing vital services such as telecommunications and transport, providing temporary shelter and emergency health care.

Disaster Recovery

Once emergency needs have been met and the initial crisis is over, the people affected and the communities that support them are still vulnerable. Recovery activities include rebuilding infrastructure, health care and rehabilitation.

These should blend with development activities, such as building human resources for health and developing policies and practices to avoid similar situations in future. Disaster management is linked with sustainable development, particularly in relation to vulnerable people such as those with disabilities, elderly people, children and other marginalised groups. Myths and Realities of Disaster Assistance summarises some of the common misunderstandings about disaster management.

CHEMICAL DISASTER MANAGEMENT AND RISK ANALYSIS

INTRODUCTION

Mining and allied activities are associated with several potential hazards both to the employees and the public at large. A worker in a mine should be able to work under conditions that are adequately safe and healthy. At the same time the environmental conditions should be such as not to impair his working efficiency.

The various safeguards to be taken to ensure the safety of the mine and that of employees are provided in the Mines Act, 1952.

IDENTIFICATION OF HAZARDS

There are various factors, which can cause disaster in the mines.

These hazards are as follows:

- Drilling;
- Blasting;
- Overburden handling;
- Heavy Machinery; and
- Explosives storage.

Drilling and Blasting

Most of the accidents from blasting occur due to the projectiles, as they may some times go even beyond the danger zone, mainly due to over charging of the shot holes as a result of certain special features of the local ground.

Flying rocks are encountered during initial and final blasting operations. Vibrations also lead to displacement of adjoining areas.

Dust and noise are also problems commonly encountered during blasting operations.

Overburden Handling

The overburden dumps may cause landslides. High overburden dumps created at the quarry edge may cause sliding of the overburden dump or may cause failure of the pit slope due to excessive loading, thereby causing loss of life and property. Siltation of surface water may also cause run-off from overburden dumps.

Heavy Machinery

Most of the accidents during transport of dumpers, trucks, proclains, ripper dozers and other heavy vehicles are often attributable to mechanical failures and human errors.

DISASTER MANAGEMENT

Measures Suggested to Avoid Accidents Due to Blasting

- Shots shall not be fired except during the hours of day light or until adequate provision is made for artificial lighting and the holes charged on a particular day shall be fired on the same day;
- Shots, if fired after hours of daylight, should be muffled so that the flying fragments from the blasting material do not project beyond a distance of 10 m from the place of blasting;
- Adequate shelters or other protective structures shall be provided to the workers at all times;
- The shot fired shall give sufficient warning by effective signal over the entire area falling within a radius of 500 m;
- Where any permanent building or structure is damaged within the danger zone, the aggregate maximum change in all the holes fired at any particular time shall not exceed 2 kg;
- If a single shot exploder is used or if blasting is done with ordinary detonator, the shot-firer shall not fire more than fifty shots in one shift, but if multishot exploder is used, the number can go up to eighty;
- During the approach and progress of an electrical storm, adequate precaution shall be taken;
- No shot hole shall be drilled in the overburden above the underground galleries.

Measures to Prevent the Danger of Overburden

- A stone wall should be built around the toe of each active dump at a distance of about 50-m from the toe;

To prevent the failure of overburden slopes, especially during the rainy season, the following precautions shall be taken:

- Proper terracing of the dump slopes, with a maximum dump height of 10 meters should be maintained;
- In flat areas where the dumping operations have come to an end, the slope angle should be flattened by about 5° lower than the angle of repose, which varies from site to site but not less than 25°;
- Planting vegetation as early as possible over the overburden dump slopes;
- Provide drainage channels along the overburden dump toe for additional protection, in such a way that a distance of 15 m should be maintained left between the overburden dump and the bench; and
- If a mine is abandoned, the bench and overburden dump should be separated from each other by digging a trench of 6 to 10 m width.

Measures to Prevent Accidents Due to Trucks and Dumpers

- All transportation within the main working area should be carried out under the direct supervision and control of the management;
- The vehicles must be maintained in good repairs and checked thoroughly at least once a week by a competent person authorized for this purpose by the management;
- Broad signs should be provided at each and every turning point specially for the guidance of the drivers at night;
- To avoid dangers while reversing the trackless vehicles, especially at the embankment and tripping points, all areas for reversing of lorries should, as far as possible, be made man free, and there should be a light and sound device to indicate reversing of trucks; and
- A statutory provision of the fence, constant education, training etc will go a long way in reducing the incidence of such accidents.

STORAGE OF FUELS AND EXPLOSIVE MATERIALS

The explosives will be stored in a magazine of 25-T capacity. Based on the study of accidents in chemical industry in India over a few decades, a specific legislation was enacted and enforced by the Government Of India in conjunction with Environment Protection Act, 1986, referred to as "GOI rules". These rules are for the purpose of identifying major hazardous installations applying certain criteria on toxic, flammable and explosive properties of chemicals. Besides, the criteria list of hazardous substances with their threshold quantities are provided in part II of schedule I of the rules. The of storage of flammable and explosive materials used in mines to determine the Threshold quantities as notified GOI Rules 1989 and the applicable rules are identified. The major hazardous materials stored and used in the mines are Diesel, Ammonium nitrate and Nitroglycerine.

Table. Applicability of Goi Rules to Hazardous Materials Storage

Sr. No.	Chemical	Annual Requirement/	Listed in Schedule No.	Threshold GOI Rules	Qty as Per Storage
1	Diesel	40 KL	1(2)	(5, 7-9, 13-15	10-12)
		(10 KL storage)		25 MT	200 MT
2	Ammonium Nitrate	540 T (25 T Magazine)	1(2)	(4,5 7-9 350 T	10-15) 2500 T

The storages of all hazardous materials in the mines are much less, when compared with threshold storage quantities. It is advised to follow the Indian Explosive Act and Rules 1983 for handling of explosives.

RISK ASSESSMENT AND DISASTER MANAGEMENT STUDIES

Risk assessment studies represent the first step of the cycle for disaster reduction. These are essential elements for planning measures and taking actions in the event of a catastrophe, and for developing an adequate risk management. A risk assessment also represents a rigorous study in which various sciences converge, through the analysis the climatic, geological, political and social characteristics of a given territory. The study must be updated on a regular basis to incorporate emerging situations, new experiences and investments, and even scientific and technical discoveries

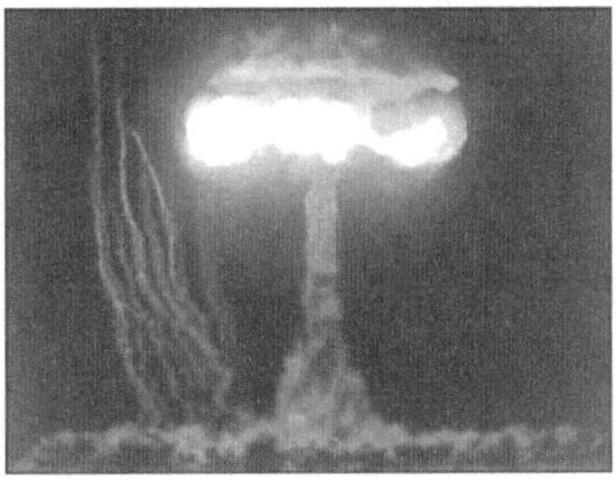

Today's total Risk Manager is the person who can combine art with science to master the challenges and opportunities of a fast-changing world and RM can be used as an effective tool to guarantee a systematic, transparent and future-oriented corporate governance.. Hazop Study a part of Risk Assesment is one of the most effective and widely used hazard identification techniques, employed all over the world, mainly for chemical and petrochemical processes. It involves a systematic analysis of the consequences, of all the possible causes of deviation in a process from the original design intention

NAPESCO's Risk Assesment Services includes:

- Comprehensive Safety Audit
- Safety Perception Survey
- Disaster Management Planning
- Risk Management Studies
- Process Risk Assessment
- Risk Analysis Studies
- Hazop Studies
- Chemical Safety Audit
- Fire Safety Audit/Fire Risk Assessment
- Lightning Protection Consultancy
- Electrical Hazards Consultancy

Some of the Risk Assesment studies being conducted by NAPESCO are:

- Hazop, QRA and PHSER studies for Installation of New Smokeless Flares at GC-25, KOC for Client KCC
- Hazop and QRA studies for Installation of New Air Assisted Flares at GC–3,6,8 and 19 at KOC for Client: ISCO

NAPESCO have also partnered with various International Reputed Safety and Risk Consultants to provide multi disciplinary Safety and Risk Consultancy services.

WASTE ANALYSIS

WHY WASTE ANALYSIS

Waste products must be used or disposed of with environmentally sound management practices in order to prevent damage to our natural resources. Farms' food-processing plants, textile manufacturers, pharmaceutical companies, wood and paper producers, and municipalities all generate a variety of waste products—the disposal of which must be managed somewhat differently depending upon the source and the intended use. Most waste must undergo some form of processing before it can be applied to the land. As landfill space becomes increasingly limited, waste producers are being forced to seek alternative disposal sites or potential recycling opportunities. Land application is one of the safest and most common alternatives provided that best management practices (BMPs) are followed. Waste products are generally applied to the land because they contain nutrients or liming materials beneficial to plant growth.

Waste analysis is the most accurate and efficient way to measure the nutrient or lime value of different waste products. Because the amount of these beneficial components can vary among waste products, laboratory analysis lets the producer know the proper amount of the waste material to apply to meet the specific plant needs for each site.

When management decisions are made without waste-analysis information, even well-intentioned users can reduce plant growth and yields or endanger the environment. Composting can reduce volume, improve uniformity, and sometimes alter the nutrient availability of waste products. Because of this, samples from the final material that will be applied must be analysed. Nutrient concentrations vary in most organic waste products. Table, for example, depicts the wide range in nutrients from animal wastes analysed by the NCDA Agronomic Division. Note that the maximum and minimum values for nitrogen, phosphate, and potash differ by more than 100-fold. These numbers should send a clear message to waste users and environmental policymakers: average nutrient estimates are not adequate guides for the safe and efficient use of waste materials.

Table. Variations in Poultry and Swine Manure Nutrient Levels.

Minimum	Maximum	Average	
Poultry, Broiler House	**Pounds Per Ton**		
Nitrogen	4	137	72
Phosphate	21	146	78
Potash	12	78	46
Swine, Liquid Lagoon	**Pounds Per 1,000 Gallons**		
Nitrogen	2	345	136
Phosphate	1	197	53
Potash	5	369	133

Waste users who fail to test each waste material are faced with a number of questions they simply cannot answer. Are they supplying plants with adequate nutrients? Are they building up excess nutrients that may ultimately move to streams or groundwater? Are they changing the soil pH to levels that will not support plant production? Are they applying heavy metals at levels that may be toxic to plants and permanently alter soil productivity? Because environmental damage and losses in plant yield and quality often happen before visible plant symptoms, growers and other users should always have their wastes analysed by a competent laboratory and their application rates determined by a knowledgeable agronomist.

WASTE ANALYSIS SERVICES

The Waste Advisory of the NCDA Agronomic Division analyses wastes, interprets analytical results, and provides management recommendations for citizens of North Carolina. A good analytical service should always determine the concentrations of essential plant nutrients, including nitrogen (N), phosphorus (P), potassium (K), calcium (Ca), magnesium (Mg), sulfur (S),iron (Fe), manganese (Mn), zinc (Zn), copper (Cu), and boron (B). Analyses of certain municipal and industrial wastes should also include tests for heavy metals like nickel (Ni), cadmium (Cd),and lead (Pb), as well as elements such as sodium (Na) and chlorine (Cl). The neutralizing value (calcium carbonate equivalent, CCE) of lime-stabilized products or materials suspected of having liming characteristics should also be determined.

SAMPLING PROCEDURES

Proper sampling is the key to reliable waste analysis. Although laboratory procedures are extremely accurate, they have little value if the samples fail to represent the waste product. The importance of careful sampling becomes clear when one recognizes that laboratory determinations are made on a portion of the sample submitted that is as little as 0.02 pound (1 gram) for solid materials or less than a tablespoon (10 milliliters) for liquid materials.

Waste samples submitted to a laboratory should represent the average composition of the material that will be applied to the field. Reliable samples typically consist of material collected from a number of locations. Precise sampling methods vary according to the type of waste. Ideally, growers should not base application rates on laboratory test results from previous years because nutrient concentrations can change significantly, particularly when the waste has been exposed to the environment.

For example, nutrient levels in an anaerobic lagoon can be influenced by rainfall. Stockpiled litter or other wastes may also change significantly if left unprotected. Municipal and industrial wastes also vary as production demands alter inputs and processing.

Liquid Wastes

Liquid waste samples submitted for analysis should meet the following requirements:

- Place sample in a sealed plastic container with about a one-quart volume. Glass is not suitable because it is breakable and may contain contaminants.
- Leave 1 inch of air space in the plastic container to allow for expansion caused by the release of gas from the waste material.
- Refrigerate samples that cannot be shipped on the day they are collected; this will minimize chemical reactions and pressure buildup from gases.

Ideally, some liquid wastes should be sampled after they are thoroughly mixed. Because this is sometimes impractical, samples can also be taken in accordance with the suggestionsthat follow.

Lagoon Liquid

Premixing the surface liquid in the lagoon is not needed, provided it is the only component that is being pumped. Growers with two-stage systems should draw samples from the lagoon they intend to pump. Samples should be collected using a plastic container similar to the one shown in Figure. One pint of material should be taken from at least eight sites around the lagoon and then mixed in a plastic container.

Waste should be collected at least 6 feet from the edge of the lagoon at a depth of about a foot. Shallower samples from anaerobic lagoons may be less representative than deep samples because oxygen transfer near the surface sometimes alters the ehemistry of the solution. Floating debris and scum should be avoided.

One quart of mixed material should be sent to the laboratory. Galvanized containers should never be used for collection, mixing, or storage due to the risk of contamination from metals like zinc in the container.

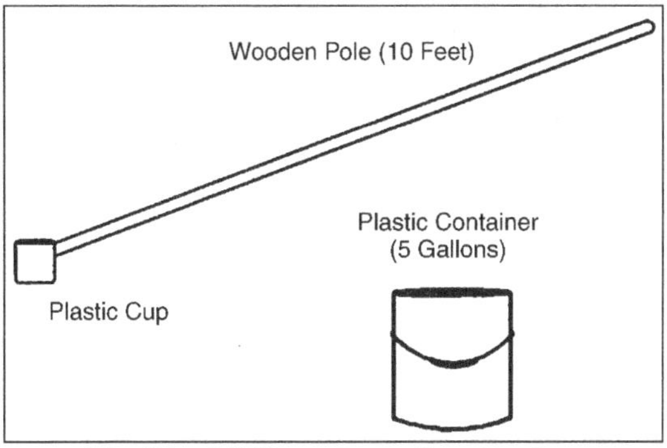

Fig. Liquid Waste Samp.ling Device.

Liquid Slurry

Waste materials applied as a slurry from a pit or storage basin should be mixed prior to sampling. Waste should be collected from approximately eight areas around the pit or basin and mixed thoroughly in a plastic container. Figure shows a useful collecting device.

An 8 to 10 foot section of 0.5-to 0.75-inch plastic pipe can also be used: the pipe should be extended into the pit, and the thumb pressed over the end to form an air lock; the pipe is then removed from the waste, and the air lock is released to deposit the waste in a container.

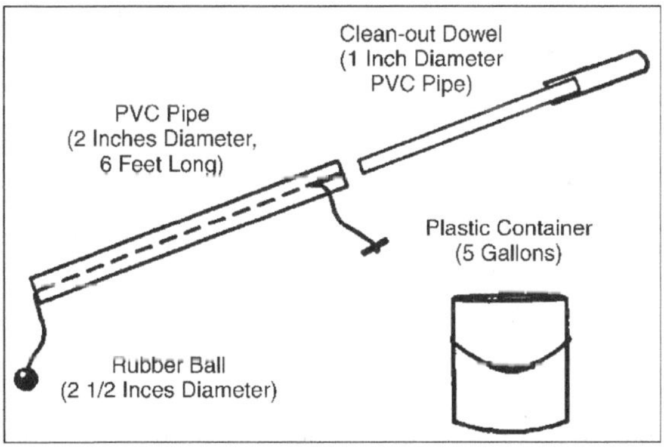

Fig. Slurry Sampling Device.

For analysis, the laboratory requires 1 quart of material in a plastic container. The sample should not be rinsed into the container because doing so dilutes the mixture and distorts nutrient evaluations. However, if water is typically added to the waste prior to land application, a proportionate quantity of water should be added to the sample.

Solid Wastes

Solid waste samples should represent the average moisture content of the waste. A one-quart sample is required for analysis. Samples should be taken from approximately eight different areas in the waste, placed in a plastic container, and thoroughly mixed. Approximately one quart of the mixed sample should be placed in a plastic bag, sealed, and shipped directly to the laboratory. Samples stored for more than two days should be refrigerated. Figure shows a device for sampling solid waste.

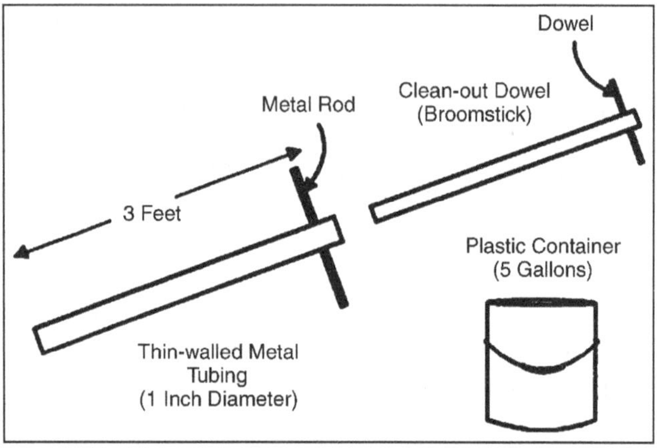

Fig. Solid Waste Sampling Device.

Poultry In-House Manure Sampling

Nutrient concentration varies widely in poultry litter both from house to house and within each house. If waste is to be applied by house, each one should be sampled separately. Waste samples should be collected from 6 to 12 locations in the house. Each sample should extend from the top to the bottom of the accumulated waste.

Samples taken around waterers, feeders, and brooders should be proportionate to the space these areas occupy in the house. The collected material should be combined in a plastic container and mixed thoroughly. The 1 quartlaboratory sample should be taken from this mixture.

Poultry Below-House Manure Sampling

In a high-rise system, manure is deposited below the poultry house. If the system is properly managed, the manure should be fairly uniform in moisture and appearance. Approximately eight samples should be collected throughout the storage area. If manure in certain areas differs in appearance, take samples proportionate to the size and number of these areas. For example, if 10 per cent of the manure differs from the bulk pile, then 10 per cent of the total sample should be taken from this area. The collected material should be combined in a plastic container and mixed thoroughly. The 1-quart laboratory sample should be taken from this mixture, placed in a plastic bag, sealed, and shipped to the laboratory for analysis. If the sample can not be shipped within one day of sampling, it should be refrigerated.

Stockpiled Litter

Ideally, stockpiled waste should be stored under cover on an impervious surface. The weathered exterior of uncovered waste may not accurately represent the majority of the material. Rainfall generally moves water-soluble nutrients down into the pile. If an unprotected stockpile is used over an extended period, it should be sampled before each application. Stockpiled waste should be sampled at a depth of at least 18 inches at six or more locations. The collected material should be combined in a plastic container and mixed thoroughly. The one-quartlaboratory sample should be taken from this mixture, placed in a plastic bag, sealed, and shipped to the laboratory for analysis. If the sample cannot be shipped within two days of sampling, it should be refrigerated.

Surface-Scraped Waste

Surface-scraped and piled materials should be treated like stockpiled waste. Follow the same procedures for taking samples. Ideally, surface-scraped materials should be protected from the weather unless they are used immediately.

Composted Waste

Ideally, composted waste should be stored under cover on an impervious surface. Although nutrients are somewhat stabilized in these materials, some nutrients can leach out during rains. When composted waste is left unprotected, samples should be submitted to the laboratory each time the material is applied. Sampling procedures the same as those described for stockpiled waste.

UNDERSTANDING THE WASTE ANALYSIS REPORT

Samples submitted to the NCDA Agronomic Division will be analysed and the sender will receive a report that lists the concentration of each plant nutrient and several potentially harmful elements. Specific concentrations of nutrients and other elements are reported on a dry-weight basis for solid wastes; results for liquid wastes are reported on a volume basis.

The most useful information is nutrients available for the first crop. These levels are predicted on an as-is or wet basis. Nutrient availability is predicted by estimating the nutrient release rate from the waste and a nutrient loss for a specific application method. Nutrients listed in the report as "available for the first crop" should be used in determining the actual application rate to meet a specific plant nutrient requirement. For the availability prediction to be reliable, growers must have properly identified the type of waste and the application method on the information sheet submitted to the laboratory.

For waste materials suspected of containing liming materials, such as stack dust or lime-stabilized waste, a calcium-carbonate equivalent (CCE) determination should be requested. These materials are reported on a dryweight basis for solid and semi-solid materials and on a volume basis for liquids. The CCE can be used to compare waste materials to agricultural lime for effectiveness in neutralizing soil acidity. The agricultural lime equivalent (ALE) is also calculated on a wet basis. This indicates the amount of the waste product that must be applied to have the same liming potential as one from agricultural lime with 90 per cent CCE.

MONITORING AND RECORD KEEPING

Growers who use waste materials as fertilizer or a source of lime should maintain records of the analytical results, application rates, and soil tests for each application site. Growers are also advised to take plant samples to evaluate their nutrient management programme, identify corrective actions for current crops, and plan improvements for future crops. Owners of waste application sites may also wish to sample surface and groundwater supplies once a year to confirm that nutrient-management programmes are not adversely affecting the environment. Where waste products have been applied regularly for a number of years, growers should also monitor the buildup of metals that can affect long-term soil productivity, particularly zinc and copper. For municipal and industrial waste sites, nickel, cadmium, lead, and sodium should also be monitored.

BIO-MEDICAL LIQUID WASTE

An expansion in the number of health facilities across the country and the burgeoning problem of un-treated biomedical waste had led to the passing of the Biomedical Waste (Management and Handling) rules 1998, but almost eight years down the line, much more needs to be done on the ground. Handling of bio-medical waste is proving to be an overwhelming challenge for the government and the health sector. However, within the broader theme of bio-medical waste, liquid bio-medical waste is emerging as particularly difficult to handle. Liquid biomedical waste is far more mobile and moves to a wider area after entering the subsurface water bodies or underground aquifers.

CHALLENGE OF LIQUID BIO-MEDICAL WASTE

Most existing systems and technologies being used in handling liquid bio-medical waste are failing to address this problem. For instance, the routine exercise of pouring biomedical liquid waste is being questioned for posing higher infection threat to medical staff due to its susceptibility to spilling, splashing and aerosolizing. Liquid bio-medical waste, if untreated, contains a wide variety of material that poses health hazards.

LIQUID BIO-MEDICAL WASTE STANDARDS

According to the *Biomedical Waste (Management and Handling) Rules 1998*, liquid pathological and chemical waste should be appropriately treated before discharge into the sewer. Pathological waste must be treated with chemical disinfectants, neutralised and then flushed into the sewage system. Chemical waste should first be neutralised with appropriate reagents and then flushed into the sewer sysrem.

These limits are applicable to hospitals that are either connected with sewers without terminal sewage treatment plant or not connected to public sewers for discharge into public sewers with terminal facilities, the general standards as notified under the Environment (Protection) Act, 1986 should be applicable.

Section (3) of the Act states: "For the purpose of protecting and improving the quality of the environment and preventing and abating the environmental pollution, the standards for emission or discharge of environmental pollutants from the industries, operations or processes shall be specified in schedule I or IV." The schedule contains general standards for discharge of effluents. Thirty-five parameters are specified for those to be discharged into municipal sewage.

MINIMAL SAFETY REQUIREMENTS

Where medical establishments cannot afford treatment of biomedical liquid waste, following measures should be undertaken to reduce risks:

- Patients with enteric diseases should be isolated to wards where their excreta can be collected in buckets for chemical disinfection. This is of utmost importance in cases of cholera outbreaks.
- No chemicals or pharmaceuticals should be discharged into the sewer.
- Sludges from hospital cesspools should be dehydrated on natural drying beds and disinfected chemically (for exmple, with sodium hypochlorite, chlorine gas, or preferably chlorine dioxide).
- Sewage from these establishments should never be used for agricultural, aqua-cultural, drinking water, or recreational purposes.

TREATMENT OF LIQUID BIO-MEDICAL WASTE

ON-SITE TREATMENT OR PRETREATMENT OF WASTEWATER

Many hospitals, in particular those that are not connected to any municipal treatment plant, have their own Sewage Treatment Plants (STPs) or Effluent Treatment Plants (ETPs). These plants carry out primary, secondary and tertiary treatment of liquid bio-medical waste followed by sludge treatment.

HOSPITALS WITH EFFLUENT TREATMENT PLANTS

HIMALAYAN INSTITUTE OF HOSPITAL TRUST

This is a 750-bed hospital near Dehradun and caters to the healthcare needs of 700 villages. The ETP here was set up on January 2004 at a cost of Rs

2,00,000, with treatment capacity of 100 m3 / day. It is based on aerobic activated sludge process and controls the BOD, COD, pH and total suspended solid. It was set up with the aim of preventing groundwater pollution, energy conservation, meeting water needs and maintaining the ground water table. Some of the treated effluent is recycled as fertilizer for gardens on the hospital premises spread over 300 acres. Some of this is also sold for use in the fields nearby. The savings in costs and also in the ground water has encouraged the institute to get another STP constructed, which will recycle 2,00,000 litre of water per day. This water will be supplied to the campus and hostels.

Fig. *ETP at Himalayan Institute of Hospital Trust.*

SIR GANGA RAM HOSPITAL

Sir Ganga Ram is a 625-bed multi-specialty hospital located in New Delhi. The ETP in the hospital was installed in the basement of the hospital and is operated round-the-clock and is monitored by its maintenance and sanitation department. The treatment process employed in this system is Extended Aeration, Suspended growth process using fine bubble diffused aeration system. Raw wastewater is collected from old and new building by gravity in to the collection tank out side the E.T.P and the raw Influent from laundry comes directly into flocculation tank. From flocculation tank it passes through tube settler for sedimentation process and finally collects in equalization tank for further aerobic treatment done in aeration tank through suspended growth process using diffused membrane aeration system. The secondary clarification of aerated mixed liquor takes place in Hopper Bottom Secondary clarifier and is followed by chlorination for disinfection. Filtration and de-chlorination of excess chlorine is done using multi grade filter and activated carbon filter. Treated water is then collected in water storage tank. Treated water is reused for flushing and gardening and the treated sludge is subjected to thickening through filter press and used as manures for plants. The results of effluent testing before and after the ETP are given in Table.

Table Physico-chemical and bacteriological analysis of effluent water

BEFORE					AFTER
Parameters	**Domestic**	**Laundry**	**Kitchen**	**Boiler**	**Entire Building**
Peak flow Kl/day	385	75	30	10	
Oil & Grease mg/L	10-20	50-75	150-175		<1
Suspended solids mg/L	100-150	150-200	300-400	200-250	<1
B.O.D. mg/L	200-250	100-150	500-600	20-30	6
C.O.D. mg/L	400-600	600-800	1000-1100	40-50	29
pH	-	-	-	-	7.3

CHOITHRAM HOSPITAL AND RESEARCH CENTRE

Choithram Hospital and Research Centre is a 350-bed tertiary care center in Indore, with a daily OPD attendance of 475 patients.. The total water requirement of the hospital is 5,00,000 litres. The ETP plant here was set in November 2001. The analysis of the hospital effluent before and after treatment is shown in Table all the physicochemical parameters are within the specified limits.

Table Physico-chemical and bacteriological analysis of effluent water

Parameter	Value before ETP	Value after ETP	Limit
Total viable bacterial count	9 X 104	Nil	-
MDR Coli-form [ ]	1.5	Nil	Nil
Chem. Oxygen Demand [mg/liter]	280	22.56	<250
Biological oxygen demand	45	3.6	<30
Total Solids	1066	630	<2200
Total dissolved solids >mg/ltr.	942	630	<2100
Total suspended solids mg/ltr.	124	<2	<100
pH	7	8.8	6.5-9

This is a 750-bed hospital near Dehradun and caters to the healthcare needs of 700 villages. The ETP here was set up on January 2004 at a cost of Rs 2,00,000, with treatment capacity of 100 m3 / day.

The chlorination results in complete inactivation of the Multiple Drug Resistant bacteria and thus makes the effluent water safe. The daily input of effluent is approximately 3,39,000 litres and approximately 3,00,000 litres of treated water is recovered. The treated effluent water is used for irrigation and sanitary cleaning. The hospital does not face water shortage any longer. Moreover, more than 5,000 kg. of dried sludge is available every month as manure for its gardens.

ALTERNATIVE USE FOR BIOTECHNOLOGY PRODUCTS

Yashraj Biotechnology Limited is a Mumbaibased company manufacturing diagnostic antigens from native source. It specialises in the field of isolation and purification of native antigenic proteins from biological fluids. Ward fluids in disease state (like ascites/pleural fluids, cerebrospinal fluid), normal state (like post delivery residual blood in cord), urine and donated or rejected blood are collected by the company for isolation of human proteins and native biological markers that are used in manufacture of In Vitro Diagnostics as calibrators and controls.

The collection of these fluids is done in leak proof plastic bottles (duly labeled with biohazard symbol and the company's address) containing preservatives (anti-microbial and protein stabilisers). Once collected the bottles are transported to their manufacturing facility in Mumbai under four layer safety packaging on lines of WHO and US Federal laws. This packaging offers safety at four levels beginning with nonleaking unbreakable bottles, followed by individual secondary self-sealing bag, jumbo bags, hard plastic container secured an sealed with strips. Any leftovers are chemically disinfected using one percent hypochlorite solution and disposed in CETP lines, as per guidelines in *Biomedical Waste (Management & Handling) Rules, 1998*. They are authorised by MPCB for these activities under contract with Mumbai Biomedical Waste Management Co. Records are maintained for such activities. The company does not offer any monetary benefit to the hospital and participation is completely voluntary.

BEST MANAGEMENT PRACTICES FOR LIQUID BIO-MEDICAL WASTE MANAGEMENT

- Medical establishments in remote locations should provide for minimal treatment of wastewater through affordable means (for examle, use of lagoons to achieve an acceptable level of purification, followed by infiltration of final effluent to the land).
- Sewage containing such waste should never be used for agricultural or aquaculture purposes.

- Sewage should not be discharged into or near water bodies that are used for drinking water.
- A mercury spill kit should be at hand and staff should be trained to recover the spill using correct techniques.
- A properly sized grease interceptor should be installed and maintained to reduce the discharge of oil and grease from kitchen and food preparation areas to the sanitary sewer system.
- Where feasible, solvents should be recovered for reuse.

There is no doubt that liquid biomedical waste management is a major problem for healthcare facilities. However, technology and treatment solutions do exist. These solutions, combined with proper training in handling of waste will enable healthcare organisations to diffuse this critical problem while safely, and cost effectively, managing their liquid biomedical waste.

4

Hazardous Waste Management

RADIOACTIVE WASTE

Any activity that produces or uses radioactive materials generates radioactive waste. Mining, nuclear power generation, and various processes in industry, defence, medicine, and scientific research produce byproducts that include radioactive waste. Radioactive waste can be in gas, liquid or solid form, and its level of radioactivity can vary.

The waste can remain radioactive for a few hours or several months or even hundreds of thousands of years. Because it can be so hazardous and can remain radioactive for so long, finding suitable disposal facilities for radioactive waste is difficult.

Depending on the type of waste disposed, the disposal facility may need to contain radiation for a very long time. Proper disposal is essential to ensure protection of the health and safety of the public and quality of the environment including air, soil, and water supplies.

Radioactive waste disposal practices have changed substantially over the last twenty years. Evolving environmental protection considerations have provided the impetus to improve disposal technologies, and, in some cases, clean up facilities that are no longer in use. Designs for new disposal facilities and disposal methods must meet environmental protection and pollution prevention standards that are more strict than were foreseen at the beginning of the atomic age. Disposal of radioactive waste is a complex issue, not only because of the nature of the waste, but also because of the complicated regulatory structure for dealing with radioactive waste.

There are a variety of stakeholders affected, and there are a number of regulatory entities involved. Federal government agencies involved in radioactive waste management include: the Environmental Protection Agency (EPA), the Nuclear Regulatory Commission (NRC), the Department of Energy (DOE), and the Department of Transportation. In addition, the states and affected Indian Tribes play a prominent role in protecting the public against the hazards of radioactive waste.

TYPES OF RADIOACTIVE WASTE

SPENT NUCLEAR FUEL AND HIGH-LEVEL RADIOACTIVE WASTE

In addition to being used to generate commercial electricity, nuclear reactors are used in government-sponsored research and development programmes, universities and industry; in science and engineering experimental programmes; at nuclear weapons production facilities; and by the U.S. Navy and military services. The operation of nuclear reactors results in spent reactor fuel. The reprocessing of that spent fuel produces high-level radioactive waste (HLW).

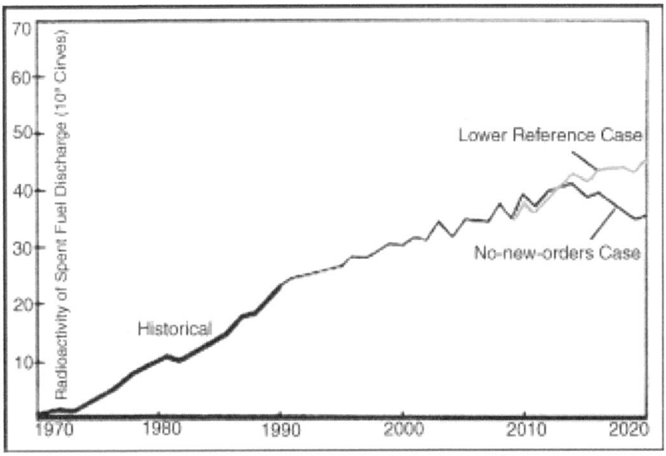

Fig. Projected Accumulated Radioactivity of Commercial Spent Fuel Discharges for the DOE/EIA

The fuel for most nuclear reactors consists of pellets of ceramic uranium dioxide that are sealed in hundreds of metal rods. These rods are bundled together to form what is known as a "fuel assembly." Depending upon the type and size of the reactor, a fuel assembly can weigh up to 1,500 pounds. As the nuclear reactor operates, uranium atoms fission (split apart) and release energy. When most of the usable uranium has fissioned, the "spent" fuel assembly is removed from the reactor. Until a disposal or long-term storage facility is operational, most spent fuel is stored in water pools at the reactor site where it was produced. The water removes leftover heat generated by the spent fuel and serves as a radiation shield to protect workers at the site. The operation of nuclear reactors over the last twenty years has substantially added to the amount of radioactive waste in this country. As shown in Figure, by the year 2020, the total amount of spent fuel is expected to increase significantly. HLW is the liquid waste that results when spent fuel is reprocessed to recover unfissioned uranium and plutonium. During this process, the fuel is dissolved by strong chemicals, and this results in liquid HLW. Plans are to solidify these liquids into a form that is suitable for disposal. Solidification is still in the planning stages. While currently there are no commercial facilities in this country that reprocess spent fuel, spent fuel from defence programme reactors has been routinely reprocessed for use in producing nuclear weapons or for reuse in new fuel.

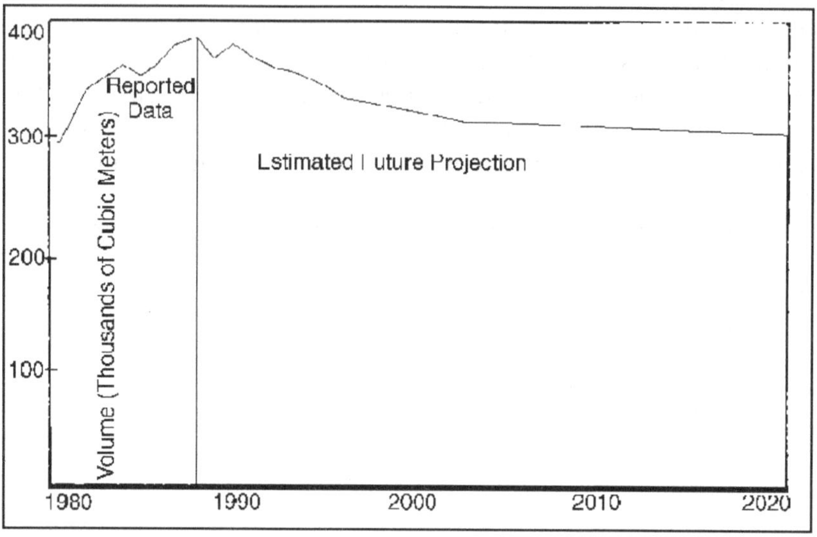

Fig. Historical and Projected Inventories of Defence High-Level Radioactive Waste

Compared to the total inventory of HLW, the volume of commercial HLW from the reprocessing of commercial spent fuel is almost insignificant, less than one per cent. Defence-related HLW comprises greater than ninety-nine per cent of the volume of HLW. Figure shows the historical and projected volume of defence-related HLW through the year 2020. The effect of the end of the "Cold War" on these projections is uncertain.

HLW is now stored in underground tanks or stainless steel silos on federal reservations in South Carolina, Idaho, and Washington and at the Nuclear Fuel Services Plant in West Valley, NY. These facilities have begun programmes to solidify and structurally stabilize the waste in preparation for disposal at a national repository.

Some elements, such as plutonium, in HLW and spent fuel are highly radioactive and remain so for thousands of years. Therefore, the safe disposal of this waste is one of the most controversial environmental subjects facing the federal government and affected states. The federal government (the EPA, the DOE, and the NRC) has overall responsibility for the safe disposal of HLW and spent fuel.

The EPA is responsible for developing environmental standards that apply to both DOE-operated and NRC-licensed facilities. Currently, the NRC is responsible for licensing such facilities and ensuring their compliance with the EPA standards. DOE is responsible for developing the deep geologic repository which has been authorized by Congress for disposing of spent fuel and high level waste. Both the NRC and the Department of Transportation are responsible for regulating the transportation of these wastes to storage and disposal sites.

In the early 1980's, the DOE formally adopted a national strategy to develop mined geologic repositories as disposal facilities for spent fuel and high-level radioactive waste. In 1983, the DOE identified nine potentially acceptable sites and, in 1984, selected three sites as candidates for further characterization. In 1987, Congress directed the DOE to pursue the investigation of only the Yucca Mountain, NV site in order to determine whether the site is suitable for development as a repository.

The DOE has designed a comprehensive "site characterization" programme to evaluate the suitability of the Yucca Mountain site.

The objectives of this programme are to:

- Determine the geologic, hydrologic, and geochemical conditions at Yucca Mountain;
- Provide information needed to design a package for the disposal of radioactive waste;
- Provide information for the design of the repository facility; and
- Evaluate whether Yucca Mountain can meet NRC and EPA protection and safety requirements.

The DOE is also developing plans for the siting and development of a potential Monitored Retrievable Storage (MRS) facility. The MRS facility could be used to receive and store spent fuel from commercial power reactors for subsequent shipment to a repository when such a facility becomes operational.

In 1985, the EPA published final regulations that established generally applicable environmental standards for the management and disposal of spent nuclear fuel, HLW, and transuranic (TRU) wastes. The disposal portion of these standards was successfully challenged in the courts and returned to the Agency for revision. The court was primarily concerned that the regulations might not adequately protect ground water and individuals from radioactive contamination. Following the court's ruling in 1987, the EPA worked to re-promulgate the disposal portion of these standards. In October 1992, two laws were enacted, the Waste Isolation Pilot Plant (WIPP) Land Withdrawal Act and the Energy Policy Act, that affected EPA's development of standards for the management and disposal of spent nuclear fuel, HLW and TRU wastes. The Energy Policy Act directs the EPA to issue environmental standards, which protect public health and safety and are specific to the Yucca Mountain site. The Act also requires that the National Academy of Sciences (NAS) conduct a study to provide findings and recommendations related to the form and content of environmental radiation protection standards for Yucca Mountain, Nevada. The EPA's standards for Yucca Mountain must be developed based upon the findings and recommendations of the NAS and must be issued within one year from the time ' the EPA receives the NAS recommendations. NRC, as the licensing authority for this site, must incorporate the EPA's environmental standards in their overall licensing regulations for HLW disposal (10 CFR 60).

TRANSURANIC RADIOACTIVE WASTE

Transuranic (TRU) waste materials have been generated in the U.S. since the 1940's. Most of this waste originates from nuclear weapons production facilities for defence programmes. "Transuranic" refers to atoms of man-made elements that are heavier (higher in atomic number) than uranium. The most prominent element in most TRU waste is plutonium. Some TRU waste consists of items such as rags, tools, and laboratory equipment contaminated with radioactive materials. Other forms of TRU waste include organic and inorganic residues or even entire enclosed contaminated cases in which radioactive materials were handled.

Some TRU waste emits high levels of penetrating radiation; this type requires protective shielding. However, most TRU waste does not emit high levels of penetrating radiation but poses a danger when small particles of it are inhaled or ingested. The radiation from the particles is damaging to lung tissue and internal organs. As long as this type of TRU waste remains enclosed and contained, it can be handled safely. Another problem with TRU waste is that most of its radioactive elements are long-lived. That is, they stay radioactive for a long time. For example, half of the original amount of plutonium-239 in the waste will remain harmful after 24,000 years. Disposal must be carefully planned so that the waste poses no undue threat to public health or the environment for years to come.

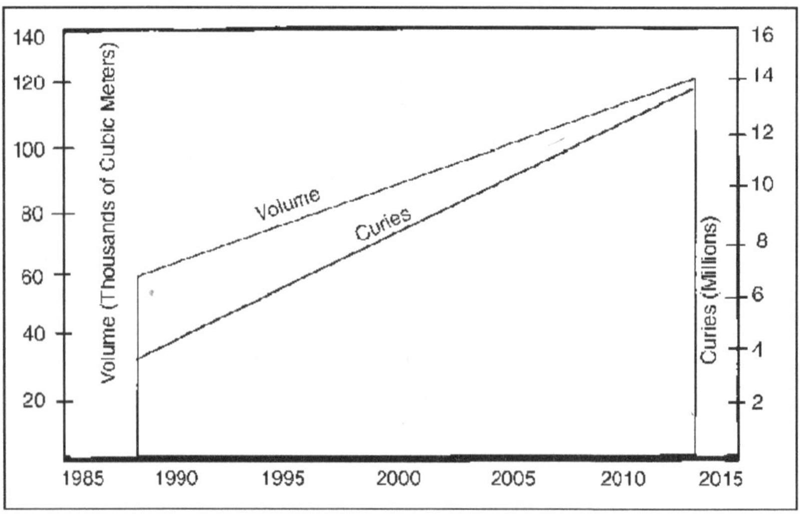

Fig. DOE Accumulated TRU Waste

The total volume of TRU waste and TRU contaminated soil is estimated at around one million cubic meters. Figure provides the historical and projected amounts of TRU wastes to the year 2015.

In the past, much of the TRU waste was disposed of similarly to low-level radioactive waste, *i.e.,* in pits and trenches covered with soil. In 1970, the Atomic Energy Commission (predecessor to the DOE) decided that TRU waste should be stored for easy retrieval to await disposal at a repository.

The DOE has evaluated several alternatives for managing buried waste and contaminated soil including:

- Leaving it in place and monitoring it;
- Leaving it in place and improving the containment; and
- Removing, processing, and disposing of the waste in a repository.

As a first step in developing a permanent disposal site for TRU waste, the DOE is developing an underground, geologic repository called the Waste Isolation Pilot Plant (WIPP), near Carlsbad, NM. This site has been excavated in a salt bed about 2,100 feet underground. The WIPP will have to meet environmental standards established by the EPA before it can be used as a permanent disposal site. If the WIPP site is eventually determined to be suitable for the disposal of TRU waste, the underground disposal area is planned to cover 100 acres. It will have a design capacity of over 2 million cubic meters, or about 850,000 barrels, of TRU waste.

As stated earlier, the EPA established environmental standards applicable to spent fuel, HLW and TRU waste, but they were returned to the Agency by the courts for revision. While the Energy Policy Act specifies procedures for developing standards for a repository at Yucca Mountain, NV, the Waste Isolation Pilot Plant (WIPP) Land Withdrawal Act requires the EPA to promulgate final standards applicable to WIPP and all other spent nuclear fuel, HLW, and TRU waste disposal facilities other than those developed under the Nuclear Waste Policy Act of 1982.

The WIPP Land Withdrawal Act reinstated all of the EPA's 1985 radioactive waste disposal standards except for the sections that the court found problematic, *i.e.,* the Individual and Ground-Water Protection Requirements of the disposal standards. The reinstated sections consist primarily of containment requirements and assurance requirements. These requirements are designed to help ensure that the wastes will be disposed of in a manner that limits the release of radioactive materials. In 1993, EPA finalized amendments to the standards to address the court's concerns. Individual radiation protection standards will limit a person's total annual radiation exposure, considering the sum of all possible exposures.

Under the WIPP Land Withdrawal Act, Congress gave EPA the responsibility for implementing its radioactive waste disposal standards at the WIPP. The Act also requires the EPA to review and approve of the DOE's plans for testing and retrieving waste at the WIPP. EPA must also ensure compliance with all federal environmental laws and regulations.

In order for the WIPP to become a permanent disposal facility, the EPA must certify that the facility complies with its disposal standards. If the EPA does not certify the WIPP, the DOE must decommission the facility. Even if the EPA certifies the WIPP, the Agency will have to determine, on an ongoing basis, whether it continues to comply with the disposal standards as well as all other federal environmental laws, regulations, and permit requirements that apply. In particular, DOE must demonstrate that the WIPP complies with the Clean Air Act; the Comprehensive Environmental Response, Compensation, and Liability Act; the Solid Waste Disposal Act; the Safe Drinking Water Act; and the Resource Conservation and Recovery Act.

URANIUM MILL TAILINGS

Uranium mill tailings are the radioactive sandlike materials that remain after uranium is extracted by milling ore mined from the earth. Tailings are placed in huge mounds called tailings piles which are located close to the mills where the ore is processed. The most important radioactive component of uranium mill tailings is radium, which decays to produce radon. Other potentially hazardous substances in the tailings are selenium, molybdenum, uranium, and thorium. Uranium mill tailings can adversely affect public health.

There are four principal ways (or exposure pathways) that the public can be exposed to the hazards from this waste. The first is the diffusion of radon gas directly into indoor air if tailings are misused as a construction material or for backfill around buildings. When people breathe air containing radon, it increases their risk of developing lung cancer. Second, radon gas can diffuse from the piles into the atmosphere where it can be inhaled and small particles can be blown from the piles where they can be inhaled or ingested.

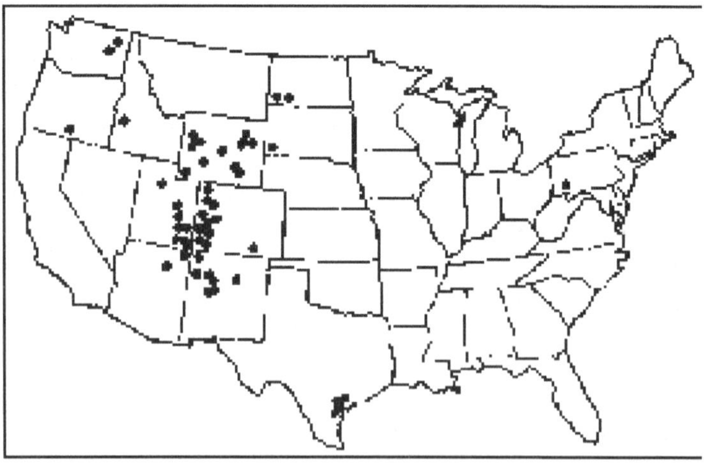

Fig. Uranium Mill Tailings Piles

Third, many of the radioactive decay products in tailings produce gamma radiation, which poses a health hazard to people in the immediate vicinity of tailings. Finally, the dispersal of tailings by wind or water, or by leaching, can carry radioactive and other toxic materials to surface or ground water that may be used for drinking water.

The NRC and some individual states that have regulatory agreements with the NRC have licensed 26 sites for milling uranium ore. However, most of the mills at these sites are no longer processing ore. Another 24 sites have been abandoned and are currently the responsibility of DOE. All the tailings piles except for one abandoned site located in Canonsburg, PA, are located in the West, predominantly in arid areas. The licensed tailings piles contain a combined total of approximately 200 million metric tons (MT), with individual piles ranging from about 2 million MT to about 30 million MT. (A metric ton is 2,200 pounds.) The 24 abandoned sites contain a total of about 26 million MT and range in size from about 50 thousand MT to about 3 million MT. It is unlikely that there will be much additional accumulation of mill tailings in the U.S., because foreign countries now produce uranium much more cheaply than can domestic producers.

The EPA issued two sets of standards controlling hazards from uranium mill tailings in 1983, under the authority of the Uranium Mill Tailings Radiation Control Act of 1978. These standards provide for the cleanup and disposal of mill tailings at abandoned sites and the disposal of tailings at licensed sites after cessation of operations. They are implemented by DOE, NRC, and some states through agreements with NRC, and require a combination of active and passive controls to clean up contaminated ground water as well as tailings that have been misused at off-site locations, and to dispose of tailings in a manner that will prevent misuse, limit radon emissions, and protect ground water.

Active controls include building fences, putting up warning signs, and establishing land use restrictions. Passive controls include constructing thick earthen covers, protected by rock and designed to prevent seepage into ground water, over the waste. Earthen covers also effectively limit radon emissions and gamma radiation and, in conjunction with the rock covers, serve to stabilize the piles to prevent dispersion of the tailings through erosion or intrusion. In some cases, piles may be moved to safer locations.

The standards were amended in 1993 to require that all licensed sites that have ceased operation undergo remedial action as soon as possible. The EPA is in the process of enacting revised ground-water protection standards that will require the same treatment of ground water at the abandoned sites as is now required at the licensed sites. In addition, EPA enacted Clean Air Act standards in 1989 limiting radon emissions and restricting the length of time that abandoned piles may remain uncovered with no controls on radon emissions. EPA also requires that any piles that may be constructed in the future meet requirements that limit radon emissions and inhibit ground-water contamination during their operational phase. Licensed mills also are subject to the Uranium Fuel Cycle standard which regulates radionuclide emissions other than radon.

LOW-LEVEL RADIOACTIVE WASTE

Low-level radioactive waste (LLW) is radioactively contaminated industrial or research waste such as paper, rags, plastic bags, protective clothing, cardboard, packaging material, organic fluids, and water-treatment residues. It is waste that does not fall into any of the three categories previously discussed. Its classification does not directly depend on the level of radioactivity it contains. LLW is generated by government facilities, utilities, industries, and institutional facilities.

In addition to 35 major DOE facilities, over 20,000 commercial users of radioactive materials generate some amount of LLW. LLW generators include approximately 100 operating nuclear power reactors, associated fuel fabrication facilities, and uranium fuel conversion plants, which together are known as nuclear fuel-cycle facilities. Hospitals, medical schools, universities, radiochemical and radiopharmaceutical manufacturers and research laboratories are other users of radioactive materials which produce LLW. The clean-up of contaminated buildings and sites will generate more LLW in the future.

Figure provides a historical look at the overall volume of LLW produced through 1990. It also projects that the volume will double by 2020. Figure below shows the volume of low-level radioactive waste disposed of by major sources in the United States.

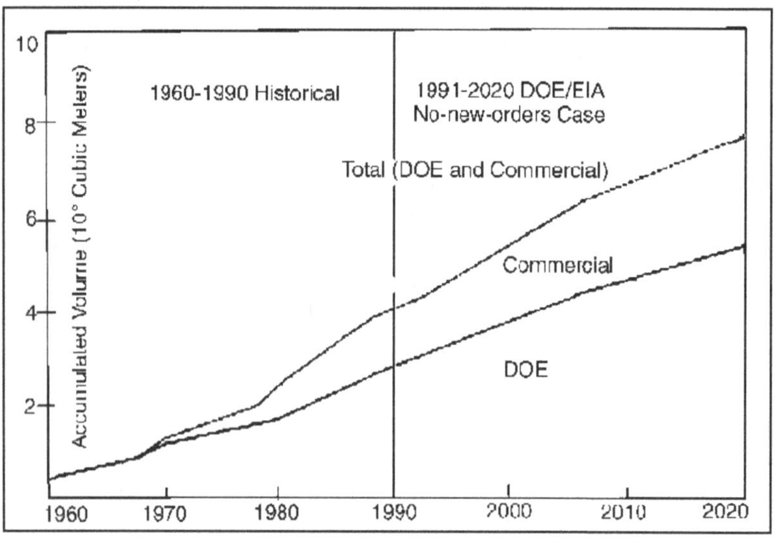

Fig. Historical and Projected Accumulated Volumes of LLW

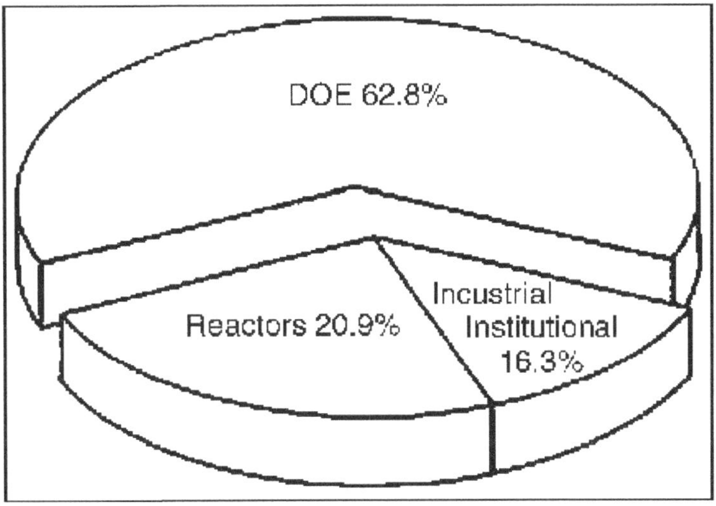

Fig. Volume of LLW Disposed

The EPA has the authority to set generally applicable environmental standards for LLW disposal; such standards would be implemented by the NRC and the DOE. DOE is planning the clean-up of radioactively contaminated sites which will result in considerable volumes of LLW.

Because of this, EPA is developing cleanup regulations as well as general environmental standards for LLW disposal. EPA plans to propose the disposal standards at the end of 1994.

The standards will facilitate planning and reduce costs for clean-up and disposal. The NRC and some individual states that have regulatory agreements with NRC regulate all disposal of commercial LLW. In 1982, the NRC improved its regulatory requirements. That year, the NRC established disposal site performance objectives for land disposal of LLW technical requirements for the siting, design, operation, and closure for near-surface disposal facilities; technical requirements concerning waste packaging for land disposal; classification of waste; institutional requirements; and administrative and procedural requirements for licensing a disposal facility.

Though the 1982 NRC regulations exempted existing NRC disposal site licensees, the NRC and the states are working to incorporate such requirements into those licenses. In 1988, the DOE, which is self-regulating, issued its own orders governing the DOE disposal sites. The general regulatory framework for the disposal of LLW has changed to account for new technology, what we have learned from past disposal practices, and current wisdom about environmental protection.

As a result of increasing costs of LLW disposal at existing sites, pre-disposal waste processing (*e.g.,* volume reduction) is a more common practice. The waste is processed by separating radioactive from nonradioactive components and by compacting bulk waste before packaging for disposal. Consequently, while the volume of waste to be disposed of is reduced, the concentration of radioactivity is greater. This waste requires more stringent safeguards for its disposal.

The first of six regional, commercial LLW disposal sites was licensed in 1962. Since then, four of the commercial sites have closed, mainly because of problems with site instability.

These problems included the collapse of the earth covering the waste and difficulties in managing surface-and ground-water contamination. Since then the technology and requirements governing disposal sites have been upgraded. New disposal facilities must be designed to avoid two kinds of failures: those caused by long-term processes such as subsidence and those caused by more unpredictable events such as human intrusion (either intentional or unintentional) and natural disaster. The Low-Level Radioactive Waste Policy Act of 1980 and subsequent amendments direct states to take care of their own LLW either individually or through regional groupings, referred to as compacts.

The states are now in the process of selecting new LLW disposal sites to take care of their own waste. The selection process for these new sites is complex and varies because of many factors including the regulations for site selection. This selection process will be affected by EPA's new LLW standard.

DISPOSAL OF NATURALLY OCCURRING AND ACCELERATOR-PRODUCED WASTES

Accelerator-produced radioactive waste is produced during the operation of atomic particle accelerators for medical, research, or industrial purposes. The accelerators use magnetic fields to move atomic particles at higher and higher speeds before crashing into a preselected target. This reaction produces desired radioactive materials in metallic targets or kills cancer cells where a cancer tumor is the target.

The radioactivity contained in the waste from accelerators is generally short-lived, less than one year. The waste may be stored at laboratories or production facilities until it is no longer radioactive. An extremely small fraction of the waste may retain some longer-lived radioactivity with half lives greater than one year. There are no firm estimates of the amount of this type of radioactive waste; however, it is generally accepted that the volume is extremely small compared to the other wastes discussed.

Naturally occurring radioactive materials (NORM) generally contain radionuclides found in nature. Once NORM becomes concentrated through human activity, such as mineral extraction, it can become a radioactive waste.

There are two types of naturally occurring radioactive waste:

1. Discrete and
2. Diffuse.

Estimates of the volumes of discrete NORM waste are imprecise, and the EPA is conducting studies to provide a more accurate assessment of how much of this waste requires attention. Because of its relatively high concentration of radioactivity, this type of waste poses a direct radiation exposure hazard. The second type, diffuse NORM, has a much lower concentration of radioactivity, but a high volume of waste. This type of waste poses a different type of disposal problem because of its high volume.

The safe disposal of radioactive waste is a very important issue today. Radioactive waste disposal standards have changed substantially with improved technology and evolving environmental protection considerations.

SOURCES OF HAZARDOUS WASTES

Hazardous wastes can be solids, gases, liquids, or semi-liquids like mining sludge and drilling mud. Most of the wastes listed by the EPA are liquids or semi-liquids. Thousands of waste materials are considered hazardous. These include familiar items like used motor oil and mercury, agricultural pesticides, and industrial materials such as asbestos and polychlorinated biphenyls (PCBs). United States industries, farms, mines, military facilities, cities, and small businesses generate roughly 200 million tons of hazardous wastes each year. Furthermore, the EPA estimates that there are presently 6,500 facilities in the United States that require hazardous waste clean-up under the directives of the 1976 Resource Conservation and Reclamation Act (RCRA) and its 1984 Hazardous and Solid Waste Amendments (HSWA).

Hazardous waste management is also an international issue. Each year, industrialized nations with strict environmental regulations export more than two million tons of hazardous waste for disposal in poorer developing nations with less stringent wastedisposal oversight. Developed nations also locate large corporate, industrial, and military facilities in countries that have lax environmental restrictions. Hazardous wastes often cause problems for years after their disposal. Many industrial waste disposal sites were established, filled, and buried long before establishment of present-day standards for management and disposal of hazardous chemicals.

Toxic, flammable, corrosive, and reactive chemicals are often long-lived, and sometimes the dangers they posed to the environment and to human health were unknown at the time of their disposal. The industries responsible for many pre-1970 hazardous waste sites are no longer in business, and sometimes the sites themselves are difficult to locate. Even modern legislation gives industries fairly broad leeway to produce chemicals, police their own waste disposal practices, and to contest cases of possible environmental or human health damage. It is often extremely difficult to prove a scientific link between an incident of drinking water poisoning, or a human disease cluster, and a facility that improperly handles industrial chemicals.

Hazardous wastes are by-products of human activities that could cause substantial harm to human health or the environment if improperly managed. The United States Environmental Protection Agency (EPA) classifies liquid, solid, and gaseous discarded materials and emissions as hazardous if they are poisonous (toxic), flammable, corrosive, or chemically reactive at levels above specified safety thresholds.

In the United States, the term hazardous waste generally refers to potentially dangerous or polluting chemical compounds; other potentially hazardous industrial, military, agricultural, and municipal byproducts, including biological contaminants and radioactive waste, are regulated by other government agencies than the EPA's hazardous waste division.

The handling of hazardous wastes became a major political issue in the late 1970s in the United States and other industrialized nations when a number of high-profile human health and environmental pollution crises focused public attention on the problem. Since then, many governments have greatly expanded regulation of hazardous waste management, disposal practices, and clean-up. In the United States, the EPA oversees hazardous waste regulations that attempt to prevent new cases of environmental and human contamination, as well as the so-called "Superfund" programme that addresses clean-up of sites contaminated in the past.

INDUSTRIAL HAZARDOUS WASTES

Four types of industry account for about 90% of industrial hazardous wastes generated in the United States: chemical manufacturing, primary metal production, metal fabrication, and petroleum processing. Large chemical plants and petroleum refineries, and other "large quantity generators" that produce more than 2,200 lb (1,000 kg) of hazardous wastes per month, are the most visible and heavily regulated facilities in the United States. However, businesses of all sizes generate dangerous chemicals; the EPA currently lists more than 250,000 facilities as "small-quantity generators" of hazardous waste. These diverse, smaller producers account for about 10% of the potentially harmful substances produced each year.

Pesticides like malathion, DDT, and diazanon are hazardous chemicals; some of them have been banned, but many are still manufactured and used in the United States. Pesticides are designed to kill pest insects, plants, and other organisms that threaten agricultural crops, destroy municipal and residential landscaping, and carry human diseases. Most pesticides are dangerous chemicals themselves, and their manufacture produces additional hazardous waste.

The EPA's Hazardous Waste division regulates handling, disposal, and clean-up of pesticides during their production, but environmental pollution and human health effects caused by pesticides after application are not included in hazardous waste regulations. (The EPA's Office of Pesticide Programmes oversees pesticide use and handles cases where pesticides in agricultural or landscaping run-off pollute air and water or compromise human health.)

OTHER SOURCES

Other types of hazardous wastes are associated with military bases, mines, residential communities, and small businesses. Though large industry produces the majority of hazardous waste in the United States, the small quantity generators (SQGs) that produce between 220 and 2,200 lbs (100–1,000 kg) of hazardous waste per month present particular regulatory challenges:

- The chemicals used by auto garages, dry cleaners, construction companies, scientific labs, photo developers, printers, large offices, and farmers are often toxic.
- Hazardous wastes generated by SQGs are much more varied than those produced by large companies. Each chemical, be it a month's supply of dry cleaning fluid or a house-worth of residential insulation, requires its own handling and disposal strategy.
- SQGs, who do not have the legal and administrative support common at large companies, often have difficulty deciphering hazardous waste regulations. Noncompliance can result from simple ignorance of a small business's responsibility to follow environmental laws.

United States military bases have some of the most serious hazardous waste problems in the nation, an issue only recently addressed by government and private environmental agencies. About 19,000 sites at 1,800 military installations show some degree of soil or groundwater pollution. More than 90 military bases have been on the EPA's Superfund list of high-priority, hazardous waste cleanup sites.

Moreover, a law passed in 1992 allows federal and state regulatory agencies to levy fines against the military if their hazardous wastes are not properly managed. Prior to this, the armed forces were not subject to state or federal environmental laws.

Consequently, the military now has a range of programmes to clean up hazardous waste problems at its bases. Mining waste, a type of industrial waste, often includes hazardous substances. Mining operations commonly use hazardous chemicals, and sometimes naturally toxic substances are released into the environment during mining and the disposal of its waste materials. For example, gold mining in the Amazon Basin of South America results in the release of 90–120 tons of mercury into rivers every year. This has resulted in elevated levels of mercury in fish and humans in the region.

Mercury poisoning results in severe birth defects, neurological disorders, kidney failure, and a number of other serious health effects. Chemical separation of ore minerals like lead, iron, and zinc from their host rocks creates socalled acid-mine drainage that contains both the toxic chemicals used in the separation process like arsenic and sulfuric acid, and poisonous heavy metals like lead and mercury. Acid-mine drainage from metal mining in the American West has contaminated drinking water and caused serious ecological damage since the mid-1800s. Household hazardous wastes are discarded products used in the home, which contain dangerous substances. Examples include paint, motor oil, antifreeze, drain cleaner, and pesticides.

In the 1980s, many local governments in the North America began to set up regular collection programmes for household hazardous wastes, to ensure that they are properly disposed or recycled. Local or state/provincial governments usually pay the costs of such programmes.

However, a system used in British Columbia, Canada, requires consumers to pay an "eco-fee" on paint they buy. This, along with funds provided by the paint industry, helps pay for a collection programme for waste paint from households.

HALF-LIFE PERIOD

Physicists have discovered that the number of nuclei decays on a time unit is proportional to the number of all nuclei in the sample. The quantity of the number of decays in the period of time in which they proceeded is called the activity of the radioactive source:

$$A = \frac{N}{t}$$

The unit for *A* is *1 becquerel* (1 Bq). The source has the activity of one becqerel, if during each second one nucleus decays. Further researches have shown that the activity of the sample decreases as the time passes accordingly to the formula:

$$A = A_0 \cdot e^{-kt}$$

where: *A0* is the initial activity, *e* is the Euler number, *A* is the activity after the time *t*, *k* is the quantity called the decay constant and is different for different/various radioactive sources. And if we use the fact that the activity of a source is proportional to the number of nuclei in the sample,

we get:

$$N = N_0 \cdot e^{-kt}$$

During the decay the number of radioactive nuclei decreases exponentially as the time passes. The period of time after which the number of radioactive nuclei of the particular element decreases twice is referred to as the *half-life period* (*T*) of that radioactive element. This period can be calculated from the formula below:

$$T = \frac{\ln 2}{k}$$

because *N* = *N0/2*.

The half-live periods for various sources are given in the table below:

Isotope		Half–life
Carbon	14C	5700 years
Iodine	131I	8 days
Polonium	214Po	1.6 × 10–4 second
Radium	226Ra	1620 years
Uranium	238U	4.5 × 109 yerars

The course of the radioactive decay is not strictly determined. On our pages some phenomena of the atom described by the probability. It is the same with the radioactive decay.

Whether the particular nucleus decays in the next minute or not, is given with some probability, characteristic for each radioactive isotope. Because of that, in a sample of some radioactive material some atoms would decay in the first minute of the observation, some other in the hundredth minute, and some other even in a couple of days or even years.

The radioactive decay is described by the laws of statistics. If there is some number of atoms of some radioactive substance, then we can say how many of them would approximately decay in the first or in the hundredth minute. But no way we can say which ones these would be or give the precise number of the decays.

HOW TO CALCULATE HALF-LIFE

Half-life is the time period taken by a chemical substance that decays to decrease to half of its initial amount at a given time period. Half-life is usually calculated for radioactive elements.

This article on how to calculate half-life explains calculation of half-life using a formula and simple steps. Half lives are calculated for exponential as well as non-exponential decays.

In case of exponential decay the half-life is constant throughout the life of decay while in case of non-exponential decay half-life of the substances varies throughout the decay process. It is usually seen that radioactive elements undergo exponential decay. The half-life of a substance is denoted by t1/2. The half-life period of a substance was initially called as 'dating'. Well, it has nothing to do with 'dating' a boy or girl!

The original formula for calculating half-life of a substance is given as, In the above formula,

- "N0" is the original amount of radioactive isotope that is present before any decay has taken place.
- "Nt" it the amount of radioactive isotope that is left after a certain time period t.
- "t" is the time period after which the number of atoms within a radioactive element changes from N0 to Nt.
- "t1/2" is the half-life of the decaying substance

Using the above formula you can easily calculate the amount of radioactive left after a certain time period t.

You can also calculate the half-life of the radioactive decay, but to make it simple, let us evaluate the above formula. Simplifying the above formula to calculate half-life we get,

$$t1/2 = (t \times \log2)/\log (N0/Nt)$$

- To calculate the half-life of a substance you need to know the initial quantity of the radioactive substance and the amount of substance left after a time period t.
- You should also know the time period after which the substance has decayed to a particular quantity.
- Substituting the above values in the formula you can easily calculate the half-life of any radioactive substance.
- You also need a logarithmic chart and a calculator to perform the calculations.
- If you are not familiar with finding the logs using the charts then you can either use scientific calculators or online calculators to find the logarithmic values.

Let us illustrate this using a simple example.

Suppose the number of atoms of a radioactive isotope is 1676 at time 0 and after a certain time, say 4 minutes, the number of atoms left behind are 1358.

From the above information,

- N0 = 1676
- Nt = 1358
- t = 4 minutes

Substituting the above vales in the formula for calculating half-life,

$$t1/2 = (t \times \log2)/\log (N0/Nt)$$
$$t1/2 = (4 \times \log2/\log (1676/1358)$$
$$t1/2 = 4 \times 0.3010/0.09131$$
$$t1/2 = 13.1858 \text{ minutes}$$

Therefore, half-life of this radioactive isotope *i.e.,* the time taken by the isotope to decay half of its atoms every time is 13.1858 minutes.

Instead of using the formula for calculating half-life of a substance you can use a manual method for calculating half-life of a substance. Suppose the initial number of atoms of a radioactive isotope is 2016 and after 35 days it decays to 63. Calculate the half-life of the substance.

Here,

- N0 = 2016
- Nt = 63
- t = 35 days

Now, divide the initial amount of the substance (2016) by 2 until it is reduced to the 63. Doing this we get the values as,

- First half-life = 2016/2 = 1008
- Second half-life = 1008/2 = 504
- Third half-life = 504/2 = 252
- Fourth half-life = 252/2 = 126
- Fifth half-life = 126/2 = 63

Therefore, the substance takes five half lives to undergo a decay from 2016 to 63. This means that it takes 35 days to complete 5 half lives. Therefore,

Each half-life = t1/2 = 35/5

Therefore,

t1/2 = 7 days

RADIOACTIVE HALF LIFE EQUATION

The half life period of a radioactive substance is defined as the time required for one half of the radioactive substance to disintegrate. The following graph shows the amount of radioactive substance a compared to original amount Ao. T is the half life of the radioactive element.

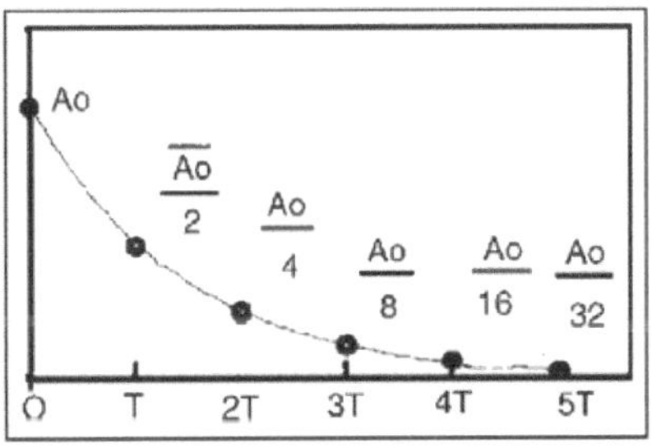

Fig. Explanation of Graph

For a given radioactive element, at the end of time only 50% of the radioactive element remain unchanged; at the end of 2 only 25% remain unchanged after 3 12.5%, after 4 6.35% and so on.

Rutherford and Soddy found that the rate at which a particular radioactive material disintegrates was independent of physical and chemical conditions. The number of atoms that break up at any instant is proportional to the number of atoms present at that instant. Let N be the number of atoms present in a particular radio element at a given instant t. Then the rate of decrease $\frac{-dN}{dt}$ is proportional to N

$$\therefore -\frac{dN}{dt} = \lambda N$$

where l is the decay constant of the radioactive element. l is defined as the ratio of amount of the substance which disintegrates in a unit time to the amount of substance present.

$$\lambda = -\frac{\frac{dN}{dt}}{N}$$

Equation 1 is written as

$$\frac{dN}{N} = -\lambda t$$

Integrating,

$\log_e N = -\lambda t + C$————(2)

where C is integration constant. Let the number of radioactive atoms at time t=0 is N0

$\therefore \log_e(N_0) = C$

Plugging in the value of C in 2

$$\log N = -\lambda t + \log(N_0)$$

or

$$\log_e\left(\frac{N}{N_0}\right) = -\lambda t$$

$N = N_0 e^{-\lambda t}$————(3)

This equation shows the number of atoms of a given radioactive substance decreases exponentially with time. We use this equation to derive the half life equation of radioactive elements.

Derivation of Radioactive Half Life Equation

$T_{\frac{1}{2}}$ is the half life period

At time t= $T_{\frac{1}{2}}$, N = $\frac{N_0}{2}$

$$\therefore \frac{N_0}{2} = N_0 e - \lambda t$$

$$\Rightarrow e^{\lambda T\frac{1}{2}} = 2$$

$$\Rightarrow \lambda T\frac{1}{2} = \log_e(2)$$

$$\Rightarrow T_{\frac{1}{2}} = \frac{\log_e(2)}{\lambda}$$

$$\Rightarrow T_{\frac{1}{2}} = \frac{0.6931}{\lambda}$$

This is the equation of half life of radioactive elements.

HALF LIFE IN NUCLEAR CHEMISTRY

The half-life of radioactive elements is a part of nuclear chemistry. Half-life occurs naturally in some of the radioactive elements while it could be artificially stimulated in some other elements. This article gives a brief introduction to half-life in nuclear chemistry. Nuclear chemistry is a sub-branch of chemistry. This branch deals with the nuclear processes, radioactivity and nuclear properties. Chemical reactions are the result of the interaction of electrons on the nucleus of an atom while nuclear reactions are different from the traditional chemical reactions and involve the changes in the composition of the nuclei.

A nuclear reaction releases enormous amount of energy. The field of nuclear chemistry was expanded in 1896, when Henri Becquerel discovered that the uranium emitted radiation. Marie Sklodowska Curie turned her focus on studying radioactivity. She propounded the theory that radiation is proportional to the amount of radioactive element present at a give time. She also found out that radiation was a property of an atom. In her lifetime she discovered the two radioactive elements polonium and radium. In 1902, another scientist, Fredrick Soddy, discovered that when a radioactivity occurs; a nuclear reaction changes the nucleus of an atom resulting in the change in the atom. He proposed that all naturally radioactive elements would decay into lighter elements.

The half-life of a radioactive element is the time required for the element to decay to half of the original amount. For instance, half-life is the time period during which half of the atom of a radioactive element undergoes a nuclear process to be reduced into a lighter element.

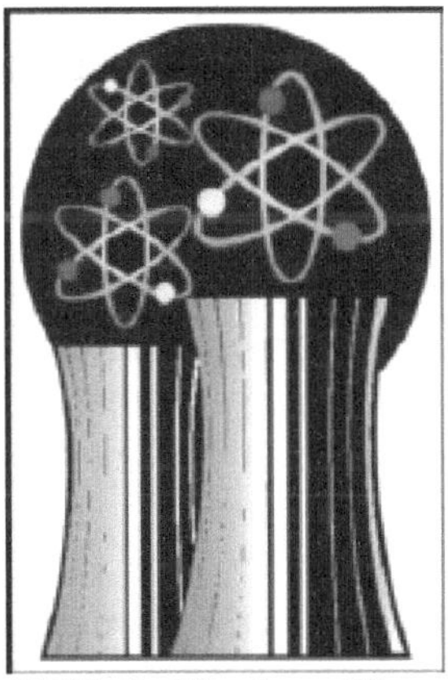

As mentioned above, half-life in Nuclear Chemistry is a decay process of a radioactive element. Each and every radioactive element has its own half-life. For instance, 238U has a half-life of 4.5 billion years. That is, sup>238U would take 4.5 billion years to decay into other lighter elements. Another interesting fact is half-life of 14C is 5730 years and this is very helpful in geological dating of any archaeological material. You must know, the nuclear half-lives of various radioactive elements would range from tiny fractions of a second to many billion years. You wouldn't be able to predict when a nucleus of a radioactive element would decay but you can calculate how much of the element would decay over a given period of time. For instance, if you have 5 grams of a radioactive element, after decaying there would be just half the amount of the original *i.e,* 2.5 grams. After another half-life, the amount of radioactive element left would be 1.25 gram. Here is a formula to calculate half-life of a nuclear element.

AE = Ao * 0.5t/t1/2

Where

AE = Amount of substance left

Ao = Original amount of substance

t = Elapsed time

t1/2 = Half-life of the substance

Try this problem out as an example. For instance, if you are given 157 grams of 14C, how much of 14C would be left after 2000 years. The half-life of 14C is 5730 years.

AE = 157 *.52000/5730

Amount of 14C left after 2000 years would be 123 grams.

Three types of natural radioactive decay include alpha radiation, beta radiation and gamma radiation. An alpha radiation is the emission of two protons and two neutrons. An alpha emission is a positive charge and has a helium nucleus. A beta radiation emits more neutrons than protons and has negative charge. In a gamma radiation, the nucleus emits rays in the gamma part of the spectrum. Another interesting fact is a gamma ray has neither mass nor a charge. While many radioactive elements decay naturally, you can also stimulate a nuclear reaction artificially. The artificially stimulated nuclear reactions are nuclear fusion and nuclear fission.

EFFECTS ON PLANTS

With advances in veterinary medicine, radiation therapy is increasingly being used to treat cancerous tumors in animals. Radiation can affect normal and cancer cells, but the localized rays of radiation can cure or control tumors that may not be killed by surgery or chemotherapy alone.

FUNCTION

Cancer in animals works much the same way as it does in humans—dysfunctional cells begin to over-multiply, and this growth causes them to eat and destroy the healthy cells around them. Radiation therapy works by sending a concentrated dose of ionizing radiation to the tumor site and destroying the DNA of the cancerous cells so they can no longer reproduce.

EFFECTS

Veterinarians will commonly use radiation in conjunction with surgery or chemotherapy to control or kill tumors that have not metastasized, or spread to other parts of the body. In cases in which it does not totally destroy the tumor, radiation can be used to palliative effect, shrinking the mass and relieving signs of the disease, thus improving quality of life for the animal.

TIME FRAME

Animals normally receive radiation therapy in a series of treatments spanning from two to five weeks and in 10 to 15 minute increments. The number of treatments and the length of dosage time depend on the size, type and location of the tumor and will be determined by the veterinary oncologist.

CONSIDERATIONS

Nasal and oral tumors often respond well to localized radiation therapy. Radiation may also be used in treating some small skin cancers and has been successfully used in animals with brain cancer. In cats and dogs, radiation therapy in conjunction with chemotherapy, has been successful in treating some lymphomas.

Radiation therapy is also commonly used in the management of bone cancer, called osteosarcoma. Another consideration for owners to remember is that their pets have to be perfectly still during the duration of the treatments, so they will need to be repeatedly anesthetized. This is not usually a problem for most animals as the down time coincides with the length of the treatment and is often quite short. Side effects of radiation therapy usually occur within three months after discontinuing treatment and may include dry, itchy skin, alopecia (hair loss) and hyperpigmentation (discolouration) of the skin around the tumor site. If the tumor was a nasal or oral tumor, the mucosal areas of the nose and mouth may become inflamed and irritated. In addition, these particular tumors often release a disagreeable odour as the cancerous cells die. More serious side effects may include some nerve damage and either the death or hardening (called fibrosis) of healthy tissue.

PREVENTION/SOLUTION

When skin conditions develop after radiation, regular cleaning of the affected area is usually recommended. Veterinarians may also prescribe pain medications and require that animals wear an E-collar so they cannot lick or chew the skin. Mucosal irritation associated with radiation therapy of oral or nasal tumors can be decreased with tea or warm-water flushes. While these conditions are temporary and require some nursing care, skin discolouration and loss of hair is often permanent. Plants do not have to worry much about radiation. Experiments have been conducted that show that radiation is really only a problem when a plant is in the stage of a seed. Still, large amounts of radiation can destroy any material, including plant material.

SEED

High doses of radiation can cause seeds to not sprout, grow slowly, lose fertility or develop genetic mutations that can change characteristics of the plant.

EFFECTS OF RADIATION ON PLANT GROWTH AND DEVELOPMENT

- Prevents Seed Growth : Ultraviolet radiation affects plant growth and development in many ways. First, it gradually stops seed growth and sprouting, depended on the how much radiation is released. Soil can become compacted and lose the nutrients needed for plants to grow. The results of various lab experiments supplying Ultraviolet radiation through filtered lamps proved that higher doses of radiation administered to the plants were very damaging.
- Disrupts Stomata Resistance : The stomata is a small air hole within a plant leaf that also controls water levels. If there is too much evaporation due to intense radiation, the stomata closes to reserve water. If the stomata is unable to open for a long period of time, the growth of the plant is stunted. Prolonged periods of radiation can completely damage the stomata and destroy the plant.
- Damages Plant Cells : The cells of living organism are also damaged and killed by Ultraviolet radiation. What allows plants to grow is the division and expansion of cells as they take up water. Cells contain chromosomes, the genetic material responsible for plant reproduction. If the cell is overly damaged by radiation, then reproduction is hindered.
- Increases Cell Mutations : Because ultraviolet radiation destroys cells, the chances of mutation are great. Affected plants are often small and weak with altered leaf patterns.
- Reduces Plant Fertility : Prolonged radiation can completely destroy the fertility of a plant. The plant gradually dies. The surroundings become poisoned and prevent the growth of future offspring. Not all radiation is bad. Sunshine is a type of radiation that is needed for photosynthesis and normal plant growth.

EFFECTS ON HUMAN AND ANIMALS

WHICH TYPE OF RADIATION IS THE MOST HARMFUL

This question, like many is difficult to answer with few words. Many readers may not have even known that different kinds of radiation exist. If you don't, see What are the different types of radiation?

To determine which type of radiation is most harmful, we must first determine how far each one can travel.

The distance that radiation travels is important for two reasons:

1. The further it travels the more easily it will get to your body.
2. The distance it travels in your body, affects how much damage it does.

There are various things to consider when determining how far radiation will travel. For a discussion on this, see How does radiation get stopped? Alpha particles can not even penetrate a piece of ordinary paper, beta particles are stopped by a thin sheet of aluminum, while it takes an inch of lead (at least) to stop gamma rays. Thus, alpha and beta particles can not even penetrate through a person's skin, while gamma rays can get into the body and cause damage. For external radiation, Gamma rays are the most harmful

Of course, to every rule, there is at least one exception. If you eat or inhale an isotope that is an alpha emitter, it doesn't have to penetrate your skin anymore to get into the body. Some alpha emitters, when inhaled, can even pass into your blood and irradiate your whole body that way. In these situations, the alphas are most harmful because the side effect of slowing down quickly is that they deposit all their energy in a short distance, thus concentrating their effect.

It is because of this effect that smokers receive a much higher annual dose of radiation than non-smokers. Radioactive polonium (from the radon decay chain) gets deposited from the air onto tobacco leaves when they are dried. When the smoker inhales the smoke, they are also inhaling polonium and other isotopes in the decay chain, all of which are alpha and beta emitters. This radiation is harmful once it gets into the lungs.

THE EFFECTS OF ANIMALS

At the end of the Pleistocene Epoch, 11,000 years ago, wild horses roamed Alaska. There were steppe bison and musk oxen and wooly rhinos. Saiga antelopes, their bizarre-looking bulbous noses an adaptation to breathing cold dry air, were common here and in Siberia and throughout the Mammoth Steppes, as this type of habitat was called, as, of course were wooly mammoths, the quintessential Ice-Age creature. At times during the Pleistocene, which began 1.8 million years ago, mastodons lived here too, elephant-like creatures covered with long hair. Mastodons are browsers; they use their long trunks to pluck leaves from trees and woody shrubs. Horses and mammoths, on the other hand, eat mostly grass.

Fig. Musk Oxen like these Roamed the Earth During the Ice Ages.

In fact, of the 31 species of large herbivores that left fossil remains in the far north, 25 were primarily grazers, dependent on grass. Today, interior Alaska is a mosaic of spruce and birch forest, not the open, grassy expanse it was in the Pleistocene. "We're hard-pressed to find many grazers here today," said Eric Post, a Penn State ecologist who studies the interactions of climate change and animal populations in Alaska, Greenland, Norway, and Sweden.

During the Pleistocene, temperatures rose and fell several times, and the ice spread and retreated. Yet by the end of the epoch the average temperatures were about five degrees C higher than they had been. In this warmer environment, shrubs grew into and replaced the grasslands. Trees took hold. Humans extended their hunting grounds farther north. By 10,000 years ago, the horses and mammoths were extinct. But other Pleistocene creatures survived in the far north until today. Not mastodons, of course, but musk oxen, a mixed feeder that eats both grass and leaves, can still be found in isolated pockets. Caribou and moose likewise, along with the Saiga antelope.

The change predicted by the Terrestrial Ecosystem Model, a computer simulation used to predict the productivity of vegetation, is on the order of the change from the Pleistocene to today, assuming a doubling of the amount of carbon dioxide in the atmosphere. "But the warming now is expected to occur much more quickly," said Post, "on the order of one century, not several thousand years."

That warming will likely change the mix of plants and animals that live in the far north. But how? Because plants use carbon dioxide to photosynthesize, it's often suggested that a rise in carbon dioxide will benefit at least some species of plants. As long as the temperature is not high enough to cause the species heat stress, plants will be healthier, greener, and will push out more leaves. Animals that eat those plants should likewise prosper.

But Post found, studying caribou in western Greenland, that there was no simple correlation between herd size and rising temperatures. "Greenland is really a ring of islands separated by an enormous mass of ice called the Inland Ice," he explained.

"In historic times, caribou were found throughout Greenland, but they're gone now from most of the places they used to be." Using records of hunting kills to estimate the health of the remaining populations, Post and his colleagues learned that the herds have increased since the 1960s. "Is warming associated with that increase? Not really," Post said. "If you look at the temperature trends overall, in western Greenland there's been cooling. Western Greenland is an interesting anomaly. We see an increase in caribou because caribou is a Pleistocene species adapted to cold dry temperatures."

The musk oxen in northeastern Greenland likewise show a complicated pattern of response to temperature. "This is one of the few places where natural and sustained populations of musk oxen still exist," Post noted. Six distinct herds are separated by tongues of the ice sheet. They do not interbreed because, unlike caribou, Post explained, "musk oxen are not very mobile animals"; they can't cross the ice. Scientists have made yearly counts of each herd.

For the red deer in Norway, a creature like the North American elk, Post and his colleagues found that the effects of warming, while still complicated, were more clear. "Two years after a warm winter," Post explained, "the female segment of the red deer population increased—but not the male segment." This increase, the researchers determined, correlated with the time that coltsfoot and wood anenome, the earliest flowers, bloomed in the spring. "When they bloom early, the females that are pregnant have access to a very good source of food just when they need it. Their calves are more likely to survive and, if they're females, to reproduce as soon as they're mature, at two years." Elk on Raspberry Island in southwestern Alaska, Post said, showed a similar response. What can we draw from all these examples? Not much, unfortunately," Post remarked. "There are few consistent patterns. We can't really say if warming is good or bad for large mammals in the far north."

Yet by studying these herds of caribou, musk oxen, red deer, or elk, by trying to tease out what effects climate change might have on them, Post began to see that another important question needed to be asked: What effects might the animals themselves have on climate change? "Large mammals can have profound influences on the ecosystems in which they exist," Post said. "They may be components in how the larger system reacts to climate change." By preferring to eat some plants over others, herbivores suppress the growth of their favourite species while allowing "inferior competitors" to stay in the system. Moose on Isle Royale in Lake Michigan, for instance, prune balsam fir down to shrubs each winter, while ignoring nearby spruce. In Alaska, when researchers set up high fences to keep grazing animals out of a plot of grassland, they found more small flowering plants inside the protected space than outside. On grass, on the other hand, the effect of grazing can be positive, as the enclosures also demonstrated. "We call it the lawn-mower effect. The grass is adapted to having its top mown off, and it comes in much more lush."

The animals also influence how nutrients cycle through the soil. "This is the fertilizer effect. Where animals feed, the availability of nitrogen is much higher," Post said. Using what he called "very conservative estimates," Post calculated that five million caribou and reindeer directly contribute 264 million pounds of available nitrogen per year to their tundra habitat. Experiments on vegetation in the far north have shown that tundra vegetation is most limited by nitrogen availability. Plants there only respond to a rise in carbon dioxide if it is accompanied by a rise in temperature. The temperature rise increases the activity of the soil microbes that turn over nitrogen through the processes of rot and decay. Only with the additional nitrogen can the plants make use of additional carbon dioxide.

The Terrestrial Ecosystem Models currently used to predict the extent of climate change contain an estimate of nitrogen flux, yet so far the animal contribution has not been factored into it. Nor are the effects of browsing and grazing figured into how plants might respond to climate change, and those effects could be significant: The same five million caribou eat an estimated 3.3 billion pounds of green matter each year.

"We think of plants as carbon sponges, draining the carbon dioxide out of the atmosphere as we are putting it into the atmosphere," Post said. "If these large animals have such an effect on which plants grow, and if plants have such an effect on global warming, then we need to put the whole picture together, don't we? "It's a provocative question: Do large animals have the potential to influence climate change? The answer will vary by the kind of vegetation, by the type of herbivore, and by the extent of nitrogen limitation in the system. Field experiments will help us figure this out. But I want the question to be considered."

HUMAN

Radiation occurs when unstable nuclei of atoms decay and release particles. There are many different types of radiation. When these particles touch various organic material such as tissue, damage may, and probably will, be done. Radiation can cause burns, cancers, and death.

UNITS OF MEASUREMENT

The unit used to measure radiation dosage is the rem, which stands for roentgenequivalent in man. It represents the amount of radiation needed to produce a particular amount of damage to living tissue. The total dose of rems determines how much harm a person suffers. At Hiroshima and Nagasaki, people received a dose of rems at the instant of the explosions, then more from the surroundings and, in limited areas, from fallout. Fallout is composed of radioactive particles that are carried into the upper atmosphere by a nuclear explosion and that eventually fall back to the earth's surface.

EFFECTS OF RADIATION EXPOSURE ON HUMAN HEALTH

Although a dose of just 25 rems causes some detectable changes in blood, doses to near 100 rems usually have no immediate harmful effects. *Doses above 100 rems cause the first signs of radiation sickness including:*

- Nausea
- Vomiting
- Headache
- Some loss of white blood cells

Doses of 300 rems or more cause temporary hair loss, but also more significant internal harm, including damage to nerve cells and the cells that line the digestive tract. Severe loss of white blood cells, which are the body's main defence against infection, makes radiation victims highly vulnerable to disease. Radiation also reduces production of blood platelets, which aid blood clotting, so victims of radiation sickness are also vulnerable to hemorrhaging. Half of all people exposed to 450 rems die, and doses of 800 rems or more are always fatal. Besides the symptoms mentioned above, these people also suffer from fever and diarrhea. As of yet, there is no effective treatment—so death occurs within two to fourteen days. In time, for survivors, diseases such as leukemia (cancer of the blood), lung cancer, thyroid cancer, breast cancer, and cancers of other organs can appear due to the radiation received.

MAJOR RADIATION EXPOSURE IN REAL LIFE EVENTS

Many people at Hiroshima and Nagasaki died not directly from the actual explosion, but from the radiation released as a result of the explosion. For example, a fourteen-year-old boy was admitted to a Hiroshima hospital two days after the explosion, suffering from a high fever and nausea. Nine days later his hair began to fall out. His supply of white blood cells dropped lower and lower. On the seventeenth day he began to bleed from his nose, and on the twenty-first day he died.

At Hiroshima and Nagasaki, the few surviving doctors observed symptoms of radiation sickness for the first time. In his book *Nagasaki 1945*, Dr. Tatsuichiro Akizuki wrote of the puzzling, unknown disease, of symptoms that "suddenly appeared in certain patients with no apparent injuries. Several days after the bombs exploded, doctors learned that they were treating the effects of radiation exposure. We were now able to label our unknown adversary 'atomic disease' or 'radioactive contamination' among other names.

But they were only labels: we knew nothing about its cause or cure... Within seven to ten days after the A-bomb explosion, people began to die in swift succession. They died of the burns that covered their bodies and of acute atomic disease. Innumerable people who had been burnt turned a mulberry colour, like worms, and died... The disease, wrote Dr. Akizuki, "destroyed them little by little. As a doctor, I was forced to face the slow and certain deaths of my patients."

Doctors and nurses had no idea of how their own bodies had been affected by radioactivity. Dr. Akizuki wrote, "All of us suffered from diarrhea and a discharge of blood from the gums, but we kept this to ourselves. Each of us thought: tomorrow it might be me... We became stricken with fear of the future." Dr. Akizuki survived, as did several hundred thousand others in or near Hiroshima and Nagasaki. In fact, at least ten people who had fled from Hiroshima to Nagasaki survived *both* bombs. The survivors have suffered physically from cataracts, leukemia and other cancers, malformed offspring, and premature aging, and also emotionally, from social discrimination. Within a few months of the nuclear explosions, leukemia began to appear among the survivors at an abnormally high rate. Some leukemia victims were fetuses within their mothers' wombs when exposed to radiation. One child who was born two days after the Hiroshima explosion eventually died of acute leukemia at the age of eighteen. The number of leukemia cases has declined with time, but the incidence of lung cancer, thyroid cancer, breast cancer, and cancers of other organs has increased among the survivors.

THREE MILE ISLAND

On a Wednesday morning, maintenance workers cleaning sludge from a small pipe blocked the flow of water in the main feedwater system of a reactor at Three Mile Island near Harrisburg, Pennsylvania. The sift foreman heard "loud, thunderous noises, like a couple of freight trains," coming. Since the reactor was still producing heat, it heated the blocked cooling water around its core hot enough to create enough pressure to have popped a relief valve.

Some 220 gallons of water per minute began flowing out of the reactor vessel. Within five minutes after the main feedwater system failed, the reactor, deprived of all normal and emergency sources of cooling water, and no longer able to use its enormous energy to generate electricity, gradually started to tear itself apart. The loss of coolant at the reactor continued for some 16 hours. Abort a third of the core melted down.

Radioactive water flowed through the stuck relief valve into an auxiliary building, where it pooled on the floor. Radioactive gas was released into the atmosphere. An estimated 140,000 people were evacuated from the area. It took a month to stabilize the malfunctioning unit and safely shut it down. The reactor was a total loss and the cleanup required years of repair and hundreds of millions of dollars. No one was reported injured and the little radiation that leaked out was quickly dispersed. Although this accident did cost lots of money and time, no one was hurt.

CHERNOBYL

A far more serious accident occured at Chernobyl, in what was then still the Soviet Union. At the time of the accident, the Chernobyl nuclear power station consisted of four operating 1,000 megawatt power reactors. Without question, the accident at Chernobyl was the result of a fatal combination of ignorance and complacency. "As members of a select scientific panel convened immediately after the... accident," writes Nobel laureate Hans Bethe, "my colleagues and I established that the Chernobyl disaster tells us about the deficiencies of the Soviet political and administrative system rather than about problems with nuclear power."

Although the problem at Chernobyl was relatively complex, it can basically be summarized as a mismanaged electrical engineering experiment which resulted in the reactor exploding. The explosion was chemical, driven by gases and steam generated by the core runaway, not by nuclear reactions. Flames, sparks, and chunks of burning material were flying into the air above the unit. These were red-hot pieces of nuclear fuel and graphite. About 50 tons of nuclear fuel evapourated and were released by the explosion into the atmosphere. In addition, about 70 tons were ejected sideways from the periphery of the core. Some 50 tons of nuclear fuel and 800 tons of reactor graphite remained in the reactor vault, where it formed a pit reminiscent of a volcanic crater as the graphite still in the reactor had turned up completely in a few days after the explosion. The resulting radioactive release was equivalent to ten Hiroshimas. In fact, since the Hiroshima bomb was air-burst—no part of the fireball touched the ground—the Chernobyl release polluted the countryside much more than ten Hiroshimas would have done. Many people died from the explosion and even more from the effects of the radiation later. Still today, people are dying from the radiation caused by the Chernobyl accident. The estimated total number of deaths will be 16,000.

MEDICAL TREATMENT

For a more in-depth view of current medical technologies available to the treatment of radiation. There is currently no effective medical treatment available for potentially fatal radiation doses. The case of the Japanese boy mentioned above illustrates an important fact about radiation sickness. The boy had probably received a dose of 450 rems or more, yet his symptoms were about the same as those of a person who received about 300 rems. Medical science has no way of telling the difference between people who have received fatal doses and will die despite all efforts and others who received less radiation and can be saved. Treatment for the ones that can be saved includes blood transfusions and bone-marrow transplants. Bone-marrow transplants rejuvenate the supply of white blood cells which was affected by the radiation.

HIGH AND LOW LEVEL RADIOACTIVE WASTE

DESCRIPTION

The fuel for a nuclear reactor is in the form of ceramic pellets of uranium oxide, each about inch in diameter and 3/4 inch long, lined up and sealed inside metal tubes about 12 feet long and inch in diameter. About 50 of these "fuel pins" are bound together, leaving space for water to circulate between the pins, to form a "fuel assembly." A large reactor might contain 200 of these fuel assemblies arranged in a lattice, with a total of 110 tons of uranium. A typical fuel assembly remains in the reactor for about 3 years. During this time, a small percentage of the uranium nuclei are struck by neutrons, causing them to undergo fission or other nuclear reactions. These reactions transform them into other nuclei, "the high-level radioactive waste." At the end of this 3-year period, the fuel is "spent" and must be replaced by fresh fuel. The subject we examine here is disposal of this spent fuel containing the radioactive waste.

One option is to dispose of the spent fuel directly by sealing fuel assemblies into canisters and burying them. A much more rational approach from the standpoint of long-range planning is to put the fuel through a chemical reprocessing operation to separate out the uranium and plutonium which are valuable for future use as fuels, and to convert the residual material into a form suitable for burial. If we follow the first option, our uranium resources will run out sometime during the next century, whereas the second option can provide all of the energy humans will need for as long as they inhabit planet Earth, without an increase in fuel costs.

Unfortunately, decisions are not made by long-range planners, but rather by business executives and politicians who base their decisions on short-term economics. Even from this standpoint, reprocessing is the more favourable option, albeit by a rather narrow margin. Consequently, reprocessing plants have been an important part of nuclear industry planning in the United States. In the late 1960s and early 1970s, three commercial plants were built, one of them was operated for a few years, and still other plants reached the advanced planning stage. However, the opposition to nuclear power in the late 1970s caused severe setbacks for the reprocessing industry, leading to its demise. Therefore, current U.S. plans are to bury the spent fuel directly.

The situation is very different in other countries. Great Britain has been reprocessing spent fuel since the 1950s and is currently constructing a large new plant. France has been operating two reprocessing plants for many years and its third plant is nearly complete. Germany has been operating a small reprocessing plant since 1971, and a much larger one is under construction with a 1996 start-up date. Japan has a small plant in operation; a much larger one, under construction, is scheduled to come on line in 1995.

The Japanese also send some spent fuel to France and Great Britain for reprocessing. Belgium, Italy, Switzerland, and the Netherlands also utilize the French and British facilities. India has one reprocessing plant in operation and has recently begun construction of another. China, where nuclear power is in its infancy, is planning to operate a pilot plant by 1995 and a full-scale unit by 2010.

The Soviet Union reprocesses its spent fuel, and Eastern bloc countries as well as Finland make use of the Soviet facilities. Sweden, Canada, and Spain are providing for long-term storage of spent fuel, and are therefore deferring a decision on reprocessing. Only the United States has a full-scale programme in operation leading to burial of spent fuel, although it would be very easy to change it to include reprocessing. This option will remain open for a long time, since even after burial the spent fuel will be retrievable for several decades.

While I fully understand the basis for the U.S. policy of burying spent fuel and I support it, I cannot believe that it will persist for more than 20 years or so. I therefore base the risk evaluations on the assumption that we will eventually do reprocessing. If I am wrong on this matter and spent fuel is permanently buried, the risks we will be discussing will be increased about 10-fold. Nevertheless it will be evident that this would not appreciably affect the conclusions of our discussion.

HAZARDS AND PROTECTIVE BARRIERS

Probably the most frequent question I receive about nuclear power is, "What are we going to do with the radioactive waste?" The answer is very simple: we are going to convert it into rocks and put it in the natural habitat for rocks, deep underground. The next question is usually, "How do you know that will be safe?" Answering that question is our next topic for consideration.

This discussion will be in terms of the high-level waste produced by one large power plant (1,000,000 kW) in one year. The high-level waste from such a plant is contained inside the fuel. If we are to have reprocessing, the 35 tons of spent fuel will be shipped to a chemical reprocessing plant where it will be dissolved in acid and put through chemical processes to remove 99.5% of the uranium and plutonium that are valuable as fuels for future use. The residue—1.5 tons of high-level waste—will then be incorporated into a glass in the form of perhaps 30 cylinders, each about 12 inches in diameter and 10 feet long, weighing about 1,000 pounds. There is a great deal of research on materials that may be superior to glass as a waste form, but far more is now known about glass, a material whose fabrication is simple and well developed. There is no evidence that it is not satisfactory. Many natural rocks are glasses, and they are as durable as other rocks.

This 15 tons of waste glass, roughly one truckload, will then be shipped to a federal repository, where it will be permanently emplaced deep underground. The U.S. Department of Energy is now spending over '200 million per year in developing this waste storage technology. The programme is paid for by a tax on nuclear electricity; about '6 billion was collected by the end of 1989. The estimated cost of handling and storing our one truckload of waste is '5 million, which corresponds to 0.07 cents per kilowatt-hour, about 1% of the cost of electricity to the consumer.

I have often been told, "We don't want a waste dumping ground in our area." This conjures up a picture of dump trucks driving up and tilting back to allow their loads of waste to slide down into a hole in the ground. Clearly it doesn't cost `5 million for each truckload to do this, especially on a mass-handling basis. What is planned, rather, is a carefully researched and elaborately engineered emplacement deep underground in a mined cavity. It may be of incidental interest to point out that the present `5 million price tag on storing one year's waste from one plant is several hundred times higher than the cost of the original plan as formulated in the 1960s. Those conversant with the earlier plan are still convinced that it provided adequate safety, although the added expenditures do, of course, contribute further safety. This tremendous escalation in the scope of the project is a tribute to the power of public hysteria in a democracy like ours, whether or not that hysteria is justified. It is also an application of Parkinson's Law—it was clearly acceptable to devote 1% of the cost of electricity to disposal of the waste, so the money was "available," and being available, the government has found ways to use it.

There have been many safety analyses of waste repositories, and all of them agree that the principal hazard is that somehow the waste will be contacted by groundwater, dissolved, and carried by the groundwater into wells, rivers, and soil. This would cause contamination of drinking water supplies or, through pick-up by plant roots, contamination of food. It could thereby get into human stomachs. The chance of this waste becoming suspended in air as a dust and inhaled by humans is very much less because groundwater rarely reaches the surface; moreover, we inhale only about 0.001 grams of dust per day (and 95% of this is filtered out by hairs in the nose, pharynx, trachea, and bronchi and removed by mucous flow), whereas we eat over 1,000 grams of food per day. On an average, an atom in the top inch of U.S. soil has 1 chance in 10 billion per year of being suspended as a dust and inhaled by a person, whereas an atom in a river, into which groundwater normally would bring the dissolved waste, has 1 chance in 10 thousand of entering a human stomach.10 Thus, an atom of waste has a much better chance of becoming absorbed into the body with food or water than with inhaled dust.

External irradiation by radioactive materials in the ground is also a lesser problem. Rock and soil are excellent shielding materials; while the waste remains buried, not a single particle of radiation from it can ever reach the surface. Compare this with the 15,000 particles of radiation from natural sources that strike each of us every second. If radioactivity is released by groundwater, this shielding is still effective as long as it remains underground or dissolved in river water. If the radioactivity does somehow become deposited on the ground surface, it will soon be washed away or into the ground by rain.

The great majority of the radiation is absorbed by building materials, clothing, or even the air. Thus, there would be relatively little exposure to the human body due to radiation originating from materials on the ground. Quantitative calculations confirm that food and water intake is the most important mode of exposure from radioactive waste, a position agreed upon in all safety analyses. Hence we will limit our consideration to that pathway. In order to estimate the hazard, we therefore start by determining the cancer risk from eating or drinking the various radioactive materials in the waste. The ordinate is the number of cancer deaths that would be expected if all the waste prouced by one large nuclear power plan in one year were eaten by people. The individual curves show the toxicity of the individual radioactive species in the waste (as labeled), and the top black curve shows their sum, the total toxicity. The horizontal dashed line shows the number of deaths expected if the uranium mined out of the ground to produce the fuel from which this waste was generated were fed to people. The scale on the right shows the deaths per year expected according to the risk analysis.

The method for calculating this is explained in resultsare shown in Figure For present purposes we need only look at the thick line which is above all the others in the figures. This is a plot of the number of cancers that would be expected if all of the waste produced by one plant in one year were fed to people. If this were done shortly after burial, according to Figure we would expect 50 million cancers, whereas if it were done after 1,000 years there would be 300,000, and if after a million years there would be 2,000. Note that we did not specify how many people are involved because that does not matter.

If nuclear power was used to the fullest practical extent in the United States, we would need about 300 power plants of the type now in use. I have authored over 250 scientific papers over the past 35 years presenting tens of thousands of pieces of data, but that "over 10 billion" number is the one most frequently quoted. Rarely quoted, however, are the other numbers given along with it: we produce enough chlorine gas each year to kill 400 trillion people, enough phosgene to kill 20 trillion, enough ammonia and hydrogen cyanide to kill 6 trillion with each, enough barium to kill 100 billion, and enough arsenic trioxide to kill 10 billion.

All of these numbers are calculated, as for the radioactive waste, on the assumption that all of it gets into people. It hope these comparisons dissolve the fear that, in generating nuclear electricity, we are producing unprecedented quantities of toxic materials. One immediate application of Fig. is to estimate how much of the waste glass, converted into digestible form, would have a good chance of killing a person who eats it—this may be called a "lethal dose." We calculate it by simply dividing the quantity of waste glass, 15 tons, by the values given by the curve in Figure and the results are as follows:

Shortly after burial	0.01 oz.
After 100 years	0.1 oz.
After 600 years	1 oz.
After 20,000 years	1 lb.

Selenium compounds	0.01 oz.
Potassium cyanide	0.02 oz.
Arsenic trioxide	0.1 oz.
Copper	0.7 oz.

Note that the nuclear waste becomes less toxic with time because radioactive materials decay, leaving a harmless residue, but the chemicals listed retain their toxicity forever. By comparing these two lists we see that radioactive waste is not infinitely toxic, and in fact it is no more toxic than some chemicals in common use. Arsenic trioxide, for example, used as an herbicide and insecticide, is scattered on the ground in regions where food is grown, or sprayed on fruits and vegetables. It also occurs as a natural mineral in the ground, as do other poisonous chemicals for which a lethal dose is less than one ounce.

Since the waste loses 99% of its toxicity after 600 years, it is often said that our principal concern should be limited to the short term, the first few hundred years. Some people panic over the requirement of security even for hundreds of years. They point out that very few of the structures we build can be counted on to last that long, and that our political, economic, and social structures may be completely revolutionized within that time period. The fallacy in that reasoning is that it refers to our environment here on the surface of the earth, where it is certainly true that most things don't last for hundreds of years. However, if you were a rock 2,000 feet below the surface, you would find the environment to be very different. If all the rocks under the United States more than 1,000 feet deep were to have a newspaper, it couldn't come out more than once in a million years, because there would be no news to report. Rocks at that depth typically last many tens of millions of years without anything eventful occurring. They may on rare occasions be shaken around or even cracked by earthquakes or other catastrophic events, but this doesn't change their position or the chemical interaction with their surroundings.

One way to comprehend the very long-term toxicity in the waste is to compare it with the natural radioactivity in the ground. The ground is, and always has been, full of naturally radioactive materials—principally potassium, uranium, and thorium. On a long-term basis (thousands of years or more), burying our radioactive waste would increase the total radioactivity in the top 2,000 feet of U.S. rock and soil only by 1 part in 10 million. Of course, the radioactivity is more concentrated in a waste repository, but that doesn't matter. The number of cancers depends only on the total number of radioactive atoms that get into people, and there is no reason why this should be larger if the waste is concentrated than if it is spread out all over the country.

In fact, quite the opposite is the case: Being concentrated in a carefully selected site deep underground with the benefit of several engineered safeguards and subject to regular surveillance provides a given atom far less chance of getting into a human stomach than if it is randomly located in the ground. Incidentally, it can be shown that the natural radioactivity deep underground is doing virtually no damage to human health, so adding a tiny amount to it is essentially innocuous.

When I point out that concentration of the waste in one place does not increase the health hazard, listeners often comment that it does mean that the risks will be concentrated on the relatively small number of people who live in that area. That, of course, is true, but it is also true for just about any other environmental problem. We in Pittsburgh suffer from the air pollution generated in making steel for the whole country; citizens of Houston and a few other cities bear the brunt of the considerable health hazards from oil refineries that make our gasoline, and there are any number of similar examples. The health burden from these inequities is thousands of times larger than those from living near a nuclear waste repository will ever be.

Figure shows the toxicity of the uranium ore that was originally mined out of the ground to produce the fuel from which the waste was generated. Note that it is larger than the toxicity of the waste after 15,000 years; after that the hazard from the buried waste is less than that from the ore if it had never been mined. After 100,000 years, there is more radioactive toxicity in the ground directly above the repository (*i.e.,* between the buried waste and the surface) than in the repository itself due to the natural radioactivity in the rock.

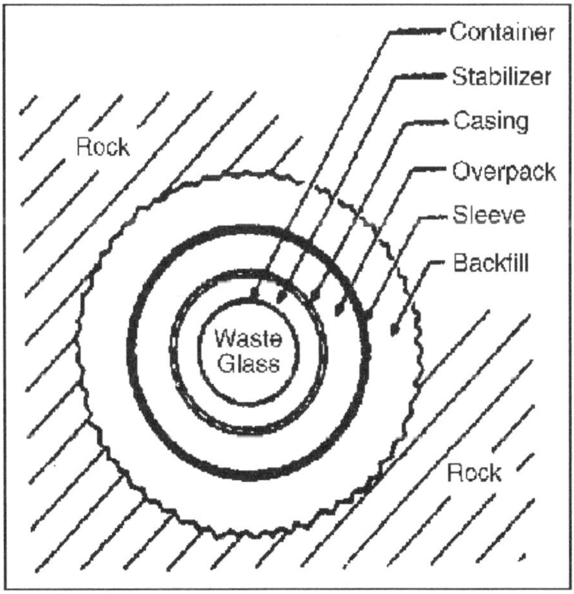

Fig. Schematic Diagram of Buried Waste Package.

Components are as follows: waste glass—the waste itself, converted into a glass; container—stanless steel can in which glass is originally cast; stabilizer—filler material to improve physical and chemical stability of the waste; casing—special material highly resistant to corrosion by intruding water, which it should keep out; overpack—provides additional corrosion resistance and structural stability; sleeve—liner for hole, gives structural support; backfill—material to fill space between waste package and rock, swells when wet to keep water out; if waste becomes dissolved, backfill absorbs it out of the escaping water.

A schematic diagram of the waste package, as buried, is shown in Figure. It is enlightening to consider the protections built into the system to mitigate the hazards. For the first few hundred years, when the toxicity is rather high, there is a great deal of protection through various time delays before the waste can escape through groundwater. First and foremost, the waste will be buried in a rock formation in which there is little or no groundwater flow, and in which geologists are as certain as possible that there will be little groundwater flow for a very long time.

If the geologists are wrong and an appreciable amount of water flow does develop in the rock formation in which the waste is buried, it would first have to dissolve away large fractions of that rock—roughly half of the rock would have to be dissolved before half of the waste is dissolved. This factor might seem to offer minimal protection if the waste is buried in salt, since salt is readily dissolved in water. However, in the New Mexico area, where a repository for defence waste has been constructed, if all the water now flowing through the ground were diverted to flow through the salt, it would take a million years to dissolve the salt enclosing a repository. The quantity of salt is enormous, while the water flow is not a stream but more like a dampness, slowly progressing through the ground. The next layer of protection is the backfill material surrounding the waste package. This will be a clay, which tends to swell when wet to form a tight seal keeping water flow away from the package. If water should penetrate the backfill, before it can reach the waste it must get past the metal casing in which the waste glass is to be sealed. Materials for this casing have been developed that give very impressive resistance to corrosion.

One favourite is a titanium alloy, which was tested in a very hot (480°F versus a maximum expected repository temperature of 250°F) and abnormally corrosive solution, and even under these extreme conditions, corrosion rates were such that water penetration would be delayed for a thousand years. Under more normal groundwater conditions, these casings would retain their integrity for hundreds of thousands of years. Thus, the casings alone provide a rather complete protection system even if everything else fails.

The next layer of protection is the waste form, probably glass, which is not readily dissolved. Glass artifacts from ancient Babylonia have been found in river beds, where they have been washed over by flowing river water—not just by the slowly seeping dampness which better describes groundwater conditions—for 3,000 years without dissolving away. A Canadian experiment with waste glass buried in soil permeated by groundwater indicates that it will last for a hundred million years—*i.e.,* only about 1/100 millionth dissolves each year. But suppose that somehow some of the waste did become dissolved in groundwater. Groundwater moves very slowly, typically at less than 1 foot per day—in the region of the New Mexico site it moves only about 1 inch per day and at the Nevada site which is under investigation it moves only 0.03 inches per day.

Furthermore, groundwater deep underground does not ordinarily travel vertically upward towards the surface; it rather follows the rock layers, which tend to be essentially horizontal, and hence it typically must travel about 50 miles before reaching the surface. In the New Mexico area it must travel over a hundred miles and at the Nevada site at least 30 miles. Anyone can easily calculate that to travel 50 miles at 1 foot per day takes about 1,000 years, so this again gives a very substantial protection for the few hundred years that most concern us here.

(Long-term effects will be considered later.) But the radioactive material does not move with the velocity of the groundwater. It is constantly filtered out by adsorption on the rock material, and as a result it travels hundreds or thousands of times more slowly than the groundwater. If the groundwater takes a thousand years to reach the surface, the radioactive materials should take hundreds of thousands or millions of years. Moreover, there are abundant opportunities along the way for waste materials to precipitate out of solution and become a permanent part of the rock.

We thus have seven layers of protection preventing the waste from getting out during the first few hundred years when it is highly toxic:

1. The absence of groundwater,
2. The insolubility of the surrounding rock,
3. The sealing action of the backfill material,
4. The corrosion resistance of the metal casing,
5. The insolubility of the waste glass itself,
6. The long time required for groundwater to reach the surface, and
7. The filtering action of the rock.

But even if all of these protections should fail, the increased radioactivity in the water would be easily detected by routine monitoring, and the water would not be used for drinking or irrigation of food crops; thus there would still be no damage to human health.

QUANTITATIVE RISK ASSESSMENT FOR HIGH-LEVEL WASTE

Our next task is to develop a quantitative estimate of the hazard from buried radioactive waste. Our treatment is based on an analogy between buried radioactive waste and average rock submerged in groundwater. We will justify this analogy later, but it is very useful because we know a great deal about the behaviour of average rock and its interaction with groundwater. Using this information in a calculation outlined in the demonstrates that an atom of average rock submerged in groundwater has one chance in a trillion each year of being dissolved out of the rock, eventually being carried into a river, and ending up in a human stomach.

In the spirit of our analogy between this average rock and buried radioactive waste, we assume that this probability also applies to the latter; that is, an atom of buried radioactive waste has one chance in a trillion of reaching a human stomach each year. The remainder of our calculation is easy, because we know from the consequences of this waste reaching a human stomach. All we need do is multiply the curve in by one-trillionth to obtain the number of fatal cancers expected each year.

This is done by simply relabeling the vertical scale, as shown on the right side of. For example, if all of the waste were to reach human stomachs a thousand years after burial, there would be 300,000 deaths, according to the scale on the left side of, but since only one-trillionth of it reaches human stomachs each year, there would be (300,000/1 trillion =) 3 X 10–7 deaths per year, as indicated by reading the curve with the scale on the right side of. This result is equivalent to one chance in 3 million of a single death each year. What we really want to know is the total number of people who will eventually die from the waste. Since we know how many will die each year, we simply must add these up. Totalling them over millions of years gives 0.014 eventual deaths. One might ask how far into the future we should carry this addition, and therein lies a complication that requires some explanation. From the measured rate at which rivers carry dissolved and suspended material into the ocean each year, it is straightforward to calculate that the surfaces of the continents are eroding away at an average rate of 1 meter (3.3 feet) of depth every 22,000 years. (All the while the continents are being uplifted such that on an average the surface remains at about the same elevation.)

Nearly all of this erosion comes from river beds and the minor streams and run-off that feed them. However, rivers change their courses frequently; changing climates develop new rivers and eliminate old ones (10,000 years ago the Arizona desert was a rain forest); and land areas rise and fall under geological pressures to change drainage patterns. Therefore, averaged over very long time periods, it is reasonable to assume that most land areas erode away at roughly this average rate, 1 meter of depth every 22,000 years. This suggests that the ground surface will eventually erode down to the level of the buried radioactive waste. Since the waste will be buried at a depth of about 600 meters, this may be expected to occur after about (600 × 22,000 =) 13 million years. When it happens, the remaining radioactivity will be released into rivers, and according to estimates developed in the one part in 10,000 will get into human stomachs.

Therefore, the process of adding up the number of deaths each year should be discontinued after 13 million years; that was done in calculating the number of deaths given above as 0.014. To this we must add the number of deaths caused by release of the remaining radioactivity. A simple calculation given in the shows that this leads to 0.004 deaths. Adding that number to the 0.014 deaths during the first 13 million years gives 0.018 as the total number of eventual deaths from the waste produced by one power plant in one year.

Recall now that air pollution, one of the wastes from coal burning, kills 75 people in generating the same amount of electricity; perhaps new pollution control technology may reduce this number to 15 deaths per year. Even if this comes to pass, we see that this one waste from coal burning would still be a thousand times more injurious to human health than are the high-level nuclear wastes. Another way of understanding the results of our analysis is to consider a situation in which all of the present electricity used in the United States has been provided by nuclear power plants—about 300 would be required—continuously for millions of years. We would then expect (300 × 0.018 =) 5.4 cancer deaths per year on an average from all of the accumulated waste. Compare this with the 30,000 deaths each year we now get from coal-burning power plants. Before closing, readers with a scientific bent may be interested in the justification for the basic assumption used in arriving at our estimate, the analogy between buried radioactive waste and average rock which is submerged in flowing groundwater.

Actually, there are three ways in which the waste may be less secure:

1. The radioactivity in the waste continues to generate heat for some time after burial, making the buried waste considerably hotter than average rock. There has been some fear that this heat may crack the surroundIng rock, thereby introducing easy pathways for groundwater to reach the waste and/or to carry off the dissolved radioactivity. This question has been extensively studied since the late 1960s, and the conclusion now is that rock cracking is not a problem unless the temperature gets up to about 650°F. The actual temperature of the waste can be controlled by the extent to which it is diluted with inert glass and by the intervals chosen for burial of the waste packages. More dilution and larger spacings result in lower temperatures. In the repositories now envisioned, these factors will be adjusted to keep the temperature below 250°F, which leaves a large margin of safety relative to the 650°F danger point. If it is decided that this margin should be larger, the easiest procedure would be to delay the burial, since the heat evolving from the waste decreases tenfold after a hundred years, and a hundredfold after 200 years. Storage facilities for waste packages have been designed, and there would be no great difficulty or expense in building them.
2. The waste glass will be a foreign material in its environment and hence will not be in chemical equilibrium with the surrounding rock and groundwater. However, chemical equilibrium is a surface phenomenon. When groundwater reaches a foreign material it rapidly

dissolves off a microscopically thin surface layer, replacing it with material that had been dissolved out of neighbouring rocks. As this surface layer builds up in thickness, it shelters the material beneath from further interaction with the groundwater. This interaction is therefore effectively stopped after only a minute quantity of the foreign material is dissolved. The foreign material is thereafter no longer "foreign," as its surface is in chemical equilibrium with its surroundings. The fact that the waste glass is a foreign material in its rock environment is therefore not important.

3. Shafts must be dug down from the surface in order to emplace the waste packages. This might provide access routes for intrusion of water and subsequent escape of dissolved waste that are not available to ordinary rock. The seriousness of this problem depends on how securely the shafts can be sealed. That is a question for experts in sealing, and I am not one of these. However, the general opinion among the experts is that the shafts can be sealed to make them at least as secure as the original undisturbed rock.

Since we have discussed the three ways in which buried waste may be less secure than the average rock used in our analogy, it is appropriate to point out ways in which it is more secure. In the first place, burial will be in an area free of groundwater flow, whereas the rock we considered was already submerged in flowing groundwater. Second, it will be in a carefully chosen rock environment, whereas the rock in our analogy is in an average environment; it might, for instance, be in an area of extensive rock fracturing. Third, the waste package will be in a special casing which provides extreme resistance to water intrusion, a protection not available to average rock; this casing should provide adequate protection even if everything else imaginable goes wrong. And finally, if any radioactive waste should escape and get into food and water supplies, it would very probably be detected by routine monitoring programmes in plenty of time to avert any appreciable health consequences.

In balancing the ways in which buried waste is more secure and less secure than the average rock submerged in groundwater with which we compared it, it seems reasonable to conclude that our analogy is a fair one. If anything, it overestimates the dangers from the waste. It should be pointed out that there are other methods than the one presented here for quantifying the probability for an atom of material in the ground to enter a human stomach. For example, we know the amounts of uranium and radium in the human body from measurements on cadavers, and we know the amounts in the ground. From the ratios of these, we can estimate the probability per year for an atom of these elements in the ground to enter a human body. This gives a result in good agreement with that of the calculation we presented. Sometimes when I complete a demonstration like the one above of the safety of buried radioactive waste, a listener complains that the demonstration is invalid because we don't know how to bury waste. How anyone can possibly be so naive as to believe that we don't know how to bury a simple package is truly a challenge to my imagination.

Many animals bury things, and people have been burying things for millions of years. Any normal person could easily suggest several different ways of burying a waste package. Why, then, are we devoting so much time and effort to developing a waste burial technology? The problem here is to decide on the best way of burying the waste to maximize its security. Whether it is worthwhile to go to such pains to optimize the solution is highly questionable, especially since we have shown that even the haphazard burial of average rock by natural processes would provide adequate safety. But the public's irrational worries about the dangers have forced our government to spend large sums of money on the problem. Actually, we are paying for it in our electricity bills. Fortunately, it only increases our bills by one per cent.

LONG-TERM WASTE PROBLEMS FROM CHEMICAL CARCINOGENS

The only reason buried radioactive waste has a calculable health effect is because we are using a linear dose-response relationship, assuming, for example, that if 1 million mrem causes a given risk, 1 mrem will cause a millionth of that risk. This linear relationship does not apply to most toxic chemicals, like carbon monoxide poisoning, for which there is a "threshold" exposure required before there can be any harm. However, it is now widely believed that a linear, no-threshold relationship is valid for chemical carcinogens (*i.e.,* chemicals that can induce cancer) just as for radiation. Basically, the reason for this thinking in both cases is that cancer starts from injury to a single molecule on a single chromosome in the nucleus of a single cell, often induced by a single particle of radiation or by a single carcinogenic molecule.

The probability for this simple process is not dependent on whether or not other carcinogenic molecules are causing injury elsewhere. Thus the probability of cancer is simply proportional to the number of carcinogenic molecules taken into the body, as described by a linear relationship. This linear, no-threshold, dose-response relationship for chemical carcinogens has now been officially accepted by all U.S. Government agencies charged with responsibilities in protecting public health, such as the Environmental Protection Agency, the Occupational Safety and Health Administration, and the Food and Drug Administration. The particular carcinogens of interest in our discussion are the chemical elements cadmium, arsenic, beryllium, nickel, and chromium. There is a considerable body of information indicating that all of these cause cancer and enough quantitative information to estimate the risk per gram of intake. All of them are present in small amounts in coal. Therefore, when coal is burned, they are released and eventually, by one route or another, end up in the ground. Small amounts of each of them are also contained in food. All such materials in food, of course, are taken in from the ground through the roots of plants.

As in the case of radioactive waste, the principal problem in evaluating the hazard is to estimate the probability for an atom of these elements in the ground eventually to reach a human stomach. However, the problem is simpler here because the toxicity in these carcinogenic elements does not decay with time, as does that of radioactive waste. Since some quantity of these elements is ingested by humans every year, if an atom remains in the ground indefinitely, eventually after a long enough time, it has a good chance of reaching a human stomach. However, there are other processes for removing materials from the ground. The most important of these is erosion of soil, with the materials being carried by rivers into the oceans. The probability for an atom in the ground to enter a human stomach is therefore the probability for this to happen before it is washed into the oceans. This is just the ratio of the rate for entering human stomachs to the rate of removal by erosion.

The rates for both of these are known. From chemical analyses of food and the quantity consumed each year, we can calculate the rate at which cadmium, for example, enters human stomachs in the United States. From the rate at which American soil is washed into oceans and the measured abundance of cadmium in soil, we can calculate the rate at which cadmium is carried into oceans. We thus can determine the probability for an atom of cadmium in the soil to enter a human stomach. It turns out to be surprisingly high, about 1.3%. It is 5 times smaller for arsenic, 20 times lower for beryllium and nickel, and 60 times lower for chromium (cadmium atoms are more easily picked up by plant roots because of their chemical properties). Since we know the quantities of each of these carcinogenic elements deposited into the top layers of the ground as a result of coal burning, the probability for them to be transferred from the ground into humans, and their cancer risk once ingested, it is straightforward to estimate the number of deaths caused by coal burning. The result is about 50 deaths due to one year's releases from one large plant. These deaths are spread over the time period during which the top few meters of ground will be eroded away, about 100,000 years.

If one takes a much longer-term viewpoint, these deaths would have eventually occurred even if the coal had not been mined and burned, because after several millions of years, erosion would have brought this coal near the surface, where its cadmium, arsenic, beryllium, chromium, and nickel could have been picked up by plant roots and gotten into food. However, the fact that the coal was mined means that its turn near the surface is taken by other rock which, we assume, has the average amount of these carcinogenic elements in it. This carcinogenic material represents a net additional health risk to humankind due to the use of coal. Taking this into account, the final result is that there would be a net excess of 70 deaths.

Note that this is thousands of times larger than the 0.018 deaths from high-level radioactive waste. The chemical carcinogens also have an impact on the long term health consequences of electricity produced by solar energy. We have already pointed out that producing the materials for deployment of a solar array requires about 3% as much coal burning as producing the same amount of electricity by direct coal burning. The quantity of chemical carcinogens released in the former process is therefore 3% of those released in the latter, so in the very long term we may expect about 2 eventual deaths (3% of 70) from an amount of solar electricity equivalent to that produced by a large nuclear or coal-fired power plant in one year. This is a small number, but it is still a hundred times the 0.018 deaths from nuclear plant waste.

But there may be much more important problems. A prime-candidate material for future solar cells is cadmium sulfide. When these cells deteriorate, that material will probably be disposed of in one way or another into the ground. The cadmium introduced into the ground in this way is estimated to eventually cause, 80 deaths for the quantity of electricity produced by a large nuclear plant in one year. Most of the cadmium used in this country is imported. Thus, in contrast to the situation for coal, it would not have eventually reached the surface of U.S. soil without this technology. Again we encounter consequences thousands of times higher than the 0.018 deaths from radioactive waste.

SHOULD WE ADD UP EFFECTS OVER MILLIONS OF YEARS

Many may be bothered by the idea of adding up effects over millions of years. Personally, I agree with them. The idea of considering effects over such long time periods was introduced by opponents of nuclear power, who often insist that it be done. The analyses presented above show that such a procedure turns out very favourably for nuclear power. However, there are many good reasons for confining our attention to the "foreseeable future," which is generally interpreted to be 100–1,000 years. Several groups, including most government agencies, have adopted 500 years as a reasonable time period for consideration, so we will use it for this discussion. The reason for ignoring lives that may be lost in the far future is not because those lives are less valuable than our own or those of our closer progeny. There surely can be no moral basis for any such claim. But there are at least three reasonable and moral bases for ignoring the distant future.

One such basis is the improvement in cancer-cure rates. In recent years, they have been improving by about 0.5% per year. It is unlikely that cure rates will continue to improve at this rate. More probably they will stagnate before long, or on the other hand there may be a breakthrough leading to a dramatic improvement. But most knowledgeable people agree that there is a good chance that cancer will be a largely curable disease in 500 years. The deaths we calculate to occur after that time will therefore probably never materialize. The second basis for ignoring deaths calculated to occur in the distant future is what I call the "trust fund" approach. We showed in that there are many ways that money can be used to save lives at a rate of at least one life saved per ` 100,000 spent. But even suppose that so many improvements are instigated that it will cost `1 million to save a life in the distant future (all our discussions discount inflation). There is a continuous record extending back 5,000 years of money always being able to draw at least 3% real (discounting inflation) interest.

Each dollar invested now at 3% interest is worth '2.5 million after 500 years and will therefore be capable of saving more than one life. It is therefore much more effective in saving far future lives to set up a trust fund to be spent in their time for that purpose rather than for us to spend money now to protect them from our waste. One might wonder about the mechanics and practicality of setting up a trust fund to be transmitted to future generations, but this is no problem. By overspending, we are now building up a public debt that they will have to pay interest on, so rather than actually set up a trust fund, we need only reduce our spending and thereby leave future generations with more money to use for lifesaving. By not spending profligately on waste management, we are doing just that. A third basis for ignoring the distant future in our considerations is the "biomedical research" approach. If we don't feel comfortable with the "trust fund" approach of putting aside money to be spent in the future for saving lives, we can save future lives by spending money today on biomedical research. One study concludes that the '68 billion spent on such research between 1930 and 1975 is now saving 100,000 lives per year in the United States, one life per year for every '680,000 spent. Another study estimates that the '20 billion spent in 1955–1965 is now saving 100,000 lives per year, or one life per year for every '200,000 spent. Age-specific mortality rates in the United States have been declining steadily in recent years; if one-fourth of this decline is credited to biomedical research, the latter is now saving one life per year for every '1 million spent.

As the easier medical problems are solved and the more difficult ones are attacked, the cost goes up. Let us therefore say that for the near future, it will cost '5 million to save one life per year in the United States, not to mention that it will save lives in other countries. Over the next 500 years, saving one life per year will avert a total of 500 deaths, a cost of '10,000 per life saved. If we extend our considerations beyond 500 years, the price drops proportionally. Since we are now spending many millions of dollars per future life saved in handling our radioactive waste, it would clearly be much more beneficial to future generations if we put this money into biomedical research. The straightforward way to implement this alternative would be for the nuclear industry to contribute money to biomedical research rather than to improved long-term security of nuclear waste, but even that may not be necessary. The nuclear industry pays money to the government in taxes, and the government spends roughly an equal sum of money to support biomedical research. All that is necessary to implement an equitable programme from the viewpoint of future citizens is that 0.1% of this cash flow from the nuclear industry to government to biomedical research be redefined as support of biomedical research by the nuclear industry.

If it would make people happier, the government tax on the nuclear industry could actually be raised by 0.1% and this money could be directly added to the government's biomedical research budget. No one would notice the difference since it is much less than a typical annual change in these taxes and budgets. As a result of any one of the above three rationales, or a combination of them, many people, including myself, feel that we should worry only about effects over the next 500 years. For their benefit we now develop estimates of the health effects expected during that time period, from one year's operation of a large power plant: For the high-level radioactive waste, we take the number of fatalities each year from using the scale on the right side of and add them up over the first 500 years. The result is 0.003 deaths, most of them in the first 100 years. However, this ignores all the time delays and special protections during this early time period that were outlined above: geologists feel confident that no groundwater will intrude into the waste repository for at least a thousand years; the corrosion-resistant casing is virtually impregnable for several hundred years; it takes groundwater a thousand years to get to the surface; and so on. Moreover, since it is quite certain that some sort of surveillance would be maintained during this period, any escaping radioactivity would be detected in plenty of time to avert health problems. These factors reduce the dangers at least 30-fold, to no more than 0.0001 deaths. This is close to a million times less then the number of deaths due to air pollution from coal burning. The chemical carcinogens released into the ground in coal burning do about 1 per cent of their damage during the first 500 years; we may consequently expect 0.5 deaths in that period. With a 500-year perspective, there is no need to consider the much later effects of the coal reaching the surface by erosion if it had not been mined. We see that the effects of chemical carcinogens from coal burning are 5,000 times worse than those of nuclear waste (0.5/0.0001). By similar reasoning, the chemical carcinogens from solar electricity will cause 0.015 deaths due to the coal used in making materials for it; if cadmium sulfide solar cells are used, they will cause 0.8 deaths. Again these are far greater than the 0.0001 deaths due to the waste from nuclear power.

SITING A WASTE REPOSITORY

As a consequence of public fear, siting a repository for high-level waste has become a very difficult and expensive process. The NIMBY syndrome—

Not in my back yard—receives its fullest expression here because there is little obvious benefit and enormous perceived harm to the area that accepts the waste. There is even a stigma attached to being the place where the nation's "atomic garbage" is sent. The issue is made to order for local environmental groups. By opposing the repository they get lots of media coverage, which is the essential ingredient needed for them to prosper. The issue is also made to order for local politicians who can garner lots of votes by posing as the defender of the home territory against the intrusion of the federal government and the commercial interests of the rest of the nation. There are few votes to be gained by supporting the local siting of a repository.

The U.S. Department of Energy (DOE), which is charged with the responsibility for managing the waste, has faced this difficult situation by adopting the position that repository site selection is strictly a scientific problem, requiring a tremendous research effort which it is more than happy to undertake. The money for it is available from the 0.1 cent per kilowatt-hour tax on nuclear electricity. Through 1989, '6 billion had already been collected. Managing a large research programme is clearly advantageous to the careers of those in charge, and it also delays the pain of making a decision. The longevity of individuals in top government positions is such that they personally will probably never have to make a final decision—for a government bureaucrat that is the ideal situation.

As a result of these factors, selection of a repository site has been painfully slow. The current status is that a tentative site has been selected, under Yucca mountain in Nevada, 100 miles northwest of Las Vegas, and research is proceeding to determine whether it is suitable. The research plan, published in December 1988, runs more than 6,300 and cost '30 million! The research project itself was estimated to take 7 years and cost '2 billion. It was to include drilling and blasting two shafts 1,000 feet deep to the repository level, and carving out an underground laboratory there for carrying out experiments that simulate the underground environment. In addition, there were to be over 300 drill holes to explore the geology and hydrology beyond the laboratory.

A year later, the new Secretary of Energy decided that the entire research plan should be revised. As part of the new procedure, the repository will not become operational until 2010. Yucca mountain is in a very barren desert region, adjacent to the nuclear weapons testing facility, an area larger than the state of Rhode Island known as the Nevada Test Site (NTS). The NTS itself was originally part of, and along with Yucca mountain is still surrounded by, a much larger U.S. Air Force bombing and gunnery range. Because of the NTS, radioactivity is not a stranger to the area. About 100 nuclear bomb tests were conducted in the atmosphere there between 1951 and 1963, and since 1963, 600 more announced tests have been conducted underground. Additional tests were not announced to the public. In the late 1980s, an average of 14 tests per year were announced. Each underground bomb test can be considered as a miniature high-level waste repository. One can stand on high ground overlooking Frenchman's Flat and see many dozens of craters, each caused by surface subsidence above a cavity caused by an underground nuclear explosion. One can see heavily damaged buildings and bridges exposed to the earlier tests in the atmosphere. The most spectacular sight is Sedan crater, 1,280 feet in diameter and 320 feet deep, created in a test of the potential use of nuclear bombs for large excavation projects—that one bomb removed 12 million tons of earth. But most testing is now conducted in "rooms" leading off of tunnels drilled into the sides of mountains.

Yucca mountain is several miles away from the part of NTS used for bomb testing. The NTS areas nearby have been used for testing nuclear reactors developed for spaceship propulsion, a project that has now been abandoned. Any possible effects of the bomb testing on the security of the waste repository will be carefully considered. The rock under Yucca mountain is welded tuff, a volcanic lava which oozed out of the earth 13 to 18 million years ago and remained at high temperature and out of contact with air for a long time. This caused it to become tightly welded into a dense, nonporous rock.

Yucca mountain is one of the driest places in the United States, with only 6 inches of rainfall per year, only 5% of which (0.3 inches per year) soaks into the ground. The water table is more than 2,500 feet deep, so that the 1,200-foot-deep repository will be 1,300 feet above it. Only a tiny amount of moisture can therefore contact the buried waste. The rock below the repository is especially rich in zeolites, materials with chemical properties that make them efficient at absorbing dissolved radioactive materials out of water passing through. It is estimated that water percolating down would take 2,000-8,000 years to travel this 1,200 feet from the repository to the water table.

If any radioactive waste should be dissolved out, and if it should somehow escape adsorption in the zeolites and reach the water table, consequences would still be minimal. Groundwater in the region moves especially slowly, only about 1 foot per year! The nearest place it could reach the surface is 30 miles away—150,000 years at 1 foot per year—in the Amargosa desert, which is a closed drainage basin—water flowing into it stays there until it evapourates. Note that the 1 foot per year flow rate applies to the water; as explained previously, materials dissolved in it move hundreds or thousands of times more slowly. For them to travel 30 miles would take many millions of years! In summary, there is virtually no moisture to dissolve the waste, which is in any case in insoluble form and protected by casings and backfill material. If any material is dissolved, the only escape path is downward 1,300 feet to the top of the water table through rock that is highly efficient at adsorbing out the dissolved materials. If it should reach the water table it would take many millions of years to reach the surface, and that would leave it trapped in the middle of a virtually uninhabited desert with no way to get out. Note that this is very much safer than the situation assumed in our risk analysis above for average underground conditions in which the waste is submerged in groundwater that moves at a velocity of 1 foot per day, and flows into a river through a region of U.S. average population. There are other matters to consider, including the potential effects of climate change, volcanoes, and earthquakes. All of these now seem to be of minimal concern. The closest major earthquake was 90 miles to the west in 1872, and there has been no major faulting or folding of rocks for over 10 million years. The climate has been arid for over 2 million years, and there have been no volcanoes for several million years. But investigating these matters is an important part of the research programme.

In spite of all this, the Las Vegas area, which has lived with nuclear bomb testing at similar or closer distances for nearly 40 years, is alive with opposition, including citizens' alliances, residents' coalitions, governor's commissions, study committees, and the like. They are composed of ordinary people—secretaries, teachers, iron workers, printers, lawyers, real estate brokers. In accordance with the law, some of these are funded by the DOE out of funds from the tax on nuclear electricity. They say that, in accepting the nuclear bomb testing facility, Nevada has done its share, so some other state should accept the nuclear waste. Nevada's governors and senators have opposed the repository. The state legislature passed resolutions opposing it, refusing to yield jurisdiction and withholding consent. It even passed a law making it a crime for anyone to store high-level radioactive waste in the state punishable by fines and imprisonment. That law is being tested in the courts.

The state has filed several law suits against the DOE, and the legal situation is cluttered with countersuits and appeals. Some Nevadans favour the repository as a diversification of industry for the state, which is highly dependent on tourism and gaming. Some fears have been expressed that other industries may be deterred from moving to the area, but in 1988–89, 50 businesses moved into Nevada and none raised the repository issue as a concern. Some Nevadans are more concerned with negotiating the best possible deal in terms of payments from the DOE for accepting the repository. There is every indication that the state will be well compensated.

If the legal problems can be worked out, and if the technical evaluation of the site does not encounter serious problems, the Yucca mountain repository will be built and operating by about the year 2010. The cost will be tremendous, but it will be covered by the 0.1 cent per kilowatt-hour tax which adds only 1% to the cost of nuclear electricity.

WHY THE PUBLIC FEAR

If the picture does not omit important aspects of the problem, and is not misleading, it is difficult for me to understand why people worry about the dangers of high-level radioactive waste. The material presented here has been published in the appropriate scientific journals for some time. It had been approved by scientific referees and editors to get there. There have been no critiques of it offered.

I have presented it at international, national, and regional scientific conferences, and in seminar talks at several major universities, all without receiving substantive criticisms or adverse comments. I therefore know of no evidence that my treatment is not a correct and valid assessment of the problem based on scientific analyses.

There have been other scientific analyses of the high-level radioactive waste hazards using very different approaches that I believe to be less valid than mine, but they come out with rather similar results. They also find the health effects to be trivial.

Why, then, is there so much opposition? What is the basis for the public worry about this problem? There have been a few scientific papers that concoct very special scenarios in which substantial—but still far from catastrophic—harm to public health might result, but they never attempt to estimate the likelihood of their scenarios.

All of them are obviously extremely improbable. Note that in my treatment the probabilities of all scenarios are automatically taken into account as long as they apply equally to average rock.

Nevertheless, there can be no question but that the fear abounds. A segment on a network TV morning show opened with the statement "[this waste] could possibly contaminate the environment. The result, of course, would be too horrible to contemplate; it could eventually mean the end of the world as we now know it." I cannot imagine any situation in which this last statement is meaningful short of feeding all of the people in the world directly with the waste.

As has been pointed out, there are many other substances that would serve with greater effectiveness if this were done. Probably the best evidence for this fear is that our government is willing to spend huge sums of money on the problem.

The fear is surely there. Perhaps the most important reason for it is that disposal of high-level waste is often referred to as an "unsolved problem." When people say this to me, I ask whether disposal of the waste from coal burning—releasing it as air pollution, killing about 30,000 Americans each year—is a "solved problem."

They usually say "no" but add that air pollution is being reduced. Actually we can hardly hope to reduce it to the point of killing fewer than 5,000 Americans per year. It is therefore difficult to understand how that converts it into a "solved problem." When I point out that the radioactive waste problem is not unsolved, since there are many known solutions, the usual retort is "then why aren't we burying it now?" The answer to that question is we are in the process of choosing the best solution. This is about as far as the discussion goes, but the real difficulty is that it rarely goes that far. The great majority of people are still hung up on "it's an unsolved problem."

I like to point out that nobody is being injured by the high-level waste, and there is no reason to believe that anyone will be injured by it in the foreseeable future—compare this with the 30,000 deaths per year from the wastes released in coal burning.

The usual reply is "how do you know that nobody is being injured?" The answer is that we constantly measure radiation doses in and around nuclear facilities and throughout our environment, and nobody is receiving any such doses from high-level waste.

If there is no radiation dose, there can be no harm. I don't believe any scientist would argue this point, but I'm sure most people continue to believe that high-level waste (or the spent fuel from which it is to be derived) actually is doing harm now. The real difficulty with public understanding of the high-level waste problem is that the scientists' viewpoint is not being transmitted to the public.

Transmitting information from the scientific community to the public is in the hands of journalists, who have chosen not to transmit on this question. I'd hate to speculate on their motives, but they are doing great damage to our nation. These are the same journalists who constantly trumpet the claim that the government is suppressing information on nuclear energy. What more despicable suppression of information can there be than refusing to transmit the truth about important questions to the public? It's every bit as effective as lying.

PESTICIDE AND XENOBIOTIC CONVCRSION

PESTICIDE USE AND SAFETY

Pesticides may be useful when non-chemical methods fail to provide adequate control of pests and when pest populations reach a level of economic injury. The suffix "cide" literally means kill. The term pesticide refers to a chemical substance that will kill pests. Since it is physically impossible to eradicate an entire population of pests, pesticides are used as a tool to control or manage pest populations to a level of tolerance. Because of government regulations, chemicals used to attract or repel pests and to regulate plant growth or function are also classed as pesticides.

PESTICIDE CONVERSION CHARTS

The measurements given below are approximate and should be used as a general guideline if the directions for mixing small quantities are not given on the pesticide label.

Table. Concentration of Active Ingredient in Formulation

Rate Desired Pounds/A	100%	90%	80%	75%	70%	60%	50%	40%	30%	25%	20%	10%	5%
(Grams of Formulation Per 100 Square Feet)													
1	1.04	1.16	1.30	1.39	1.49	1.74	2.08	2.60	3.47	4.17	5.21	10.4	20.8
2	2.08	2.31	2.60	2.78	2.98	3.47	4.17	5.21	6.94	8.33	10.4	20.8	41.7
3	3.12	3.47	3.90	4.17	4.46	5.20	6.25	7.81	10.4	12.5	15.6	31.2	62.5
4	4.17	4.63	5.21	5.55	5.95	6.94	8.33*	10.4	13.9	16.7	20.8	41.7	83.3
5	5.21	5.79	6.51	6.94	7.44	8.68	10.4	13.0	17.4	20.8	26.0	52.1	104
6	6.25	6.94	7.81	8.33	8.93	10.4	12.5	15.6	20.8	25.0	31.2	62.5	125
7	7.29	8.10	9.11	9.72	10.4	12.1	14.6	18.2	24.3	29.2	36.4	72.9	146
8	8.33	9.26	10.4	11.1	11.9	13.9	16.7	20.8	27.8	33.3	41.7	83.3	167
9	9.37	10.4	11.7	12.5	13.4	15.6	18.7	23.4	31.2	37.5	46.9	93.7	187
10	10.4	11.6	13.0	13.9	14.9	17.4	20.8	26.0	34.7	41.7	52.1	104	208

**Example:* To put out a 100 sq. ft. plot at the rate of 4 lbs./A active ingredient using a formulation containing 50% active ingredient, use 8.33 grams of the 50% formulation and distribute evenly over the 100 sq. ft.

Table. Concentration of Active Ingredient in Formulations, lbs./gal.

Rate Desired Pounds/A	1	2	2.5	3	4	5	6
(ml of formulation per 100 square feet)							
1	8.67	4.33	3.47	2.89	2.17	1.73	1.44
2	17.3	8.67	6.93	5.78	4.33	3.47	2.89
3	26.0	13.0	10.4	8.67	6.5	5.20	4.33
4	34.8	17.4	13.9	11.6	8.69	6.95	5.79
5	4.34	21.7	17.4	14.5	10.9*	8.68	7.24
6	52.1	26.0	20.8	17.4	13.0	10.4	8.68
7	60.8	30.4	24.3	20.3	15.2	12.2	10.1
8	69.4	34.7	27.8	23.1	17.4	13.9	11.6
9	78.1	39.0	31.2	26.0	19.5	15.6	13.0
10	86.7	43.3	34.7	28.9	21.7	17.3	14.4

Example: To put out a 100 sq. ft. plot at the rate of 5 lbs./A active ingredient using a formulation containing 4 lbs./gal. active ingredient, use 10.9 mL. of the 4 lbs./gal. formulation and distribute evenly.

Table. Emulsifiable Concentrate Per cent Ratings in Pounds Actual Per Gallon

%EC	lbs/gallon
10–12	1
15–20	1.5
25	2
40–50	4
60–65	6
70–75	8
80–100	10

Table. Proportionate Amounts of Dry Materials

Water		Quantity of Material			
100 gallons	1 lb.	2 lbs.	3 lbs.	4 lbs.	5 lbs.
50 gallons	8 oz.	1 lb.	24 oz.	2 lbs.	2 1/2 lbs.
5 gallons	3 tbs.	1 1/2 oz.	2 1/2 oz.	3 1/4 oz.	4 oz.
1 gallon	2 tsp.	3 tsp.	1 1/2 tbs.	2 tbs.	3 tbs.

Table. Proportionate Amounts of Liquid Materials

Water	Quantity of Material		
100 gallons	1 qt.	1 pt.	1 cup
50 gallons	1 pt.	1 cup	1/2 cup
5 gallons	3 tbs.	5 tsp.	2 1/2 tsp.
1 gallon	2 tsp.	1 tsp.	1/2 tsp.

PESTICIDE FORMULATIONS

The formulation describes the physical state of a pesticide and determines how it will be applied. Pesticides are rarely applied full strength. The chemical in the pesticide formulation that actually kills the pest(s) is termed the active ingredient. The added chemical(s), those which make the product easy and safe to formulate or apply, are termed the inert ingredients. Common pesticide formulations follow.

Emulsifiable Concentrates (EC or E): The active ingredient is mixed with an oil base (often listed as petroleum derivatives) forming an emulsion which is diluted with water for application. ECs are common in the home garden trade, being easy to mix and use. They can cause a minor surface bronzing of light-coloured fruit. They should be protected from freezing temperatures which can break down the emulsifier.

- Solutions (S): These formulations are premixed, ready to use. They are often used in household pest products.
- Flowables (F or L): A flowable, or liquid, can be mixed with water to form a suspension in a spray tank.
- Aerosols (A): These are very low-concentrate solutions, usually applied as a fine spray or mist. They are generally sold in aerosol cans and are a very expensive source of pesticide.
- Dusts (D): Made by adding the active ingredients to a fine, inert powder or talc; generally used dry.
- Granules (G): Granular formulations are made by adding the active ingredient to coarse particles (granules) of inert material like fired clay particles.
- Wettable Powders (WP or W): Wettable powder formulations are made by combining the active ingredient with a fine powder. They look like dusts, but they are made to mix with water. These formulations

need continuous agitation to maintain a suspension and are thus difficult for home gardeners to use. When mixing a WP, first mix the measured quantity with a small amount of water, forming a slurry, (a paper cup with a popsicle stick makes a good disposable mixing container) then add it and the additional water to the spray tank. The spray tank must be frequently shaken to maintain the suspension.

- Soluble Powders (SP): Made of an active ingredient in powder form; dissolves in water.
- Baits (B): A bait formulation is made by adding the active ingredient to an edible or attractive substance. Baits are often used to control slugs, snails, ground-dwelling insects, and rodents.Gardeners often attempt to compare a spray with a dust. It should be noted that dusts are a type of formulation, but sprays are not a formulation; they are one means of applying several different formulations such as wettable powders or emulsifiable concentrates that are mixed with water.

SURFACTANTS, ADDITIVES, OR ADJUVANTS

When added to a pesticide, a surfactant reduces the surface tension between two unlike materials, such as a spray film and a solid surface. For example, by adding a surfactant to a sprayer, oil and water will mix and can be sprayed on plant surfaces. With increasing emphasis on safe application of pesticides, such factors as droplet size, spray pattern, and pesticide drift have focused more attention on surfactants to give ideal coverage for pesticides.

Surfactants include: activators; compatibility agents; deflocculators; detergents; dispersants; emulsifiers; foam and drift suppressants; and spreading, sticking, and wetting agents. These materials are added to a spray mix to help keep the pesticide in suspension; improve cohesiveness and dispersion of the spray; and increase the wetting (or coverage) of the leaves, fruits, and stems. This will focuses on surfactants that act as spreading, sticking, and wetting agents. They are most useful when spraying the hard-to-wet foliage of such plants as azalea, boxwood, camellia, carnation, conifer, euonymus, gardenia, gladiolus, holly, iris, narcissus, peony, rose, and yew. Whether a spray rolls off or sticks to a plant surface depends on the physical and chemical properties of the spray mixture and the physical properties of the surface itself. If the surface tension of the mixture is high, or if the plant surface is waxy, the spray droplets will roll off.

A spreader or film extender (spreader-activator) is a substance that, when added to a pesticide mix, increases the area that a given volume of spray will cover and improves the contact between the pesticide and the plant surface. A spreading agent builds spray deposits and improves weatherability. Most wettable powder insecticides benefit from the addition of a spreader. A sticker or adhesive is a material that, when added to a spray mix or dust, improves the adherence (tenacity) to a plant surface rather than increasing the initial deposit. Commercial sticking agents are oily in consistency and increase the amount of suspended solids retained on plant surfaces by coating the particles with a resin or varnish-like film. Most fungicides, especially wettable powders, benefit greatly from the use of stickers. Stickers may be judged in terms of resistance to wind and water, length of adherence, and mechanical or chemical action.

A wetting agent is a material that, when added to a pesticide, lowers the interfacial tension between a liquid and a solid; in this case, a plant surface. Effectiveness is measured by the increase in spread of a liquid over a solid surface and the ability of the spray film to make complete contact with it. When a wetting agent reduces surface tension, spreading naturally occurs. The pesticide label should state whether a surfactant is needed or should be added to a spray mix for certain applications and should indicate restrictions in the selection of compatible surfactants. In many cases, surfactants have been designed specifically for use with fungicides, insecticides, or herbicides.

All commercial spreading, sticking, and wetting agents should be mixed strictly according to label directions. Adding more surfactant than recommended may cause excessive run-off, resulting in a poor spray deposit and reduced pest control. In general, if the spray mix contains one or more pesticides produced or formulated by the same company, use a surfactant sold or recommended by that company. Surfactants are sold separately from pesticides and are not subject to EPA registration. Although choosing an effective surfactant to accompany a specific pesticide is no simple task, the label will state whether a surfactant is needed and the brand that should be used.

PESTICIDES AND THE ENVIRONMENT

- Direct Kill : Fine mists of herbicides can drift to nearby crops or landscape plants and kill them. Bees and other pollinators can be killed if a crop is treated with a pesticide when they are in the field. The natural enemies of pest insects can also be killed by pesticides. Life in streams or ponds can be wiped out by accidental spraying of ditches and waterways, run-off from sprayed fields, and careless container disposal. If more than one pesticide will control the pest, choose the one that is the least hazardous to the environment and most useful for the situation. To protect beneficial insects, avoid excessive use of insecticides—spray only when crop and pest populations require.
- Protecting Insect Pollinators : Gardeners should give special consideration to protecting insect pollinators, such as the honey bee, from insecticide poisoning. Insecticides highly toxic to bees have restricted application times when being applied to crops frequented by honey bees. Bees are not active in late evening and early morning.

Do not apply insecticides when temperatures are unusually low because residues will remain toxic much longer.

- Persistence and Accumulation : Although most pesticides break down quickly, remaining in the environment only a short time before being changed into harmless products, some pesticides break down slowly and stay in the environment for a long time. These are called persistent pesticides. Some persistent pesticides can build up in the bodies of animals, including man. These pesticides are called accumulative. Most persistent pesticides have very limited usage or have been removed from the market. For example, chlordane is a persistent pesticide and its use was limited to termite and fire ant control but has been removed from the market.
- Pesticides Move in the Environment : Pesticides become problems when they move off target. This may mean drifting off the target if in the form of dust or mist, moving with soil particles by erosion, leaching through the soil, being carried out as residues on crops or livestock, or evapourating and moving with air currents.
- Safe Use Precautions : Following safety precautions and using common sense can prevent harm from pesticides. Here are the minimum safety steps you should take. Before buying a pesticide, identify the pest to be controlled. Then find out which pesticide will control it. If there is a choice of several, choose the least hazardous product. Before purchase, read the label of the pesticide you intend to buy to ensure that the host plant (and pest) are listed on the pesticide label and that the pesticide is not phytotoxic to the plant being protected. Also check safety conditions for use, such as special equipment, protective clothing, restrictions on use, and environmental precautions needed. Before applying the pesticide read the label again. Be sure of proper application and safety measures, including protective clothing and equipment needed, the specific warning and precautions, with what it can be mixed, mixing instructions, application to harvest period for fruit and vegetables, crops to which it can or cannot be applied, and other special instructions.
- Compatibility : Compatibility occurs when two or more pesticides can be mixed together without reducing their effectiveness or harming the target. For instance, carbaryl (Sevin) is often combined with a miticide such as Kelthane in order to kill both insects and mites at one time. Synergism is the action of two materials of the same type which used together produce a greater effect than the sum of the materials when used alone. One of the materials when used alone may not affect the pest, but greatly increases the total effect of the two when used together. *Example:* Chemical A kills 60%, Chemical

B kills 20%, Chemical A and B together kill 98% of the pests. Synergism may increase control or require less chemical. It may also be more harmful to a nontarget organism. A synergistic effect can also be undesirable, causing death or damage to the organism that is being protected. It should be stressed that no chemicals should be mixed together unless the label specifically says they are compatible.

- Home Garden vs Commercial Pesticides : Some pesticides are packaged specifically for home garden use. These products are packaged in small quantities, *i.e.,* pints, quarts, ounces, or pounds. They are seldom highly toxic pesticides and are usually in low concentrations. The label rate is given in spoonfuls per gallon or pounds per 1000 square feet. Because of the small label size, home garden products may not list all of the plants and/or pests for which the product may be registered for use. For example, one manufacturer sells Diazinon 25% EC as Fruit and Vegetable Insect Control and Diazinon Insect Spray. Both are basically the same product, but plants and pests listed vary greatly. This situation causes some confusion in pesticide application and stimulates the purchase of excessive amounts of pesticides. Products packaged for the commercial grower may appear to be less expensive, but consumers should not be tempted to use them. They are generally more toxic than those for home use and require special protective clothing and equipment for application. These products are more concentrated and in larger containers than the consumer could expect to use or safely store, and are much more difficult to calibrate and mix correctly, since rates are usually based on a per-acre system. A few products extremely toxic to humans or the environment are classified by the EPA as restricted use pesticides. The label will state "restricted use pesticides for retail sale to and application only by certified applicators, or person under their direct supervision." A license from the State Department of Agriculture is required by law for purchase and use of restricted use pesticides. This licensing is intended for commercial growers and does NOT automatically clear the use of these products by the home gardener. If you must use pesticides from the commercial trade, use extra caution to protect yourself, your family, and the environment.
- Pesticides and Organic Gardening : Although it is questionable whether we could raise all crops without the use of pesticides, it is certainly true that we can reduce the amount of pesticides we use by careful and efficient use. There are some steps to consider before automatically turning to a pesticide. First, determine if control measures are really needed. Is the problem severe enough to warrant

treatment? If the cost of treatment is less than the predicted loss, the economic threshold has been reached, and treatment is necessary. Consider alternative control measures. Some examples are cultivating instead of using an herbicide, and removing and destroying diseased plant parts rather than using a pesticide. The next step is integrated control. This is probably the best answer to pest control. In this situation, the wise use of pesticides is combined with alternative methods, such as conservation practices, to encourage natural enemies of the pest. For example, a simple integrated control programme could be used on a golf course for grub-proofing against Japanese beetle larvae. A chemical pesticide would be used to protect the more valuable sodded areas of the fairways. Milky spore disease, which is a commercially produced biological control for Japanese beetle larvae, would be applied in the roughs. The chemical pesticide would give immediate protection to the sodded areas while the milky spore disease becomes established in the rough. Then, as the chemical breaks down in the more valuable areas, milky spore disease would move in. Once milky spore disease is established, no more chemical treatment is usually needed to protect the turf.

- Pesticides and the Law : The registration and use of pesticides are governed by the E.P.A. and the Arizona Department of Agriculture and Consumer Services. Under the amended Federal Insecticide, Fungicide, and Rodenticide Act (Federal Environmental Control Act of 1972) it is illegal to use a pesticide on a crop unless the crop is listed on the label. You may not exceed the given rate of application on the label. Fines and other penalties change and vary according to laws broken. Under the law you are liable for misuse of pesticides on your property. Recent court rulings extend your liability to include misuse by commercial applicators you hire. Serious misuse by gardeners usually results from drift, leaching of a pesticide onto non-target plants, or the direct treatment of the plant by a wrong pesticide.

XENOBIOTIC

Modeling methods allow the identification and analysis of determinants of reactivity and specificity in enzymes. The reaction between glutathione and 1-chloro-2,4-dinitrobenzene (CDNB) is widely used as a standard activity assay for glutathione S-transferases (GSTs).

It is important to understand the causes of differences between catalytic GST isoenzymes and the effects of mutations and genetic polymorphisms. Quantum mechanical/molecular mechanical (QM/MM) molecular dynamics simulations have been performed here to investigate the addition of the glutathione anion to CDNB in the wild-type M1-1 GST isoenzyme from rat and in three single point mutant (Tyr6Phe, Tyr115Phe, and Met108Ala) M1-1 GST enzymes.

We have developed a specifically parameterized QM/MM method (AM1-SRP/CHARMM22) to model this reaction by fitting to experimental heats of formation and ionization potentials. Free energy profiles were obtained from molecular dynamics simulations of the reaction using umbrella sampling and weighted histogram analysis techniques.

The reaction in solution has also been simulated and is compared to the enzymatic reaction. The free energies are in excellent agreement with experimental results. Overall the results of the present study show that QM/MM reaction pathway analysis provides detailed insight into the chemistry of GST and can be used to obtain mechanistic insight into the effects of specific mutations on this catalytic process.

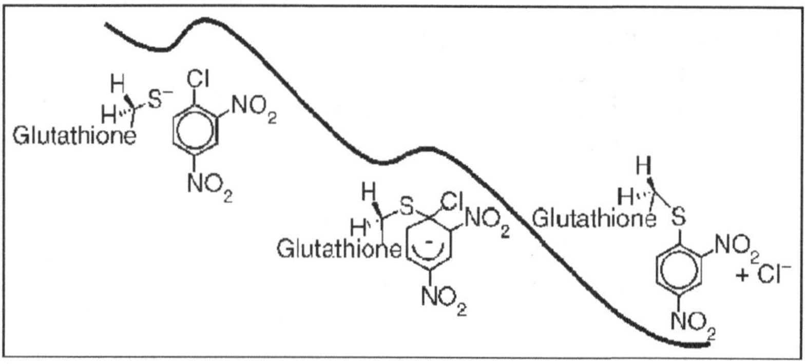

DEGRADATION OF PESTICIDE

Composting is a process in which *microorganisms* rapidly consume organic matter, using it as an energy source and converting it into carbon dioxide, water, *microbial biomass*, heat and *compost*. *Feedstock* used to fuel the composting process may originate from a number of different sources, including yard trimmings, manure, biosolids, and agricultural residues. These materials may contain a number of synthetic organic compounds or *xenobiotics*, including *pesticides*.

Many different physical and chemical factors help determine the overall *persistence* of a pesticide. In general, composting provides an optimal environment for pesticide destruction. This publication discusses the potential for a pesticide to become *inactivated* and degraded during composting.

THE COMPOSTING PROCESS

Compost is well-suited for pesticide degradation because:

- The elevated or *thermophilic* temperatures achieved during composting permit faster biochemical reactions than possible under ambient temperatures, accelerating pesticide degradation. The high temperatures can also make pesticides more *bioavailable*, increasing the chance of microbial degradation.

- Some microorganisms may co-metabolize pesticides, where the microbes rely on the feedstock for food and energy while breaking down an adjacent pesticide. Co-metabolism means that the microorganism does not receive any energy or potential food from the secondary reaction (in this case, from breaking down the pesticide). The many different organic matter *structures* in compost help to promote co-metabolism of numerous objectionable compounds, even *recalcitrant* xenobiotics such as *DDT*, *PCB* and *TCE*.
- Compost feedstock contains numerous and diverse *active* microorganisms, all with their own characteristics and capabilities. This diversity means a greater chance that a pesticide will encounter a microbe that can degrade it.

MECHANISMS AFFECTING PESTICIDES DURING COMPOSTING

Biological Degradation

Microorganisms have developed many *enzymes* that can break down natural compounds. Modern scientists, though, have created pesticides with chemical structures not found in nature. These unique structures are often responsible for a pesticide's effectiveness and also explain why pesticides can persist in the environment.

A pesticide's environmental persistence largely depends on its chemical structure and on the presence of unusual *functional groups*, which are large sub structures within the pesticide molecule. The chemical structure helps determine its *water solubility* and consequently, its bioavailability, since microbes more readily assimilate water-soluble compounds.

When a pesticide's functional groups are attached with weak or *labile* bonds, it can degrade more rapidly. Many modern pesticides have such bonds designed into them to avoid problems of extended persistence. Adding water may break many labile bonds.

This process is called *hydrolysis* and the enzymes that promote hydrolysis are termed hydrolytic. Malathion is an example of an insecticide containing many such labile bonds that may be broken using hydrolytic enzymes (for example, esterase and phosphatase). Other pesticides capable of hydrolytic degradation are: carbamate pesticides, urea derivatives, pyrethroids, diazinon, dicamba, dichloropicolinic acid, dimethoate, phenylalkanoic ester, dimethoate, phenylalkanoic pyrazon, atrazine, linuron, propanil, chlorpyrifos, and 2,4-D.Two other classes of enzymes, mono-and di-oxygenases, are also commonly associated with pesticide degradation. These enzymes introduce one or two oxygen atoms, respectively, into the structure of a pesticide. This *oxidation* process often makes the pesticide more amenable to further degradation by increasing its water solubility, thereby increasing its bioavailability. Degradation may begin at the extracellular level and then proceed further at the intracellular level.

Extracellular Decomposition

Many of the same enzymes microorganisms use to break down cellulose, hemicellulose, and lignin—the primary natural compounds in most plant material—may also degrade pesticides during composting. The large *polymeric* structure of these natural compounds prevents their passage into the microorganism for consumption. To deal with this problem, microorganisms begin breaking down chemicals outside their "body," or extracellularly. They excrete enzymes out of their cells that react with the bonds in cellulose, hemicellulose, and/or lignin, breaking them down into smaller components. The shortened polymers can then be subjected to further degradation. Extracellular enzymes can have very low "specificity," working like a key that fits different locks. They can, therefore, react with many different chemicals. If the enzyme finds a pesticide before reaching its "intended" substrate (for example, cellulose, hemicellulose, lignin), it may react with it, changing the pesticide into a possibly less toxic and less hazardous form. Such co-metabolism appears to play a significant role in degrading pesticides found in compost and soil.

Fungi are the source of most extracellular enzymes. Some fungi often associated with compost and soil organic matter are in the genera *Trichoderma*, *Gliocladium*, *Penicillium*, and *Phanerochaete*. Fungi grow through the development of hyphae (long strings of cells) that extend throughout compost or soil organic matter.

The hyphae release extracellular enzymes, which break down the pesticide and allow it to pass into the cells. This allows the production of additional hyphae and/or energy. Although fungi are present in compost feedstock, they contribute more to composting in its later stages. As bacteria exhaust the easily degraded organic matter from the feedstock, fungi then begin to degrade the more recalcitrant polymeric organic matter.

Intracellular Decomposition

After extracellular enzymes begin breaking down a pesticide or if it is otherwise bioavailable, a pesticide may enter the cell of a microorganism. To pass into a cell efficiently, the pesticide must be dissolved in water. Generally pesticides containing more oxygen, nitrogen, and sulfur tend to be more water soluble due to *hydrogen bonding*. Once inside a cell, a pesticide may undergo varying degrees of degradation. *Mineralization* reduces the pesticide to carbon dioxide, water, and other inorganic components. Typically, it accounts for only a small portion of the "disappearance" of a pesticide through composting.

Adsorption

Water-insoluble pesticides tend to *adsorb* onto and within organic matter, making them even less bioavailable. The chemistry of the functional groups in the pesticide and the organic matter dictates the strength of this pesticide-organic matter interaction. Adsorbed pesticides are generally much more resistant to breakdown than water-soluble pesticides. Consequently, highly adsorbed pesticides are not considered bioavailable, enabling them to persist for months or even years.

However, when a pesticide is adsorbed to organic matter that eventually decomposes, it may once again become bioavailable. Additional factors can make adsorption a likely outcome for even water-soluble pesticides. For example, many pesticides contain acidic and nitrogen-containing functional groups that can adsorb due to the presence of a negative or positive charge, respectively. A negatively charged pesticide will adsorb to positively charged functional groups on organic matter, while positively charged pesticides will adsorb to negatively charged functional groups on organic matter and clays.

Volatilization

Volatilization occurs when a pesticide *partitions* from the solid or *aqueous phase* to the gas phase. Once volatilized, a pesticide may *diffuse* into the atmosphere and either be destroyed or continue as an environmental risk. When mixing disturbs a soil contaminated by a pesticide or other organic compound, a 30 per cent or greater loss of the soil contaminant through volatilization is not unusual. Volatilization of a pesticide is highly temperature dependent; thermophilic temperatures typically increase pesticide losses. The tendency for a pesticide to volatilize also depends upon its size, structure, and function. Moisture also affects volatilization rates. Water may physically impede the flow of a gas phase pesticide by obstructing the *pores* through which gases travel. Water may also promote volatilization by liberating weakly adsorbed pesticides.

Leaching

Water-soluble pesticides have a tendency to be "rinsed away" through a process called leaching, that is, the movement of a chemical within percolating water. Typically, leaching is of concern when the pesticide moves into groundwater or another location, posing an increased risk to humans and/or the environment. Many pesticides are not highly soluble in water, readily adsorbing onto the organic matter fraction. For this reason, use of composts in agricultural soils tends to reduce the threat of pesticide leaching losses.

CASE STUDIES

Many studies have been conducted on the fate of pesticides during composting, some of which are summarized in an article in the Winter 2000 issue of *Compost Science and Utilization*. During composting, pesticides will probably behave differently than they do when in soil. This is because of increased temperature, microbial diversity, microbial activity, and organic matter during composting. While many of these studies showed a significant reduction in detectable pesticides, they also showed only a small percentage of pesticide is typically lost to mineralization.

Besides mineralization, the "disappearance" of pesticides may occur by volatilization, adsorption, leaching, or other methods noted earlier. A pesticide adsorbed to a compost molecule, while technically present, may also be inactivated and could permanently lose its pest control function. Many of the studies showed that concentrations of organophosphate and carbamate pesticides were lower after composting. However, recalcitrant organochlorine insecticides (for example, DDT) and pyridine carboxylic acid herbicides (for example, *clopyralid* and *picloram*) are more resistant to degradation.

Lemmon and Pylypiw studied the persistence of chlorpyrifos, diazinon, isofenphos, and pendimethalin after composting with grass clippings. The authors found the pesticides undetectable shortly after application, and they disappeared quickly after composting. Vandervoort *et al.* showed a similar result: decreasing concentrations of chlorpyrifos, 2,4-D, isoxaben, triclopyr, clopyralid, and fluprimidol after composting with grass clippings. Pesticide levels were below the routine detection limit after 128 days. They were typically lower in samples from inside of compost piles that had been turned versus the exterior and static piles.

Muller and Korte found that only 12 per cent of the initial aldrin, 3 per cent of the dieldrin, and less than 15 per cent of monolinuron and imugan added to municipal solid waste and biosolids feedstock were degraded after composting. In contrast, 55 per cent of the herbicides buturon and heptachlor were degraded. Without any evidence for pesticide mineralization, the authors concluded that composting might not be suitable for treating feedstock contaminated with these persistent pesticides. Critics of this study think the three-week period too short to evaluate the potential for removal of persistent pesticides.

Racke and Frink also presented data on the limited mineralization of a pesticide during composting. Approximately 97 per cent of the insecticide carbaryl was transformed during composting of municipal biosolids, but only 5 per cent of this could be attributed to mineralization. Racke and Frink ended their experiment after a short time (20 days), also drawing criticism. But both studies suggest that appreciable mineralization of a pesticide during composting may take more processing time.

Other studies focused on volatilization and mineralization in pesticide degradation. Petruska *et al.* showed the importance of volatilization in the remediation of pesticide-contaminated compost. Losses due to volatilization reached 22 per cent for diazinon and 50 per cent for chlordane after three weeks of cow manure and sawdust composting. Chlordane was not substantially mineralized, and diazinon was considerably transformed, but again with a low rate of mineralization. Rao *et al.* also found minimal mineralization of the herbicide atrazine during composting with several different wood-derived substrates. After 160 days of composting, there was no detectable atrazine, yet a maximum of 7 per cent had been mineralized. The unmineralized atrazine apparently leached or complexed with the humic components, preventing further *transformation*. While many of the studies have shown significant decreases in detectable pesticides after composting, some of the pesticides were not completely degraded or mineralized. Instead, some were transformed to other chemical compounds, volatilized, adsorbed to the humic fraction, or leached out of the compost. The issue of pesticide toxicity after these types of changes is complex and varies significantly among pesticides. Some pesticides may increase in toxicity once changed, while others may be inactivated. Additional studies are necessary to better understand the fate of pesticides during composting.

POSSIBLE PRECAUTIONARY MEASURES

Consumers and composters should note the possibility that persistent pesticides can endure the composting process at damaging levels. For example, as little as 10 parts per billion of clopyralid can be toxic to legumes, potatoes, sunflowers and tomatoes. Clopyralid and picloram are of concern because they have shown up in compost on at least two occasions. In particular, after the inadvertent composting of contaminated grassy material or manure at two separate Washington composting facilities, routine laboratory tests on the resulting compost by the commercial composting facility did not indicate the presence of pesticides. Subsequent tomato damage first surfaced during 2000 and prompted more sensitive laboratory analysis of the compost that indicated 31–75 parts per billion of clopyralid. Extensive testing of materials used to make the compost identified clopyralid contaminated lawn clippings from Spokane. Later that year another herbicide-laced compost was attributed to picloram contaminated bedding and manure in Pullman. At the same location clopyralid contaminated hay and straw purchased for animal feed, and the resulting manure was also composted during 2001.

Clopyralid is apparently more problematic than picloram since the different registered uses of the two pesticides suggest that materials typically coming into a composting facility are less likely to be contaminated with picloram. As a minimum precaution, operators should become familiar with the supplier and source of each material and enquire regarding persistent herbicide usage. Bioassays by facility operators or highly sensitive analytical tests may be advisable on incoming materials and outgoing products. Washington State

University staff offers bioassay guidelines and colour images of clopyralid-damaged plants at.

Growers and landscapers concerned about pesticide or herbicide residues may also wish to take one or more precautionary measures before applying compost. A few herbicides are phytotoxic below detectable analytical levels, so the above bioassay guidelines may help assess the safety of a compost pile. A simple seed germination test will ensure that a split-sample of compost is mature and any salts present are not phytotoxic. If either bioassay results in no germination or the young plants show symptoms of herbicide damage, it is advisable to perform analytical tests on the remainder of the sample that include tests for suspected herbicides (parts per billion sensitivity), salinity, and compost maturity. Users also can apply the compost in a small test plot before covering an entire garden or farm.

IMPORTANCE OF MICROBIAL PESTICIDES

DESCRIPTION

Studies of natural epizootics of entomopathogenic bacteria and fungi during the latter half of the nineteenth century and the first half of the twentieth century, stimulated man's interest in employing them as microbial pesticides and myco-insecticides to control agricultural pests. Mass production of the selected bacteria and fungi is a necessary prerequisite for any large-scale field application, and the methodology involved was developed at an early stage to suit a number of different pest-pathogen situations. However, this technology stagnated as disillusionment as to the practical value of virus, bacteria and fungi as biological control agents of arthropods and their efficacy against a range of pests became dominant in various parts of the world, following the initial overwhelming success of chemical pesticides.

The revival of interest in microbial insecticides over the last 20 years, has led to large-scale production of *Bacillus thuringiensis*, a promising fungi candidate, and to the marketing of the first bacterio-insecticides Dipel, Thuricide, Bactospeine, Vectobac, Tecnar, Bactimos, Baturin 82 and Myco-insecticides Mycotal, Vertalex based on the formulation of *Verticillium lecani* and Metaqino which is based on the formulation of *Metarhizium anisopliae*. While, the production of bacterio-insecticides is common worldwide, there is little information available on the biotechnology of entomopathogenic fungi, and their industrial production is still relatively unsophisticated.

A microbial toxin can be defined as a biological poison derived from a microorganism, such as a bacterium or fungus. Pathogenesis by microbial entomopathogens occurs by invasion through the integument or gut of the insect, followed by multiplication of the pathogen resulting in the death of the host, *e.g.*, insects. Studies have demonstrated that the pathogens produce insecticidal toxin important in pathogenesis. Most of the toxins produced by microbial pathogens which have been identified are peptides, but they vary greatly in terms of structure, toxicity and specificity. Toxins of *Bacillus thuringiensis* are the most widely investigated example. The organism was first isolated in 1902 by Ishiwata, but it was not until the 1950's that the diamond-shaped crystals or "parasporal bodies" in sporulating cells of B.t. were recognized as being involved in killing insect larvae. Later it was demonstrated that the crystals were mainly protein "polypeptides" and Angus showed that the crystal caused paralysis of the midgut and cessation of feeding in the silkworm, Bombyx mori, while the spores were necessary for the establishment of septicemia.

Many compounds, such as *Beauvericin*, and the destruxin of *Metarhizium anisopliae, aphidicolin* of *Verticillium lecanii* are highly toxic to insects. The more widespread acceptance and use of myco-insecticides will depend on improvement in a number of key areas.

Widespread use of myco-insecticides in China, Brazil and USSR may be repeated in the low-input labour-intensive agricultures around the world. In the short term, with our present level of knowledge, it seems likely that commercial production of myco-insecticides is going to be restricted to small-scale production in specific areas.

At present there appears to be a situation in which biological control agents including fungi would provide a viable commercial option, where conventional chemical control gives insufficient control or where there is insecticide resistance; where conventional chemicals are too expensive; or where government restricts application of chemicals.

Despite these problems many of the multinationals are now pursuing projects on biological control. However, predictably, most interest appears to be focused on microbial toxins, with the view of expressing pathogen toxin genes in plants or using the toxins themselves as starter molecules for developing new chemical insecticides.

PRODUCTION AND COMMERCIALIZATION OF PATHOGENS

The practical use of microbial agents which kill insects is being carried out by many scientists and horticulturists throughout the world. Other alternatives to chemical pesticides are also under investigation, including novel pest control systems based on parasitic and predatory insects, predatory mites, fungi, bacteria, viruses, protozoans, nematodes and pheromones which modify the behaviour of insects for man's benefit. However, most of these novel systems have not yet been exploited in agricultural practice on a commercial scale. This is due to the series of sometimes lengthy and sometimes expensive steps which must be carried out before new pest control systems can be offered to the grower.

- Steps Leading to Commercialization : Once any new system has been identified and characterized in the laboratory, the following steps must be completed before it can be successfully commercialized.

Process Development: A process must be developed which can be carried out on a large enough scale to ensure that an adequate amount of the material can be made. This process must be sufficiently reliable to provide a product which is both safe and effective. In addition, the production cost must allow manufacturers to make a profit.

Product Development: Many systems for controlling pests are successful in the laboratory. However they fail when tried in the greenhouse or in the field. This is one of the many problems which must be solved by product development. Products must be manufactured and formulated in a way which makes them stable for the longest possible time, as convenient as possible to use, and as immune as possible to "use and abuse" *i.e.* the failure of many people to store or use the product as directed and then to blame the product for poor performance. Recommendations must be developed for the use of the product in actual agricultural practice.

Normally these recommendations cannot be so novel or so complex or require such unconventional equipment that people refuse to use the product. Often the recommendations are developed in collaboration with the appropriate advisory service to ensure that they will be accepted by the trade. For novel products, testing is necessary to establish that they are safe to use; in addition, quality control tests must be devised which will ensure that every batch will be safe and effective. Once any testing is completed and quality control protocols developed, the appropriate government authority must be approached for permission to sell the product; at present, this must be done individually for every country in the world. Once a product has been sold, it is often helpful to visit growers who have used it, either to confirm its success or if it has failed, to investigate and determine the cause. Further development work can than be carried out to find ways of avoiding product failure in the future.

Local Marketing and Sales: Once made, the product must be sold and used if all the effort spent in development is to be worthwhile. There are many obstacles to selling alternative pesticides, especially fungi. Users are unfamiliar with how to use these types of products and how they work. Marketing requires extra efforts both to familiarize growers with the new product and to provide a substantial back-up service for the product.

- Process Development and Production: Before one can sell a live micro-organism as a pest control agent, a reliable method of production must be developed which yields large quantities for which a product specification can be drawn up.

Organism Storage: The first problem in producing a micro-organism is storing it in a way that ensures the retention of desirable features. The most obvious feature to be retained is pathogenicity; the second is productivity in terms of yield in the commercial production process. This is typically measured either by total biomass, or by number of infective propagules, *i.e.* spores or fragments of mycelium, produced per litre-hour of fermentation time. Many microorganisms are known to lose desirable features either on storage or after repeated sub-culturing. Among insect pathogens, Beauveria bassiana has been reported to have reduced virulence after subculturing whereas both Verticillium lecanii and Metarhizium anisopliae are reported as being undiminished in virulence after many passages. Organisms which lose virulence may sometimes be restored to their former potency by passing them through their normal host, *i.e.* the target insect; however, such a technique would be cumbersome as a routine part of a production process and always presents the risk of contamination. Therefore the problem is often avoided by storing a large number of elements of a single spore isolate in a deep frozen or freeze-dried condition. Samples are checked periodically to make certain that virulence and productivity have not diminished with time.

Fermentation Method: The standard method of production of microorganisms is the process of fermentation. There are many types of fermentation; the two most common are "submerged" and "semi-solid". Submerged or deep-tank fermentation is, as the name implies, a growth of micro-organisms in a fully liquid system. There are a number of advantages to fully liquid systems which include the ability to hold temperature and pH constant, the ability to pump large quantities of air into the system and disperse it by means of stirring impellers, and the ability to generate reasonably homogeneous conditions to maximize the growth of micro-organism. Despite the many advantages of submerged fermentation some fungi will not yield a satisfactory product by this technique.

Semi-solid fermentation offers an alternative in which the fungi grow primarily on the wet surface of a solid material, often some form of processed cereal grain to which nutritional adjuvants have been added, though attempts are made frequently to use "waste" materials or media of low value, such as straw. This allows fungi to grow in conditions more similar to those found in nature; spores, the infective propagules by which the fungus survives and infects insects, are produced in the air and are consequently more durable. Semi solid fermentations are relatively easy to develop on a small scale. Scaling them up to the sizes necessary for commercial product presents numerous problems; aeration becomes a major difficulty as the volume of a semi-solid mass increases more rapidly than the available surface area. This requires either a very large area of relatively shallow media, *e.g.* on trays, or in a vessel which can agitate or tumble the media. On any scale, trays are very difficult to sterilize and keep sterile. *The development of large vessels for semi-solid media fermentation requires the invention of a number of techniques or pieces of equipment for:*

Keeping the media friable after sterilization. Its tendency is to set solid when it cools, rather like oatmeal.

- Inoculation with the desired fungus without contamination
- Aeration and agitation during fermentation

Drying the material prior to opening the fermenter in order to avoid contamination, etc.

Medium Development : Which ever type of fermentation is chosen, nutrients must be provided so that the micro-organism can grow. Which nutrients are chosen will markedly affect how fast the organism grows, how much is produced and often, how infective the final product is. Nutrients to be provided include a carbon source, *e.g.* glucose or molasses, nitrogen source, *e.g.* soybean meal or yeast extract, and a "defined", in which case the precise nature and quantity of every nutrient is known, or, alternatively, they can contain ingredients of an indeterminate and occasionally variable nature *e.g.* molasses; most commercial media are latter type.

THEORETICAL BACKGROUND OF INDUSTRIAL PROCESSING IN BIOTECHNOLOGY

The two main disciplines which determine the trends of small and large-scale industrial microbiology are theoretical micro-biology (including microbial genetics, physiology and bio-chemistry) which forms the theoretical ground, and microbial engineering which creates the basis for the application of engineering aspects in microbial processes. A successful microbial process on a small or large scale requires the research and development [R&D] of methods satisfying providing for the following demands: Maintenance of stability of the production culture, both in its initial form (preservation) and as subcultures infrequently propagated via sporulation or vegetative generations. Maintenance of suitable conditions ensuring reproducible yields.

This entails the use of row materials of appropriate quality, especially complex organic compounds, and the development of analytical methods for controlling both culture processes and the quality of the raw materials used. Application of the technology for maintaining strictly aseptic conditions; this factor is important in the biotechnology of most products, in the isolation steps, and in the conversion of the product to the final form. Increase in production yields of a particular product by modifying the medium composition and the genetic properties of the production strain.

Laboratory Processing

- *Cleanliness and Safety:* The normal technical procedures designed to keep cultures sterile or pure and prevent cross-infection of laboratory materials contribute considerably to the safety of the individuals an most laboratory workers observe reasonably high standards of personal hygiene and wash their hands after handling cultures of any kind and before touching the rest of their person, handling their food or smoking. The maximum standards of safety can be achieved only if every laboratory worker has a real understanding of the basic principles and is able to apply them to reduce the risk in each particular circumstance.

- *Safety Cabinets "FLOWBOX" :* There are cabinets which are fitted with filters which remove particles down to 0.01 mm and discharge their effluence into the laboratory air.
- *Ultra-violet Light:* Continuous irradiation of the air above eye level is possible and reduces the bacterial content. Ultra-violet light can be used to disinfect the insides of protective cabinets but to much reliance should not be placed on this as a disinfecting agent. Chemical methods should also be used (75% ethylalcohol). Ultra-violet light does not penetrate surfaces.
- *Use of the Microscope:* One important microbiological technique will be introduced: the use of the oilimmersion objective is essential to most microscopic studies of bacterial cells. The best type of microscope is with Phase-contrast.

Preparation of Dilution

- Examples of Dilutions :

1 × 10-2 or 1: 100; 1.0 ml + 99.0 ml or 1.0 ml: (99 ml) = 1/100

2 × 10-2 or 1: 50; 2.0 ml + 98.0 ml

5 × 10-3 or 1: 200; 0.5 ml + 99.5 ml

2 × 10-4 means 2/10.000 = 1/5.000

- *Dilution Plate Counting and Distribution of Bacteria: Preparation of Dilutions:* Shake each stock dilution well. Using aseptic techniques, transfer 0.1 ml of the 100 stock dilution to a 9.9 ml dilution blank (1:10,000 dilution). Mix well to obtain even distribution of organisms. With a pure pipette, place 1.0 ml of the 1:10,000 dilution into a sterile Petri plate and with the same pipette transfer 1.0 ml to a 9.0 ml dilution blank (1:100,000). Discard the pipette and mix the dilution to a fresh 9.0 ml dilution blank (1:1,000,000). Mix. with a fresh pipette transfer 1.0 ml of the final dilution to a sterile Petri dish. Pour approximately 15-20 ml of nutrient agar which has been steam-pressure sterilized (autoclaved) and cooled to 45oC in a water bath; then rotate each plate to mix the inoculum and medium. After the agar has completely solidified (15-30 minutes) invert the plates and place in incubator space to dry off excess surface moisture. Time of incubation is 2 days at 25 or 28oC. After incubation count the number of colonies.

Pure Culture Techniques Tube Transfers : Transfers from agar plates to tubes, and from tube culture to tube is a common and simple procedure, but requires careful attention to certain details. Transfer from a colony on an agar plate to an agar slant or tube of broth may be made either a straight wire or a loop.

Pure Culture : Pure cultures of different microbial species and subspecies may be isolated from the highly complex mixed populations in nature by a variety of methods, the most common of which will be used is a dilution plating. Each discrete colony which arises in or on a well prepared dilution plate is assumed to be composed of cells, all of which are descendant of a single cell. Sub-cultures from such a colony should produce colonies all of the same kind, any one of which is composed all of the same kind of cells as the original colony. After culture purity has been established in subcultures, a stock culture of the organism is established. The stock culture may be maintained on an agar slant kept in the refrigerator, but unless it is transferred at suitable intervals to establish a fresh stock, it may loss its viability (its capacity to reproduce). Viability of agar slant cultures may be prolonged by covering the slant with a layer of sterile mineral oil to exclude oxygen and prevent evaporation. Since frequent transfers of stock cultures encourage accumulation and selection of mutations, microbiologists often preserve pure cultures virtually unchanged for identifinite periods by lyophilization (a suspension of cells is quick-frozen at about-60oC, rapidly dried under high vacuum, then hermetically sealed in a glass tube) or by immersion in liquid nitrogen (-195oC).

- *Preparation and Testing of Culture Media :* Copper or zinc containers must not be used. Small quantities of these metals will dissolve in the culture media and are bactericidal and fungicidal. Large quantities of media can be made in stainless steel buckets such as are used in dairy and food trades. Smaller amounts can be made in resistance glass laboratory flasks. Distilled water of commercial bulk supplier quality may contain substances which inhibit bacterial growth, *e.g.* oil materials from stripper stills attached to steam lines. Manesty-type distilled water, glass-distil water and deionized water should be used, although it must be realised that some "trace elements" necessary to bacterial growth are in fact supplied by the distilled water, by glassware, or by recognized impurities analytical quality reagents. Dextrose, when autoclaved with salts such as phosphate may yield inhibitory substances. It is best to add this and other carbohydrates as sterile solutions after the medium has been sterilized. Excessive heating, and remelting may destroy growth factors and gelling capacity and cause darkening or pH drift of culture media.

Adjustment of Ph : Pipette 10 ml of the medium into a 152 mm × 16 mm test-tube and measure pH with indicator test-paper; according to scale can be seen the pH value, and can be corrected by N/20 HCl or N/20 NaOH. *Example*: 10 ml of medium at pH 6.4 requires 0.6 ml of N/20 NaOH to give the required pH 7.2, than the bulk medium will require

$$\frac{19 \times 1000\text{ml}}{20 \times 10} \text{ of N.NaOH per liter} = 3.0 \text{ ml}$$

All final readings of pH must be made with the medium at room temperature because hot medium will give a false reaction with some indicators.

Sterilization : The usual objective in heat sterilization is the destruction of all microorganisms with the least possible damage to the material being sterilized. "Sterilization", as commonly understood, is not necessarily absolute; for example, instrument sterilizers may kill all infection—causing bacteria, but not all sporeforming bacteria. The aim in sterilization of culture media is the destruction of all life without rendering the medium ineffective for cultivation because of physical and/or chemical damage to its ingredients. Methods employing moist or dry heat, or filtration are used in the sterilization of culture media and of materials and equipment used in the bacteriological laboratory.

Steam Sterilization : Steam under pressure in a closed system (autoclave) is frequently used to sterilize heat stable culture media, heat stable chemicals, dilution blanks, rubber articles, and to sterilized heat stable culture media (antibiotic) must be sterilized before being added aseptically to be sterilized, cooled media. A temperature of 121oC at 1.5 MPa pressure for 15 minutes generally is required for moist heat sterilization.

The most important point in the operation of the autoclave is the removal of all air from the chamber. The temperature rather than the pressure is the lethal agent. Therefore, it is important that the desired temperature is reached before timing the sterilization cycle. Adequate time must be allowed for heat convection current to penetrate the centre of the material. Preheating large quantities of media is often desirable to reduce the over-exposure to sterilization temperature. Viscosity reduces convection, and therefore, a long period of time is required for sterilization of agar than of broth. Two to five minutes must be added for agar sterilization. Never autoclave solidified agar in a flask; most of the autoclaving time is required to melt the agar. Premelt the agar in a boiling water bath prior to sterilization.

Flaming : Although not achieving red heat, flaming is a method commonly used for decontaminating the mouths of bottles, flasks, culture tubes, glass slides, scalpels etc. by passing them though a Bunsen flame without allowing them to become red hot.

Hot Air : The process of sterilization by hot air ovens is simple in principle and the materials to be processed can be prepacked in craft paper or sealed in metal containers. The method is used for sterilizing such articles as glass syringe etc. Material such as dry powders, fats, oils and petroleum jelly in small shallow containers can also be sterilized by this method. Air is not a good conductor of heat so that hot air sterilization poses problems of penetration. Special apparatus "fan" is needed to ensure that all parts of the load have been maintained at the required temperature. The hot air must circulate between the packages. The Heating-Up Period is the time taken to reach sterilization temperature; this may take about 1 hour. *The Holding Periods at different sterilization temperatures recommended are:*

160oC for 45 min.
170oC for 18 min
180oC for 7 min

The Cooling-Down Period is carried out gradually to prevent glassware from cracking as a result of a too rapid fall in temperature. This period may take up to 2 hours. The full sterilizing process from loading the oven to unloading it may therefore take about 3–4 hours, depending on the size of load. Long exposure to a lower dry heat temperature has been a method of sterilization recommended like a dry heat cycle of 135oC for 22 hours.

Preservation of Strains

Variability, one of the characteristic features of microorganisms, tends to increase with increasing productivity of producer strains. The variability can result in transient, non-hereditary changes, or in permanent changes of hereditary character. In some cases the properties of the whole culture change, in others the culture becomes heterogeneous. Heterogeneous cultures comprise a number of cell variants with diverse morphological, physiological or biochemical properties. The heterogeneity or homogeneity of a culture can usually be examined by plating individual spores or cells onto a solid medium and comparing the properties of the resulting cultures. Transient changes on the cultures are usually easily eliminated since they depend mostly on the composition of the media used for culture and on other ambient conditions. The Development of Uniform and Stringently Defined Culture Procedures to Eliminate the Transient Variability of Production Cultures. Close attention must be paid to the permanent, hereditary changes in the cultures. In most cases the change does not affect the whole culture and the homogeneous parent culture thus becomes heterogeneous.

The strain heterogeneity is currently thought to be brought about by uncontrolled environmental factors. Its appearance depends on the ambient conditions in the broadest sense of the word; for instance, certain sporulation media give rise to a larger number of variants than others. Strain heterogeneity is more conspicuous with a spore inoculum than with a vegetative one.The culture requires a strict regulation and control of ambient conditions (temperature, aeration and mixing intensity, composition of medium etc.); equal care should be exercised to ensure the highest yields and the highest stability of the strain. A variety of methods have therefore been developed for culture preservation. To preserve a strain properly means to maintain it under conditions ensuring the longest possible stability of the culture; in other words, under conditions minimizing the occurrence of permanent hereditary changes leading to strain heterogeneity.

Production strains can be preserved in several ways depending on the type of microorganism:

- Preservation of cultures on sporulation agar slopes at low temperatures.
- Preservation of cultures on agar slopes which are, after inoculation, overlaid with sterile liquid paraffin. This technique is suitable for preserving nonsporulating fungi and yeasts.
- Lyophilisation or freeze-drying is based on freezing vegetative cells or spores to temperatures far below the freezing point and drying them under a high vacuum. The suspension obtained by washing the culture from the surface of the medium which contains agar is transferred to test tubes containing either a protective colloid such as broth, blood serum, whey, or a mixture of soil and sand. The samples are frozen in solid carbon dioxide in ethanol and then dried in a vacuum of about 7–70 Pa. The test tubes are then sealed under vacuum. The resulting stock cultures so preserved (about 1g) can serve to inoculate only a small number of subcultures.

Preservation of cultures in liquid nitrogen. Cultures sealed in glass ampoules are rapidly frozen by placing them in a container with liquid nitrogen.

Elaboration of a Processing

The development of a process includes three steps: elaboration on laboratory scale, small scale and pilot large scale production and finalization of product *e.g.* formulation of microbial pesticides.

Laboratory Scale

The goal of the laboratory research is to develop

- Preservation of the culture
- Culture of the strain on solid media and its propagation,
- Nutrient medium of a suitable composition,
- Techniques of laboratory submerged or semi-solid scale culture.

The medium for propagation of the strain has to meet several demands. It has to ensure perfect growth and sporulation and, at the same time, guarantee a satisfactory stability of the strain. Both the strain and its culture conditions, *i.e.* the composition of the nutrient medium, incubation temperature, time of incu-bation, etc., should be conceived as forming an integral system which can be severely disturbed by changing only some of the conditions.

The appropriate preservation techniques are to be determined by studying the stability of the production strain preserved by different techniques, in long-term experiments. Each type of stock culture should be prepared in a sufficient amount even when the preserved strain is not yet optimal for production. This procedure ensures the supply of a uniform inoculation material for sufficient periods of time; the stability of the strain in the spectrum activity to target organisms and the efficiency of preservation must be examined in long-term studies over several years.

The composition of the nutrient medium is determined at the initial stages of research; the medium should, above all, ensure reproducible yields. The quality and quantity of raw materials used, and the technique of media preparation (sterilization, etc.) should be adjusted accordingly. Apart from productivity, a number of additional factors determine the medium composition suitable for scale-up purposes. These include the accessibility and price of individual raw materials, their sterilizability, requirements for an economical isolation procedure and final formulation of the product.

The next step is the elaboration of the process on a laboratory scale when the culture is usually grown on reciprocal or rotary shakers, the latter affording a more intensive aeration of the culture. The optimum aeration regime for laboratory cultures can be attained by using shakers with different types of motions, changing the shape of the culture flasks and the volume of the nutrient medium. The aeration intensity is to some extent inversely proportional to the amount of the medium in the flask.

With optimum aeration intensity defined, other factors are determined which could affect the product yields and the length of time necessary to attain maximum yield. Another important facet is the determination of a strain stability during vegetative transfers. Experiments conducted in flasks on laboratory shakers provide fundamental information on the production strain, the composition of the medium, suitable type of inoculum, etc., but they provide meagre data on technological factors such as the choice of construction materials, aeration, measuring and control devices, etc. All this information is obtained from experiments with laboratory and seed fermenters.

Small Scale Production

The first task in small scale production is the development of a basic culture procedure affording reproducible results. Absolute production yields are of secondary importance, the main emphasis being put on the expected standard course of the microbial process with the attendant changes in growth, pH, consumption of nutrients, production of metabolites, and in the physiological state of the microorganisms. On attaining reproducible results the search for individual optimum conditions can begin. The first factors to be explored are usually aeration and stirring. Next to be examined is the effect of changes in the ratio of individual components of the nutrient medium, with special reference to the source of carbon and nitrogen and their mutual proportions.

The effect of different types and amounts of antifoam agents is also studied since the physical action of these agents can affect the dispersion of air in the culture and respiration of the microorganisms; some antifoam agents (vegetable oils, lard oil) can be utilized by the microorganisms, thus changing the metabolism of the culture. Fluid from laboratory and small scale fermenters can be used for tentative isolation of metabolites and preliminary tests of their quality.

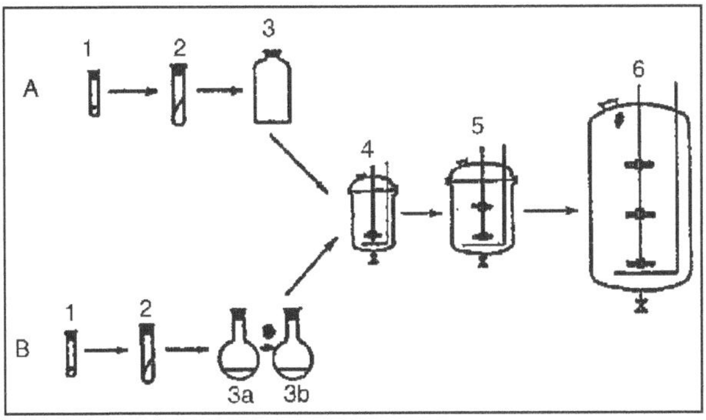

Fig. Preparation of a Microbial Product

A-spore inoculum, B-vegetative inoculum;

1- Stock culture of production strain,

2- Sporulation generation I on agar slant,

3- Sporulation generation II on solid medium in a Roux flask 3a,3b-generations I and II on liquid medium in a flask,

4- Preseeding fermenter,

5- Seeding fermenter,

6-main fermenter (50-500 or 1,000 litres) of small scalc production. Pilot plant for large-scale production have 5,000—50,000 litres fermenters.

Problems of Contamination of Microbial Processes

Microbial contamination of fermentation processes and principles and techniques for its elimination should be appraised from several viewpoints:

- Type of the metabolite produced;
- Specific properties of the culture;
- Machinery and equipment used in the process;
- Nutrient medium and the raw materials used for its preparation;
- Technology adopted in the process.

Contaminating microorganisms affect negative the microbial process by:

- Destroying the cells of the production strain,
- Inactivating the synthesized metabolites,

- Producing substances affecting the producer‘s metabolism and thus decreasing the production of the required metabolite,
- Exhausting compounds crucial for growth and product synthesis from the medium.

However, the presence of a contaminating microorganism need not always results in a drop in metabolite or spores production; in the absence of this drop, it is often difficult to detect contamination. In semi-solid fermentation process, contamination need not always lead to failure. The term "protected fermentation" is used for such processes in which foreign contamination is suppressed by the presence of an antimicrobial agent. This agent is added to the medium in suitable form.

Sterility of Microbial Process

Checks of the absence of alien microorganisms are required during all crucial stages of the process, culture, product isolation, and its final formulation. Identification of microbial contamination is done by microscopic and culture methods. Microscopic examination represents a useful tool for immediate detection of massive contamination of cultures with an alien microflora. In most cases viable cells are difficult to distinguish from dead ones. The differentiation is somewhat aided by the so-called vital test which, however, is not always fully reliable. The most reliable method for identification of alien microorganisms is by culturing.

The following procedure is currently used in laboratories: Samples are transferred under aseptic conditions into sterile flasks. A volume of 1 ml serves to inoculate two tubes with 5ml broth each and, using a loop, blood, blood agar in a Petri dish. Incubation is then carried out for 24-48 hours at 37oC. Both microscopic and macroscopic counts of alien microorganisms are then taken. If the results are not unequivocal then 1 ml of culture from the test tubes and colonies on the Petri dishes is used to inoculate another four test tubes (2 + 2) and counts are taken again after 24 hours of incubation at 37oC. A macroscopic indication of the presence of contaminating microorganisms is often a different growth form.

Sensitivity of Microbial Processes to and Protection against Contamination

From this viewpoint, microbial processes can be divided into:

- Processes that do not require stringent control and protection against the proliferation of a foreign microflora in the medium,
- Processes requiring strictly aseptic conditions-the so-called aseptic processes-microbial insecticides.

Pilot-Plant-Fermenters

Although crucial technological factors may be assessed in laboratory fermenters, it is often necessary to verify the laboratory results in devices more closely resembling industrial fermenters. These devices are pilot-plant fermenters; they serve to complete, modify and verify the data obtained in laboratory fermenters and to test the suitability of construction, regulation an monitoring devices.

Since, with the same type of agitator with dimensions proportional to fermenter dimensions, laboratory fermenters require higher impeller speed to achieve the same aeration effect as in large fermenters, and since the aeration effect depends largely on the transfer of mechanical force into liquid via the impeller, the verification of agitation and aeration conditions is of utmost importance. Different types of agitators, their relative size, different types and dimensions of baffles, aeration systems, and the effect of their position inside the fermenter are also studied on pilot-plant scale.

Sterility criteria. A basic feature of most microbial technology is the stringent requirement for the absence of foreign microorganism during the process (without contamination).

This has to be maintained throughout the process from the moment of opening of stock culture to the termination of growth. Large fermenters offer a greater possibility of culture contamination, being much more complicated than laboratory devices.

The presence or absence of contaminating microorganisms is determined by the so-called sterility test. The fermenter is supplied with a relatively rich medium but not inoculated. A conventional process is then carried out including agitation, air feed and sampling and for duration at least equal to that of the real process. Samples of medium are then subjected to sterility tests in a laboratory.

These tests are necessary since each unsuccessful pilot-plant and, especially, industrial scale run represents a considerable economical loss owing to the large volume of medium and high operating costs involved. To meet the demand for the absence of foreign microorganisms, the device has to be sterilized thoroughly and the possibility of contamination by undesirable microorganisms must be excluded.

Pilot-plant fermenters, their pipelines and fittings are sterilized prior to medium sterilization, sometimes together with air filters. After medium sterilization, the outlet valve at the bottom of the fermenter is briefly opened to remove air bubbles and the medium is cooled down.

When the pressure inside the fermenter drops to 0.05 MPa, air is introduced by means of the aeration device. During sterilization all valves and connecting lines are flushed with steam. Flange packing and seals are used as rarely as possible and, wherever possible, are replaced by welding. When using flanges, the packing has to be selected carefully.

The packing must not be made of porous materials but even the most common nonporous material, rubber, has to be of high quality, without textile ply, and has to be resistant to high sterilization temperatures without losing elasticity or cracking. Valves are mounted in such a way that their packing is located underneath the steam seal, usually in a horizontal position. The mounting of valves on a fermenter deviates from conventional rules; here the streaming liquid does not flow against the valve cone.

The valves are mounted so that the cone shaft packing communicates with the valve steam seal, not with the fermenter interior. This is because of the risk of microbial contamination by growth through the packing, which is especially acute in valves with large construction lengths. The valves have to be placed so that no condensate is formed on the steam-blocked side since this would prevent a through heating by steam.

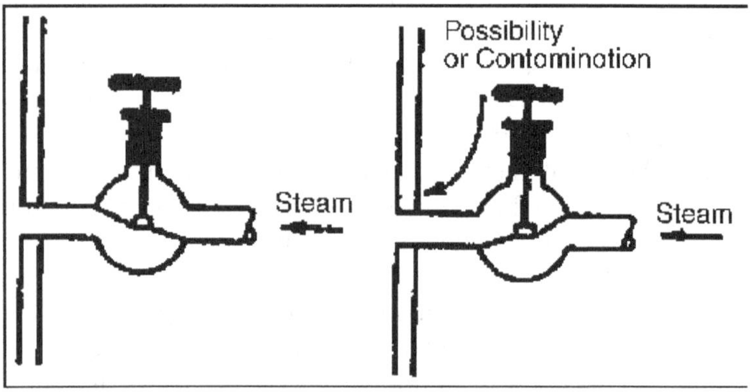

Fig. Valve Mounting

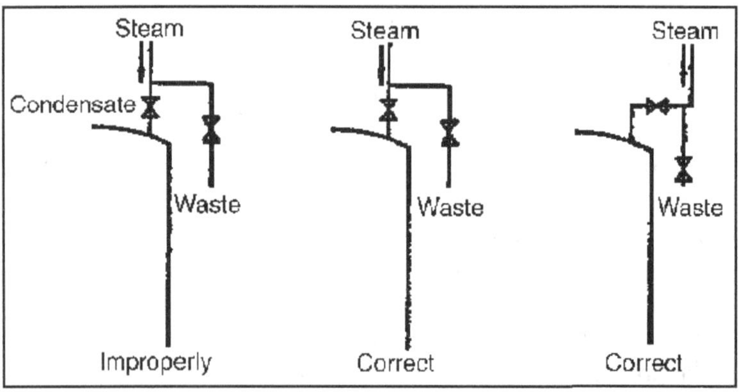

Fig. Valve Blocking Whit Sleam

Valves communicate directly with the medium in the fermenter wall, with minimum length of connecting tubes. This holds especially for medium sample collectors. It is convenient to arrange valves into a system of valve sets which take up less room and are sealed by a common steam inlet. Manometers, valves and back pressure regulators are mounted on the descending part of tubes wherever possible.

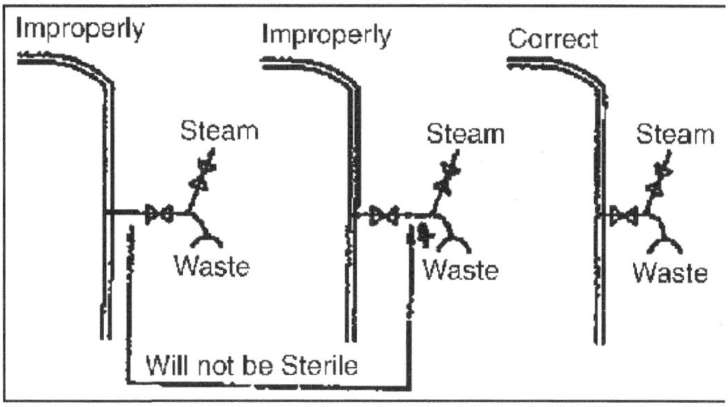

Fig. Sampling System Mounting

Contamination may often be caused by minute leakages in cooling coils or jackets. The localization of these leakages is often difficult, testing for them should include a thorough mechanical removal of medium residue adhering to surfaces and the use of relatively high water pressures. The test for leaks may be carried out using air or ammonia, with detection of the ammonia leakage by an appropriate reagent.

The correct position of packing in a flange is tested by smearing its circumference with a soap solution and observing the formation of soap bubbles at leakages points. The contamination of medium by Gram-positive microorganisms from the air is usually due to faulty packing or air filter failure whereas Gram-negative microorganisms come from water through leakages in the cooling system.

The design and construction of pilot-plant fermenters has to meet the following requirements:

- No connection should exist between sterile and nonsterile parts of tubes and fittings;
- Connection and flange packing should be made of higher-quality rubber without textile ply;
- Wherever possible, welded construction should be used;
- Valves and other fittings should be easy to sterilize and should remain sterile throughout the culture process;
- After sterilization all parts and tubes that have to remain sterile should be kept at a constant positive pressure of sterile air;
- It is necessary that every part of the device can be separately sterilized without disturbing the operation of other parts;
- Inlet and outlet valves and tubing which are not otherwise protected should be connected to a live steam inlet;
- Prior to each new fermentation the tightness of fermenter seal, tube connections, valves and other fittings should be tested.

STANDARDS FOR HAZARDOUS WASTE FACILITIES

LEGAL AUTHORITY

This rule is promulgated under 38 M.R.S.A. Section 1301, et seq., which prohibits the establishment, construction, alteration or operation of a waste facility for hazardous waste without a license and authorizes the Board of Environmental Protection to adopt rules establishing standards for the licensing of these facilities.

PREAMBLE

It is the purpose of the Department of Environmental Protection, consistent with legislative policy, to provide necessary controls over hazardous waste facilities so as to ensure the protection of public health, safety, welfare and the environment.

The Board of Environmental Protection will administer this rule in a conservative fashion because it recognizes that many unknowns remain about the shortterm and longterm impacts of hazardous waste to public health and natural ecosystems. The intent of this rule is to protect the public health, safety, and general welfare and the environment; the burden of proof shall rest with each applicant seeking a license for a waste facility for hazardous waste to affirmatively demonstrate that the intent of this rule will be met at all times.

DEFINITIONS

For purposes of this rule, terms not defined in this section shall have the meaning given them in 38 M.R.S.A., Sections 361A and 1303-C. The following terms as used in this rule shall have the following meaning unless the context indicates otherwise.

- Aboveground tank. "Aboveground tank" means a device meeting the definition of "tank" which is situated in such a way that the entire surface area of the tank is completely above the plane of the adjacent surrounding surface and the entire surface area of the tank (including the tank bottom) can be visually inspected.
- Active Life. "Active life" means the period from the initial receipt of hazardous waste at the facility until the Department receives certification of final closure.
- Ancillary equipment. "Ancillary equipment" means any device including, but not limited to, such devices as piping, fittings, flanges, valves, and pumps, that is used to distribute, meter, or control the flow of hazardous waste from its point of generation to a storage or treatment tank(s), between hazardous waste storage or treatment tanks to a point of disposal on-site, or to a point of shipment for disposal offsite.

- Claims made policy. "Claims made policy" means an insurance policy that provides coverage for an occurrence for which a claim arising out of the occurrence is made during the term of the policy or any extension thereof.
- Component. "Component" means either the tank or ancillary equipment of a tank system.
- Container. "Container" means any portable device in which a material is stored, transported, treated, disposed of, or otherwise handled.
- Corrosion expert. "Corrosion expert" means a person who, by reason of his knowledge of the physical sciences and the principles of engineering and mathematics acquired by a professional education and related practical experience is qualified to engage in the practice of corrosion control on buried or submerged metal piping systems and metal tanks.
- Such a person must be certified as being qualified by the National Association of Corrosion Engineers (NACE) or a registered professional engineer who has certification or licensing that includes education and experience in corrosion control on buried or submerged metal piping systems and metal tanks.
- Dike. "Dike" means a berm, embankment or ridge of either natural or manmade materials used to prevent the lateral movement of liquids, sludges, solids or other materials.
- Existing tank system. "Existing tank system" or "existing component" means a tank system or component used for the storage or treatment of hazardous waste that is in operation, or which installation has commenced on or prior to July 14, 1986. Installation will be considered to have commenced if the owner or operator has obtained all Federal, State, and local approvals or permits necessary to begin physical construction of the site or installation of the tank system and if either (1) a continuous on-site physical construction or installation program has begun, or (2) the owner or operator has entered into contractual obligations, which cannot be canceled or modified without substantial loss, for physical construction of the site or installation of the tank system to be completed within a reasonable time.
- Final Closure. "Final closure" means the closure of all hazardous waste management units at the facility in accordance with all applicable requirements so that hazardous waste management activities are no longer conducted, except as provided in Chapter 851, Section 8(B).
- Food chain crops. "Food chain crops" means tobacco, crops grown for human consumption, and crops grown for feed for animals whose products are consumed by humans.

- Freeboard. "Freeboard" means the vertical distance between the top edge of a tank or surface impoundment dike and the surface of the waste contained therein.
- Hazardous waste incinerator. "Hazardous waste incinerator" means an enclosed device using controlled flame combustion, a purpose of which is to thermally break down hazardous waste. Examples of incinerators are rotary kiln, fluidized bed, and liquid injection incinerators, cement kilns and boilers used to thermally treat hazardous waste.
- Hazardous Waste Management Unit. "Hazardous waste management unit" as is defined in 40 CFR 260.10.
- Hydraulic conductivity. "Hydraulic conductivity" means a recognized measure of water permeability under standard conditions of hydraulic head.
- Inground tank. "Inground tank" means a device meeting the definition of tank whereby a portion of the tank wall is situated to any degree within the ground, thereby preventing visual inspection of that external surface area of the tank that is in the ground.
- Installation inspector. Installation inspector means a person who by reason of his knowledge of the physical sciences and the principles of engineering, acquired by a professional education and related practical experience, is qualified to supervise the installation of tank systems.
- Landfill. "Landfill" is defined as is defined in 40 CFR 260.10.
- Land treatment.
- "Land treatment" means the treatment of hazardous waste by application onto or incorporation into the soil surface so that the waste is rendered nonhazardous by soil processes. A land treatment facility is a disposal facility if the waste will remain after use of the facility ceases.
- Leachate. "Leachate" means any liquid or semiliquid, including any suspended components therein, that has percolated through or drained from hazardous waste.
- Leak detection system. "Leak detection system" means a system capable of detecting the failure of either the primary or secondary containment structure or the presence of a release of hazardous waste or accumulated liquid in the secondary containment structure. Such a system must employ operational controls (e.g., daily visual inspections) or consist of an interstitial monitoring device designed to detect continuously and automatically the failure of the primary or secondary containment structure or the presence of a release of hazardous waste into the secondary containment structure.

- Abbreviated License. "Abbreviated License" means authorization to establish, construct, alter or operate a facility upon and for so long as the facility is in compliance with requirements established by Chapter 856, Section 11.
- Miscellaneous unit. "Miscellaneous unit" means a hazardous waste management unit where hazardous waste is treated, stored, or disposed of and that is not a container, tank, surface impoundment, waste pile, land treatment unit, landfill, incinerator (including boiler or industrial furnace), or underground injection well.
- Mobile treatment facility. "Mobile treatment facility" means a facility or unit capable of being moved and operated at hazardous waste sites for a limited period of time at a generator's site. In order to qualify as a "mobile treatment facility" units located at generator sites must be operational at more than one site in a calendar year.
- New tank system. "New tank system" means a tank system or component that will be used for the storage or treatment of hazardous waste and for which installation has commenced after July 14, 1986.
- On ground tank. "On ground tank" means a device meeting the definition of tank which is situated in such a way that the bottom of the tank is on the same level as the adjacent surrounding surface so that the external tank bottom cannot be visually inspected.
- Partial Closure. "Partial closure" means the closure of a hazardous waste management unit in accordance with the applicable closure requirements of Chapters 855 and 856 at a facility that contains other active hazardous waste management units.
- Principal hazardous constituents (PHC). "Principal hazardous constituents" (PHC) means the hazardous constituents identified in Chapter 850.
- Representative sample. "Representative sample" means a sample of a universe or whole which can be expected and demonstrated to exhibit the average properties of the universe or whole.
- Run-off. "Run-off" means any rainwater, leachate or other liquid that drains from any part of the facility property over land, including land which is part of the facility property as defined in Chapter 856, Section 3 and land which is not.
- Run-on. "Run-on" means any rainwater, leachate or other liquid that drains onto any part of the facility property over land, including land which is part of the facility property as defined in Chapter 856, Section 3 and land which is not.
- Seepage lagoon. "Seepage lagoon" means any lagoon in which seepage of liquid hazardous waste or leachate through its base or sides is the intended method of disposal of liquids from the lagoon.

- Storage. "Storage" means the containment of hazardous waste, either on a temporary basis or for a period of years, in such a manner as not to constitute disposal of the hazardous waste.
- Sump. "Sump" means any pit or reservoir that meets the definition of tank and those troughs/trenches connected to it that serve to collect hazardous waste for transport to hazardous waste storage, treatment, or disposal facilities.
- Surface impoundment. "Surface impoundment" means a facility or part of a facility which is a natural topographic depression, man made excavation or diked area formed primarily of earthen materials, although it may be lined with manmade materials, which is designed to hold or holds an accumulation of liquid wastes or wastes containing free liquids, and which is not an injection well. Examples of surface impoundments are holding, storage, treatment, settling and aeration pits, ponds and lagoons.
- Tank. "Tank" means a stationary device designed to contain an accumulation of hazardous waste which is constructed primarily of nonearthen materials which provide structural support.
- "Tank system" means a hazardous waste storage or treatment tank and its associated ancillary equipment and containment system.
- Thermal treatment. "Thermal treatment" means the treatment of hazardous waste in a device which uses elevated temperatures as the primary means to change the chemical, physical or biological character or composition of the hazardous waste.
- Examples of thermal treatment processes are incineration, molten salt, pyrolysis, calcination, wet air oxidation and microwave discharge.
- Treatment. "Treatment" means any method, technique, or process, including neutralization, designed to change the physical, chemical, or biological character or composition of any hazardous waste so as to neutralize such waste, or so as to recover energy or material resources from the waste, or so as to render such waste nonhazardous, or less hazardous; safer to handle; or amenable for recovery, amenable for storage, or reduced in volume.
- Trust fund. "Trust fund" means a trust, established by the owner or operator of a hazardous waste facility and administered by a financial institution with fiduciary responsibility to carry out the terms of the trust, in which funds are held for the purpose of assuring proper closure and/or post-closure care of the facility.
- Underground injection. "Underground injection" means the subsurface emplacement of fluids through a bored, dug, drilled or driven well, or a subsurface waste disposal system including, but not limited to, a

septic tank, cesspool, drainage field, seepage lagoon, salt dome formation, salt bed formation, underground mine or cave.

- Underground tank. "Underground tank" means a device meeting the definition of tank whose entire surface area is totally below the surface of and covered by the ground.
- Unfit for use tank system. "Unfit for use tank system" means a tank system that has been determined through an integrity assessment or other inspection to be no longer capable of storing or treating hazardous waste without posing a threat of release of hazardous waste to the environment.
- Waste pile. "Waste pile" means any noncontainerized accumulation of solid, nonflowing hazardous waste that is used for storage of the waste prior to treatment or disposal.
- Zone of saturation. "Zone of saturation" means that part of the earth's crust in which all voids are filled with water.

REFERENCES TO FEDERAL REGULATIONS

Portions of this rule refer to federal regulations of the United States Environmental Protection Agency (EPA). Unless otherwise specified, the federal regulations referenced are those interim final or final regulations revised as of July 1, 1988, as they appeared in volume 40 of the Code of Federal Regulations (CFR). Where specifically stated, the terms of a referenced federal regulation are hereby adopted as terms of this rule, except that in regulations incorporated thereby, "EPA" shall mean "the Maine Department of Environmental Protection (DEP)"; "Administrator", "Regional Administrator" and "Director" shall mean "the Mainc Board of Environmental Protection or its designated representative", and the phrase "treat, store, and/or dispose" shall mean "handle". In addition, where the terms of federal regulations hereby incorporated by reference differ from or are inconsistent with other terms of this Chapter or Chapters 850860, the more stringent of the requirements shall apply. Other changes to regulations incorporated hereby are as expressly made in this rule.

ENVIRONMENTAL PERFORMANCE STANDARDS

- All hazardous waste facilities shall be located, designed, constructed, altered, operated, maintained and closed in a manner that will assure protection of human health and welfare and the environment. Protection of human health and welfare and the environment shall include, but not be limited to:
- Prevention of adverse effects on ground water quality considering:
  (a) The volume and physical and chemical characteristics of the waste in the facility, including its potential for migration through soil or through synthetic liner materials;

(b) The hydrogeological characteristics of the facility and surrounding land;
(c) The quantity, quality and directions of ground water flow;
(d) The proximity and withdrawal rates of ground water users;
(e) The existing quality of ground water, including other sources of contamination and their cumulative impact on the ground water;
(f) The potential for health risks caused by human exposure to waste constituents;
(g) The potential damage to wildlife, crops, vegetation and physical structures caused by exposure to waste constituents;

The persistence and permanence of the potential adverse effects; and

(2) Prevention of adverse effects on surface water quality considering:
(a) The volume and physical and chemical characteristics of the waste in the facility;
(b) The hydrogeological characteristics of the facility and surrounding land, including the topography of the area around the facility;
(c) The quantity, quality and directions of ground water flow;
(d) The patterns of rainfall in the region;
(e) The proximity of the facility to surface waters;
(f) The uses of nearby surface waters and any water quality standards established for those surface waters;
(g) The existing quality of surface water, including other sources of contamination and their cumulative impact on surface water;

The potential for health risks caused by human exposure to waste constituents;

(i) The potential damage to wildlife, crops, vegetation and physical structures caused by exposure to waste constituents;
(j) The persistence and permanence of the potential adverse effects; and

(3) Prevention of adverse effects on air quality, considering:
(a) The volume and physical and chemical characteristics of the waste in the facility, including its potential for volatilization and wind dispersal;
(b) The existing quality of the air, including other sources of contamination and their cumulative impact on the air;
(c) The potential for health risks caused by human exposure to waste constituents;
(d) The potential damage to wildlife, crops, vegetation and physical structures caused by exposure to waste constituents;

(e) The persistence and permanence of the potential adverse effects; and

(4) Prevention of adverse effects due to migration of waste constituents in the subsurface environment, considering:

(a) The volume and physical and chemical characteristics of the waste in the facility, including its potential for migration through soil;

(b) The geologic characteristics of the facility and surrounding land;

(c) The patterns of land use in the region;

(d) The potential for migration of waste constituents into subsurface physical structures;

(e) The potential for migration of waste constituents into the root zone of food chain crops and other vegetation;

(f) The potential for health risks caused by human exposure to waste constituents;

(g) The potential damage to wildlife, crops, vegetation and physical structures caused by exposure to waste constituents; and

The Persistence and permanence of the potential adverse effects.

- The treatment or disposal of hazardous waste at a facility by means of evaporation is prohibited.
- The burning of hazardous waste in a cast iron and firetube boiler or in a boiler having a capacity level of less than 25 million Btu per hour is prohibited.
- The disposal of hazardous waste within the coastal waters of this State is prohibited. In addition, the disposal of hazardous waste in any ocean waters by a resident of this state is prohibited except that this prohibition shall not apply to ocean waters which are within the jurisdiction of another state.
- The placement of any hazardous waste into any salt dome formation, salt bed formation, underground mine or cave, and the underground injection of hazardous waste, is prohibited.

GENERAL STANDARDS

- The standards set forth in this section are applicable to all waste facilities for hazardous waste, except as specifically provided otherwise in this rule or in Chapter 856. An applicant for a license must demonstrate in his application that the facility has been designed, will be established, constructed or altered and will operate in compliance with these standards. A licensee must operate the facility so as to comply with these standards.
- The plans, specifications, descriptions and other documentation submitted by the applicant in support of his application and approved

by the Board in issuing the license constitute terms of the license which must be complied with by the licensee. These plans, specifications, descriptions and other documentation include, without limitation, those required by Chapter 856, Section 10 and this rule.

- The facility must be established, constructed, altered and operated in compliance with the following requirements:
  (1) this rule;
  (2) 40 CFR 264.12. Required Notices, which is hereby adopted and incorporated by reference, provided, however, that the phrase "of this Part and Part 270 of this chapter" in 40 CFR 264.12(c) shall mean "of this Chapter and Chapter 856";
  (3) 40 CFR 264.13 as revised on August 17, 1988 (53 FR 31211), Waste Analysis, which is hereby adopted and incorporated by reference, provided, however, that all references to 40 CFR Part 268 or sections or subparts thereof shall mean "Chapter 852", all references to "this part" shall mean "this Chapter", the phrase "Part 270 and Part 124 of this chapter" in 40 CFR 264.13(a)(1) shall mean "Chapter 856", all references to "Part 261" shall mean "Chapter 850", the reference to "Sections 264.17, 264.314, 264.341 and 268.2 of this Chapter" shall mean "this Chapter and Chapter 852", and the phrase "Section 260.22 of this Chapter" in 40 CFR 264.13(b)(7)(iii) shall mean "Chapter 850";
  (4) 40 CFR 264.14, Security, which is hereby adopted and incorporated by reference;
  (5) The daily inspection requirements of Chapter 856, Section 10B(3) and 40 CFR 264.15, General Inspection Requirements, which is hereby adopted and incorporated by reference, provided, however, that any references to sections of 40 CFR Part 264 shall mean "this Chapter";
  (6) 40 CFR 264.16, Personnel Training, which is hereby adopted and incorporated by reference. In addition, the training program must be approved by the Department prior to operation of the facility;
  (7) 40 CFR 264.17, 264.31264.37, Preparedness and Prevention, which are hereby adopted and incorporated by reference, provided, however, that references to "Section 264.13" shall mean "subsection (3) above". In addition, the precautions required to be taken by 40 CFR 264.17 must meet applicable requirements of codes, standards and rules of the Department of Public Safety (State Fire Marshal's Office); the aid agreements required by 264.37 must be in writing, on file with each party to the agreement and with the Department, readily accessible to facility personnel, and reviewed and updated annually; and the facility

owner or operator shall provide copies of the agreement to all parties thereto and shall file a copy with the Department prior to the commencement of operation of the facility and upon each update of the agreement;

(8) 40 CFR 264.51264.56, Contingency Plan and Emergency Procedures, which are hereby adopted and incorporated by reference, provided, however, that the reference in 40 CFR 264.52(b) to "Part 112 of this chapter, or Part 1510 of Chapter V" shall read "Part 112 or Part 1510 of EPA regulations";

(9) The owner or operator must keep a written record at the facility. The following information must be recorded, as it becomes available, and maintained in the operating record until closure of the facility:

(a) A description and the quantity of each hazardous waste received, and the method(s) and date(s) of its treatment, storage, or disposal at the facility, which is hereby adopted and incorporated by reference, provided that references to Section 264.73 shall mean "this subsection", and references to "Part 261 of this chapter" or sections or subparts thereof shall mean "Chapter 850";

(b) The information specified in 40 CFR 264.73(b)(2)(16) as revised on August 17, 1988 (53 FR 31211), which is hereby adopted and incorporated by reference, provided, however, that all references to Part 264 or subparts or sections thereof shall mean "applicable provisions of Chapter 852";

(10) 40 CFR 264.74, Availability, Retention, and Disposition of Records, which is hereby adopted and incorporated by reference, provided, however, that the reference to "section 264.73(b)(2)" shall mean "subsection (9)(b) above".

(11) 40 CFR 264.75, Annual Report, which is hereby adopted and incorporated by reference, provided, however, that references to sections within 40 CFR Part 264 shall mean "Chapter 854", other comparable forms may be required by the Department, and the report must be prepared and submitted annually no later than March 1st for the preceding calendar year;

(12) 40 CFR 264.76, Unmanifested Waste Report, which is hereby adopted and incorporated by reference, provided, however, that the reference to "Section 263.20(e)(2)" shall mean "Section 7B of Chapter 857", and the reference to 40 CFR 261.5 shall mean "Section 3(A)(5) of Chapter 850";

(13) In addition to submitting annual reports and unmanifested waste reports as specified in subsections (11) and (12) above, the owner/

operator must also report to the Department releases, fires, and explosions as specified in subsection (8) above, facility closures, reports as mandated in other provisions of this Chapter; and other reports, concerning quantities and handling of hazardous waste, as deemed necessary by the Department for effective management of wastes.

(14) Chapter 857, Manifest Requirements;

(15) 40 CFR 264.111264.115, closure for all facilities, and 40 CFR 264.116264.120 post closure requirements for all disposal facilities, and waste piles, surface impoundments, and tanks closing as landfills as those provisions were revised on September 2, 1988 (53 FR 34086), Closure and Post Closure Care, which are hereby adopted and incorporated by reference, provided, however, that:
   (a) references to other sections or subparts of 40 CFR 264 shall mean "this Chapter";
   (b) references to 40 CFR Part 270 or Part 124, or sections or subparts thereof, shall mean "Chapter 856";
   (c) references to 40 CFR Part 262 shall mean "Chapter 851";
   (d) 40 CFR 264.112(e) shall be deleted;
   (e) certification of closure of any unit (not just land disposal units as provided in 40 CFR 264.115) used to handle hazardous wastes shall be required within 60 days of completion of closure; and
   (f) the notification of closure required by 40 CFR 264.112(d) shall be provided at least 180 days prior to the date on which closure is expected to begin.

(16) The financial requirements of 40 CFR 264.141264.143 and 264.147264.151 for all facilities, and 40 CFR 264.144264.146 for all facilities subject to postclosure requirements, as those provisions were revised on September 1, 1988 (53 FR 33950), which are hereby adopted and incorporated by reference, provided, however that:
   (a) references to other sections or subparts of 40 CFR 264 shall mean "this Chapter";
   (b) references to sections or subparts of 40 CFR Part 265 shall mean "Chapter 855";
   (c) references to "section 3008 of RCRA" shall mean "applicable Board or Department procedures";
   (d) references to sections or subparts of 40 CFR Parts 124 or 270 shall mean "Chapter 856"; and
   (e) liability coverage shall not be demonstrated through a

financial test or corporate guarantee, therefore 40 CFR 264.147(a)(2), (b)(2) and (3),(f), and (g); and 40 CFR 151(g) and (lh2)(2) shall be deleted; and combinations of coverage shall not include the financial test or corporate guarantee.

(f) when a financial test is selected as the method of providing closure or postclosure assurance, the applicant must include in the application the most current copy of Form 10K as filed with the Securities and Exchange Commission or equivalent financial information. A current copy of Form 10K or equivalent financial information must be submitted to the Department with the annual fee each year for the term of the license.

(g) any trust agreement must provide that the trustee is prohibited from investing trust funds in Commodities, Real Estate Investment Trusts (REITs), Corporate or Municipal Bonds which have not received the highest rating by Moody's Investment Service or Standard & Poor's, equity shares of firms which are not subject to regulation by the Securities and Exchange Commission, Foreign Currency speculation or in any other investment vehicle that is not consistent with the "Prudent Man" concept as it would apply to assuring that funds are available for carrying out a future activity with vital public interest. The agreement must also provide that primary consideration in making investments must be given to prompt liquidity and face value of assets held in trust.

The owner or operator must pay into a closure or postclosure trust fund according to the following requirements:

(i) The owner or operator shall deposit 25 percent of the sum required into the trust fund on the date his facility license is issued. The license is not effective until the deposit is made.

(ii) The remaining 75 percent of the sum required, adjusted for inflation, must be deposited in the trust fund in equal installments on or prior to the anniversary of the date upon which the license was issued, in each remaining year of the term of the license. The license remains in effect only if each deposit is made. The obligation to make deposits ceases only upon an approved transfer of the license or upon full payment.

(iii) After the last annual deposit to the trust fund, subsequent annual deposits to account for inflation must be made over the life of the facility. The license remains in effect only if these deposits are made. The obligation to make deposits ceases only upon an approved transfer of the license or upon accomplishment of closure.

(iv) If the Board determines that the costs of closure or postclosure are increased, it may require the owner or operator to deposit additional funds into the trust fund by single deposit or according to a schedule. If according to a schedule, adjustment for inflation must be made for each deposit after the first. The license remains in effect only if the additional deposits are made. The obligation to make deposits ceases only upon an approved transfer of the license or full payment or upon accomplishment of closure or termination of the postclosure care period.

(v) If a license is suspended or revoked, the Board may require deposits to be made according to (i), (ii), (iii), and (iv) above or may impose an accelerated schedule or may require immediate full payment, with adjustment for estimated inflation.

(vi) When computing the annual inflation adjustment for closure or postclosure trust funds, the owner or operator must use the Implicit Price Deflator for Gross National Product as published by the Department of Commerce in "Survey of Current Business."

(i) The owner or operator must submit with his application and must submit annually thereafter proof of liability insurance for the facility for sudden and accidental occurrences. Coverage must be provided during active life and closure and, where wastes will remain on the facility property after closure, during the postclosure period. The level of coverage must be at least one million dollars per occurrence and two million dollars annual aggregate, unless because of a greater risk a higher minimum is required by the Board for a particular facility.

(j) The owner or operator of a facility that utilizes a landfill, land treatment, surface impoundment or underground storage in tanks to handle hazardous waste or of a facility where hazardous waste will or is likely to remain on the facility property after closure must submit with his application and must submit annually thereafter proof of liability insurance for the facility for nonsudden and accidental occurrences. Coverage must be provided during active life and for so long as any waste remains on the facility property but for no longer than the postclosure period. The level of coverage must be at least three million dollars per occurrence and six million dollars annual aggregate, unless because of a greater risk a higher minimum is required by the Board for a particular facility.

(k) Wording of liability insurance endorsements must be identical to the wording contained in 40 CFR 264.151(i) except that subparagraph 2(b) shall read: "The Insurer is liable for the payment of amounts within any deductible applicable to the policy, with a right of reimbursement by the insured for any such payment made by the Insurer."

(l) All liability insurance coverage amounts must be exclusive of legal defense costs.

(m)A financial test may not be utilized in lieu of liability insurance nor may an owner or operator selfinsure. If liability insurance is unavailable, a $2,000,000 letter of credit drawn on a reputable bank, the terms of which the Board must approve, may be utilized in lieu of liability insurance for sudden and accidental occurrences.

(n) If a liability insurance policy is written as a "claims made" policy, an endorsement must provide for a discovery period of at least twelve (12) months beyond the date of expiration or cancellation of the policy. The endorsement must also provide that the underwriter will notify the public according to the requirements below:

(o) At least sixty (60) days prior to the date upon which the policy will expire or be canceled, give written notification to all owners of property abutting the facility and to the chief elected official in the municipality in which the facility is located and in each of the municipalities immediately abutting the municipality in which the facility is located, that insurance for the facility will expire or be canceled, giving date of expiration or cancellation, and that claims against the insured must be filed within twelve (12) months from the date of expiration or cancellation, specifying where and how claims can be filed;

(p) During the first, third, sixth and ninth month subsequent to the date of expiration or cancellation, place in each of the State's major newspapers (Portland Press Herald, Bangor Daily News, Lewiston Sun, Kennebec Journal, and Waterville Sentinel) and in all local newspapers published or widely distributed in the municipality where the facility is located an advertisement designed to attract notice and containing the information specified in i. above.

(17) Chapter 851, Section 8 A & B, Pre Transport Requirements.

(18) 40 CFR 264.101, Corrective Action for Solid Waste Management Units, which is hereby adopted and incorporated by reference.

- No person shall own or operate a waste facility for hazardous waste without having obtained a hazardous waste facility identification number specific to the site.

(1) The identification number shall be comprised of the identification number assigned to the facility by the U.S. Environmental

Protection Agency (EPA) and/or any identifying number or letter as may be assigned by the Department.

- An applicant must demonstrate in his application sufficient financial capacity, including projections of utilization of the facility by hazardous waste generators, to construct, operate and maintain all aspects of the facility in accordance with requirements of statute and rules. A licensee must maintain sufficient financial capacity for the term of the license, including any renewal license, and at the time of renewal must demonstrate sufficient current financial capacity including current projections of utilization of the facility during the renewal term.
- For a facility at which hazardous waste will be disposed, the applicant must demonstrate that the volume of waste and the risks related to its handling will have been reduced to the maximum practical extent. For an on-site facility, the applicant shall comply with this requirement first by toxics use reduction, as described in 38 MRSA section 2302, subsection 1, then by waste reduction, as defined in 38 MRSA section 2302, subsection 3, then by treatment and volume reduction prior to disposal.
- A licensee must operate the facility to meet this requirement during the term of the license, including renewal thereof, and at time of renewal must provide a current demonstration that the requirement is met.
- An application for a mobile treatment facility may consist of two phases:
  (1) The first consisting of general operational, structural features, and generic siting criteria.
  (2) The second consisting of site specific operating and siting features.

FACILITY LOCATION IN CERTAIN AREAS

- Prohibition. No person shall establish, construct, alter, or operate a waste facility for hazardous waste, except as noted, where the facility is or would be located:
  (1) On land defined as a wetland under statutes or regulations administered by the Department, Department of Conservation, Department of Inland Fisheries & Wildlife, Department of Marine Resources, or the State Planning Office; or
  (2) Within any 100 year flood plain so designated by the Federal Insurance Agency or within the level of any documented flood of a greater magnitude. This prohibition shall not apply to a facility where hazardous waste is not handled in a landfill, land treatment

unit, miscellaneous unit, surface impoundment or waste pile or to any interimly licensed (under Chapter 855) storage or treatment facility in use on the effective date of this rule; or

(3) So that it overlies any portion of a surface or subsurface sand and gravel aquifer or a high yield bedrock aquifer. This prohibition shall apply to a facility where hazardous waste is handled in a surface impoundment, landfill, underground tank, or waste pile or a facility where hazardous waste is treated utilizing land treatment techniques; or

(4) Within the boundaries of a state or federal park or designated wilderness area. This prohibition shall not apply to a storage facility (Section 12 of this rule);

- Rebuttable Presumption. A waste facility for hazardous waste located as set forth below is presumed to pose serious threats to public health or welfare or to the environment such that a license for a facility cannot be issued. The presumption applies if:

  (1) The facility property is located on land defined as a wetland under statutes or regulations administered by the Department, Department of Conservation, Department of Inland Fisheries & Wildlife, Department of Marine Resources, or the State Planning Office; or

  (2) The facility or facility property is located within 300 feet of any 100 year flood plain so designated by the Federal Insurance Agency or within 300 feet of the level of any documented flood of a greater magnitude. Evidence that the facility will be constructed or operated in compliance with the special requirements for facilities located in a flood plain is not an adequate basis for rebutting the presumption against such siting. However, the presumption may not be rebutted unless the applicant demonstrates along with its other offer of evidence rebutting the presumption that the facility will meet all applicable standards; or

  (3) The facility or facility property overlies any portion of a surface or subsurface sand and gravel aquifer or its primary recharge zone or a high yield bedrock aquifer; or

  (4) The facility or facility property is located within one mile upgradient of any underground source of public drinking water, or within the watershed of a surface water source of public drinking water, or within 1,000 feet of any source of potable water for humans or livestock; or

  (5) The facility or facility property is located such that it may pose a threat to fisheries or wildlife or other natural resources in an

area including a sanctuary, refuge, or preserve designated as such under statutes or regulations administered by the Departments of Inland Fisheries & Wildlife or Marine Resources; a state or federal park, sanctuary, or designated wilderness area, or a critical area identified as such under statutes or regulations administered by the State Planning Office, or to fish in a fish hatchery; or

(6) The facility property is located within the boundaries of a state or federal park or designated wilderness area.An applicant seeking a license to establish, construct, alter, or operate a facility in such a location must overcome this presumption by persuasive evidence that the facility is unique in some way that allows for compliance with the intent of this rule.

ADDITIONAL STANDARDS APPLICABLE TO HAZARDOUS WASTE LANDFILLS

Performance Standards

(1) Landfills are regarded by the Board as the least preferable method of hazardous waste handling. While it is expected that the expense of landfilling will discourage its use, the Board, prior to approval of any application for a hazardous waste landfill, will consider whether alternative preferred method(s) exist for handling a waste proposed to be landfilled.

(2) A hazardous waste landfill must be designed, constructed, and installed to prevent any migration of wastes out of the landfill to adjacent subsurface soil or ground water or surface water at any time during the life, including the post-closure period, of the landfill.

(3) A hazardous waste landfill must be established, constructed, altered and operated to meet the following performance standards:

   (a) No landfilled hazardous waste or constituent or derivative thereof shall appear in ground or surface waters at a concentration above background level, or above current public health drinking water standards for Maine, including the Maximum Exposure Guidelines, or standards for aquatic toxicity, whichever is most stringent. Background levels shall be those established by the pre-construction analysis required by Chapter 856, Section 10C(11)(g) or of the upgradient monitoring well required by Section 8D(1) below, whichever is lower

   (b) No landfilled hazardous waste or constituent or derivative thereof, shall appear in the atmosphere in concentrations significantly above the background level nor exceed current ambient air quality standards for Maine at any time. Background levels shall be established by monitoring or demonstrated to have been previously established by monitoring.

Design. The provisions of 40 CFR 264.301(a), (c), and (f) (j) are hereby adopted and incorporated by reference, provided however, that:

(1) All new, replacement, or expanded portions of a landfill established in the State of Maine must be at least doublelined. The two liners are referred to below as

(a) the bottom liner, which lies adjacent to subsoil deposits; and

(b) the top liner, which is in contact with the landfilled waste.

Be properly installed on a base which is both smooth and structurally capable of supporting the entire landfill; and

(i) Be covered by a sufficient layer of well-graded fine soil material (not less than six inches in depth) so as to prevent damage to the liner due to facility operation, such as the movement of heavy equipment used at the site.

(j) Be installed to cover all surrounding earth likely to be in contact with a waste or leachate; and

(k) Be able to generate sufficient friction force between itself and the surrounding materials in order to maintain a short term factor of safety of 1.25 and a long term factor of safety of 1.50; and

(l) Be able to meet the manufacturer's minimum specifications for the material being proposed for use.Manufacturers' specifications on the standard leak rate of the liner must be specified in the application.

(7) The applicant must develop a Quality Assurance Plan (QAP) in order to ensure that design specifications and performance requirements for all hazardous waste facility components are met during construction. The QAP shall clearly describe the Construction Quality Control (CQC) and Construction Quality Assurance (CQA) measures to be implemented during construction. The QAP shall include, but not be limited to, the following:

(a) A description of the responsibility and authority of organizations and personnel involved in permitting, designing, and constructing the facility;

(b) The qualifications of the CQC/CQA personnel;

(c) The observations and tests to be used to ensure that the construction or installation meets or exceeds all design criteria, plans, and specifications for each hazardous waste facility component;

(d) The sampling activities, sample size, methods for determining sample locations, frequency of sampling, acceptance and rejection criteria, and methods for ensuring that corrective measures are implemented;

(e) Recordkeeping and reporting requirements for CQC/CQA activities;

(f) An assessment of construction equipment and manpower skills necessary to achieve design specifications and performance requirements; and

(g) A list and description of required manufacturers' product certification, installation certifications, and warranties.

(8) A leachate detection, collection, and removal system must be installed immediately above the top liner to assure that leachate is collected and removed. In addition, a leachate detection, collection and removal system must be installed between the top and bottom liners.

(9) The leachate collection system must be constructed such that:

(a) the system immediately above the top liner must be designed, constructed, maintained, and operated to collect and remove leachate from the landfill during the active life and post closure care period. The design of the collection and removal system shall be such that no more than 30 cm (1 foot) of leachate shall accumulate on the top liner at any one time.

(b) the leachate collection system between the liners must be designed, constructed, maintained, and operated to detect, collect, and remove liquids that may leak through the topliner during the active life and post closure care period.

(c) the leachate collection systems must be constructed of materials that are chemically resistant to the waste managed in the landfill and the leachate expected to be generated and of sufficient strength and thickness to prevent collapse under the pressures exerted by overlying wastes, waste cover materials, and by any equipment used at the landfill; and designed and operated to function without clogging during the active life and post-closure care period.

(10) The applicant must evaluate the potential for generation of gas within buried wastes. If a potential for build up or explosion of gases exists, a gas discharge system capable of collecting gases must be designed into the landfill cover system.

(11) The applicant must evaluate the compaction and consolidation of materials placed within the landfill. If compaction could result in ponding of drainage on the final cover system, an impermeable plastic cap or cover liner must be used to prevent infiltration. Otherwise, the final cover may be a layer of recompacted clay at least 2 feet thick with a hydraulic conductivity of less than 1 x 10-7 cm/sec.

(12) A sand and gravel drain layer must be placed over the final cover system.

(13) Final cover must be protected from disruption. Disruption due to frost heaving and penetration by burrowing rodents must be prevented by grading the site with soil material and at least six inches of topsoil. Disruption by plant roots must be prevented by the planting of shallowrooted vegetation and its maintenance in perpetuity. The final

grade of the landfill surface must be between two and ten percent grade.

(14) The applicant must evaluate the earthquake risk. The applicant must show that the facility is designed so that any disruption due to earthquake will not cause any performance standard to be violated.

(15) A buffer zone of at least 200 feet must be designed and maintained between the boundaries of the facility property and the boundaries of the landfill and of any other area of the property where hazardous waste will be handled.

(16) Fugitive emissions, including volatile organic compounds, from the facility must be controlled in accordance with a plan approved by the Board.

(17) Operation. The provisions of 40 CFR 264.303, 264.312, 254.313, 264.316 and 264.317 are hereby adopted and incorporated by reference, provided however, that:

(1) Runon must be diverted away from the facility.

(2) Runoff from the facility must be collected, analyzed and managed according to a design and plan approved by the Board.

(3) Cover material, sufficient to control odors, dispersion by wind and excessive water infiltration into a hazardous landfill cell, must be placed daily or after the landfill has received new wastes, whichever is the longer period.

(4) Access to active portions of the facility must be restricted to facility personnel needed for operation or management and to authorized federal, state and local officials while in performance of their official duties.

(5) No liquid waste shall be placed in a landfill except in accordance with the following:

(a) Bulk or noncontainerized liquid hazardous or nonhazardous waste, or hazardous or nonhazardous waste containing free liquids, must not be placed in a landfill unless, before disposal, the liquid waste or waste containing free liquids is treated or stabilized, chemically or physically, so that free liquids are no longer present and that the wastes are altered in such a way so that the materials that have absorbed the liquids will not biodegrade or release liquids when compressed.

(b) Containers holding free liquids must not be placed in a landfill unless:

(c) To demonstrate the absence or presence of free liquids in either a containerized or a bulk waste, the test method referenced in 850.

(6) Incompatible wastes must be separated horizontally by such barriers as will prevent any mixing of them in accordance with a plan approved by the Department. Vertical landfilling of incompatible wastes is prohibited.
(7) Containers placed in landfills must be:
(a) at least 90 percent full; or
(b) crushed, shredded, or similarly reduced in volume to the maximum practical extent before burial.

- Ground Water Protection. Ground water beneath and adjacent to the facility shall be protected and monitored in accordance with the requirements of:

ADDITIONAL STANDARDS FOR HAZARDOUS WASTE SURFACE IMPOUNDMENTS

- Performance Standards. A hazardous waste surface impoundment which is existing, new or laterally expanded must be established, constructed, altered and operated to meet the following performance standards:

(1) A surface impoundment must be designed, constructed, and installed to prevent any migration of wastes out of the impoundment to the adjacent subsurface soil or ground water or surface water at any time during the life, including the postclosure period, of the impoundment.
(2) No impounded hazardous waste or constituent or derivative thereof shall appear in ground water or surface water at a concentration above background level, or above current public health drinking water standards for Maine, including the Maximum Exposure Guidelines, or standards for aquatic toxicity, whichever is most stringent. Background levels shall be those established by the preconstruction analysis required by Chapter 856, Section 10C(11)(g) or of the upgradient monitoring well required by Section 8D(1) of this rule, whichever is lower.
(3) No impounded hazardous waste or constituent or derivative thereof shall appear in the atmosphere in concentrations significantly above the background level nor exceed current ambient air quality standards for Maine at any time. Background levels shall be established by monitoring or demonstrated to have been previously established by monitoring.
(4) An applicant seeking a license to treat hazardous waste in a surface impoundment must demonstrate to the satisfaction of the Board that:
(a) the waste is capable of being treated in a surface impoundment using the process proposed, based upon a trial test (a bench or smallscale pilot test) that determines the treatment technique, its effectiveness, and any limiting factors;

(b) the design measures and operating procedures will maximize the success of the treatment;
(c) the facility design and components are compatible with the hazardous waste and the treatment process; and
(d) the treatment process can and will be controlled at all times so as to prevent uncontrolled releases of hazardous waste or its constituents or derivatives and to protect the public health and safety and the environment.

- Design

(1) The provisions of 40 CFR 264221(c), and (f)(lh2) are hereby adopted and incorporated by reference provided however, that all new, replacement or expanded portions of a surface impoundment established in the State of Maine must be at least doublelined. The two liners are referred to below as a) the bottom liner, which lies adjacent to subsoil deposits, and b) the top liner, which is in contact with the impounded waste.
(2) A surface impoundment must have an impervious bottom liner of, or equivalent to, a recompacted clay layer of a minimum of 5 feet thick, with a hydraulic conductivity of 1 x 107 cm/sec or less and, in addition, have a minimum of 10 feet of similar deposits beneath it. If a suitably low permeability clay bottom liner cannot be produced by recompaction, its permeability must be decreased by addition of bentonite or other approved sealing compounds.
(3) Where the surface impoundment is located in a ground water discharge zone, an applicant must evaluate the possibility of upward rupture of the liners and design the impoundment so as to prevent such a rupture.
(4) At a minimum, a synthetic liner must be used in lieu of a clay liner if the clay cannot be made sufficiently impermeable or if organic solvents are to be handled in the surface impoundment. Any synthetic liner used as part of a surface impoundment must conform to the requirements of Section 8B(4), (6) and (7) of this rule.
(5) A leachate detection, collection and removal system must be installed, constructed, maintained, and operated immediately above a clay or synthetic bottom liner to assure that leachate is detected, collected and removed. The system must be designed so that the leachate can flow out freely, without a pressure head of leachate developing within the system.In addition, a leachate detection system must be installed immediately beneath the clay or synthetic bottom liner. The leachate collection system must be:
(a) constructed of materials that are chemically resistant to the waste managed in the surface impoundment and the leachate expected

to be generated and of sufficient strength and thickness to prevent collapse under the pressures exerted by overlying wastes, waste cover materials, and by any equipment used at the surface impoundment; and

(b) designed and operated to function without clogging during the active life and postclosure care period.

(6) The liner system in contact with the impounded waste must be:

(a) compatible with the waste;

(b) sufficiently impermeable to the waste under maximum operating conditions of hydraulic head so that the leachate system would not be filled in a period of less than one year;

(c) of sufficient strength to outlast the design lifetime of the impoundment; and

(7) Dikes must be designed with sufficient structural integrity to prevent failure when saturated, without dependence on any liner system for support.

(8) Earthen dikes must have a protective cover such as grass, shale or rock to minimize wind and water erosion and to preserve their structural integrity.

(9) Runon must be diverted away from the surface impoundment.

(10) At least two feet of freeboard must be assured at all times.

(11) An automatic shutoff or automatic diversion system must be installed in the waste feed so that flow of waste into the impoundment will stop when there is less than 2 feet of freeboard or any failure of the base or liners.

(12) An automatic alarm system to alert the operator to abnormal operations and to malfunctions must be installed.

(13) A backup containment system must be provided to contain 20% of the volume of the impoundment or 4 hours maximum flow from the influent pipe(s), whichever is the larger amount.

(14) The applicant must evaluate the earthquake risk and must demonstrate that the facility is designed so that any disruption due to earthquake will not cause any performance standard to be violated.

(15) The applicant must evaluate the compaction and settlement beneath the liners and must demonstrate that the liners will not crack or rupture under full potential load.

(16) A ground water monitoring system which meets the requirements of Section 8D of this rule must be operational before any waste is placed in the impoundment.

(17) Fugitive emissions, including volatile organic compounds, from the surface impoundment, must be controlled in accordance with a plan approved by the Board.

(18) Requirements other or less stringent than those established by Section 9B(1)(13) above may be imposed on a surface impoundment which is interimly licensed and being used for handling hazardous waste on the effective date of this rule, if the applicant demonstrates to the Board's satisfaction that the surface impoundment has not in the past violated the performance standards established herein and that the risk that it will violate the performance standards is no greater than that risk for a surface impoundment which meets the above requirements.

- Operation

(1) A surface impoundment must have at all times sufficient freeboard to prevent overtopping by overfilling, wave action or a storm. At no time shall there be less than 2 feet of such freeboard.

(2) Leachate must be removed from the leachate collection system either continuously or with sufficient regularity that no hydraulic head builds up within it.

(3) Earthen dikes must be kept free of perennial woody plants and burrowing animals and maintained so as to prevent any erosion of the dikes.

Containment System Repairs: Contingency Plans

(1) Whenever there is any indication of a possible failure of the base, liner, dike, leachate collection system or backup containment system, that part or system must be inspected in accordance with the requirements of Section 9D(4) below. Indications of possible failure include:
  (a) an unplanned nonsudden drop in liquid level in the impoundment;
  (b) liquid detected in the leachate detection system above the quantity to be expected from the design permeability of the liner;
  (c) evidence of leakage or the potential for leakage in the dike;
  (d) erosion of the dike;
  (e) apparent or potential deterioration of the liner(s) based on observation or test samples of the liner materials;
  (f) any mishandling of wastes placed in the impoundment; and
  (g) foreign objects in the impoundment.

(2) Whenever there is an indication of a failure of the base, liner, dike or leachate collection system, the surface impoundment must be removed from service. Indications of failure of the containment system include but are not limited to:
  (a) an unplanned sudden drop in liquid level in the impoundment;
  (b) quantities of waste detected in the leachate detection system in excess of three times the normal daily quantities;
  (c) leakage through the dike; or

(d) a breach (e.g., a hole, tear, crack, or separation) in the base, liner, dike, leachate collection or backup containment system.

(3) If the surface impoundment must be removed from service the owner or operator must:

(a) immediately shut off the flow of or stop the addition of wastes into the impoundment;

(b) immediately contain any leakage which has occurred or is occurring;

(c) immediately stop any leakage; and

(d) if the leak cannot be stopped by any other means, empty the impoundment into secure containers or the backup containment system.

(e) Take any other steps necessary to stop or prevent catastrophic failure.

(f) Notify the Department of the problem verbally within 24 hours and in writing within seven days after detecting the problem.

(4) The owner or operator must include as part of the contingency plan that is required to be filed with his application:

(a) a procedure for complying with the requirements of Section 9D(3) above; and

(b) a method for base, liner, dike, leachate collection and backup containment system evaluation and repair including:

(i) testing and monitoring techniques;

(ii) procedures to be followed to evaluate the integrity of the base, liner, dike, leachate collection system and backup containment system in the event of a possible failure;

(iii)actions to be taken in the event of a possible failure; and

(iv)specification of the repair techniques to be used in the event of leakage which does not require the impoundment to be removed from service.

(5) No surface impoundment that has been removed from service in accordance with Section 9D(3) above may be restored to service unless:

(a) repairs have been made; and

(b) repairs have been certified by a qualified engineer to ensure that the failure will not recur.

(6) A surface impoundment which has been removed from service and which is not being repaired must be closed in accordance with closure and postclosure requirements of this rule.

- Inspection, Surveying and Recordkeeping. The provisions of 40 CFR 264.226 and 40 CFR 264.229264.231 are hereby adopted and incorporated by reference, provided however, that the reference to

"40 CFR 264.221(a)" shall be deleted, references to sections of 40 CFR Part 261 shall mean Chapter 850, and references to "40 CFR 264.17(b)" shall mean "Section 6(C)(7) above." Furthermore, the following requirements shall apply:

(1) The owner or operator of a surface impoundment must inspect:
   (a) the freeboard level at least daily to ensure that two feet of freeboard is being maintained; and
   (b) the surface impoundment area, including dikes and vegetation thereon, at least weekly to check for any leaks or discharges and for signs of erosion, deterioration or failure of the impoundment.

(2) Where insufficient freeboard is noted, remedial action must be taken at once.

(3) The owner or operator must maintain, and keep current for as long as the facility is operated, a record of all hazardous waste handled in the impoundment by type, volume and date, all methods and times of treatment, all inspections and all records of repair, accidents and abatement measures taken. The record must be kept at the facility during its operating life and upon closure must be delivered to the Department. The Department may require that a current copy of that record be kept on file with the Department.

- Air, Ground Water and Surface Water Monitoring
   (1) Emissions, including fugitive emissions, from the facility shall be monitored in accordance with Section 8F of this rule.
   (2) Ground water shall be monitored in accordance with Section 8D of this rule.
   (3) The Board may require surface waters within or adjacent to a facility or facility property to be monitored in accordance with a plan approved by the Board.

Closure and PostClosure

(1) The owner or operator of a surface impoundment that does not meet the liner requirements of Section 9(B) of Chapter 854 shall:
   (a) include in the closure plan for the surface impoundment both a plan for complying with paragraph (2) below and a contingent plan for complying with paragraph (3) below in case not all contaminated subsoils can be practicably removed at closure;
   (b) prepare a contingent postclosure plan for complying with paragraph (3) below in case not all contaminated subsoils can be practicably removed at closure; and
   (c) base the cost estimates for closure and post-closure care required under subsection 6C(15) above on the cost of complying with the more expensive of the two closure and post closure scenarios.

(2) The owner or operator must remove or decontaminate all waste residues, contaminated containment system components (liners, etc.), contaminated subsoils, and structures and equipment contaminated with waste and leachate, and manage them as hazardous waste unless Section 3(A)(3)(d) of Chapter 850 applies; or

(3) If, after removing or decontaminating all residues and making all reasonable efforts to effect removal or decontamination of contaminated components, subsoils, structures and equipment as required in paragraph (2) above, the owner or operator finds that not all contaminated subsoils can be practicably removed or decontaminated, he must close the facility in accordance with the closure and postclosure requirements that apply to landfills.

(4) After closure, hazardous waste surface impoundments must continue to meet the performance standards.

(5) The Department may grant a variance to paragraph (2) of this subsection if the owner or operator demonstrates that the hazardous constituents in the waste will not migrate into ground water, surface water and air in violation of the performance standards in this Chapter for as long as the waste and other materials will remain on-site. Facilities receiving a variance to paragraph (2) shall close the facility in accordance with the closure and post closure requirements that apply to landfills.

ADDITIONAL STANDARDS APPLICABLE TO HAZARDOUS WASTE LAND TREATMENT FACILITIES

Performance Standards

(1) The land treatment of hazardous waste must meet the following performance standards:

(a) A land treatment facility must be designed and operated to ensure that hazardous waste placed in or on the treatment zone will not migrate beyond the zone and will be degraded, transformed, or otherwise made nonhazardous within the treatment zone within six months from the date of waste placement.

(b) No land treated waste or constituent or derivative thereof shall appear in ground or surface waters at a concentration above background level, or above current public health drinking water standards for Maine, including the Maximum Exposure Guidelines, or standards for aquatic toxicity, whichever is most stringent. Background levels shall be those established by the pre-construction analysis required by Chapter 856, Section 10C(11)(g) or of the upgradient monitoring well required by Section 8D(1), whichever is lower.

(c) No land treated waste or derivative or constituent thereof shall appear in the atmosphere in concentrations significantly above the background level nor exceed current ambient air quality standards for Maine at any time. Background levels shall be established by monitoring or demonstrated to have been previously established by monitoring.

(2) An applicant seeking a license to land treat hazardous waste must demonstrate to the satisfaction of the Board that:

(a) The waste will be rendered nonhazardous using the processes or methods proposed;

(b) The design measures and operating procedures will maximize the success of the treatment;

(c) The facility design and components including the soils, are compatible with the hazardous waste and the treatment process; and

(d) The treatment process can and will be controlled at all times so as to prevent any uncontrolled releases of hazardous waste or its constituents or derivatives and to protect the public health and safety and the environment.

- Design

ADDITIONAL STANDARDS APPLICABLE TO HAZARDOUS WASTE PILES

- Performance Standards. A waste pile must be established, constructed, altered and operated to meet the following performance standards:

(1) A waste pile must be designed and operated such that there is no migration of wastes out of the pile into adjacent subsurface soil or ground water or surface water at any time and that any particulate matter which may be subject to wind dispersal is controlled at all times.

(2) No hazardous waste or constituent or derivative thereof shall appear in ground or surface waters at a concentration above background level, or above current public health drinking water standards for Maine, including the Maximum Exposure Guidelines, or standards for aquatic toxicity, whichever is most stringent. Background levels shall be those established by the preconstruction analysis required by Chapter 856, Section 10C(11)(g) or of the upgradient monitoring well required by Section 8D(1), whichever is lower.

(3) No hazardous waste or constituent or derivative thereof shall appear in the atmosphere in concentrations significantly above the background level nor exceed current ambient air quality

standards for Maine at any time. Background levels shall be established by monitoring or demonstrated to have been previously established by monitoring.

(4) No hazardous waste may be treated in a waste pile.

- Design and Operating Requirements

  (1) The provisions of 40 CFR 264.251 and 264.259 are hereby adopted and incorporated by reference. A natural clay liner meeting the design and operation requirements of Section 8B(2) or a synthetic liner which meets the design and operation requirements of Section 8B(4), (5), (6) and (7) must underlie the waste pile. The liner must be intact beneath the waste pile and must be constructed with a raised berm around the entire waste pile.

  (2) No ignitable or reactive wastes may be stored in a waste pile.

  (3) Storage of incompatible wastes in a waste pile must be in accordance with the requirements of 40 CFR 264.257, which is hereby adopted and incorporated by reference, provided, however, that the references 40 CFR 264.17(b) shall mean "Section 6(C)(7) above".

  (4) No waste may remain in a pile for longer than 180 days.

  (5) Fugitive emissions from the waste pile must be controlled in accordance with a plan approved by the Board.

- Monitoring

  (1) Monitoring of the structure of the waste pile during construction and operation shall meet the requirements of 40 CFR 264.254, which is hereby adopted and incorporated by reference, provided however, that the reference to 40 CFR 264.251(a) shall mean "subsection (B)(1) above."

  (2) Ground water shall be monitored in accordance with Section 8D of this rule.

  (3) Emissions, including fugitive emissions, from the facility shall be monitored in accordance with Section 8F of this rule.

  (4) The Board may require surface waters within or adjacent to a facility or facility property to be monitored in accordance with a plan approved by the Board.

- Closure Requirements. The provisions of 40 CFR 264.258 are hereby adopted and incorporated by reference provided however, that references to Sections of 40 CFR Part 261 shall mean "Chapter 850", and references to other sections or subparts of 40 CFR Part 264 shall mean "this Chapter."

ADDITIONAL STANDARDS APPLICABLE TO HAZARDOUS WASTE TANK AND CONTAINER STORAGE FACILITIES

Performance Standards

(1) A hazardous waste storage facility must be established, constructed, altered and operated to meet the following performance standards:

(a) No hazardous waste or derivative thereof shall escape from the facility to ground or surface waters or to adjacent subsurface soil at any time during the life of the facility.

(b) No hazardous waste or constituent or derivative thereof shall appear in the atmosphere in concentrations significantly above the background level nor exceed current ambient air quality standards for Maine at any time. Background levels shall be established by monitoring or demonstrated to have been previously established by monitoring.

(2) The storage of hazardous waste in an underground or inground tank is prohibited unless that tank is interimly-licensed under Chapter 855 and in use on the effective date of this rule and is not prohibited under Section 7A(3).

Design

(1) The provisions of 40 CFR 264.175, 264.190(a) and (b), 264.192, and 264.193(a) (f)(3) and (i) as revised on September 2, 1988 (53 FR 34086), are hereby adopted and incorporated by reference, provided however, that references to sections of 40 CFR Part 270 shall mean "Chapter 856", and references to other sections or subparts of 40 CFR Part 264 shall mean "this Chapter".

(2) A container storage facility must have a base which is a firm working surface, such as asphalt or concrete, which is impervious and which must be kept entire. A natural clay liner meeting the design and operation requirements of Section 8B(2) or a synthetic liner which meets the design and operation requirements of Section 8B(4), (5), (6) and (7) must underlie the working surface. The liner must be intact beneath the storage facility and must be constructed with a raised berm around the entire storage facility.

(3) An interimly licensed container storage facility for hazardous waste which is being used as such on the effective date of this rule may be exempted from the requirement of a liner beneath the existing base if the applicant demonstrates to the Board's satisfaction that the facility has not in the past violated the performance standards established herein and that the facility design will provide full compliance with the performance standards at all times.

(4) Each building or separate container storage area must have a containment and collection system the capacity of which must exceed 20% of the total capacity of all containers and tanks used to store wastes or 110% of the capacity of the largest container or tank, whichever is greater. This system must also provide for sufficient

freeboard to allow for containment and collection of precipitation resulting from a 24 hour, 25 year storm, unless the storage facility is enclosed.

(5) A tank must be designed and installed so that it can be fully inspected for structural integrity, deterioration, and leaks except that a tank whose base cannot be fully inspected must be designed and installed to meet the standards of 40 CFR 264.193 (e)(3) for doublewalled tanks.

(6) Uncovered tanks must be designed to assure at least 2 feet of freeboard at all times.

(7) Overtopping of tanks during continuous feed must be prevented by a system of automatic shutoff or by automatic diversion of the waste feed into a tank having at least 30 percent of the volume of the primary tank.

(8) A building or other structure used as a hazardous waste storage facility must meet all requirements, codes and standards of the Department of Public Safety (State Fire Marshal's Office).

(9) The date of manufacture of a tank must be painted in a prominent location on the tank.

Operation

(1) A container must not be used for the storage of hazardous waste for a period of time exceeding the design life of the container.

(2) The requirements of 40 CFR 264.191 are hereby adopted and incorporated by reference, provided however, that references to 40 CFR 264.193 shall mean "Subsection (B) above", references to sections in 40 CFR Part 270 shall mean "Chapter 856", and references to 40 CFR Part 264.196 shall mean "subsection (E) below." In addition, any pipeline and pipeline valves that transfers hazardous waste to or from a tank used to store hazardous waste must be inspected and pressure tested at least annually or tested at least annually by a method approved by the Board or Department, to determine structural integrity. A pipeline that fails the test or a pipeline or tank is determined as a result of the inspection to be unsafe shall not thereafter be used to store or transfer hazardous waste. A tank, its piping and valves must be tested at least annually to determine the thickness and corrosion rate utilizing a method approved by the Board. In addition all piping valves must be internally inspected at least annually to determine fitness for use. The date of the most recent inspection and testing of a tank must be painted in a prominent location on the tank. Results of all tank and pipe testing shall be submitted to the Department within 10 days of taking place.

(3) An underground tank that is not prohibited by Section 12A(2) of this rule must be tested at least semiannually by the method(s)

recommended in Chapter 691. An underground tank that fails the test or leaks shall be removed and may not be replaced. Underground hazardous waste storage systems (tanks and piping) with secondary containment, and continuous interstitial space monitoring, need not be tested annually except to insure that the leak detection equipment is operating properly in accordance with the testing and calibration requirements of Chapter 691, Section 7(C)2 of the Regulations for Registration, Installation, Operation and Closure of Underground Oil Storage Facilities.

(4) Hazardous waste must not be stored in containers or tanks which are rusted, bulging or leaking. The requirements of 40 CFR 264.171 are hereby adopted and incorporated by reference.

(5) Containers or tanks must be compatible with the type of waste stored therein. The requirements of 40 CFR 264.172 and 40 CFR 264.194(a) are hereby adopted and incorporated by reference.

(6) Containers or tanks used to store hazardous waste must not be used to store foodstuffs or animal feed or any substance likely to come into contact with foodstuffs or animal feed.

(7) Containers or tanks holding incompatible hazardous wastes must not be stored in the same enclosure, building or structure unless they are segregated in a manner that prevents the wastes from coming into contact with one another under any circumstances, including leakage or failure of a container or tank. The requirements of 40 CFR 264.177 and 264.199 and adopted and incorporated by reference, provided however, that the references to 40 CFR 264.17(b) shall mean "Section 6(C)(7)" abovc."

(8) All hazardous waste containers must be stored in a manner that allows access for inspection and for remedial action if any container is found to be rusting, bulging or leaking or waste is spilled or discharged. In any event:
   (a) Containers with a capacity of 10 gallons or more must not be stacked in rows in excess of 4 wide and 2 high.
   (b) Aisle space between rows of containers must be sufficient to allow the unobstructed movement of personnel, fire protection equipment, spill control equipment and decontamination equipment to any area of facility operation in any emergency but in no event shall the aisle space be less than 36 inches wide. Rows not exceeding a single container in width and two (2) high may be stacked adjacent to walls or other components of the storage facility.

(9) Storage of hazardous waste in open containers or in open tanks not meeting the requirements of Section 12B(5) (7) above is prohibited.

The requirements of 40 CFR 264.173 and 264.194(b) and (c) are hereby adopted and incorporated by reference provided, however, that references to 40 CFR 264.196 shall mean "subsection (E) below".

(10) Wastes not already so labeled must, on arrival at the facility, be clearly and permanently labeled with the words "Hazardous Waste" and labeled to identify type of waste, generator and date of arrival.

(11) For any hazardous waste stored for longer than 180 days, the owner or operator of the facility must:
   (a) Pay the fee as required by 38 M.R.S.A., Section 1319I;
   (b) Prepare a written inventory of all wastes stored for 180 days and submit a copy to the Department on the 181st day, indicating when these wastes will be removed from storage for further handling and how they will be handled.
   (c) Segregate and label these wastes with the date of the 180th day.

(12) The storage of any hazardous waste for longer than 360 days is prohibited unless the owner or operator of a storage facility applies for, in writing, and receives approval to do so from the Commissioner. Any extension shall be for a period of time not exceeding 90 days, after which a new extension may be requested. In seeking approval, the owner or operator must demonstrate the maintenance of a segregated area for such waste, the continuing integrity of containers or tanks, the quantification and control of fugitive emissions, continuing security and continuing efforts to move the waste out of storage to other handling. If an approval for storage for longer than 360 days is not granted or if any request for extension is denied, continued storage of that waste is a violation of the license of the facility and, in addition, constitutes unlicensed disposal of the waste.

(13) Containers holding ignitable or reactive waste must be located at least 15 meters (50 feet) from the facility's property line. Tanks holding ignitable or reactive waste are subject to the requirements of 40 CFR 264.198, which are hereby adopted and incorporated by reference, provided, however, that references to 40 CFR 261.21 or 261.23 shall mean "Chapter 850" and references to 40 CFR 264.17(b) shall mean "Section 6(C)(7) above."

- Inspection, Surveying and Recordkeeping. The requirements of 40 CFR 264.174 and 264.195 are hereby adopted and incorporated by reference. In addition:

(1) Daily inspections shall be made to ensure that:
   (a) Two feet of freeboard is maintained at all times in uncovered tanks,
   (b) No containers, tanks, pipelines or valves are rusting, bulging or leaking.

(2) Weekly inspections shall be made to ensure that:
   (a) The working surface and the containment and collection system are in good order and free from cracks and leaks.
   (b) All safety devices, valves, spill and overfill equipment and fire extinguishing equipment are structurally sound and properly functioning.
(3) Monthly inspections shall be made to ensure that:
   (a) All tank welds, rivets, bolts, foundation supports for both tanks and piping are in good condition,
   (b) All sources of cathodic protection are tested and in good working order,
   (c) All pressure relief valves are functioning properly.
(4) Every ten years, beginning on January 1, 1994, all aboveground vertical tanks with a capacity of 31,500 gallons or more must be inspected and deemed suitable for service in accordance with the standards published by the American Petroleum Institute (API) - #653.
(5) The owner or operator of a hazardous waste storage facility must maintain and keep current a written record and/or diagram showing:
   (a) The layout of the facility and where each type of hazardous waste is stored within the facility;
   (b) The length of time each waste has been at the facility;
   (c) Details of all inspections of and repairs to the base, liners and containment and collection systems;
   (d) Details of all accidents and spills, including date and time of discharge or discovery and spill reporting, volume of spill and method of clean up;
   (e) Dates of repair or removal of rusted, bulging or leaking containers. This record/diagram must be maintained at the facility during operation and closure and must be delivered to the Department upon closure. The Department may require that a current copy of that record be kept on file with the Department.
(6) The results of annual tank and pipe testing shall be recorded at the facility.

Repairs and Response to Leaks or Spills

(1) Breaks in the liner(s) shall be repaired immediately.
(2) In the event any container is found to be rusted, bulging, leaking or otherwise unsafe, the wastes contained therein shall be transferred immediately to another container that does meet the standards provided in 49 CFR 173. If the unsuitable container is repaired so that it meets the specifications in 49 CFR 173, it may be reused.
(3) The requirements of 40 CFR 264.196 are hereby adopted and incorporated by reference, provided however, that references to other

sections in 40 CFR Part 264 shall mean "this Chapter", and references to sections in 40 CFR Part 270 shall mean "Chapter 856."

(4) The liquids must be removed from the containment structure of a storage facility which is not enclosed as soon as practicable, but in no case later than 24 hours or at another time approved by the Department after detection of the leak. Upon request by the owner or operator, the Department may extend the 24 hour time limit if the owner or operator demonstrates further removal is not necessary to prevent further harm to human health or the environment. An evaluation shall be performed as to whether such liquids are a hazardous waste prior to treatment or disposal of the liquids.

(5) If, at any time during operation, closure, or postclosure of the facility, the performance standards of this section are not being met, a corrective action program must be implemented, details of which must be specified or approved by the Department.

- Air, Ground Water and Surface Water Monitoring. The Board may require ground water, surface water and air quality monitoring in accordance with the requirements of Sections 8D, 8E, and 8F of this rule if it determines that such monitoring is necessary to ensure protection of public health and safety or of the environment.
- Closure. The requirements of 40 CFR 264.178 and 264.197 are hereby adopted and incorporated by reference, provided however, that references to other sections of subparts of 40 CFR Part 264 shall mean "this Chapter", and references to sections of 40 CFR Part 261 shall mean "Chapter 850", and no variance under 40 CFR 264.193(g) shall be allowed.

ADDITIONAL STANDARDS APPLICABLE TO HAZARDOUS WASTE INCINERATORS

- Principal hazardous constituents (PHCs) and hazardous combustion by-products must be treated to the extent required by the performance standards specified in Section 13B below. This specification will be based on the degree of difficulty of incineration of the hazardous constituents of the waste feed and its combustion by-products, their concentration or mass, considering the results of waste analyses and trial burns or alternative data submitted with the facility's license application. Hazardous constituents or by-products which represent the greatest degree of difficulty of incineration will be those most likely to be designated as PHCs or hazardous combustion by-products. Constituents are more likely to be designated as PHCs or hazardous combustion by-products if they are present in large quantities or concentrations. Trial PHCs will be designated for performance of trial burns in accordance with the procedure specified in 40 CFR 270.62 (or Chapter 856 of those rules) for obtaining trial burn permits. Trial hazardous combustion by-products will be designated under the same procedure.

- Performance Standards. A hazardous waste incinerator must be established, constructed, altered, operated and maintained to meet the following performance standards:
  (1) No hazardous waste or constituent or derivative thereof shall appear in the atmosphere in concentrations significantly above the background level nor exceed ambient air quality standards for Maine at any time. Background levels shall be established by monitoring or demonstrated to have been previously established by monitoring.
  (2) An incinerator burning hazardous waste must achieve a Destruction Removal Efficiency (DRE) of 99.99 percent or greater (except as noted in (3) below) for each Principal Hazardous Constituent (PHC) designated in its license for each waste stream to be burned. The following equation is used to determine the DRE for each PHC:

$$DRE = \frac{W\,in - W\,out}{W\,in} \times 100$$

Where: W in = Mass feed rate of one PHC in the waste stream feeding the incinerator; and

W out = Mass emission rate of the same PHC present in exhaust emissions prior to release to the atmosphere.

(3) An incinerator burning hazardous wastes F020, F021, F022, F023, F026, or F027 must achieve a destruction and removal efficiency (DRE) of 99.9999% for each principal hazardous constituent (PHC) designated in its license. This performance must be demonstrated on PHCs that are more difficult to incinerate than tetra-, penta-, and hexachlorodibenzo-p-dioxins and dibenzofurans. In addition, the owner or operator of the incinerator must notify the Board of his intent to incinerate hazardous wastes F020, F021, F022, F023, F026 or F027.

(4) An incinerator burning hazardous waste containing more than 0.5% halogens must remove at least 99% of the hydrogen halides from the exhaust gas. The stack emissions of hydrogen chlorides from any hazardous waste incinerator shall not exceed 50 parts per million (ppm) by volume, adjusted to 7% oxygen by volume.

(5) An incinerator burning hazardous waste must not emit particulate matter exceeding 180 milligrams per dry standard cubic meter (0.08

grams per dry cubic foot) when corrected for 7% oxygen. Tests may be required, if applicable, using the procedures specified by 40 CFR 60.50, Subpart E (Clean Air Act Regulations, "Standards for Performance of Incinerators").

(6) No heavy metals shall appear in the atmosphere in concentrations significantly above the background level nor exceed ambient air quality standards for Maine at any time. Background levels shall be established by monitoring or demonstrated to have been previously established by monitoring.

(7) An incinerator must destroy hazardous combustion by-products designated in its license such that the total mass emission rate of these by-products emitted from the stack is 0.011% or less of the total mass feed rate of PHCs fed into the incinerator.

(8) All combustion residues, such as fly ash, must be handled in accordance with all Federal and State statutory and regulatory requirements for their handling.

Operation

(1) An incinerator must be operated in accordance with operating requirements specified in the license. These will be specified on a case-by-case basis as those demonstrated (in a trial burn or in alternative data) to be sufficient to maintain compliance with the performance standards of Section 13B above.

(2) Each set of operating requirements will specify the composition of the waste feed (including acceptable variations in the physical or chemical properties of the waste feed which will not affect compliance with the performance standards to which the operating requirements apply.) For each such waste feed, the license will specify acceptable operating limits including the following conditions:
   (a) Carbon monoxide (CO) level in the stack exhaust gas;
   (b) Waste feed rate;
   (c) Combustion temperature;
   (d) An appropriate indicator of combustion gas velocity;
   (e) Air feed rate;
   (f) Such other operating requirements as are necessary to ensure that the performance standards are met.

(3) During startup and shutdown of an incinerator, hazardous waste must not be fed into the incinerator unless the incinerator is operating within the conditions of operation (temperature, air feed rate, etc.) specified in the license.

(4) Fugitive emissions from the combustion zone must be controlled by:
   (a) Keeping the combustion zone totally sealed against fugitive emissions; or

(b) Maintaining a combustion zone pressure lower than atmospheric pressure; or

(c) An alternate means of control demonstrated (as part of the permit application) to provide fugitive emissions control equivalent to maintenance of combustion zone pressure lower than atmospheric pressure.

(5) An incinerator must be operated with a functioning system designed to automatically cut off waste feed to the incinerator when operating conditions deviate from limits established under this section.

(6) An incinerator must cease operation when changes in waste feed, incinerator design or operating conditions exceed limits designated in its license.

(7) All hazardous waste incinerators in which halogenated wastes are burned must maintain, at a minimum, a combustion temperature of 1,000° C for a 2 second dwell time with 3% excess oxygen in the stack gas or 1,200° C for a 1.5 second dwell time with 2% excess oxygen in stack gas or an equivalent standard. More stringent operating requirements may be required by the Board, depending upon the waste involved, if it is determined by the Board to be necessary to protect the public health and safety or the environment.

(8) Hazardous waste incinerators which burn only non-halogenated wastes must maintain a combustion temperature of not less than 885° C. Specific combustion temperatures will be established in the license and will depend on the type of non-halogenated waste, its physical condition and the rate at which it is added to the normal fuel feedstock.

Monitoring, Inspections, and Recordkeeping

(1) The owner or operator must conduct waste analyses sufficient to verify that all waste feed to the incinerator is within the limits specified in his license.

(2) The owner or operator must monitor stack emissions to verify that the operating requirements established in the license achieve the performance standards.

(3) The owner or operator must monitor on a continuous basis:

(a) Combustion temperature, waste feed rate, combustion gas velocity and air feed rate;

(b) CO, at a point in the incinerator downstream of the combustion zone and prior to release to the atmosphere;

(c) Such other parameters, such as CO, CO2, O2, total hydrocarbons, and opacity, that the Board determines to be necessary to be monitored at the stack or at other locations in order to demonstrate compliance with the standards and requirements of this rule at all times.

(4) The incinerator and associated equipment (pumps, valves, conveyors, pipes, etc.) must be subjected to thorough visual inspection, at least daily, for leaks, spills, fugitive emissions and signs of tampering.
(5) The emergency waste feed cutoff system and associated alarms must be inspected daily and tested at least weekly to verify operability.
(6) The owner or operator of an incinerator must maintain and keep current for as long as the facility is operated a record of the types and quantities of hazardous waste incinerated, dates of incineration, repairs, accidents or uncontrolled releases and any abatement measures taken.
(7) The monitoring and inspection data must be recorded and all records must be placed in the operating log required by Section 6C(9) of this rule. The Department may require that a current copy of those records be kept on file with the Department. Upon closure, the operating log must be delivered to the Department.
   - Closure. At closure, the owner or operator must remove all hazardous waste and residues (including, but not limited to, ash, scrubber waters, and scrubbers sludges) from the incinerator site.

ADDITIONAL STANDARDS FOR TREATMENT IN TANKS

Performance Standards

(1) Facilities for treatment of hazardous waste in tanks must be constructed, altered and operated to meet the following performance standards:
   (a) No hazardous waste or constituent or derivative thereof shall escape from the treatment facility to ground or surface waters or to adjacent subsurface soil at any time during the life of the facility.
   (b) No hazardous waste or constituent or derivative thereof shall appear in the atmosphere in concentrations significantly above the background level nor exceed current ambient air quality standards for Maine at any time. Background levels shall be established by monitoring or demonstrated to have been previously established by monitoring.
   (c) The treatment of hazardous waste in an underground tank is prohibited.
(2) An applicant seeking a license to treat hazardous waste in a tank or tanks must demonstrate to the satisfaction of the Board that:
   (a) The waste is capable of being treated in a tank or tanks using the processes proposed, based upon a trial test (a bench or small-scale pilot test), that determines the treatment technique, its effectiveness, and any limiting factors;

(b) The design measures and operating procedures will maximize the success of the treatment;
(c) The facility design and components are compatible with the hazardous waste and the treatment process; and
(d) The treatment process can and will be controlled at all times so as to prevent uncontrolled releases of hazardous waste or its constituents or derivatives and to protect the public health and safety and the environment.

- Design. In addition to the requirements applicable to storage of hazardous waste in tanks under Section 12B, the following requirements apply to treatment in tanks:
  (1) Materials used in the construction and operation of all parts of the treatment facility must be compatible with the wastes to be treated and with any treatment chemicals or reagents utilized in the treatment process.
  (2) An alarm system to alert the operator to abnormal operations and to malfunctions must be installed prior to operation of the facility.
  (3) The facility must have sufficient excess capacity to hold all wastes undergoing treatment if an equipment malfunction or breakdown occurs during the treatment process. The wastes must be able to be held securely until the treatment equipment is repaired.
  (4) Fugitive emissions, including volatile organic compounds, from the facility must be controlled in accordance with a plan approved by the Board.
- Operation. In addition to the requirements applicable to the storage of hazardous waste in tanks under Section 12C, the following requirement shall apply to treatment in tanks.
  (1) All hazardous waste must be analyzed immediately prior to treatment, in order to ensure that:
    (a) The proper treatment technique, feed rates of treatment chemicals and reagents, and operating conditions (temperature, pressure, flow rate, etc.) are known and will be adhered to;
    (b) The treatment technique proposed will not have any detrimental effect upon any of the materials used to construct or operate the treatment apparatus;
    (c) The waste contains no components or contaminants which might interfere with or have an adverse impact on the treatment process;
    (d) The waste contains no components or contaminants which, when treated, may cause an uncontrolled release of wastes or toxic gases or fumes;

(e) The waste contains no components or contaminants which, when treated, would form substances or residues which the facility could not handle properly in accordance with State and Federal requirements.

(2) Demonstration of the treatment process must be made by trial test. The demonstration, appropriately modified for treatment in tanks, must comply with Chapter 856, Section 10G.

(3) All treatment chemicals and reagents must be stored in a manner that minimizes the potential for spills, fires, explosions or uncontrolled discharges or releases.

- Inspection, Surveying and Recordkeeping. In addition to the requirements applicable to the storage of hazardous waste in tanks under Section 12D, the following requirements shall apply to treatment in tanks:
- The owner or operator must maintain and keep current a record of:
  (a) All hazardous waste(s), by type and volume, received for treatment;
  (b) Where at the facility each hazardous waste is being held prior to treatment;
  (c) Date of treatment of each waste received, the volume treated and the method of treatment (if more than one method is permitted);
  (d) Details of all accidents and spills at the facility; and
  (e) All inspections.

This record must be maintained at the facility during operation and upon closure must be delivered to the Department. The Department may require that a current copy of that record be kept on file with the Department.

- Air, Ground Water and Surface Water Monitoring. The Department may require ground water, surface water and air quality monitoring in accordance with the requirements of Sections 8D, 8E, and 8F of this rule if it determines that such monitoring is necessary to ensure protection of public health and safety or of the environment.
- Response to Leaks or Spills and Closure. The requirements of Section 12E and 12G applicable to the storage of hazardous waste in tanks shall also apply to the treatment of hazardous waste in tanks.

ADDITIONAL STANDARDS APPLICABLE TO MISCELLANEOUS UNITS

Performance Standards

(1) A hazardous waste miscellaneous unit must be established, constructed, altered, and operated to meet the following performance standards:

(a) No hazardous waste or constituent or derivative thereof shall appear in ground or suffice waters at a concentration above background level, or above current public health drinking water standards for Maine, including the Maximum Exposure Guidelines, or standards for aquatic toxicity, whichever is most stringent.

(b) No hazardous waste or constituent or derivative thereof shall appear in the atmosphere in concentrations significantly above the background level nor exceed current ambient air quality standards for Maine at any time. Background levels shall be established by monitoring or demonstrated to have been previously established by monitoring.

(2) A miscellaneous unit shall also meet the appropriate performance standards applicable to other hazardous waste management units.

Design, Construction, Operation and Closure

(1) A miscellaneous unit must be located, designed, constructed, operated, maintained, and closed in a manner that will ensure compliance with the performance standards in subsection (A) above. Permits for miscellaneous units shall contain such terms and conditions necessary to protect human health and the environment and ensure compliance with such performance standards, including but not limited to, as appropriate, design and operating requirements, detection and monitoring requirements, and requirements for responses to releases of hazardous waste or constituents from the unit. Permit terms and conditions shall include those requirements of this Chapter applicable to other hazardous waste management units that are appropriate for the unit being permitted. Protection of human health and the environment includes, but is not limited to, the factors specified in 40 CFR 264.601(a)(c), which are hereby adopted and incorporated by reference.

- Monitoring, Analysis, Inspection, Response, Reporting, and Corrective Action

(1) Monitoring, testing, analytical data, inspections, response, and reporting procedures must ensure compliance with the performance standards of subsection (A) above, the general inspection, equipment testing and maintenance, annual reporting, unmanifested waste reporting, and additional reporting requirements specified in Section 6(C) of this Chapter; the corrective action requirements of Section 6(C)(18) of this Chapter; and any additional requirements necessary to protect human health and the environment as specified in the permit.

(2) The Board may require ground water monitoring, surface water monitoring, air monitoring, and/or soils monitoring in accordance

with a plan approved by the Board. If, at any time during operation, closure, or post closure of the facility (where applicable), the monitoring demonstrates that the performance standards are not being met by the miscellaneous unit, a corrective action program must be implemented, details of which must be specified or approved by the Department.

- Post-Closure Care. A miscellaneous unit that is a disposal unit must be maintained in a manner that complies with the performance standards of subsection (A) above and protects human health and the environment during the post-closure care period. In addition, if a treatment or storage unit has contaminated soils, surface waters, or ground water that cannot be completely removed or decontaminated during closure, then that unit must also meet the performance standards of subsection (A) above and protect human health and the environment during postclosure care. The postclosure requirements of Section 6(C)(15) of this chapter shall apply and the postclosure plan must specify the procedures that will be used to satisfy this requirement.

ADDITIONAL STANDARDS APPLICABLE TO COMMERCIAL FACILITIES

For commercial facilities, the exposure information requirements of Chapter 856, Section 10(C)(13) shall apply.

VARIANCE REQUESTS

Consistent with Federal requirements for authorization to operate the State hazardous waste management program, the Board may, on its own motion or on request, modify or waive one or more of the requirements of Sections 8B, 9B, 11B, 12B, and 14B of this rule relating to design of a specified type of facility except that no performance standard may be made less stringent. Such modification or variance must be justified on the basis that greater protection to health, safety, welfare or the environment than that provided by the performance standards is required and will thereby be provided or on the basis that no less protection than that provided by the performance standards will thereby be provided in that the design is an alternate but equivalent one.

SEVERABILITY

Should any provision of this rule be declared invalid or ineffective by court decision, the decision shall not invalidate any other provision of this rule.

Bibliography

A. Halim: *Anatomy of the Head and Neck: For Dental and Medical Students*, Ane Books Pvt. Ltd., 2009.

Ajeet Jaiswal: *Anthropo-Medical Profile of Textile Workers*, Alfa Pub, 2012.

Albert Sasson: *Medical Biotechnology : Achievements Prospects and Perceptions*, Rawat, 2007.

Aparna Rajagopalan: *Fundamentals of Medical Biotechnology*, Ukaaz Pub, 2006.

B.K. Tyagi: *Medical Entomology : A Handbook of Medically Important Insects and Other Arthropods*, Scientific, 2003.

Babul Roy: *Medical Anthropology : Studies in the Highlands of Assam*, Serials Publications, 2011.

Chittabrata Palit and Achintya Kumar Dutta: *History of Medicine in India : The Medical Encounter*, Kalpaz, 2005.

D.V. Rai: *Emerging Trends in Biomedical Science and Health*, R.C. Sobti and Raj Bahadur, I.K. Pub, 2009.

Darshan Shankar and P.M. Unnikrishnan: *Challenging the Indian Medical Heritage*, Cambridge Univ Press, Hardbound. Deep Mala Srivastva: *A Study in Medical Sociology*, Radha, 1996.

Fabian J. Theis And Anke Meyer Base: *Biomedical Signal Analysis: Contemporary Methods And Applications* , PHI Learning, 2011.

Frank Hoffmann and Martin Manning: *Herbal Medicine and Botanical Medical Fads*, Viva Pub, 2006.

G.S. Sawhney: *Biomedical Electronics and Instrumentation : Made Easy*, I.K. International Publishing House, 2012.

Geoff Dougherty: *Digital Image Processing for Medical Applications*, Cambridge University Press, 2006.

George Somerville: *Encyclopaedia of Health Education : A Complete* New, Comprehensive Health and Medical Reference Alphabetical *Guide for All Purpose*, Friends Pub, 2006.

Gyanendra Pandey: *Bhaisajya Ratnavali : Reknowned Treatise on* Applied on Pharmaceutical Therapeutics in Medical Practice, *Vol. I*, howkhamba Sanskrit Series Office, 2005.

H. Heimlich and Lawrence Galton: *Home Guide to Medical Emergencies*, Orient Paperbacks.

Jules J. Berman: *Biomedical Informatics* , Jones and Bartlett Learning, 2010.

K E Raj Pramukh: *Health, Illness and Healing : Themes and Issues in Medical Anthropology* , Serials Pub, 2009.

Lakshman Desai: *Biomedical Systems*, Paragon International Pub, 2007.

M P Gogoi: *A Doctor's Memoirs : An Inside Story of the Medical Profession*, B R Pub, 2008.

M. Ruchi Chandra and Neelma Kunwar: *Medical and Health Problems of Fasting and Non-Fasting Women*, Discovery, 2012.

Mandeep Singh: *Introduction To Biomedical Instrumentation*, PHI Learning. Manish Kapoor: *BioMEMS and Biomedical Nanotechnology*, Oxford Book Company, 2012.

Omar Hasan Kasule: *Medical Education : An Islamic Perspective*, Bangladesh Institute of Islamic Thought (BIIT), 2007.

P C Trivedi: *Medical Biotechnology* , Aavishkar, 2008.

Prem Kumar Sharma: *Medical Astrology* , Rupa, 2009.

R. Anandanatarajan: *Biomedical Instrumentation And Measurements*, PHI Learning, 2011.

R. Panjarathinam: *A Textbook of Medical Parasitology*, Universities Press, 2007.

R.K. Bag: *Law of Medical Negligence and Compensation*, Eastern Law House, 2011.

Rais Akhtar and Nilofar Izhar: *Global Medical Geography : Essays in Honour of Prof. Yola Verhasselt*, Rawat, 2010.

Rajesh Kumar: *Global Trends in Health and Medical Tourism*, SBS Pub, 2009.

Ranjan Das and Papri N. Das: *Instant Medical Biostatistics*, Ane Books Pvt. Ltd., 2009.

Robert B Northrop: *Analysis and Application of Analog Electronic Circuits to Biomedical Instrumentation*, CRC Press, 2005.

V Rajendran, B. Hillebrands, P. Periasamy and K. E. Geckeler: *Biomedical Applications of Nanostructured Materials* , Macmillan Publishers India, 2011.

V. Sujatha: *Health by the People : Sociology of Medical Lore*, Rawat, 2003.

Veena Bhasin: *Medical Anthropology : Tribals of Rajasthan* , Kamla Raj Enterprises, 2005.

Index